Fifty Million Years in Prison

Self-Help Legal Books by Ivan Denison

Flipping Your Conviction:
Post-Conviction Relief
for the Pro Se State Prisoner
(2013)

Flipping Your Habe:
Overturning Your State Conviction in Federal Court
Under 28 USC 2254
(2014)

The Essential Supreme Court Cases:
The 200 Most Important Cases for State Prisoners
(2015)

All available on www.amazon.com

Fifty Million Years in Prison

The Futility of Prisoners Seeking Justice in America

By Ivan Denison

Copyright 2017 by Ivan Denison

All rights reserved. No part of this book, with the exception of the Afterword, may be reproduced in any form, without written permission from the author. The Afterword is placed in the public domain and may be copied and distributed without violating copyright laws.

Portions of this work have been previously published at www.PrisonWriters.com and are reprinted here with permission.

Grateful acknowledgement is made to Jeremy Gross and Dujuan Emerson for their essays which first appeared in *Prison is For Real*, a 'no-copyright' publication in the public domain.

Published in the United States through www.createspace.com.
Suggested retail price: US $16.95

Denison, Ivan, 1962 –
Fifty Million Years in Prison: The Futility of Prisoners Seeking Justice in America
Non-Fiction, Narrative

ISBN: (on back cover)
   1. Criminal Justice – United States – Indiana
   2. Prisons – Prisoners – Legal Assistance
   3. Imprisonment – United States – Mass Incarceration
   4. Crime – True Crime

First Edition
                    10   9   8   7   6   5   4   3   2   1

Legal Disclaimer:
This book does not constitute nor should be construed as legal advice, and no opinion within this book is intended to be a substitute for the exercise of professional legal judgment. On all legal matters you are advised to consult a licensed attorney.

Dedicated to Kathleen Fairhurst
(1949-2016)
and Jimmi Fairhurst Evans
(1943-2017)

My lifelines to the world.

"The more we understand the human stories behind this problem, the sooner we can start making real changes that keep our streets safe, break the cycle of incarceration in this country, and save taxpayers like you money."

President Barack Obama, August 3, 2016,
after commuting 214 federal sentences in one day.

Fifty Million Years in Prison

Table of Contents

1	The Ark, The Covenant	1
2	Ascending the Granite Wall	19
3	Trust the Professionals	43
4	Defining Innocence	55
5	The Mercy of the Court	73
6	Technically, They Can't Do That	113
7	The Margins of Society	139
8	Ten Years Per Gram	167
9	One of Them Cases	193
10	Thorazine and Monster Mix	219
11	Deliberate Indifference	233
12	Mod Mania	245
13	Degrees of Innocence	263
14	Illusions	273
	Afterword: MIRA	289
	Appendices	299
	Bibliography	317
	Endnotes	321
	Acknowledgements	329
	About the Author	331

Fifty Million Years in Prison

Author's Note

This is a work of nonfiction, describing events I witnessed. No scenes are imaginary or made up. Some dialogue was, of necessity, recreated from notes and memory and condensed to arrive at the point of the conversation. Some of the events are not in chronological order; this was done to make the narrative flow in a way which would keep the reader engaged, and to avoid confusion.

Most of the individuals in this book are identified by their real names, and the crimes described are public record. However, to protect the privacy of certain people I have invented the following pseudonyms:

Weasel	Esther Coleman	Darrell
Markevious Hogan	Matthew Amalfitano	Ms. Billups
Najee Blackford	Hector	Marcus
Jerry Griner	Emily	Yasmani Salazar
Calvin Hogg	D-Bizzle	Brian Hixon
Mr. Hakenkreuz	Ben Jewell	Chad Kimbrough
Wally Pierson	Tichina Montgomery	Wally Lockhart
Lori Barton	Ned McConnell	Jeffery Hofstedter
Teresa Cortez	Martin Blair	Jelani
Adela	Melissa Nash	Janet Myerson

Factual information has been collected from published sources, publicly available court records, government reports obtained through Freedom of Information Act requests, and directly from the persons involved. The author has relied on the accuracy of these sources to tell the stories in this book; however, any or all of the above sources may be in error. Persons mentioned in this book could be proven innocent at some future date.

None of the prisoners in this book had any editorial input into this work, and none will profit from this publication.

Fifty Million Years in Prison

PROLOGUE

Fifty Million Years in Prison

I am serving a 71-year prison sentence for attempted murder. There's a story there, but this book is not about that. It's not about me. Most prisoners publish books about themselves and their own cases, and they do so with a painfully biased point of view no matter how much they try to be objective. Ultimately, they produce a narrowly-focused work nobody but their closest associates would want to read, and maybe not even them. Since I am as biased about my own case as any other prisoner, I will spare you that.

This book is about others I have met in prison, through my position as a law library clerk. It tells the story of their cases, and their struggles to get their convictions overturned or their sentences reduced. It is primarily a story of futility, as the subtitle suggests. Yet there are victories, hard-won and noteworthy due to their achievement in an environment not conducive to success.

The prisoners' stories included within this book are a fairly representative cross-section of prisoners in America. The focus here is on the guilty, and they do not form a particularly sympathetic cast of characters. Guilty people populate the pages here, just as they populate the densely-packed prisons scattered from coast to coast. Pure, unmitigated innocence, while sensational, is a rare commodity in prison, and so it is equally rare between the covers of this book.

Each prisoner's story may be considered one of the "quantum units" of incarceration – after all, one individual after another is how prisons get filled. The early chapters deal with their stories and their post-conviction legal struggles, to give the reader a feel for how the legal system operates on an individual level. The middle chapters explore the conditions and broad social and economic forces that combine to target these people for lengthy prison sentences. By the latter chapters, with knowledge of the motivations driving

Fifty Million Years in Prison

America's criminal justice system, one can gain understanding as to why America's prisons are full and overflowing.

The book's broad aim is to help the reader understand the causes of mass incarceration in the United States in the early 21st century. There are well over two million people confined in America, more prisoners than any country in the world. The incarceration rate is also the highest, roughly 5 to 6 times higher than other developed nations. While the world average, excluding the United States, is to lock up about 1 in 800 citizens, the United States confines roughly 1 in 145. When a nation leads the world in any statistic, it begs the question, *Why?* Is it necessary? How do other countries, with demographics and melting pots of ethnicities similar to ours, engineer both low crime rates and low incarceration rates simultaneously? What is it about the American social and political system that fuels the desire to lock up so many people?

If the United States had enjoyed a "normal" incarceration rate since 1980, one in conformity with the rest of humanity, we would have 80% fewer prisoners than we have today, and our facilities would have avoided a combined fifty million human-years of imprisonment. We're either on to something brilliant that the rest of the world does not yet understand – or we're doing something costly, counterproductive, and arguably inhumane. As one modern philosopher observed, "It's a fine line between clever . . . and stupid."

I come from a mathematics-based background, having worked as a land surveyor in my former life. I like numbers. I like numbers because they quantify, whereas all other descriptors are ambiguous. So, in addition to the anecdotal evidence, I have also provided some light analysis to reveal the root causes of mass incarceration. We examine the solitary prisoner as the quantum unit of incarceration, then work backwards: to the nation that incarcerates disproportionately as compared to the international community, to the state that established the sentencing framework, and to the county that sentenced him. I have been cautioned by wiser people than me, professionals within the publishing industry, to go light on the data, so I've kept it sparse. Not everybody likes numbers the way I do.

At the end of the book my hope is that the reader will realize that American penal policies, enacted by legislatures, utilized by prosecutors, and enforced by the judiciary, have caused the most massive wanton deprivation of liberty since 1865. It's not crime, but the government's response to crime, that

Fifty Million Years in Prison

has caused an abnormally high incarceration rate. Just as breaking the law is a choice, lengthy sentences are also a choice, a choice made by the people in a democratic society, through their elected officials.

When this book goes to press, in early 2017, the post-1980 human cost will be, more precisely, forty-nine million years, and counting. In 2018 the United States will hit the fifty-million-year mark. We're not in this situation because of crime, as the anecdotes and data will show, but because of underlying and intertwining factors: politics, poverty, and racial bias. That's my thesis.

Now, for the stories of these prisoners, and how I arrived at this conclusion. . . .

Fifty Million Years in Prison

CHAPTER ONE

The Ark, The Covenant

"You've got a thousand men in the water and maybe three life preservers. You better be okay with watching men drown."
– Melvin Tunstill, when I took a job in the prison law library.

    Prison is isolation. Russian writer Aleksandr Solzhenitsyn famously described Stalin-era prisons and labor camps as a string of islands – an archipelago – strewn across the Soviet Union's landscape. Solzhenitsym was referring to geographic isolation, but his metaphor was laden with a hidden dimension. Islands, as botanists and zoologists know, develop unique characteristics; and a string of islands, given time, will transform life into something much different from life on the mainland. Isolation (from the Italian *isola*, meaning "island") limits available resources, and creates a challenging environment. Natural selection, with all its brutality implied, takes effect. New species emerge, and they thrive on their island but are maladapted to the outside world. In that respect, Solzhenitsyn's island metaphor was more than geographic. It was ageless and perfect, more than he probably knew.
    America's prison archipelago has more islands and more prisoners than Stalin's at its height, but a comparison to a totalitarian regime is probably unfair. Stalin's motives were political, and his idea of due process devolved into "show trials," a warped style of justice. Ethnic groups were targeted, and purges removed their voices from political discourse. The Soviet labor camps also satisfied an economic incentive, to construct public works and open rugged Siberia to development. Stalin's gulags were purely exploitative. There's

nothing like that going on here, I presume – we have a moral, anti-crime motivation, defensible incentives, and a cautious system of due process – so it's harsh to lay the two countries' records side by side.

Except, somehow, *without* a dictator in charge, we have still managed to amass more convicted prisoners than any country in history, and have the world's highest incarceration rate, despite the existence of several countries we consider inhumanely oppressive. Just think, if we didn't have democracy, wealth, and high ideals . . . how much worse would it be?

I am an inhabitant on one of the islands, and I have taken a job in the prison law library. In all my reading of Soviet literature, I don't recall any reference to law libraries in the gulag, or jailhouse lawyers, or writs of habeas corpus. Habeas corpus is a construct of English law. Russian zeks, once screwed, stayed screwed, as far as I can tell. It's not like that here, which is another reason why America's high incarceration rate confounds me. Our system should correct injustice, act as a brake on wrongful convictions and excessive sentences, and drive the imprisonment rate downward.

My vision as a law library clerk is pretty clear. I want to see a prisoner who has been declared guilty beyond a reasonable doubt overturn his conviction and walk out the front gate, into an enraptured throng of photographers and reporters. I want to see this prisoner on the ten o'clock news, grateful for the restoration of his freedom, thanking the people responsible for his release, my name foremost among them. I want to expose the system's injustice by freeing at least one wrongfully convicted man. One victory, maybe two or three, isn't much to ask.

The opportunity to win in court seems enormous. Over several years in prison I have listened to hundreds of prisoners' stories and recognized a legitimate thread of unfairness within their complaints. Common sense leads me to believe their cases are correctable, if only the right legal pressure is applied. On the surface, case after case seems fixable. We have over 1,700 men at Pendleton, and they have over 30,000 years left to do in prison. It should not be hard to find a case I can win.

Yet, every day, I feel some hesitation. My formal legal training consists of nothing more than writing legal descriptions of property, a product of my former career as a land surveyor. I will be working with murderers, gangsters, dope dealers, and the mentally ill, most of them with long sentences, histories of violence, and with nothing to lose. If I screw up their legal work, how will they react?

It's Tuesday, cellhouse delivery day. A relentless wind penetrates our thin prison clothing and sleet assaults our faces as we four law library workers trot briskly to what the prisoners here describe as "a jail within a jail," the G-cellhouse segregation unit at Pendleton Correctional Facility. We're carrying postal bins stacked with legal books, blank forms, and printouts of case law, covered with plastic to keep everything dry. Our job is to provide legal assistance to our fellow prisoners in seg, men who have no physical access to the law library. The seg unit houses 268 on this frozen December day in 2011, 20 shy of capacity, and of those, only two or three have retained private counsel for their ongoing legal issues. The rest, if they have collateral attacks on their convictions pending or contemplated, pin their hopes on us, four guys with no legal training.

A ten-foot chain-link fence topped with razor wire parallels the brown brick cellhouse, and we're waiting at the gate, thirty feet from the cellhouse doors, hoping a guard will notice we're waiting to get in. I adopt a downwind pose, and as we wait, my mind wanders. The cellhouse dimensions remind me of the ark built to withstand the Great Flood – proportional to Noah's plan, 30 by 50 by 300 cubits, the color of faded gopherwood, seal the windows and maybe it'll rise with its foundation and float. But no, it's the anti-ark, filled with the unworthy, waiting for the Second Deluge, weighted down with two million pounds of steel, feeling gravity's pull since 1923. The floor inevitably cracked, rendering this ark unseaworthy. Besides, it wasn't built for animals two by two, innocent and destined to repopulate the Earth, but for humans one by one who've displayed their Hobbesian animal natures. One of the first occupants was John Herbert Dillinger, #14395, arriving without fanfare September 16, 1924, with an eleven-year commitment to think about. Just an ordinary prisoner, he transferred to Michigan City in 1929 and was released May 10,

1933, going on to a brief free life punctuated by fame/infamy. I doubt Dillinger ever imagined the cellhouse as watercraft.

It would take nearly 8,000 buildings like this one to house all of the prisoners in America, so I am looking at a tiny sliver of the mass incarceration phenomenon. On this day, America's prisoner head count is 2,252,500 – one-and-a-half times the population of Manhattan, squeezed into an area one-fourth the size of Manhattan. From the southern tip of the island, they wouldn't make it to the theater district. If prisoners formed their own state, it would be more populous than 15 other states, and command five electoral votes – if they were allowed to vote. Or, spread out in their respective areas of residence, they would have altered the outcome of the 2000 Presidential election. (And later, the 2016 election.) The sheer numbers are massive, with an enormous potential for political influence.

"Gate!" yells Edgar Lee, shaking me out of my daydream. "Come on with the damn gate," he mutters with impatience. "Gate!" Of our quartet, he's the one most eager to make this visit and return quickly. He's assigned to serve the 2-4-6 ranges on D-side, the most restricted area of disciplinary seg (DS). The men he'll see are arguably the most dangerous, nearly all of them in seg for violence or weapons possession. Without question they endure the most miserable living conditions – no television, no radio, no books, no commissary beyond the bare minimum hygiene items. One would think these guys would occupy their time by trying to overturn their convictions, but Edgar Lee's bin is the lightest of the four. Have the men on his ranges lost hope, lost the will to fight? "Gate! Gate! GATE!" A head appears at the door's foot-square window, and moments later a rookie correctional officer (CO) wearing a shank-proof vest is finding the key to unlock the gate's padlock. We sprint up the stairs and into the warmth of the anti-ark.

The requisite shakedown is delayed, giving us time to stash any contraband, if we have any, in the cluttered entry area. Drugs, cellphones, and shanks are slightly less prevalent in seg than in general population, but well-connected and determined prisoners still manage to get the items they want. I once walked up on a seg acquaintance using a cellphone while simultaneously snorting brown heroin from his desktop. "Nobody's slowing you down, are they, Jack?" He grinned, sniffed, and flinched like a gun-shy duck dog. "You know I gotta get mine." The inevitability of the flow of contraband perhaps explains the staff's casual attitude toward shakedowns; and whenever they do conduct a thorough inspection it alerts the prisoner that someone told staff that contraband is being muled. We don't get the predator-eyed focus from the shakedown CO today. Instead we get a blank-faced stare and automaton commands as we undress in pairs in the two booths. I'm down to boxers and socks when the CO says "good enough" and hands my clothes back through the slot. I'm about as far off their radar as a man can get.

Edgar Lee and Whatley were first to get shaken down, and they've grabbed their bins and headed to their ranges. Whatley has the 1-3-5 ranges on D-side, which is also disciplinary seg, but of the softer variety. Most of Whatley's guys have 90 days to do in seg, and all have their personal property. The only punishment is their restriction from all programs, jobs, and daily outdoor recreation. For some, that's offset by having all three meals delivered. Showers run three times a week, as does rec. Rec takes place in 10-by-20-foot "dog runs," chain-link enclosures, each sporting a worn rubber basketball and a backboard with orange hoop, sans net.

I can never pass the rec cages without thinking of the cage-match stabbing I witnessed there in May of 2011. I was a resident on D3 range and went to rec the day Weasel wriggled though a gap in the fencing to get at smart-mouthed Timothy Knapp. Weasel was a nutty kid with a long sentence, while Knapp was a rarity for Pendleton, a guy with only three years to do. Knapp was in for arson, and a "hold" for some minor offense in another state dictated his immurement behind Pendleton's 25-foot wall. He should have been in a lower-level facility, but the classification system is rather inflexible regarding detainers – any kind of detainer, you go behind the wall. He taunted Weasel incessantly, and he probably figured he could run his mouth any kind of way for eight more months, incur no retribution, go home, and laugh at the suckers he left behind. Weasel upset that plan. The two had been feuding for several days, escalating to the artillery fire of shit bombs hurled into opposing cells.

Knapp, expecting a fistfight, allowed Weasel to shimmy through the gap in the dog-run fencing. "C'mon punk-ass bitch, let's get it on!" But to Knapp's surprise, Weasel produced a nine-inch ice-pick type weapon, and the sober realization came that this would be no boxing match.

The squeak of sneakers on concrete was all we heard as thrust and parry commenced. The combatants were wordless, focused, one trying to pierce his hated enemy, the other simply trying to survive. We watched silently, on tiptoe, stretching our necks – prairie-dogging to see the action.

It wasn't until that one particular microsecond, when the victim knew the blade was on its way into his body and wouldn't be deflected or avoided, that he let out a scream in anticipation of the shank hitting its mark. It was a hearty scream, both lungs maximizing their output as his torso braced for impact. And the pitch – it's almost a joke, but experience suggests, the longer the shank, the higher the octave of the scream. A nine-incher commands a note four octaves up the scale, an operatic sopranino – *fortissimo, sostenuto*. Loud and sustained. You'll hear few screams like it during your prison stay, hopefully never emanating from yourself. As Knapp yelled out, my odd thought was, *Why scream?*

The utility of the scream is debatable. As a primeval survival mechanism, the scream may attract assistance or frighten off the attacker, but I've never seen it effectively do either. If anything, attackers seem more emboldened, more determined to keep stabbing until silence is attained. And the only persons who come running invariably stop, take in the scene, and wait for the violence to play out. Interference is risky.

Once Knapp's screaming started it continued for the duration of the stabbing. Weasel got in nine puncture wounds, five in the front, four in back, most of them lower body, none near the heart. By then Knapp was on his back, thrusting the assailant away by kicking his legs. Sometime, between the first stab and the ninth, guys in the surrounding cages started in, siding with Weasel.

"Run your mouth now, motherfucker!"

"Yeah! Ya got what you had coming!"

"Who's the punk-as bitch, now? Bleed out and die, bitch!"

Both Knapp and Weasel were exhausted, and the guards heard the commotion and came trotting down the walk, keys jangling. Seeing the shank, one officer made the radio call, "10-10 with weapons." The other officer told the little guy to drop the weapon and cuff up. Weasel dropped the shank outside the cage door, turned around, slipped his hands out the door slot, and was handcuffed. Knapp never moved.

Another radio call, "Signal 3000," alerted medical, and they came jogging with a stretcher. Knapp was whisked away, and then we were returned to our cells, some grumbling that they didn't get their full hour of rec time.

The day after the stabbing I talked to the officer who had escorted Knapp to the Infirmary. The prisoner had been lying on the table, attended by the weekend nurse. The bleeding wouldn't stop, and at one point the victim exclaimed, "I'm dying!"

The nurse replied, "It's not that bad. You're gonna be alright."

"No! I'm dying! Ya gotta get me to the hospital!"

After forty minutes, with the bleeding unstaunched and the patient getting gray, medical personnel decided maybe it would be best to get this guy to an outside hospital after all.

But according to the official record, he died in the Infirmary. He would prove a reminder to all at Pendleton, that violence can erupt at any time, even in the most tightly secure area of the prison.

As I pass D1 range I see Whatley engaged in the "throw-n-go" method, sliding the man's requested materials under his door and not stopping to answer questions. Questions only lead to more questions, and those lead to doing more work. Whatley has his own case to work on, trying to overturn a drug-dealing conviction. He sold cocaine to an informant, which is normally a Class B felony worthy of 6 to 20 years in prison in Indiana, but in Whatley's case the transaction occurred within 1,000 feet of school property, so it was bumped up to a Class A felony, carrying 20 to 50 years. Whatley ended up with 40, do 20. I've noticed that the purely geographic and seemingly unbiased 1,000-foot rule ensnares far more black defendants than whites. When prosecutors lobbied for the law and the legislature enacted it, did anyone realize that every section of "the hood"' in Indianapolis was within 1,000 feet of a school?

I related to Whatley the story of my friend Jorge Alvarez, convicted in Florida in 1989 for conspiracy to smuggle in 440 pounds of cocaine on a Cessna emanating from the Bahamas. Alvarez did less than seven years on a 15-year sentence, and that was the maximum under Florida law. Whatley delivered a quantity of cocaine that wouldn't fill one empty sugar packet, and he'll do three times as long as my Colombian friend. When I told him the Alvarez story all Whatley could do was toss his hands in the air, shake his head speechlessly, and finally exclaim, "What the fuck am I doing here?"

Tony Warren-Bey and I slide through the gate to C-side, our bins nearly overflowing. This side isn't a disciplinary unit, it's administrative segregation (AS), and these prisoners are here "under investigation." Internal Affairs (IA) officers are usually the ones who put them here, and they're also the ones who decide how long they'll stay. Per Indiana Department of Correction (IDOC) policy, AS prisoners are periodically reviewed for the necessity of continuing AS status, but the prisoner has little input into that review. Many don't believe adequate grounds exist for AS placement, and a majority exhibit anxiety from the indefinite duration of confinement. They become more contentious, both with staff and with us, and they are far more demanding than DS prisoners in their requests for legal assistance.

Administrators also deposit the dysfunctional mentally ill in AS, so we encounter displays of paranoia, delusions, aggression, hyper-sensitivity, and hyper-responsiveness. They act up. Today I'm delivering copies of a federal civil complaint to Markevious Hogan, who scribed a thirty-page diatribe against forty-four defendants, alleging unconstitutional "mind manipulation" and demanding one billion dollars. The defendant list ranges from Jennifer Lopez and Beyoncé to Anheuser Busch, Condoleeza Rice, and Cactus Annie. Hogan is indigent, so his copies were made at no charge. The state will also provide free postage. I'm tempted to ask how he'll spend the billion dollars. He has life without parole.

Warren-Bey heads to the 2-4-6 ranges where he hears Najee Blackford impatiently yelling for a law library clerk. Blackford's behind plexiglass in the first cell on C2 range due to his proclivity for throwing bodily fluids on his enemies, which includes just about anybody going by his cell. His demands are invariably unreasonable and voluminous, and he's always argumentative. "Just serve Blackford for me," Warren-Bey asks, "and I'll do everybody on 1-range for you." No deal, especially not today. I can see the nurse on 1-range now, passing out meds, and I know that range will be calm within 15 minutes.

I'm assigned to the 1-3-5 ranges on C-side, and all 72 cells are full. I start on 3-range, and as soon as I bark out "law library on three" several 1-range guys start screaming.

"You skipped 1-range!"

"You lazy motherfucker, we need law library too!"

"Chill out," I yell back. "I'll be there once the nurse is gone." If they've been here long enough, and most of them have, they know we can't be on the range at the same time as med delivery.

I proceed down 3-range, and a new face in cell 5 has a question. "I just got here from The City, and IA has me down as STG. How long I gotta stay here?" "The City" is the maximum-security prison upstate, at Michigan City, and an STG designation means he's been identified as a member of a Security Threat Group, or gang. The lightning bolts on his neck and the numbers 88 and 14 tell me he's in the Aryan Brotherhood.

"I'd say you'll be in AS until you repudiate your gang affiliation, debrief with IA, and have sat here long enough that they don't think you'll cause any problems in population."

To debrief means to tell IA what the gang's been up to. Snitching, in other words; and in this case snitching on the prisoners with the highest likelihood of responding with extreme violence. He asks, "Isn't there some kind of constitutional violation for keeping a man in seg indefinitely?"

I explain the U.S. Supreme Court decision declaring there is "no liberty interest" at stake when a prisoner is placed in seg. Seg prisoners are incredulous when they first hear this, ticking off all the liberties that come with housing in general population. Running track, weight machines, programs, socializing, hot meals in the chow hall, church services. But the courts don't define liberty by what a person can do, only by whether that person is removed from free society or not. Reducing a 31-acre prison down to a 49-square-foot cell is no "loss of liberty" to our Supreme Court justices. The landmark segregation case is *Hewitt v. Helms* (1983), and I make a note to give this guy a copy of my AS handout, a sort-of orientation pamphlet for AS prisoners.

While delivering blank forms to 15-on-3C I notice Toby Payne in cell 14, pacing rapidly, four steps forward, turn, four steps back, turn. His light is on, the only brightly lit cell in the building. Looks like he's under 120 pounds now, nervous, frail, a deathly pallor. He's got life without parole (LWOP) for a harebrained scheme where he hired a Mexican acquaintance to kill his ex-wife. Toby provided the house key to the accomplice, who employed a confederate who killed Toby's ex and the guy with whom she was having sex.

They were on the bed and oblivious to the intruder until the gun was fired. With faux sympathy, I ask Toby how he's doing. "You need anything?" He flashes a glare and keeps pacing.

Up on 5-range I reach five guys in consecutive cells who have all filed post-conviction (PC) petitions, and when I talk to the first one I notice the other four have gotten up to listen. The PC is the most crucial action a state prisoner can file – a modern day version of the Writ of Habeas Corpus, or "Great Writ," which traces its lineage to the Magna Carta in 1215. The writ has undergone many changes in 800 years, mainly a broadening of its application, but its purpose has been fundamentally the same: the petitioner contends he's unlawfully confined; that despite the guilty finding by twelve unanimous jurors and the affirmation of that verdict on direct appeal, certain fundamental rights were denied and the conviction should be held invalid. In other words, he claims he didn't get a fair trial.

The PC petition focuses on matters outside the trial record, such as witnesses that weren't called, potential evidence that wasn't used, or cross-examination questions counsel failed to ask – mistakes that seem to happen in every trial. Issues counsel failed to preserve, such as failure to object to inaccurate jury instructions, or failure to challenge a discriminatory jury selection process, are also reviewable on a PC petition. There are hundreds of possible issues. Most imply one's trial attorney or appellate attorney failed to safeguard the defendant's rights, so PC petitioners regularly allege ineffective assistance of counsel (IAC). The U. S. Constitution, Amendment V, guarantees a defendant the right to "have the Assistance of Counsel in his defence" in "all criminal matters," and the U. S. Supreme Court has interpreted this as requiring more than an attorney's mere presence, but "effective" counsel.

The Court established the standard of review for IAC claims in *Strickland v. Washington* (1984), the most well-known case in all prisoner jurisprudence. Every PC plaintiff is familiar with *Strickland*'s two prongs that must be satisfied before relief is granted: (1) counsel's performance was deficient, and (2) the errors were so serious as to deprive the defendant of a fair trial, a trial whose result is reliable. The prisoner doesn't have to prove he's innocent; he only has to show by a "preponderance of the evidence" that a "reasonable probability" exists that the verdict was wrong. Sounds easy, but experience shows it's not.

The prisoners listen attentively as I answer questions about the long, complicated PC process. My five PC petitioners have seemingly endless questions, and I wish there was a book I could hand them that would explain it all, but no such book exists. The PC rules have been in place in Indiana since 1969, but nobody has bothered to author a self-help manual to relieve these guys from the burden of having to muddle through it.

One has an urgent request – his notice of appeal deadline is seven days away. I assure him I can complete the paperwork within two days. Perhaps disappointed by others' failures, he asks for a third time, "You sure you can get it back to me in time?" This is Tuesday, and I know the form I'll draft will be in Thursday's deliveries.

"It's easy," I assure him. "I get back to the library, and I'll have it done in the time it takes you to wash your hair." He's shaven bald, swastika tattoo above the ear.

"That'd be fast," he grins, wiping his palm over his smooth dome. "You sure?"

"Word."

Word means something here. If you give your word you'll do something, your entire reputation rides on it. It's a guarantee; a covenant. For most of us, our word is sacred. We give it sparingly because it obligates us to the utmost.

He up-nods approvingly. "Right on. That's what's up." He's clearly relieved, and although he's never met me before he's 100% certain I'll come through.

I finally break away and continue down 5-range. I see a few guys I know, including an old cellmate from 2008. I've been at Pendleton six years, and while I don't know everybody, it seems like everybody knows me. Others call my name and I answer a few more ordinary questions. "How do I get a copy of my trial transcript?" "How do I get a copy of my attorney's file?" These are routine, and I promise to supplement my responses with informative handouts next week. Then I traverse down to 1-range and field an odd request from Donald Lock, wheelchair-bound in cell 1.

Lock's in his late 60's, in poor health, and wants to donate his body to science. Indiana University School of Medicine, specifically. He saw a feature on cadaver use on the local news and apparently wants to make one final contribution to the world. I happen to have the forms for a living will on my computer, and I can modify one to suit him. An Indiana statute forbids the use of prisoners' bodies for any purpose, in life or after death – prisoners can't even donate blood – but there's no point telling Mr. Lock this. I know from experience he wants what he wants and will just complain until he gets it. As I leave I tell him, "Too bad more guys don't donate their bodies, it'd put the Chinese organ thieves out of business." "Yeah," he responds, "put 'em out of business!"

I continue down C1-range and wordlessly slide Hogan's copies under his door. He's asleep, but twitching, and I'm glad I have no awareness of the visions flashing through his mind. His meds worked fast.

Next to Hogan is Michael Daniels, who always has a request ready and placed in his door slot. He's in bed, facing the wall, blanket wrapped tight around his head. Daniels spent 27 years on death row, now he's got LWOP. He senses my presence. "It's all in the envelope, self-explanatory." I take it and move on. Later, when I open the envelope, I'll see he filed a "Motion to Correct Erroneous Sentence" in county court, it was denied, and now he has appealed. His Appellant's Brief needs a lot of work, and since he's been locked up so long I decide to look into his case.

I pick up a request from cell 23, who points to his left and says, "The chomo in 24 needs to see you."

The prisoner in 24, Jerry Griner, sees me coming and thrusts a thick envelope at me. He's obese, bald, pale, wearing the oversized state-issue bifocals locally known as "chominators." They complete the classic child molester look – "chomo" is short for child molester. Jerry's in his 50's, and I immediately size him up as a person with no ability to function in general population.

"I got this in the mail," he says. "All I know is, it's from the court. I had Russell Boyd helping me, but he left."

I see the postmark, dated in August. "You've had this for four months and you don't know what it says?"

"I can't read."

I review the court order. The judge gave him 30 days to amend his PC petition or it'd get dismissed with prejudice. The next paper is the dismissal order. He has a 45-year sentence for attempted murder, with a 30-year habitual offender enhancement; 75 years total. His priors are mostly thefts, but there's a child molesting conviction there too. I see in Jerry's other papers – he's offering handfuls now that I've held still for him – he also has a long history of mental illness, with numerous in-patient stints of short duration. He was off his meds one winter day, stormed out of his mother's house in Lafayette, and robbed an elderly woman outside the Dollar General store. The woman resisted surrendering her purse, so Jerry stabbed her in the chest with a paring knife. Four dollars were taken and later found in Jerry's shirt pocket. The woman was slightly punctured, and at Jerry's sentencing she seemed most concerned with the financial loss of her bloodstained coat. He pled guilty and got five years less than the maximum. Now he wants to know what he can do to get back in court.

"Jerry, this is a mess." I promise to get back to him next week. Hope is a nasty, tenacious, blinding emotion. He's a mentally ill, illiterate, violent sex offender who pled guilty, and he's exhausted his appeals and PC petition, yet he still holds out hope for freedom.

Finished with my ranges, I discover Edgar Lee and Whatley are long gone, and Warren-Bey is trying to extricate himself from Blackford's presence. I can hear Blackford chiding Warren-Bey, "You don't know nuthin', do ya? You just a house nigga shuffling down here with the mail. Straight dumbass." Warren-Bey half grins and fires back, "At least I'm shuffling. You're stuck behind that glass, like an animal." Blackford's a prime example of how not to do one's time. He's midway through his eleventh year on a 20-do-10, and still has a year to go. He keeps losing time due to misconduct.

Blackford once sent me his trial transcript to review, and he seems to be hung up on the "bogus match" of the spandex leggings found in his room to the spandex worn by the cross-dressing bank robber. "Those spandex were brand new. I never wore 'em." Spandex or not, there was plenty of other evidence, and I commiserated for the attorneys who have had to represent him. I mentioned to Blackford that his PC attorney lived across the street from me when I was arrested in 2005. "Oh! So you're sent here to cover up for her!" That was, thankfully, the end of my involvement with his case.

Warren-Bey and I, exhausted from non-stop questioning, finally flee G-cellhouse, the wind and sleet punishing us again as we quickstep back to the law library. En route we pass two flatcarts loaded with Styrofoam trays, piled high in layers on orange bread racks. Two kitchen workers are pushing the meals to the seg units, and the trays aren't wrapped, aren't covered, and will sit in the elements for up to an hour. Prisoners occasionally file grievances about the cold, wet food, but policy allows the trays to sit for four hours – at any location, indoors or outdoors, apparently – and still be considered warm enough to serve.

Policy: A rule justifying whatever practice is currently in place.

I have a cold tray waiting on my desk when I return, but the four-hour rule doesn't concern me today. We have a microwave oven in the back room, behind the "Workers Only" sign, as well as the only toaster oven in the prison.

The law library is a spacious, high-ceilinged hive of legal activity. Prison libraries like this one have spawned some of the most influential cases in American legal history, cases that have shaped how criminal matters are handled for millions of Americans. Napue, Gideon, Brady, Boykin, Anders, Pearce, McDonnell, Batson, Barker, Faretta, Doyle, Herrera, Brecht, Conner, Miller-El, Frye, Holt, and many others – all were prisoners who began by filing rudimentary petitions and ended up as landmark cases in the U. S. Supreme Court. The prisoners occupying this room, fifteen per hourly pass line, seven lines per day, are emboldened by the knowledge that their predecessors fought from rooms similar to this one, less-equipped ones even, and successfully overturned their convictions or gave back years off their sentences. Hope and hard work combine here, and every man dreams of being the next one to get the life-changing news: "You've won your case, and you're going home."

The resources within Pendleton's law library make it comparable to any law library inside or outside prison. Foremost in utility are the computers, ten assigned to law clerks, fourteen open to the patrons. Computers are loaded with Microsoft Office software, and MS Word allows prisoners to rapidly format neat, legible documents. The clerks have compiled a bank of over 200 modifiable legal forms. The searchable legal database, LEXIS, is updated quarterly and contains court opinions, or "case law," from Indiana and all federal courts. Two desktop printers and an industrial copier never seem to rest, providing copies at ten cents per page. Colored papers and binders for preparing appellate briefs are free. Dozens of legal books are on the shelves, along with subscriptions to the *Indiana Defender, Indiana Lawyer, Prison Legal News, Indiana Law Journal,* and *Notre Dame Law Journal.* The only Internet connection belongs to the supervisor, Larry Fowler, who uses it to find requested addresses and very recent court decisions. An old IBM Selectric II typewriter sits alone at the back of the room, an anachronistic exhibit reminding prisoners of the days when research was conducted by using thick, tan volumes of the *Indiana Reporters*, while hoping the case desired hadn't been razor-sliced and stolen.

Annual law library expenditures hover around $62,000, with almost 90% of it for the computer systems. The LEXIS database is the largest single expense, $46,000 per year, and other computer costs are close to $9,000. But taxpayers need not be indignantly alarmed – prisoners pay for all of it through the Offender Trust Fund. The account is fueled from a 10% tax on commissary sales, and Pendleton's 1,750 prisoners dole out nearly $1.3 million per year for food, clothing, and hygiene items, about $750 per year per man. If that seems like a lot, realize that the distribution of prisoners' wealth is similar to the distribution of wealth on the outside – divided into the haves and have-nots. The top 20% of prisoners account for half of the commissary sales. The bottom 20% rarely purchase commissary.

Statewide, Indiana's 28,900 prisoners spend over $20 million a year on food, while the state contracts with food service provider Aramark at $25 million annually for the meals prisoners try to avoid. Figuring in Aramark's unpublished profit margin, and ballparking the amount of Aramark food that finds its rightful home in the trash, one can safely infer that close to half the average prisoner's nutrition is self-purchased. The poor food quality in the dining hall has the collateral effect of giving the prisoners better legal resources.

I'm reheating overcooked spaghetti when fellow law clerk Pete Mitchell alerts me that I have a "client" waiting. Pete has a well-rounded litigation history: state, federal, criminal, civil, IDOC grievances, and disciplinary appeals. He has the gift of being able to slice through a prisoner's thick case description and ascertain the relevant facts and issues in rapid fashion. I often consult Pete when I'm searching for a solution to a legal problem, and he does the same with me.

"Hopefully not an 'innocent' client today," I plead. "I'm too tired to go fifteen rounds again."

Pete recognizes my reference to the man we endured yesterday, Calvin Hogg. Contrary to public perception, we have very few prisoners claiming innocence, like Hogg. Hogg is legendary here for his bombastic denials, constantly asserting it wasn't rape, it was consensual sex with his ex-girlfriend. And when he gets his conviction overturned he's going to sue the state for millions. Yesterday he soapboxed for an hour, saying there was "no physical evidence" and his ex's testimony should fall under the "incredible dubiosity" rule. Hogg kept repeating that her testimony "didn't make sense," and "if it was rape why'd she wait three days to report it?" Well, it made sense to twelve jurors, and wasn't so incredible that a reviewing court would throw it out. As for physical evidence, none is required to convict for a sex offense. We understood Hogg's general assessment: the whole case devolved into simply believing the accuser, not exactly the overwhelming "beyond a reasonable doubt" standard one would expect to support a 50-year sentence. But there was nothing we could do. A conviction founded solely on testimonial evidence is almost certainly irreversible. If Hogg truly is innocent, it's unfortunate that all he knows to do is keep proclaiming it, loudly, frequently, and to no avail.

Pete assures me today's client is nothing like Hogg. "He's waiting at the far table, quiet guy. He might actually be innocent for all I know, but he sure doesn't act like Hogg. He's the one in for murder on the egg-throwing case."

The spaghetti is pure mush so I trash it, lean out the door, and give my guy a 'one-minute' signal. I grab a blank A-4 form for Mr. Hakenkreuz's Notice of Appeal, to fill out immediately. If the whole prison goes on lockdown (which is liable to happen at any time, without warning) I can still use the institutional mail system to get his form to him by Thursday. Then I reach under my desk and grab a thirty-pound bag of legal papers and carry it to the man who was convicted of murdering a 15-year-old boy for hitting him with a raw egg.

I had read his file over the weekend. The sensational case made front page headlines in Indianapolis in 2005, and carried nationwide interest. A group of teenagers, all black but one, had thrown an old mattress in the road and ambushed white drivers with eggs when they slowed to avoid the obstacle. There were several egging victims, including Lori Barton, who pulled over and called 9-1-1 as she was taunted, "Ha Ha! Stupid white bitch!" As she spoke into her cellphone an irate man in a red pick-up truck stopped by. Also egged in the head, he told her, "I've got a rifle," and drove off to chase the kids.

Two shots were eventually fired at four youths who were fleeing down a dark corridor next to the Public Storage building. One .22-caliber bullet struck Michael Dyer in the leg. The other shot struck Brandon Dunson in the back, piercing his heart. He'd taken his white shirt off, presumably to make himself more difficult to see as he played the 'escape and evade' game. He lagged behind the others and fell behind the building, the shirt still in his pocket. One of his friends found him dead hours later, around 2 a.m.

Police quickly developed a suspect, Wally Pierson, who drove a red pickup truck and lived nearby. Pierson was a registered gun owner whose license plate partially matched the partial description given by Lori Barton. Barton identified Pierson from a six-photo array as the man she saw stop and threaten to go after the kids with a rifle. She was "90% sure" it was Pierson.

Detectives tracked Pierson to his girlfriend's apartment, and when they knocked Pierson cautiously approached the peephole with a loaded 9-mm pistol in hand. Multiple officers were prepared to enter, so Pierson placed the gun on the floor, told officers it was there, and surrendered. He waived his Miranda rights, started talking, and let them search the apartment.

In Pierson's first story he didn't get home on the Sunday night in question until almost midnight. The shooting had taken place around 11:30 p.m., and yes, he'd heard about it on the news. A detective dug in the trash and found a receipt from a gas station less than two miles from the murder scene, timed for Sunday night at 11:09 p.m. Then Pierson's story changed; oh, yeah, he might've gotten home sooner than he thought.

And where had he been that day? He'd had dinner with family friends at a rural residence about 60 miles south of Indianapolis. The afternoon had been spent target shooting. With a .22-caliber rifle.

It was pretty solid policework, I recognized, similar to dozens of cases I'd read. The evidence was probably sufficient to convict Wally Pierson of reckless homicide, or possibly voluntary manslaughter committed while acting under "sudden heat," at worst. But not murder. Murder requires the killing be done "knowingly or intentionally," and a good attorney should have been able to successfully argue that shooting at dark figures running through a dark area at night would not qualify "beyond a reasonable doubt" as a knowing or intentional murder.

But there was more evidence discovered in the week after the shooting, and it pointed away from Wally Pierson. In fact, the man sitting at the prison law library table isn't Wally Pierson. Despite the evidence developed in the first 48 hours, Pierson, son of a Marion County Sheriff's Deputy, was never charged, never arrested. The man wearing a neatly pressed prison uniform sitting forlornly across from me is 43-year-old Donnie Ware. His demeanor is placid, composed, and friendly, belying his technical classification as a "violent criminal." He has a 70-year sentence, no money, no lawyer, and no idea what to do.

I want Donald Ware's case. Donnie Ware has a case I can win.

CHAPTER TWO

Ascending the Granite Wall

"While nothing is easier to denounce than the evildoer, nothing is more difficult than to understand him." – Fyodor Dostoyevsky

Easter Sunday, 1988. Yosemite National Park. I'm 26 years old and, I think, pretty good at rock climbing. I've free-styled my way up several cliffs in California, the 100 to 200-foot variety, and on this day I've committed myself to scrambling up a crease hidden between two monoliths of granite, leading to a crest at the back left behind Bridalveil Falls. I figure I'll make it to the top in an hour or two, then descend to the edge of the waterfall, all so some Japanese tourist will possess an Ansel Adams-like photo with some guy (me) giving human scale to the 620-foot drop. The things I do for art.

"What I didn't know," I explained to Tony Warren-Bey years later, "was that the incline went from 70 to 80 to 90 degrees pure vertical. When facing it, you can't see that. And since it was a gulch between two peaks, I never had the side view that would've kept me off that spot."

There are always clues that you're out of your element. In rock climbing, one is that you've shifted from using your legs to using your arms to provide upward motion. Another is that you're stretching on tiptoe to reach the next handhold. The last clue, reserved for dummies, I guess, is when you see pitons wedged into crevices around you.

I came to a halt with my left hand wrapped around the third piton, and I advised my climbing partner, "Don't come up." After a few minutes of trying to find a way to reverse course I told Harry, "I'm gonna need a rope and a harness."

While Harry was gone I managed to spin around, put my back to the cliff, and hold the piton above my head with my right hand. It was a beautiful vista, the tops of the pine trees forming a flat carpet across the valley, like the surface of a dark green reservoir. A few hundred feet below three experienced climbers on a cross-trail came into view. They were headed down. "Yo!" I yelled. Up came a man with hands like Spiderman and legs like a grasshopper, his rapid ascent mocking my recent labor. He had extra gear. A nylon cord was slipped through the piton, I was harnessed, and we frog-hopped down. A park ranger, not amused, told me they have to get somebody off Penny-Nickel Gulch about once a week. "It's deceptive," he said.

"The moral of the story," I concluded, "is that despite your previous success, despite your confidence, and despite the appearance of ease of the task before you, you still have to allow for the possibility . . . that you don't really know what you're doing."

None of the dozen of us law clerks were burdened by the delusion of overconfidence, a characteristic distinguishing us from the braggadocio of the cellblock's jailhouse lawyers and the self-righteous certitude of the do-it-yourselfers wrapped up in the details of their own petitions. Experience in most subjects lends to a rise in one's confidence, but in the field of law there's a curvilinear relationship: confidence rises at first, crests on a rounded hilltop, then abruptly falls, taking a long glide down an infinite ski slope. The descent is triggered when one begins losing cases for reasons that aren't easily explained. Precedent is ignored, facts are tossed aside. The law sheds its appearance of a logical science and cloaks itself in a mist disguising its true form: the art of persuasion, with outcomes determined non-scientifically, by humans forming opinions. Every appellate and supreme court case is titled just that: "Opinion." In jurisprudence, there is no Pythagorean Theorem, no Boyle's Law, no theory on the conservation of mass and energy. It's just people. People, basically, making up shit as they go along. With enough experience, one's confidence in any legal outcome, like the end of a ski run, levels out and approaches zero.

We twelve resided at different points along the confidence curve, our guys forming a representative cross-section of the prison litigator's life cycle. At the nascent stage was Walker Whatley, who thus far had only worked on his own case, and so had yet to experience failure. He approached his PC petition and his appeal like a Rubik's Cube – he'd figure it out, plop down the solution, and the court would be compelled to agree. He sat at the computer to my left. I'd see him type a sentence, edit it, lean back and unconsciously fiddle with his near-Afro, mumble the sentence, then edit again. Close that window, open another, and re-read the controlling case law. And back. He'd ask, "How can they prove I was within 1,000 feet of a school when nobody went out there and measured it?" At trial they'd had a county employee familiar with the GIS map – Geographical Information System – testify he'd scaled the distance from property line to property line at 821 feet. Straight line. But to walk from door to door would be about 1,200 feet. To Whatley, every detail under close examination spelled an opportunity to overturn his conviction. Read the law. Read it again. He was thorough in his pursuit, which is how law clerks are made. Surely, surely, there was a way out of this.

Atop the hill, overflowing with optimism, was Michael Lane, aka Mongoose. He knew enough about the law to believe the legal system could provide justice to the wrongfully convicted, but he lacked the hands-on, hard-knocks experience that would've shown him how difficult it is to obtain that justice. He lacked the side-view of Penny-Nickel Gulch; he believed most cases were winnable. A rail-thin black man in his forties, he'd preserved the healthy exuberance of his long-gone twenties, his age belied only by the gray now sprouting from his ever-crisp short haircut and his occasional reliance upon reading glasses. Nearly twenty-five years in prison had given him that gray, and for the entirety of that time, from arrest to trial to what should have been the brink of hopelessness, he'd maintained his innocence. As had his two codefendants, also at Pendleton, who both vehemently denied a rape had occurred, and believed that, somehow, the post-conviction process would rescue them. One codefendant, Robey, never came to the law library – he was a sullen, defeated man – but Blakemore and Lane trolled the LEXIS database incessantly, like prospectors panning for nuggets in the stream of an abandoned claim.

Like many of the wrongfully convicted, Mongoose and his cohorts desired DNA testing – but the evidence, apparently, was gone. There's no law on the books requiring police or prosecutors to preserve evidence, although most agencies do so against the possibility of a retrial. Once that possibility is extinguished – conviction upheld on direct appeal – the county agency may elect to clean the clutter out of the evidence room. Tactically, it's probably the prudent thing to do, especially if the conviction was based mainly on unsubstantiated victim testimony.

Mongoose, or Goose as we frequently called him, was dedicated to delivering the kind of help to others he hoped to receive for himself one day. "These guys in the hole need research done," he'd say, spurring us on to an effort beyond what was written in our job description. Really, all we had to do was deliver blank forms and specifically requested case law. But Goose had done a bit of seg time too. Coupled with a firm belief in his own innocence, he identified with the most beleaguered men at Pendleton. If there's one thing that separates the innocent in prison from those who falsely claim they're innocent, it's this: the innocent believe there are others like themselves in prison; the pretenders think everybody's guilty and others who claim innocence are liars . . . like them.

Sliding down the confidence slope in an accelerating fashion was Tony Warren-Bey, whose petition for certiorari was pending in the U.S. Supreme Court. He'd lost his PC in the county and on appeal, transfer to the Indiana Supreme Court was denied, his petition for writ of habeas corpus was drubbed out of U.S. district court, no appeal was allowed in the Seventh Circuit, and now he waited for an official date of death to put on his case's tombstone. It's the last thing written on a fully exhausted claim: *cert denied*. The odds that the U.S. Supreme Court would intervene on a nondescript state PC case were so remote as to defy calculation, and I'm sure Warren-Bey knew that. A hellbound snowball could've read his cert petition and thought, *Maybe I don't have it so bad.* He had the look I'd come to know from others who had traveled so far: *Okay, so what do I do now?*

I never delved into the details of Warren-Bey's case. All I knew was that it was murder, and from Indianapolis. Collectively, we read hundreds of cases, but we had little interest in our fellow clerks' cases. Why burn my time with *your* case when you're up here 45 hours a week just like me? I'd skimmed through a few of Warren-Bey's filings and I saw he knew how to properly format his work, and he wrote fairly well – whether that meant he knew how to argue his case was still, to me, an open question, which is why I'd related to him the Penny-Nickel Gulch story.

Stretched out on the flattening curve where experience is long and confidence in the outcome is low were Mike Lindsey, Pete Mitchell, Bill Woodford, and me. Between us, we'd battled in the courts for over 60 years, filing thousands of documents. Our success rate, well, that would depend on how one defines the term "win." Total victory – the enemy's war-torn capital hoisting a white flag – never happens. But we all had tales of getting satisfaction for ourselves or others. Success at the law is measured by degree.

Mike Lindsey, with his pre-1985 five-digit prison number, had been wrangling with the courts the longest. He was in his early 50's, with densely-rooted dark hair erupting out of his scalp, like the brow of a woodchuck wakened from slumber. After an inch or two of vertical effort, Mike's hair laid parallel to his head, partless, neatly coifed, as all former barbers wear it long after they've disengaged from the barber shop. Square-rimmed prescription glasses hid the lines radiating from around his eyes, and a square jaw completed a look I likened to a research chemist at Eli Lilly. He had a bachelor's degree from Ball State, and wonderfully concise legal writing, honed, no doubt, from years of practice. His wit was equally concise – dry humor, founded on paradox. He grew up in Northern Indiana and was a big fan of Notre Dame football, a team I detested for the purely logical reason that the cop who beat me when I was arrested was a former Fighting Irish football player. I'd been face down with two other cops on my back, motionless, when Frank Poskon came over and punched my head repeatedly, until he broke his own hand. Mike's explanation: "He didn't hear the whistle." And it was my own fault for not wearing a helmet on the play.

Mike kept his law practice concise, maintaining a very small case load by cherry-picking the most promising cases. He'd work on three or four cases at a time, in addition to his own. Whatever his offense was, it was something about which I knew nothing. I was pretty sure it was his second time in. His outdate was the same year as mine, in 2037. I didn't ask about his case; there was no reason to breach prison etiquette by inquiring. (The question, *What are you in for?* could be met several ways, most of them counterproductive. *Why are you asking? What business is it of yours? What are YOU in for?* Or, the question could tripwire a series of lies – *I'm in for arson* when it was really a sex offense.) Whatever Mike was in for, I knew it couldn't be too hideous or he'd have never been hired to work in the law library. Larry Fowler, for whatever reason, didn't hire child molesters.

Pete Mitchell, who never answered to his given name (Richard), was the social loner of our group. He didn't have any buddies to hang out with, rarely laughed or smiled, and exuded pessimism with a force nearly equal to Mongoose's optimism. While Mongoose's personality attracted conversation, even if only light banter, Pete's persona deflected small talk. His clients were likewise pessimists, sour and withdrawn. Six-foot, with thinning blonde hair and gray-rimmed oversized bifocals, he held fast to his desk, intently focused on his computer screen, seldom joining in conversation. Late in the day he'd get in an hour or so on some shoot-em-up video game.

Pete had a Class B felony conviction, armed robbery, with a habitual offender enhancement, so he'd been to prison twice before, beginning in 1985. Each prison term taught him more about post-conviction law. On his current conviction he was enduring the frustration of trying to get DNA testing to prove his "innocence," a claim none of us believed. Our pronouncement was probably unfair – none of us were familiar with the details of his case. Our doubt was based on nothing more than the feeling we got when listening to his denials. The same subjective method had us believing in Mongoose's innocence, evidence unseen.

In Pete's case, the armed robber at a bar in Kosciusko County had, undisputedly, used a beer glass that was later tested for prints and DNA. The prints didn't match Pete, and the "major" DNA found wasn't Pete's. There were four "minor" bands of DNA found, considered by the forensic specialist at the Indiana State Police crime lab as too minimal to deserve further analysis. Pete wanted those four DNA profiles developed and compared to the national Combined DNA Index System (CODIS) database – but the PC court refused, and the higher courts upheld the refusal. Indiana law allows a prisoner to get DNA testing done when it could prove innocence, but if it doesn't definitively exculpate the convicted person, a test doesn't have to be done. Prosecutors argue (usually successfully) against all post-conviction DNA testing requests on the grounds that the rest of the evidence is "overwhelming" (whether it is or not). Even top-notch attorneys and Innocence Project specialists may have to file years of petitions and appeals just to get the evidence examined. Pete, despite his experience with the process, could get nowhere doing it alone.

At the desk adjacent to the supervisor sat Bill Woodford, a clerk few liked because, as Edgar Lee put it, "he thinks he runs the place." Even Mongoose, who seemed to like everybody, would roll his eyes, shake his head, and say, "I don't know what to say about Bill." It wasn't Bill's assigned job, but he did assume the air of de facto office manager. The monthly reports on law library activity – patrons served, supplies used, payroll required – were Bill's exclusive province, as was the database he'd built, tailor-made for the law library's needs. He'd earned a business degree from Grace College, scoring high marks, and was meticulous and well-organized by personal habit. "I'm going to outlive this sentence," he once told me, "and when I do, I want to have some usable job skills."

Had Bill been physically less imposing the others may have been more directly confrontational, but he was in excellent condition and probably would have quashed a fight quickly. He was around my age, 50, over six feet tall, lean and muscular from a strict workout regimen. He favored weight training, alone, followed by a trodding half-jog several times around the track. For several months he occupied the bunk next to mine in K-dorm, his bed perfectly made every day, personal items stored rank-and-file. A desktop book nudged half an inch would gain his attention. (I know – I nudged.) The books he studied were work-related tomes by Justices Scalia and Breyer, how-to books on legal writing, and a thick primer discussing DNA analysis.

His one recreational diversion was chess. He had organized the prison chess club, ran the tournaments, and played at a very respectable level, one we calculated as firmly 'Class A', just below the Expert level in the U.S. Chess Federation. Class B patzers and below were players who habitually let their hand hover over the board, and sure sign of indecision and low aptitude – neither of which described Bill. He favored the Budapest Defense, deploying that line monomaniacally in our weekend games. We always played on the clock at the time control of one hour per player per game, a pace nobody else could tolerate. Most prison chessplayers enjoy rapid chess – Bang! Snatch! Grab! – gladiator-style, but Bill chose to move like he was participating in a European grandmaster clash at Baden Baden. He liked to think. Precision in all things was his unspoken mantra.

Bill's speech was also precise. Like actor Morgan Freeman, he never dropped the final syllable of a word, and he always clearly enunciated the final consonant. He scoffed condescendingly at the widespread use of Ebonics, as if those who employed the dialect were consciously attempting to reject assimilation into American society. Together, Bill's dignified mannerisms annoyed black prisoners – *who do you think you are* – far more than they affected anyone else.

I liked Bill, and I liked his business-like approach to the law library. I'd told Larry Fowler about my background as a business owner, providing land surveying services, and how that guided my relationship with library patrons. "I treat this job like it's my own business, and I treat them like paying customers." At the beginning of an hourly pass run, as a dozen or so guys streamed in, I'd announce that if they had questions, they could come see me. This allowed clerks who were working on cases to continue undisturbed, and it allowed the less-enthusiastic clerks, five or six of them, to not have to hide for the first ten minutes past the hour. It also dispelled the popular notion, often grumbled aloud, that the clerks were all lazy / stupid / no help at all.

Internally, I felt as optimistic as Mongoose about post-conviction cases, but like many attitudes we hold about ourselves, I eventually learned some didn't see me as upbeat and hopeful. Our second-in-command, supervisor Kamil Serour, pulled me aside one day and told me, "You shouldn't be so hard on people with your opinion about their cases." I was surprised to hear this, and told him I was just being honest, "brutally honest," about the issues they thought they had. "I can't lie to them," I protested. "If the issue is a loser, I feel it's the responsible thing to do to tell them so." Serour pointed out another function of the PC process – not to provide legal redress, but to provide something else prisoners needed. "You kill their *hope*," said Serour. From then on I crafted new ways to respond to a prisoner's dead-in-the-water issues. I'd point out the pitfalls he'd face, describe them as challenges to overcome, and let the man figure out the hopelessness for himself.

Even if my bedside manner lacked sophistication, I was still a popular choice for those seeking legal help. Some welcomed brutal honesty, even if it meant rethinking their entire petition and rewriting dozens of pages of argument. Others, I suspect, simply recognized my certainty in what I was doing – even though I bespoke no confidence, and made no promises, in the ultimate outcome. I was like a ballplayer who took a good cut at the ball – they wanted me in the line-up because there was a good chance I'd put good wood on the ball and maybe drive one out of the park. Sure, a strikeout is the most likely result (we're facing Roger Clemens on steroids), but the swing looks good, and we've taken this guy deep before.

A pathetically minuscule level of success at legal work in prison gets blown out of proportion, amplified by the telling and retelling through the prison grapevine. In 2010 I'd won a case in the Seventh Circuit Court of Appeals, entirely pro se, overturning a district court's summary judgment entered in favor of the cops who, I alleged, used excessive force both during and after my arrest. I'd been arrested, and convicted, of attempted murder and resisting arrest. Summary judgment, dismissing the civil suit, had been granted by Judge David Hamilton because the excessive force claim, if proven, would "necessarily render the criminal conviction invalid." Hamilton cited *Heck v. Humphrey* (1994), where the Supreme Court barred civil claims by prisoners when those claims were nothing more than an end-around run at developing a second collateral attack on a felony conviction.

Prisoner lawsuits are *Heck*-barred daily in the United States, but I found a common-sense argument that worked: if excessive force was used *after* any resistance had ended, then proving excessive force post-resistance would not impugn the conviction for resisting. A finding to the contrary, I argued, would allow the police to continue to wail on a handcuffed arrestee indefinitely, under the premise that once an arrestee resists you can beat him all you want (which is pretty much how police operate).

Chief Judge Easterbrook agreed, although with much more articulate language than I could muster. He cited as authority a Fourth Amendment case, *Wallace v. Kato* (2007), an opinion both I and opposing counsel had overlooked. (I then read *Wallace* two dozen times before I figured out why Easterbrook used it.) Summary judgment was overturned, and the case was sent back to the district court for trial. I was waiting for the trial date to be set, and it would take time because it wouldn't be in Hamilton's court – he'd been appointed to sit on the Seventh Circuit, next to Easterbrook, in Chicago. My win established a landmark case, was written up in university law journals, and began to be cited in other decisions around the country. To the prisoners at Pendleton attuned to legal issues, though, it represented an enormous victory – no pro se prisoner in Indiana had won anything in the Seventh Circuit (besides overturning prison disciplinary reports) in twenty-five years.

I had worked that case in my spare time, while I was shouldering a full load in my final year at Ball State. I was assigned to the law library in 2011, and by then my own PC petition had been pending for five years. The state PC process, viewed broadly, resembled the habeas corpus process I'd encountered in federal prison in the 1990's, at FCI-Oxford (Wisconsin) and FCI-Cumberland (Maryland). I hadn't attacked my counterfeiting and bank fraud convictions then, but I'd helped others petition under 28 U.S.C. 2255 in over 120 cases. We'd "won" twice – new sentencing hearings, not released from prison – exceeding the 1-in-80 average success rate. Those victories, like every one I ever had, were argued from common-sense interpretations of the law, the only approach I came to believe would work, coming from a lowly prisoner. Prisoners pushing erudite arguments packed with legalese, I'd noted, inevitably failed. Judges don't like non-attorneys acting like they know the law. The common-sense style also convinced prisoners I knew what I was doing because I could explain my legal arguments in a way they could understand. Simple works best. Clarity sells. Complexity in law can be overcome by basic, broad-as-a-barn-door, common-sensical judgment.

Or so we believed. Intuitively, we sensed an enormous opportunity to overturn convictions and reduce sentences, based on nothing more than America's abnormally high incarceration rate. "Something's out of whack," said Mike, "when we've got the highest incarceration rate in the world, five times higher than the world average." There exist two – and only two – plausible conclusions: either Americans, for whatever reason, are five times more criminally prone than the other 95% of the world, or the sentences, determined by the government (legislators, prosecutors, judges), are five times too severe.

"Even when someone argues that locking up two million people keeps the crime rate in check," Mike deduced, "they imply that Americans have a criminality found nowhere else in the world." We'd be unique, as if the convergence of Old World populations between 30 and 49 degrees latitude in North America mutated and formed a sociologically inferior race, *Homo americanus criminalis.*

"They're still looking for the crime gene in human DNA," I told Mike.

He snickered. "Yeah, they'll find it next to the poverty gene."

We pondered what the American criminal justice scene would look like if our government responded to crime like other developed countries. "Ya know," I said to Mike, "if America's incarceration rate was in conformity with the rest of the world, four out of five people currently in prison wouldn't be incarcerated. Around 1.8 million of the 2.3 million in America's jails and prisons would be out in the free world." Other countries manage to do it without enduring a crime wave; the United States hasn't figured it out yet.

A thunderous voice intruded: "All you guys are in prison because you broke the law." We looked over to see who'd rambled into our conversation. It was CO Riggs, or "Red," as we called him. He had flaming red curls, unruly sideburns, and black-rimmed glasses, and the officer's uniform lent him the appearance of a Georgia infantryman, circa 1863, defending the approaches to Missionary Ridge. A generally surly demeanor was useful for playing traffic cop at the school's entrance. No pass? Forgot it? Too bad, go back to the dorm. No library for you. "But my name's right there on the list!" Nope, go back. "Bathroom's full, Red, can I use the one down the hall?" Nope, not today. (Not tomorrow, either.) Red suspected every one of us was up to no good. He was obnoxious. We relished his days off.

"That's right," Red declared, "the only way to get here is to be convicted of a crime. You either admitted it and pled guilty, or you denied it, and twelve jurors said you did it, without a doubt."

"Not everyone in here should've been found guilty," Pete offered. "The jury doesn't know everything, and they get the wrong answer sometimes."

"You can't tell me 80% of you are innocent!" Red had been eavesdropping from his desk outside the door. "Maybe a few got screwed, sure; but there are so few truly innocent people in prison that it's major news whenever an innocent person is discovered and let out."

A focus on the innocent, in my opinion, blinded everybody from seeing the real problem. In a perverse way, the release of an exonerated prisoner worked to *affirm* the public's faith in the justice system – when only 150 prisoners per year are cleared, out of 1.5 million in America's prisons, the public believes the system is getting it right 99.99% of the time.

"You ever get a speeding ticket?" I asked.

"Yeah, a long time ago."

"How much did it cost you?"

"I forget. About $100."

"What if you, and only you, had to pay $500 for that ticket – would that be fair?"

"We're not talking about speeding tickets, we're talking about *real* crimes. Murder, burglary, rape, robbery."

"And drugs," said Whatley, to keep Red from ignoring one-fourth of Indiana's prisoners.

"Yeah, and drugs. The state shouldn't go easy on any of those crimes."

"Nobody's asking the state to *go easy* on crime," I countered. "We're asking the state to just have a *normal reaction* to crime, not five times more punitive than the rest of the world."

"Well," Red concluded, "you were born in the wrong country." And with that he went back to his desk.

We couldn't do anything about the sentencing ranges set by the legislature, but we could challenge how prosecutors and judges acted within those ranges. Prosecutors overcharged crimes; judges let them get away with it. Prosecutors used unfair tactics at trial; judges let it slide. Prosecutors argued for sentences on the high side; judges "tough on crime" agreed. A majority of judges were former prosecutors.

Defense attorneys, an astonishing amount of the time, stood by mute. Defendants were whisked off to prison, showing up in our library, expecting us to straighten it all out. We could give them maybe four or five guys who could help, for a population of over 1,700. If they thought public defenders' case loads were too heavy, this was worse. And we weren't even attorneys. It's no wonder, that when the lawyers were gone, most had to learn the law and fight their convictions on their own.

Their learning process was excruciating to watch. Kenny Allen came back to his desk after helping a prisoner and exclaimed, "You can't tell me there's no such thing as a stupid question. He wanted to know the meaning of the word, *that*."

"What's that?"

"Yeah."

"Yeah, what?"

"That."

"Oh, *that*. And what *is* that?"

"That's the question."

"Didja tell him, *that's* whatever?"

"That's not whatever, *that* is specifically something."

"And what *is* that?"

"That's for him to decide."

We'd seen MS Word documents with no Return key ever entered – all space bar entries. I'd had a guy point to the semicolon key and ask, "How do you get *that* to appear on the page?" Uh . . . you push it. I checked to see if his semicolon key was stuck or malfunctioning; it wasn't. Guys refused to use spell check: "It takes too long." We had a guy sit at the keyboard and screen, certainly for the first time, and ask, "Where does the paper go?" Another, who'd been locked up since 1980, told me he didn't want the document I'd promised to produce if it was going to be printed on "computer paper." He wanted it on typing paper. He objected to the "holes" in the computer paper, which confused me until I realized he was thinking of the 30-year-old dot-matrix printers.

One of our dullard patrons was Tom Cat, who pestered the U.S. Patent and Trademark Office with trademark requests he wanted applied to a riffraff of ink drawings. He had no clue how to save a file – then he learned to save it in so many versions in so many places that he could never find the last version he'd worked on. So he'd blame the clerks for sabotaging his files. We were amused when he got into a fight in E-dorm, lost, and complained he'd been sucker punched. His opponent had a tattoo across the front of his neck, four-inch block letters: SUCKER PUNCH. How do you get sucker punched by a guy whose nickname is Sucker Punch? Who has a warning sign posted on his neck? Tom Cat went back and fought him two more times, tapping out each time. Oh-for-three. Persistent. But in the end, convinced.

Along with the office hardware insanity, we'd see profoundly confused legal writing. "Counsel was ineffective for not protecting my Twelth Amendment right to a indictment." Uh, Twelfth Amendment? That's the manner of choosing President and Vice President. And there's no right to an indictment; and even if there were, counsel has nothing to do with the indictment stage. Another cited *Plessy v. Ferguson* (1896), using the "separate but equal" clause to argue for an all-black jury. Once a month somebody would ask about suing the judge, the prosecutor, or the State of Indiana for not providing a fair trial. Sorry, not possible, they all have immunity. "Well, that's not fair!" That's the way it is. "So they just do whatever they want and answer to nobody?" They answer to the voters, every four years. Or this: "I was denied the right to plead insanity." That's crazy! A look of bewilderment, then, "Yeah, it *is* crazy!" No, I mean you claiming such a right exists is crazy. "It *does* exist!" In *your* mind, maybe, but it doesn't exist under the Constitution.

Kenny Allen was our front man on answering questions. He had no pressing legal work of his own, having pled guilty to three murders in order to avoid the death penalty. Post-conviction relief for Kenny was highly unlikely, like a major leaguer hitting five home runs in a game – and Kenny couldn't get his foot in the door of the stadium. He and I had been in the Marion County Jail at the same time, and we had gotten similar special treatment from the guards escorting us to court – handcuffed, with a movement-limiting black box over the cuffs, legs shackled, and held by two COs as we shuffled through the tunnel connecting the jail with the courthouse. Six COs walked in front, and six more guarded the rear, as if we'd arranged for ninjas to pop out of the tunnel walls and rescue us from captivity. Kenny, I'd noticed, seemed to enjoy the notoriety. He was in his twenties then, and authorities had found three people buried under fresh cement in his basement – his mother, and his maternal grandparents. It wasn't something he ever felt the need to talk about.

Having never done a PC, Kenny knew little about the process, save for what he picked up hearing the rest of us talk. He was more concerned with prisoners' rights issues, as befitting a prisoner with LWOP, whose future would only be behind prison walls. Conditions of confinement and disciplinary matters. The guiding cases were *Wolff v. McDonnell* (1974) and *Sandin v. Conner* (1995), and his expertise centered on these and their progeny. I was glad to have Kenny nearby to deal with questions coming from what were, mainly, knuckleheads. He handled them well, I thought, given his limited formal education.

Kenny was nearly six feet tall and cellblock pale, sporting a Home Depot haircut, with stray long hairs springing randomly, like rambunctious weeds. He had the unreformed mass and girth of a physically imposing man, heavy enough to play offensive tackle, but the weight distribution was low on the body, as if he'd been cast from candle wax and left to sit on a hot floor register. From afar he reminded me of the ungainly elephant seals on the California beach below the Hearst Mansion. He chirped a country twang and overused the word *beings*, as in, "The petitioner shouldn't be barred from filing a notice of appeal *beings* how he never got notice of the court's denial in the mail." We once disagreed on the meaning of *dicta* – he held that *dicta* dictated how other courts should rule; I proposed he look it up and see that *dicta* was merely a court's commentary and did not establish precedent. I doubt he ever looked it up – he wasn't the dictionary-consulting type.

We also had clerks who did no legal work whatsoever, but fulfilled other duties, and so were valuable members of our team. Donald Brunk, an electrician by trade, manned the copy machine, kept the blank forms in stock, and wrangled with the books and IDOC policies loaned to seg prisoners. Mid-30's, with a shaved head to combat a horseshoe hairline, one might have presumed he was skinhead-affiliated if not for the dearth of skin ink and an unfailingly pleasant demeanor with all, black and white. His son was the same age as my nephews, and we commiserated over our inability to be involved in their lives. Brunk arrived in prison in 2009, and wouldn't be leaving until 2039.

Elliott Tyson laboriously wrote a hundred passes a day. The four-inch square papers were sorted and delivered to prisoners' locations in the evening. The pass was shown to get out of one's dorm or cellblock, but if the CO knew the man had been issued a pass he didn't need to see the actual slip in order to open the door. A pass could be left behind, and when it was, the prisoner would hope Leo was on the schoolhouse door, not Red. Leo, a black CO with a casual, friendly attitude, figured things ran just as well, probably better, if he wasn't an asshole twelve hours a day.

Leo had the radio tuned to Rush Limbaugh in the afternoons, and one day I asked him why he listened to such a right-wing radio program. "Gotta keep an eye on what they're up to," he said. "Yeah," I teased, "God forbid a black man be a Republican."

Ol' Tyson had only one legal concern – getting his own sentence reduced. He had a Class A drug dealing conviction, with a 30-year enhancement for the habitual offender, and he sought to get the Class A dropped down to a Class B. He theorized he'd been entrapped into dealing within 1,000 feet of a school, and he may have been right, but the narcotics agents in Marion County had fallen upon an unimpeachable way to avoid the entrapment argument. Tyson, on a cell phone, had proposed a location for the dope to be picked up. The undercover, for whatever excuse, couldn't agree to that location, and told Tyson to pick another spot. "Pick a location, and I'll meet you there." I read the transcript of the call, and this line cleverly put the choice unambiguously in the hands of Tyson. It was like a hustler playing a shell game – if the sucker picks a spot outside 1,000 feet, play off some excuse to not meet there, then con him into picking a new spot, upping the odds of getting a Class A felony from zero to something above zero. Tyson chose a vacant high school parking lot. Bingo. The sentencing range ballooned from 16 to 50 years, to a die-in-prison range of 50 to 80 years. His outdate, one he'd never live to see, was in 2040.

Another clerk was Ronald Covington, who, like Kenny Allen, had three murders and pled guilty to avoid the death penalty. I never pried into the circumstances of Ron's crime. It takes four murders to be classified as a serial killer, and when a guy is one short, one tends not to meddle in the man's business. Ron was extremely quiet and studious – he read books most of the day – and very polite. Nothing murder-ish about him. Like most convicted of murder, he was honest and forthright, possessing good character, considerate of others. Most murderers, I'd noted, had lived pretty normal lives and had had a problem with only one individual (a big, intolerable problem, apparently, that led to homicide). He didn't seem to have a temper, and he avoided conflict. He was intelligent, educated, and did his job well. His presence at Pendleton with LWOP, in short, confused me.

Ron's sole assignment was to serve the protective custody wing, R-2, housed upstairs in O-Building. The "check-ins" resided there, wishing for a transfer elsewhere. Some waited years to get moved. And when they did transfer, word would hit their new population in a flash that they'd checked in at Pendleton, and could not be trusted. Nor respected. To successfully check in and transfer, a prisoner had to reveal the source of the problem – *Who, exactly, is threatening you?* Some, like former cops or COs, would say, *Everybody.*

A former Indiana State Trooper on Ron's R-2 range was David Camm, convicted twice of killing his family in New Albany. Camm contended he had nothing to do with the murders of his wife and two small children – that

Charles Boney, an ex-convict, had committed the crime and falsely claimed the two conspired in the deed. Camm's first conviction was overturned on appeal in 2006 because of prosecutorial misconduct when the prosecutor focused on Camm's long string of alleged infidelities. He was convicted a second time, and in 2009 the conviction was overturned again. Once again it was for prosecutorial misconduct – the prosecutor inferring that Camm had molested his daughter and she may have recently told her mother about it. (There was only speculative evidence to support this.) Now he was awaiting his third trial date.

He had good attorneys, the best in the state (Stacy Uliana and Richard Kammen), and that made all the difference. I read Camm's lengthy published opinions and noted that any other poor slob, presenting the same issues pro se or with a public defender, wouldn't have gotten anywhere near as much ink from the higher court, and surely wouldn't have gotten a reversal with similar facts.

Camm's case was perhaps the most sensational criminal case in the state, and I asked Ron how Camm was doing up there, isolated from the world. "He never asks for anything," said Ron. "I guess his attorneys on the outside are taking care of it for him." Must be nice, I thought. Nearly everybody else who'd been in his situation, after about ten years of confinement, would be floundering around with a pro se PC petition. At best.

Clerk Phillip Lee, who went by Edgar Lee, overheard me asking about Camm. "That motherfucker got slick, conspiring with Boney to kill his family, and it all blew up in his face. There wasn't no way Boney would go into a rich-ass neighborhood like that unless Camm invited him in. Camm was scheming to lay it all on Boney from the start." Well, that was roughly the same reading one got from the court's opinion in *Boney v. State* (Ind. App. 2008).

Charles Boney resided in J-cellhouse, and perhaps Edgar Lee had talked to Boney and learned some inside info. Hard to tell. But we all knew this: in unresolved crimes, jailhouse chatter was 99% unreliable. Clever jailhouse snitches would listen, figure out what the prosecutor wanted to hear most, then deliver the "phrase that pays." Even if Edgar Lee heard a story straight from Boney, it was unlikely Boney was being 100% truthful. In effect, every bit of talk coming out of a jail or prison about another man's case was inherently worthless. But that didn't deter prosecutors from using it, or jurors from believing it.

Edgar Lee was one of the most impatient people I'd ever encountered. Years earlier, I'd checked out a book on economics from the state library loan system, and it had been due back to our library on a Friday. Edgar Lee was responsible for collecting the inter-library loan books, and he came to my dorm two days early, found me kicked back, reading the book, and wanted to know if I was done yet. "Uh, no." Pretty obvious I wasn't done, I had it in my hand. "Well, I need it back *now*." I had two days left to go before it was due. "No, I gotta have it today to get it back on time." I figured, whatever, I'll just check it out again. I gave him the book. He walked away briskly, shaking his head like I was some kind of idiot.

Now we worked side-by-side as law clerks, and we both pretended the former incident never took place. Edgar Lee's impatience with everything included his reluctance to wait for a person to finish his sentence, and he'd watch a person's mouth and anticipate how the sentence would end. "Edgar Lee," I'd say, "I need you to screen these guys better, keep them away from my desk." He'd say along with me, a tenth of a second behind, "…from my desk." "I want you to find me a case I can win." He'd stare at my lips and finish with me, "…I can win." Sometimes I could deliver all but the last few words of a sentence and he'd accurately fill in the line. "Edgar Lee, tell that dogbreath who wouldn't shut up yesterday to get…" "…the fuck away from your desk." Perfect.

One morning, as we prepared toast, I told him, "You're not bringing me any worthy clients. You keep dragging in carp. I want a keeper now and then, like a bass or a bluegill." He shook his head and chuckled. "Man, there ain't nothing on the line but carp, suckers, and bullheads." He motioned toward to the row of fish-eyed prisoners staring at computer screens. "They ain't got a clue." He pulled his toast out, half done, and skedaddled. Most of his day was spent playing solitaire.

The one time Edgar Lee talked about the law was in reference to his own case, where he had won a PC claim in the trial court, only to have the appellate court overturn the grant of relief. The state presented an argument based on the "blue pencil doctrine." "What kind of shit is that?" he asked. "Blue pencil doctrine is supposed to be for contracts or civil law or some shit like that. They tried to use it to screw me." The case was reversed on other grounds, not the blue pencil doctrine, but it showed how far-reaching the Indiana Attorney General's office would go to get a court to deny a prisoner relief.

At the end of a long day wrestling with other people's problems I often unwound in the dorm by playing out the day's events with the one guy I could depend upon to listen – really listen – to my exasperation. Melvin Tunstill, or Mel-T, was nine years my senior, almost to the day. A big fan of Barack Obama, he relished the coincidence of sharing a birthday with Michelle Obama – January 17th. Mel-T and I minored in Anthropology and Sociology at Ball State, and we had teamed up on class projects, giving our cultural work a black-white perspective. In our studies he ran across the word *steatopygia*, which he soon proclaimed his favorite word of all time, as in, "That Nikki Minaj sho' has some steatopygia goin' on." He possessed no ample backside of his own because he ate little – his major intake was zero-calorie black coffee. His body was withering to a freeze-dried appearance, skin concaved around bone and sinew, like a desiccated Incan corpse at the crest of an Andean mountain. Brass, oval-rimmed bifocals perfected the look of the wise old African, sage of the Yoruba tribe, keeper of the mysteries of life.

Mel-T had come of age in the 60's, and his first "moment of political consciousness" came in April 1968, when he was 15. Dr. Martin Luther King had just been killed, and as nightfall approached he was preparing to do what other young black men were doing as sunsets descended east to west across America: *riot*. King himself had said, "A riot is the language of the unheard." Emotionally-torn denizens of the black neighborhoods on the near north side of Indy congregated near a park and were about to speak that devastating language, by the thousands. "Then we heard a loudspeaker, and the mass of people gravitated toward it. The man speaking was Robert F. Kennedy." Kennedy was running for President, present in Indiana for the Democratic Primary, but on this night he had nothing to say about his personal ambition. "He spoke like he *knew* us, like he felt what we were feeling. He also made sense. For the first time in my life I realized that not all white people were against us."

"Just most of 'em," I joked.

"Yeah!"

"Anyway," he continued, "that speech was powerful, and I saw that *words* could hold back *an army*." Indianapolis was the only major city in America that didn't explode in civil disorder that night. RFK's impromptu speech was credited for the calm. "Kennedy's oratory, combined with his own assassination a couple months later, convinced me that political organization was the *only* way to achieve equality in this country." At 18 he joined the Black Panther Party.

I asked him what the Black Panther agenda was really about back then.

"Building up the black community," he replied; then, fixing me squarely in the eyes, "and self-defense. Protecting ourselves from the cops, mainly. I'm sure the white community just viewed the Black Panthers as 'niggers with guns'."

"If there's an iconic image of the Panthers," I observed, "it's probably Huey Newton, dressed in fatigues, shotgun cradled, clenched fist raised high. Black power."

"And black power is the *last* thing white people wanted to see."

He never detailed for me the incident, or incidents, that led to his appearance in criminal court in 1971 ("fund-raising activities"), but it culminated in an option young defendants are no longer afforded: plead guilty and go to prison, or enlist in the military. Vietnam needed bodies more than the penitentiary did. Mel-T chose to join the U.S. Army.

Enlistment took him to Fort Hood, Kentucky, where he was the only black man in the barracks. "I was 5-foot-7 and 124 pounds and I fought every last man in my platoon. There were many times I thought I'd made the wrong choice, like I'd have been better off in prison." He served out his commitment under the thumb of superiors who never let him ship out to fight in Southeast Asia. "Putting me 'in country' with an M-16 would've been too easy on me, is what they prolly figured. If I was them, I wouldn't have given me live ammo in the jungle either." Honorably discharged, he returned to Indy, worked, and raised a family. His record wasn't perfect, but in an environment where over half the black men had felony records, Mel's criminal history was unexceptional.

If one were to narrowly define Melvin Tunstill by his current conviction, he was a drug dealer. He had a Class A felony for dealing cocaine, 5.7 grams, netting a 30-year sentence, with a 30-year habitual offender enhancement. Sixty years, do thirty. But he didn't consider himself a "drug dealer." He once asked me, "You ever sell a car?" Well, sure, a few times, most people have. "So does that make you a car dealer?"

I'd read Mel-T's legal work to get a feeling for writing a motion for sentence modification, and it was no ordinary drug-dealing case. Quite a few prisoners cry that the cops "were out to get me," but in Mel's case it was no bare claim – the prosecutor and undercover agent admitted Mel had been specially targeted. Mel was in their crosshairs because he'd gotten a homicide conviction overturned on appeal. The killing had taken place at a liquor store at 16th and College, after midnight, when a belligerent drunk's threats prompted Mel to take out the knife he carried. He held it defensively, at chest level, blade pointing out, and the mouthy drunk charged. Whether he saw Mel's knife or not, we'll never know, but he impaled himself upon it, taking the blade directly into his heart. The rarest of all stabbing deaths – one injury, nothing more.

As Mel put it, "He fell on my knife."

Mel had a right to a self-defense instruction, and the court's impairment of that right caused his conviction to get tossed. He did a couple years in prison, then walked free. Naturally, the Marion County Prosecutor's Office didn't like it, and before his heels hit the pavement they'd arranged for Jeff Avington, from the Metro Drug Task Force, to get close to Mel and induce Mel to sell him cocaine.

Most people are two or three degrees of separation from a drug dealer – you know someone who knows someone – but a black ex-convict in Marion County's Center Township is always one degree of separation away. Of course Mel knew where to get dope. And here was this black guy playing the part, convincingly, earning Mel's confidence, eventually getting Mel to deliver two eight-balls, enticed by a $100 profit that would supplement his janitorial income from Wishard Hospital. That C-note would wind up costing Mel the rest of his life.

Mel's public defender negotiated for the 30-year advisory sentence on the dealing charge, then argued for the low end of the 10-to-30 range for the habitual. On this point he was confused; the habitual on a Class A felony was a flat 30, no range, no options. The prosecutor and the judge set him straight and Mel wound up with 60, do 30.

The public defender's ignorance of the sentencing statute (beyond ignorant – it's like an English major not knowing how to conjugate a verb) set Mel up for a post-conviction claim of ineffective assistance. Mel had taken the guilty plea as a result of bad advice, so he argued for the plea to be vacated. Former Pendleton law clerk Joseph Everroad helped Mel, but the petition failed. The Indiana Court of Appeals was unwilling to set Mel free a second time. They declared that Mel's 60-year sentence was 20 years less than the maximum, so he received a "substantial benefit" from pleading guilty, rendering his lawyer's profoundly ignorant advice "harmless error."

He caught the drug case when he was 43. Now he was 59. He had maxed out on his education time cuts – four years' worth – and he still had 10 years left to do.

"So, youngster," Mel joked, "did you get anybody out of prison today?"

"You ain't heard? Watch the ten o'clock news."

"And when they walk up to the cameras, they're gonna give you all the credit."

"That's the deal. I don't do this for pay, I do it for the glory."

I related some of the challenging clients I'd dealt with throughout the day, and then I got serious. "I've been working on Donnie Ware's case since December, and I'm afraid I don't even know how steep the climb is gonna get. It's the worst kind of case – he might actually be innocent."

"First degree innocence – I thought that was the kind of case you always wanted."

"Not really," I explained. "If he's innocent and I fail him, I have to live with that. I'd rather operate like a *real* lawyer – get some guilty person off. That's the law at it's finest, using the system to get the result you want, to hell with right and wrong."

"Ware's in for shooting the black kids who threw eggs at him?"

"Right."

"Has he told you he's innocent?"

I shook my head. "You know my routine, Mel. First interview, I tell them I don't care if they're innocent or not. I don't need to know; I'll work just as hard for them either way." I didn't want guys thinking I'd only work hard if I believed in their innocence, because they'd just lie to get my best effort. They do that with their attorneys, pre-trial, all the time. The lies were invariably poorly told, and exhausting. Most of them didn't employ the Webster's definition of *innocent* anyway. We were better off never bringing up the word.

Mel considered my position, and advised me to employ a flexible strategy. "You owe it to him to put up an argument that preserves his ability to claim innocence. You have to walk that fine line where you don't admit he did it, and you don't exclude the possibility that he didn't do it."

"Carefully worded lawyer talk?"

"That's what the courts enjoy hearing."

He was right, of course. I had read Donnie's record, and there were two possible defenses, both then and now: he didn't do it, or, he did it and it wasn't technically a murder, but a lesser offense. I didn't have to know the truth – I only had to cleverly construct an argument that left open both possibilities. The truth? That wasn't for me to decide. My obligation was to get Donnie up that cliff, over that wall.

CHAPTER THREE

Trust the Professionals

"Justice is to mankind what conscience is to the individual."
– Georges Nivat

I finally get a full afternoon scheduled with Donnie Ware, and my first question is, "How did they *not* arrest Wally Pierson for this crime?"

Wally did everything that would get the ordinary person placed in cuffs – lied to the cops about his location when the egg-throwing kids were shot, admitted using the same kind of rifle hours before the shooting, no longer possessed the rifle, punched in late to work the next morning and punched out sick thirty minutes later, answered the door clutching a pistol when the cops came to get him, was identified by another egging victim with 90% certainty, drove a red truck matching the shooter's truck, had a partial match on his license plate, and a receipt put him two miles from the scene twenty minutes before the shots were fired. A 15-year-old boy was dead, another shot, and the public clamored for the police to make an arrest. One would think they had enough to place Wally Pierson in custody, but he never saw the inside of a jail cell, not even temporarily.

"His dad was a cop," said Donnie, "a retired Marion County Deputy. And the family friend he'd visited that day, where he shot the rifle for target practice, was an appellate court judge." Ware's discovery file, I knew, confirmed all this.

The retired deputy surrendered a .22 rifle for ballistics tests, the weapon Wally said he'd used at the judge's house. A late night phone call was placed to the judge, who confirmed Wally's story – although nobody could pinpoint the time Wally and his girlfriend left for Indianapolis. Wally explained why he answered the door with gun in hand – his girlfriend's ex had made threats and had been stalking them. Wally was fully cooperative, never lawyered up, and had no criminal record, so the detectives found an arrest unnecessary.

Next day, they put Wally's picture in a six-person array for Officer Tracy Nash. Nash was the first patrolman responding to 9-1-1 dispatch and had pulled behind a red truck stopped on Rockville Road in front of the Public Storage building at about 11:30 p.m., later determined to be within one minute of the shooting. A man had gotten out of the truck, pointed toward the fleeing youths, and told Nash they'd thrown eggs at him. Nash instructed the man to stay put. Nash went after the boys, but when he returned minutes later the truck was gone. Nevertheless, Nash had gotten a good look at the man in his headlights. He scanned the faces in the photo array and did not select Pierson.

Then the ballistics result, a rush job, came back from the Indiana State Police Crime Lab: no match to the Pierson rifle.

Meanwhile, an anonymous caller gave police Donald Ware's name, description, address, cell phone number, truck description, and the unpublished knowledge that the irate driver had been egged "in the face." Detectives pulled up Ware's record. Three felony convictions: possession of cocaine, operating while intoxicated, resisting arrest. And thirteen misdemeanors. Three probation violations. They put Ware's most recent arrest photo in an array and called in Officer Nash. Nash picked out Ware. They met with Lori Barton again and showed her a new photo array. Shaken, she picked out Ware this time. Her confidence, curiously, rose from the 90% level she had with Pierson, to 100% with Donald Ware. At Ware's trial she would explain the second photo array was upsetting because she realized she'd previously identified an innocent man with near certainty.

"There's a joke," I told Donnie, "that 70% of all statistics are made up on the spot." When Barton claimed 90% certainty, where'd she get that number? If she'd undergone testing on her ability to recall a stranger's face and succeeded nine times out of ten, she'd have a scientific foundation for her 90% accuracy. "And then," I concluded, "oddly enough, she *increases* confidence to 100% while admitting she'd just fingered an innocent man two days before. After her mistake, you'd think she'd never venture anywhere near the 90% level again."

We have copies of the photo arrays used. I find it odd that Ware and Pierson, other then being thirty-something white males with straight brown hair, look nothing alike.

"You think she was influenced," Donnie asks, "to pick me out?"

"We'll never know." The detectives' encounters with both Nash and Barton weren't filmed, so if detectives were suggestive, even unintentionally, there's no evidence for Donnie to examine. Barton must have inferred her identification of Pierson was wrong when she was brought in to look at a second array, but what, exactly, was she told? Those who've studied exonerations relate that 64% involve mistaken eyewitness identification, and the Innocence Project calls it the leading cause of wrongful convictions.

The anonymous tip formed the basis for a probable cause affidavit to obtain a search warrant. Arriving at Donnie's house they found eggshells in the driveway and dried egg on his truck, which was parked out of public view, on the grass behind the house. A gang of cops stormed through the front door, guns drawn, loud and boisterous, terrifying the only two occupants – Teresa Cortez, Donnie's long-time girlfriend, and their three-year-old daughter, Adela. The toddler wet her pants and ran crying to her mother, who was blitzed with questions from angry and demanding black-clad men with badges.

Teresa had no idea where Donnie was, an answer the cops took as evasion. Not a good idea to hide a man wanted for murder, they told her. Then they found a small baggie of marijuana in their bedroom, 49 grams, and the heat went up. Miranda rights were read. A cop beside her with a menacing glare clacked his handcuffs expectantly. The only friendly face in the room sat across from her, placidly telling her how it would be: she was looking at jail time, maybe prison. Uncooperative people don't get good deals from the prosecution. Child protective services will be here soon, and . . . and you better start telling us everything we need to know.

Of course she started talking. I've had numerous prisoners ask me if it's legal for the police to threaten a witness to get the witness to talk, and the answer is yes – as long as the "threat" is merely a statement of legal consequences. It's not unconstitutionally coercive unless the police threaten the witness with something they can't legally do. The 1986 Supreme Court case, *Colorado v. Connelly,* allows police to pressure suspects and witnesses in exactly the manner used to get Teresa Cortez to spill everything she knew.

Yes, Teresa admitted, Donnie had been hit with eggs. He owned a rifle. He'd talked about the incident and said he'd "fired some rounds." She gave them every location Donnie might be. Satisfied, detectives allowed Teresa to stay home, avoid charges, and keep Adela out of foster care.

At Donnie's trial Teresa recanted, saying she only talked because she was afraid. Nevertheless, the state contended, her first statement was believable, and strong evidence of Donald Ware's guilt.

The clincher, though, was a time-stamped security video from the storage facility. The video recorded the boys running past the store front, with a pickup truck partially in view, parked at the spot where two .22-caliber shell casings were found, the same spot where Officer Nash encountered the egged driver who fled, whom Nash identified as Donald Ware. If Nash's identification was sound, Ware was the guy.

Only one other detail spiked my curiosity – three of the boys reported that the truck contained *two* men, one driving, another standing in the truck bed. Nash didn't see another person with Ware, but did Donnie have an accomplice? Or was there a second truck, similar to Donnie's, with two men in it?

"That was one more thing my attorneys used to raise reasonable doubt," Donnie explained. "They pointed the finger at Wally Pierson, mainly, but they said the jury might also believe someone with me fired the shots, or that there was another truck like mine after the kids."

His attorneys, privately retained, went with the obvious strategic choice: Donnie didn't do it, and make the state prove he did. Whether Donnie really wanted this defense or whether some other defense may have fared better is irrelevant post-trial, as *Strickland* declares that "strategic choices made after thorough investigation of law and facts relevant to plausible options are virtually unchallengeable." The decision to anchor the defense on suspicion of Wally Pierson was a reasonable one, one almost every attorney would have used. Unfortunately for Donnie, Pierson's existence, initially thought to be helpful, locked Donnie into a defense that was doomed to fail.

Ware's attorneys also had a strong objection to the warrant, derived, as it was, from an anonymous source. If police were allowed to enter someone's home or make an arrest on every anonymous tip they received it might make vengeful ex-girlfriends happy, but it would render the Fourth Amendment's search and seizure clause a nullity. The Supreme Court held in *Illinois v.*

Gates (1983) that uncorroborated hearsay from a source of unknown credibility is insufficient to support a probable cause affidavit and search warrant. A subsequent investigation corroborating an anonymous tip, however, may establish the informant's trustworthiness, but not from "facts easily observable and within the public domain." The only non-public information in the tip on Ware was his unpublished cell phone number, and the easily surmised fact he'd been egged "in the face." This issue, coupled with the other evidence potentially raising doubt, practically forced counsel's hand. Even if he were to lose at trial, Ware had a good shot at overturning the conviction on appeal.

"When the trial began, you must've thought you had a pretty good chance of walking away from all this, huh?" I regretted the tone I used as the question came out; it sounded accusatory, as if his only concern was for himself. Donnie wore the 'you don't understand' expression, so I rephrased it. "What I mean is, were you happy with the defense chosen when you went to trial?"

"Well, yeah . . . I guess," he recalled. "I don't know anything about the law. I didn't know what to do, so I just listened to the people I'd hired."

"So you never told your attorneys exactly what kind of defense you wanted?"

"Well, no," Donnie replied, "I left it all up to them. They're the professionals; they're supposed to know what to do. You know, it seems like from the moment I got arrested, all of the decisions have been out of my hands. They tell you when you're arrested, 'You've got the right to remain silent,' and everyone will tell you, staying silent is what you better do. Then you're charged, and automatically you enter a not guilty plea. Then you see your attorneys, and they tell you there are four or five ways to beat the case, and they know what they're talking about, and you're gonna listen to them."

I sorted through the copies of his trial exhibits until I came to a photo of the corridor between the buildings where the boys were shot. A large-leafed tree obstructed part of the view, and the corridor would have been partly illuminated at night. I flipped to State's Exhibit #1, the photo of Dunson face down in the grass, shirtless, tiny hole in his back. He had fallen next to a circular, slatted storm drain while his cohorts sped away. I wasn't trying to be mean, but I wanted to gauge Donnie's reaction.

He was silent for nearly a full minute, and I waited.

"He wasn't a bad kid," he said, softly.

No, he wasn't. Brandon's friends and family described him as a good kid who would have grown into being a good man. He was looked up to and adored by his younger brother. He had good parents who showed up for every one of Ware's court proceedings, no matter how minor. It was hard to tell from the cold record whether they were bitter and vengeful, or if they were merely looking for a truth they could accept, but it was clear they were heartbroken.

Donnie's attorneys had tried to get some photos of the boys shown to the jury – they'd congregated at Burger King hours before the shooting and taken pictures of themselves flashing "gang signs," the attorneys alleged. They resided on the west side of Indy, and the hand sign 'W' was displayed, the same one rappers Snoop Dogg and Dr. Dre used to represent the West Coast. Brandon's in the center of every picture, unemotionally focused on the camera while the other kids played silly around him. They were no "gang," just kids goofing off on a summer night. The judge excluded the pictures – prejudicial and not relevant to any trial issue. Donnie's two previous jailhouse lawyers wanted to make something of this discretionary exclusion, but the court's ruling was unimpeachable.

As we looked at the excluded photos Donnie listened to my explanation of why they're irrelevant. He understood me, but had one objection.

"The prosecutors said this was a racially-motivated crime, but the kids were the ones who brought race into it," he pleaded. "They chose to hit me and everybody else because we were white. They planned it, bought the eggs, threw the mattress in the road to slow us down, and when we were hit – an egg can hit pretty hard, by the way – they yelled racist things at us. I heard, 'stupid white bitch' and 'fuck you, redneck.' They just kept it up the whole time. I'm not saying this excuses what happened to those kids, I'm just saying if there was a racial element to it, it came from the kids, not from me or anybody else."

According to Lori Barton, the angry white male had responded in kind, calling them "little nigger bastards" before mentioning he had a rifle. Those three words were emphasized in the final sentence the prosecutor spoke before the jury retired for deliberations.

"I do not remember saying that," Donnie said.

"You were pretty hot, though, right?"

"Oh, yeah! Not thinking straight, at all."

On count one, Ware's jury was given instructions on three charges, each having a distinct degree of culpability: murder, voluntary manslaughter, and reckless homicide. Murder was described first – "knowingly or intentionally" killing another person. Voluntary manslaughter has the same description, but with the caveat that the defendant was under the influence of "sudden heat." This instruction can only be given when some evidence of sudden heat is in the record, and the state bears the burden of disproving the existence of sudden heat, beyond a reasonable doubt. Reckless homicide was described last – "recklessly" causing death, as opposed to a knowing or intentional killing. Both voluntary manslaughter and reckless homicide are described to the jury as "lesser included offenses," and as scores of published cases attest, juries often fail to understand that only one of the three offenses can apply. Juries have been known to simultaneously return guilty verdicts on all three charges, fundamentally misconstruing the instructions.

One might presume an instruction on lesser included offenses would be simple to draft. After describing the elements of each offense, on separate instructions, the jury could be given a verdict form like this:

> On Count One, homicide, pick ONE:
> 1. Guilty of Murder
> 2. Guilty of Voluntary Manslaughter
> 3. Guilty of Reckless Homicide
> 4. Not Guilty

The courts, of course, through two centuries of opinions, have never allowed it to be that simple. Attorneys for both sides, but primarily prosecutors, have successfully argued that the above format leads to compromise verdicts. Prosecutors prefer juries to begin deliberating on the most serious felony first, and hopefully never consider the lesser offenses. The structure and wording of the instructions become crucial, and in no type of case is this more true than in a murder case.

In Ware's case, the convoluted homicide instruction was a 493-word behemoth, Instruction 21A, comprising the definitions and elements of all three offenses, with a structure and language specifically directing the jurors that their consideration of the lesser offenses was unnecessary. The murder elements came first:

> 1. The Defendant, Donald Ware;
> 2. Knowingly or intentionally;
> 3. Killed;
> 4. Brandon Dunson, a human being.
>
> If all four elements are found beyond a reasonable doubt, the Defendant is guilty of murder. If you find the Defendant is not guilty of the charged offense, then you may consider whether the Defendant is guilty of the included offenses.

Farther down the page, Instruction 21A states a finding of sudden heat "mitigates" the offense, then the elements for voluntary manslaughter and reckless homicide are enumerated. Of course, the plain language atop the page clearly tells the jurors everything below the murder charge is superfluous if they've found the Defendant guilty of murder. Problem is, the elements of voluntary manslaughter are the same four as for murder, but with a fifth element added:

> 1. The Defendant, Donald Ware;
> 2. Knowingly or intentionally;
> 3. Killed;
> 4. Brandon Dunson, a human being.
> 5. And the Defendant was acting under the influence of sudden heat.

The state's cleverly crafted instruction makes it impossible for this fifth element to be considered because the jury is instructed to stop deliberating upon finding the first four elements. To be fair to the defendant, a proper murder instruction (where sudden heat is in dispute) should have five elements, not four, with the fifth being:

> 1. The Defendant, Donald Ware;
> 2. Knowingly or intentionally;
> 3. Killed;

4. Brandon Dunson, a human being.
5. And the Defendant was NOT acting under the influence of sudden heat.

"Donnie," I say, "this isn't *my* interpretation of the law. I didn't dream this up. It's the opinion of the Seventh Circuit Court of Appeals." In January of 2005 their ruling in *Sanders v. Cotton* struck down a homicide instruction substantially identical to Ware's Instruction 21A, and in 2006 the Indiana Supreme Court responded by drafting a new pattern jury instruction to include the fifth element. "Donnie, your trial was in December 2005. Had Indiana not dragged its feet for sixteen months before drafting a clear and fair homicide instruction, you would've had an instruction allowing the jury to consider voluntary manslaughter instead of stopping deliberations upon finding the elements for murder."

And in Donnie's case, the evidence for sudden heat was abundant. Every witness described the shooter unambiguously – angry, mad, irate. Lisa Barton, the teens, and Officer Nash, who said he saw Ware one minute after the shots were fired, all noted the shooter's agitated demeanor. Even at Ware's sentencing, the judge remarked that Ware acted because he was "angry and upset," prompting Ware's attorneys to move for a directed verdict of voluntary manslaughter, which the judge refused.

"With all this overwhelming evidence of physical provocation, verbal provocation, and witness descriptions of sudden heat," I tell Donnie, "the only way you got convicted of murder and not manslaughter is because the instruction wouldn't let the jury consider manslaughter."

Because *Sanders* was published in January 2005, and because attorneys have a professional responsibility to be current on the law, we have an ineffective assistance claim. "But Donnie," I tell him, "the court doesn't want to entertain this argument coming from some convicted prisoner working pro se. You need an attorney for this."

Donnie already knew the importance of having an attorney. "I have family and friends taking up a collection, pooling their money together, to get me an attorney." It'll take at least five thousand dollars to get a good PC attorney, and he thinks they'll come through for him.

I'm doubtful. "How much has been collected so far?"

"Teresa has $500, and a friend has promised to put in $300." He pauses. "There'll be more," Donnie adds, in a way that tells me he's trying to convince himself more than he's trying to convince me.

"Well, Donnie," I reply, "the way to go about this is for me to pretend – at this point – that I'll be doing all the work myself. When you've hired an attorney, I'll have the case ready to hand off. For now, though, we've got to get your petition filed, and stop the federal habeas corpus time clock." He's used eight months of his one-year time limit under the AEDPA. The ability to file in federal court is important in his case because the primary argument will rely upon a Seventh Circuit opinion.

Then I tell him there's a second issue, one that should get his two Class D criminal recklessness convictions overturned. Two shots were fired, but Donnie was convicted for four separate crimes. One shot killed Dunson; that was the murder. The other shot struck Dyer's leg; that was the battery. Those same two shots were also used to convict on two counts of criminal recklessness because James Peterson and Jude Sayles were nearby when Dunson and Dyer were shot. A common law definition of double jeopardy should preclude any convictions beyond the two for Dunson and Dyer because there were no "separate acts" committed against Peterson and Sayles.

I didn't have to search LEXIS very long to find Indiana cases on point with this double jeopardy claim. In one, *Clark v. State*, (Ind. App. 1992), Clark had fired two shots into a room with four people in it. Initially, Clark had four convictions, but the appellate court reduced it to two, an attempted murder on the person shot, and one criminal recklessness for the three people nearby when the second shot was fired. The logic should be obvious – what if a defendant fired a single shot into a crowd of twenty people, killing one person? Without double jeopardy's application, the defendant could get 65 years for murder, plus nineteen two-year sentences, running consecutive, for a total of 103 years. Or, as I would later argue for Donnie, what if the shots were fired at two victims amid a crowd at an Indiana Pacers game? Per the trial court's understanding, that'd be murder, battery, and 18,000 counts of criminal recklessness.

Ware was convicted of murder (60 years), battery (6 years), and two counts of recklessness (2 years each), all running consecutive, for an aggregate 70-year sentence. He'd do 35 on that, getting released in 2040, at age 72, if we can't get him any PC relief. My hope, I tell him, is to get a retrial on the homicide and get the last two counts dropped. On retrial, he'd probably want to argue for voluntary manslaughter more forcefully, get 40 on it, along with the 6 for battery, allowing him to do 23 years instead of 35. "Or, you never know," I say, "you might end up with a good plea bargain and get less."

He seems hopeful now, and can envision a future on the outside, albeit one far away, and only after lengthy legal proceedings. His daughter is growing up without him, and her mother is struggling to make ends meet without Donnie's income. He works in the prison laundry and sends a majority of his state pay home, about fifty dollars a month. He wants to pay me for my work, which would be equivalent to taking money from his family. Instead, he puts me on his laundry service list – my whites washed in bleach (something general population doesn't get), and I'm atop the list for new clothes when I need them.

"There's one more thing I need you to do," I tell Donnie before he leaves. I've wanted to ask the simple, direct question: *Did you do it?* – but the question was inappropriate. "I know you never testified, Donnie, and you have never given a statement. So I need you to still admit nothing and say nothing about your case. We could win a new trial, and if we do, I don't want one of your neighbors here writing to the prosecutor, trying to be a witness for the state. It's a strategic choice, to say nothing. Same as when you were arrested."

"Strategic?" Donnie seems perplexed. "Where's strategy gotten me so far? What about the truth? It seems like the truth should matter the most, and that the truth . . ." He was at a loss for words. "The truth! What really happened should matter. The truth should be what this whole thing should be focused on."

"I'm afraid not, Donnie. The system – it just doesn't work like that."

Donnie stared at the table, pondering having to contain his side of the story at least a few more years.

"*Now* is not the time to tell anybody what really happened," I stressed. "You have to play the game the way it is, and the truth card can't be played yet. You would lose if you brought it out now."

"I know." Donnie was exasperated with the justice system. "All along, I've just done what people told me was the best thing to do. The attorneys – they're professionals, I trusted them. There's never been an opportunity for me to tell my side of it. The attorneys said I shouldn't testify, so I didn't testify. There's never been an opportunity for me to let anybody know exactly what happened and why."

I could see that Donnie possessed a particularly sensitive conscience, to a degree rarely seen at Pendleton. Whether he was an intentional shooter, or accidental shooter, or accomplice, or witness, or totally innocent, he bore some level of guilt and wished to unburden himself.

I talked to Mel-T about Donnie's case for an hour after lights out that night. We talked about the degrees of conscientiousness we had seen, shades of light and dark in every man. Some were dark – very dark, unreachable. Others were pained by what they had done, but had no way to make it right.

In the end, we identified the ineluctable conflict: people, possessing degrees of conscience, guilt, and innocence; versus a system that painted in only black and white, guilty or not guilty. Two colors, one brush. And to the outside world, all of us behind the wall were painted identically.

CHAPTER FOUR

Defining Innocence

"Everybody's innocent in here. Don't you know that?"
– Andy DuFresne, to Tommie, in *The Shawshank Redemption*

    A common perception about prisoners is the well-worn statement, delivered with a roll of the eyes, "They all claim they're innocent." It's exasperating to hear an obviously guilty person persistently maintain his innocence, and that's one reason why we seldom hear it within the prison community. Lie to the cops, sure. Lie to the court, no big deal, we understand. Even lie to your attorney if you have to, whatever it takes to get that 'not guilty' verdict. But once the trial's over there's no need to lie to us, or lie to yourself. We've been there, we know better, and we don't want to hear it. Prisoners are the toughest audience, and actual innocence claims are rarely voiced here.
    I've met thousands of prisoners, and confidentially reviewed hundreds of cases, and between 1% and 2% say they had absolutely nothing to do with the crime. Innocence in the first degree. By this metric, one might conclude the criminal justice system is doing a pretty good job. But this statistic misdirects our focus, and is not the true measure of the system's effectiveness. More accurate is to focus on imbalance – whenever the process results in a person doing more time than necessary, the system has failed. Overpunishment is an imbalance, and imbalanced scales are the very symbol of injustice.
    When defendants are overcharged, oversentenced, or denied due process, they may be classified as "wrongfully convicted." The wrongfully convicted prisoner knows instinctively he simply should not be in prison, and in his parlance he is "innocent." Rather than a denial of responsibility, it's an expres-

sion of one's awareness of injustice. And by that definition, there are hundreds of innocent prisoners here at Pendleton, and well over a million nationwide.

"Man, look here, you ain't understandin' me." Nate was arguing with me from the back of his cell during one of my runs to the admin seg unit. "I''m tellin' you, the judge couldn't have took my plea because at the same time I was pleadin' guilty, I was maintainin' my innocence."

It's true that a judge cannot accept a guilty plea from a person who claims innocence. Judges routinely ask the defendant if they understand the charge, and they usually ask them to specifically outline what they did to violate the law.

"But you admitted in open court that you and your brother robbed the pharmacy – that's not *innocent*."

"See, you don't understand. I pled guilty to a Class A felony, drug dealing over three grams, but I never admitted it was my intent to sell any of the drugs I stole."

"Yeah, I get you," I countered. "But you've got a couple problems to overcome. One is that you pled guilty, and by law, if you read *Norris v. State*, you cannot come back on a PC challenging any of the facts. The facts are not challengeable at this point. That's simply the way the law reads. And two, even if you *could* raise such a thing on a PC, the mere fact that you possessed $24,000 worth of stolen drugs implies an intent to sell. There are plenty of cases on that point. You'll lose either way."

"But I'm *innocent* of Class A dealing! I'm an addict, and I was gonna *do* the drugs, not sell them." There were eight types of narcotics stolen, so he wants me to believe he was hooked on all eight.

"Look, Nate," I finally say, "I read your sentencing hearing transcripts. You were asked what you intended to do with the drugs, and your codefendant brother said you'd do most of them, and sell some too. I don't know how you're gonna get that admission around the Indiana Attorney General."

"So you're telling me you won't do my appeal for me?"

"I see no way to make an argument that makes any kind of sense; so, no, I won't be writing it."

"You don't understand what I'm saying . . ."

I walk away, and the familiar refrain begins. In the distance I hear Nate telling his neighbors, "These clerks don't wanna help nobody…"

Sure, Nate had a point. The pharmacy robbery was a Class B felony, but that didn't satisfy the prosecutor's zeal for punishment, so the Class A felony for dealing in a Schedule I narcotic was charged, ensuring a harsher penalty. Nate wound up with 25 years.

Innocence is a wildly defined term in prison. Another guy, caged down the range from Nate, said, "I was there when my codefendant beat the victim, but nobody was trying to kill the guy. It was a simple battery. But they charged it as attempted murder, and I got convicted. But ya see, I'm *innocent* of that."

"You're overcharged," I try to reason with him, "not innocent. Leave that word for guys who did absolutely nothing wrong."

"Whatever."

"I get what you're saying. Instead of four years, the advisory sentence on a Class C simple battery, you got thirty years, the advisory for a Class A attempted murder. And that's wrong."

"Yeah, that's what I mean."

Since he should have been justly confined for only two years, the release point on a four-year term, one can appreciate his sentiment – during the last 13 years of his incarceration he's in prison needlessly, wrongly, unjustly, no different that if he were completely innocent.

After my conference with Donnie Ware, which culminated in me agreeing to draft a PC petition, I peel into Jerry Griner's case file. Hopeless Jerry. Illiterate, mentally ill, history of child molesting, with 75 years for attempted murder. It'd be easy to look at him, or at his description as written by authorities, and not care what happened to him. Within minutes I discover that Jerry – like Donnie, like Nate – has been overcharged.

An attempted murder conviction requires specific intent to kill. An action that could conceivably result in death is insufficient – the perpetrator had to desire that, at the end of the incident, the victim would be dead. The purpose of the attack had to be murder. And in Jerry's case, where he stuck a paring knife into an elderly lady outside the Dollar General store, no such intent was in the record – not initially, at least. I examine the earliest evidence: a post-arrest interview with the Tippecanoe County detective.

Jerry waived his Miranda rights; no surprise, given his level of intelligence, that he would waive his rights despite his numerous arrests. I find the portion of the interrogation where the detective, who's fully aware of the elements required for attempted murder, squarely addresses Jerry's *mens rea*, or criminal intent:

> DET. – When she wouldn't let go of her purse, what did you do?
> JERRY – I tried to get it away.
> DET. – And when you couldn't get it away, what did you do?
> JERRY – Stabbed her.
> DET. – How many times?
> JERRY – One time.
> DET. – On what part of her body?
> JERRY – Chest.
> DET. – You know she could have died?
> JERRY – Yeah.
> DET. – Is that what you wanted to happen?
> JERRY – No, I just wanted her to let go of the purse.
> DET. – But you agree, stabbing her in the chest could have killed her?
> JERRY – Yeah, I guess so.
> DET. – You guess so? Come on, Jerry, you know that stabbing someone in the chest can kill them, right?
> JERRY – Yeah.
> DET. – So you tried to kill her, right?
> JERRY – Yeah.

And here's where the prosecutor comes in, drafting an information in support of the attempted murder charge: "Griner was asked directly if he tried to kill the victim, and Griner replied in the affirmative." That's what prosecutors do – ignore the substantial meaning of the conversation, and cherry-pick the phrases needed to support the highest felony possible.

As any experienced cop, prosecutor, or coroner will tell you, a true murder attempt with a knife will involve either one enormous knife or multiple stab wounds. A stabbing is not like a Shakespeare play, one thrust and the victim wails and hits the floor. I recall a Florida prisoner in for murder, 32 stab wounds inflicted, and I asked him why he stuck the guy so many times. "Because he wouldn't quit fighting!" Stabbing victims die from loss of blood, and this usually takes time; meanwhile, most of them fight, which means there'll be more stab wounds, *if* the intent is murder.

One thrust with a paring knife is not attempted murder, and Jerry's initial response, before being manipulated by the detective, showed no intent to kill. The proper charge was a Class B felony aggravated battery, carrying 6 to 20, with a habitual offender enhancement of an additional 10 to 30 years. So, 16 to 50 years, do half. Or the charge could have been a Class B robbery – same result. By overcharging the case, and lacking any effort by the public defender to defend Jerry on this point, Jerry was relegated into a sentencing range of 50 to 80 years – 20 to 50 for attempted murder, and a flat 30 for the habitual. He pled guilty to attempted murder – a crime he did not do – and got 75 years. His cooperation got him five years less than the maximum, but probably 30 more years than he should have gotten.

His plea agreement waived the right to appeal, as most agreements do, so there was no appellate review. After a few years Jerry heard about this PC thing as a way to "get back in court," and a clerk drafted a "bare bones" petition for him, simply alleging ineffective assistance, with no details as to how counsel was ineffective. Like nearly all guilty plea convictions, the state public defender's office took no interest in the case. That left Jerry, with all his unique faculties and resources, to prosecute the PC pro se. He bungled that, and now it's in my lap.

I'd like to get Jerry's PC petition reinstated by explaining Jerry's situation, but the PC was dismissed "with prejudice," meaning the court will hear no more about it. And he can't go to a higher state court because there's no appealable order in the county court. Besides, a notice of appeal must be filed within 30 days. Federal court is out too – to qualify for U.S. district court, the prisoner had to exhaust appeals in the highest state court, and have filed his habeas petition within one year of sentencing. All that remains for Jerry is a successive PC, sometimes called a PC-2.

The successive PC can't be filed directly to the county court. Instead, the Indiana Court of Appeals acts as gatekeeper for all successive PCs. The prisoner must first draft a proposed PC petition, then ask the appellate court for permission to file it in the county court. Permission will be granted if the prisoner can show a "reasonable probability" he is entitled to relief.

Sounds easy. But it's not. The court's definition of "reasonable probability" gets excruciatingly narrow when applied to a PC.

I draft a simple PC petition for Jerry – a concise one is superior to a long, complex claim that would only be scanned with impatience – alleging IAC because counsel did not provide "reasonably competent advice," as required for guilty pleas per *McMann v. Richardson* (1970). I make the subclaim alleging there was "no factual basis for the plea," per *Patton v. State* (Ind. 2003), stressing Jerry's initial denial of lack of intent to kill.

However, I also know Jerry's already exhausted his IAC claim from his first PC, and a petitioner is required to put *all* of the grounds for ineffectiveness within the initial IAC claim. If any grounds were overlooked and omitted – too bad. The IAC claim is *res judicata*, already adjudicated, and won't be reconsidered. So I try to dance around this outcome be showing his original PC was never amended to include all IAC grounds, and was never adjudicated by full due process on the merits. I attach an affidavit outlining Jerry's illiteracy, mental illness, lack of assistance, and segregation status.

It takes another three weeks to get it mailed, after wrestling with the G-cellhouse counselor to get Jerry's signature notarized, copies made, envelopes addressed, and postage procured. Each step, I have to write instructions for Jerry to present to others – it's like pinning a note on a kindergartener. I see Jerry's hopes rise. I give him no encouragement, knowing how these usually turn out. At one point he tries to give me a bag of coffee for helping him. I tell him I'm paid by the IDOC (25 cents an hour) and a simple 'thank you' will do.

Roughly a third of the law library clerks charge others prisoners for legal services; another third, like me, work for free; the remaining third do a little of both, charging only those who can obviously afford it. The decision on whether to charge or not depends primarily on the clerk's financial situation, not the client's. Clerks without savings or family support, or those with expensive habits – tobacco, drugs, cellphone bills – see the work as a 'hustle,' a semi-legitimate source of prison income. Most who labor for the $45 monthly state pay need a little extra to get by comfortably.

There's an undercurrent of lack of confidence in the quality of work provided by law library clerks – let's face it, there are no law degrees hanging on the library's walls. And, like professional attorneys who promise absolutely nothing, experienced prison clerks also provide no guarantees. Combine this with the adage, "you get what you pay for," and one understands why many prisoners elect to hire one of the costly "jailhouse lawyers" advertising their services back in the cellhouse. The jailhouse lawyers have another advantage – an unabashed proclamation of utter confidence in the outcome of the proceedings, which sounds much better, to the untrained ear, than the one-in-twenty success rate the clerks quote, a statistic based on hard data.

As one of my pro bono clients, Chris Turner, related to me, "The guys up in K-Dorm said, if you don't charge for your work, it must not be worth much." They had the same opinion regarding their public defender's trial work, and a majority believe the difference between a guilty verdict and acquittal was merely their inability to hire a paid lawyer.

While many high-profile examples prove the value of a top-dollar attorney, the presumption that legal fees *always* directly correlate to the quality of service is nonsense. Based on my reading of trial records, some paid attorneys are absolutely atrocious, and many public defenders do outstanding work. In general, yes, it's true that defendants with retained counsel obtain better outcomes, on average, than those with public defenders; numerous studies support this fact. And a super-expensive attorney does seem to have the magical ability to get anybody out of anything, as many celebrity criminal proceedings attest.

"Every case is winnable," said Edgar Lee, "if you have enough money. Just look at O.J." O.J. Simpson spent $50,000 *per day* on his defense.

"I'd like to find a way to quantify exactly how much money matters to everyday defendants," I told Edgar Lee. "We need some hard data to prove how the system is screwing the poor, if that's what's really going on here."

I make a note to get data on poverty, race, crime rates and incarceration rates, in order to resolve the competing theories I've heard for years. Some prisoners believe they've been unfairly railroaded into prison because they're poor; minorities often believe the system targets them purely out of racial bias. In opposition is the conservative mantra, that we are all in prison due to making bad choices, and blame lies solely with the individual and his decision to break the law. As CO Red sometimes reminded us, "There are plenty of poor people out there who don't break the law, people of all different races and colors and backgrounds. If they can obey the law, you can too."

One perplexed and uneasy about my pro bono service is Louis Amalfitano, a rambunctious kid in his early 20's with a 46-year sentence. Louis and his father, Luigi, are here on the same case, one qualifying as "high-profile" in tiny Madison County. The elder Amalfitano has a 34-year sentence, courtesy of a plea agreement promising the non-filing of the habitual offender enhancement, thereby avoiding an extra 10 to 30 years. Louis went to trial on eight felony charges, lost, and got the maximum sentence on every count, all sentences to be served consecutively. Since it was a highly publicized case, by local Anderson, Indiana, standards, I expect to find many irregularities in both the trial and sentencing, and I'm not disappointed.

As I find in any high-profile case, there are now four stories and four sets of facts to contend with: the direct appeal opinion with a section titled "Facts"; the trial transcripts; the news media accounts; and the defendant's version. I begin by tuning out the defendant's story, mainly because it won't be useful until I hear how it will fit with the evidence accepted by the court. I prefer to hear the worst version first, to see what I'm really fighting against, and for that I can always depend on the news media to have written the most sensational and inaccurate story.

Reporters are puddy in law enforcement's hands. They slurp up whatever craftily spun info the cops release, then spew out the most outlandish, headline-making, rag-selling tale they can create.

A disgusted public heard the tale of the vagabond Amalfitano clan, originally from Brooklyn, and how they befriended 65-year-old Esther Coleman, duped her into residing with them, then locked her in a small room for six months while cashing her social security checks, hijacking her Xanax prescription, and beating her on a regular basis. A tip led the Anderson police to doing a welfare check on her, whereupon they rescued a confused and exhausted Esther from a hot, filthy, feces-strewn utility room. She was "near death." Luigi, Louis, and 12-year-old Matthew were jailed after Esther identified those three as responsible for her confinement, injuries, and stolen property.

The media description leaves much to the imagination and isn't really clear on, specifically, who did what. The question for me is, What exactly did Louis do?

The trial record gets closer to the truth. First, the charging information alleged Esther was confined some time between April 9, 2010, and May 27, 2010, a seven-week period, not six months. She'd been living with the Amalfitanos for six months, traveled to New York and back with them, and had willingly shared her social security money to help cover expenses. They'd taken her to doctor's appointments, the pharmacy, and grocery shopping. She toted a puppy around, and kept the dog in her room, a converted back porch adjacent to the kitchen.

A couple weeks before she was rescued, Esther testified, young Matthew had beaten her up, giving her a black eye. She thought Louis was involved too. After that, her door was locked from the outside. When she banged on the door Louis' girlfriend would open it and escort her to the bathroom. (The girlfriend, I'd later discover, was the source of the tip sent to police.) While confined, Esther's social security check was cashed without her consent, and her Xanax prescription was picked up at the pharmacy. Evidence showed Louis responsible for the transactions.

A cop testified he found feces in her room, on the floor, and in a plastic bag hanging on the doorknob. A doctor determined Esther was dehydrated and suffering from hypokalemia – low potassium – a "potentially fatal" condition. Other witnesses who saw Esther during the seven-week period outlined in the charging information helped narrow down her actual confinement period to the thirteen days prior to May 27th. Louis did not testify, per his public defender's insistence.

Louis was convicted on all eight counts: (1) Class B criminal confinement with serious bodily injury, 20 years; (2) Class C battery, 8 years; (3) Class D exploitation of endangered adult, 3 years; (4) Class D financial exploitation of endangered adult, 3 years; (5) Class D theft, 3 years; (6) Class D theft, 3 years; (7) Class D possession of controlled substance, 3 years; and (8) Class D possession of controlled substance, 3 years. Judge Rudolph Pyle III, a former state trooper, ran the sentences wild, for an aggregate 46 years, do 23.

The direct appeal couldn't do anything for Louis because his public defender hadn't preserved any worthwhile issues. A perfunctory brief was opposed by a brief from the Indiana Attorney General's office that spent most of the paper railing on the reprehensible conduct heaped upon the poor elderly woman. The resulting "Facts" section of the appellate court's opinion read like it was culled from the media reports, including the "fact" that Esther was confined for six months. The appellate court largely incorporated the version written by the state and electronically filed with the court – a process enabling the court to blindly cut-n-paste any "fact" alleged in the state's brief. Obviously the appellate court made no attempt to fact-check their opinion with the trial record, which is, experience tells me, quite normal.

Last, I get to Louis' versions of events. He tells me the problem started with Esther and Matthew unable to get along. Matthew was disgusted with Esther's lack of hygiene, with her untrained puppy defecating all over the house, and with Esther's high-handed pronouncements that Matthew was an evil child on his way to Hell. On May 14th Matthew exploded after Esther called him an "evil little bastard," and he punched her in the eye. Louis forcibly broke up the altercation, and Luigi decided it would be a good idea to keep them apart – the dog restricted to one room also – best accomplished by keeping Esther in her room.

Louis doesn't say it, but I suspect they planned to keep her in her room until she healed, so as not to be accused of abuse. One accusatory word, and things would not be good for father or son, both of whom had felony records and would not be believed by the first cops on the scene. Louis admits cashing her check and getting her Xanax from the pharmacy. He's incredulous regarding the blood draw that determined Esther was hypokalemic: "She ate bananas every day!" The hypokalemia was a crucial point, as it established the "serious bodily injury" element necessary to raise Count 1 from a Class D to a Class B felony.

Luigi independently gives me the same story. Both insist the feces in her room were from the dog, not Esther, and that she'd gotten out regularly to visit the bathroom. "They exaggerated everything," says Luigi, "and it was like we had no attorney at all."

While none of the Amalfitanos could be called "innocent," it's clear Louis has landed the trifecta of wrongful incarceration: overcharged, an unfair trial, and oversentenced.

On Count 1, no question, criminal confinement occurred when her door was locked. But at trial it was never determined who locked the door; and if Louis didn't do it he shouldn't have been convicted. Then, to establish the element of serious bodily injury (SBI), the state needed an injury that caused "loss or impairment of a bodily function" or "created a substantial risk of death." The prosecutor came up with hypokalemia. From my LEXIS research, it appears to be the first time in legal history a potassium deficiency was used to allege "serious" injury. Since it elevated the penalty by 17 years, counsel should have contended against it – but did nothing. How do we know Esther wasn't hypokalemic prior to the incident? No previous bloodwork was in evidence. Where's the testimony from the lab technician? And was the risk of death truly "substantial"? I have a researcher perform an on-line search and find 12% of the nation's cardiac patients live with hypokalemia, and there is no data on hypokalemia as an independent cause of death.

Then I turn to the six Class D felonies. Counts 3 and 4 should be void because Esther didn't qualify as an "endangered adult." The statute defines an endangered adult as a person age 18 or over, "incapable by reason of mental illness, mental retardation, dementia, habitual drunkenness, excessive use of drugs, or other mental or physical incapacity" of providing self care. None of those conditions were found at trial – merely being 65 doesn't cut it. She cared for herself both before and after May 2010.

Then there's the argument that double jeopardy should have cut the six Class D felonies down to only two counts. Counts 3, 4, and 5 were based on one act, the theft of Esther's social security check. It's well established under common law that a defendant cannot be punished for separate crimes that rely on a single act. For example, if you steal a car, you can't be punished for theft, auto theft, and possession of stolen property simultaneously. The double jeopardy principle predates the enactment of the Bill of Rights by a hundred years, and its application has been standardized through numerous Supreme Court decisions. Yet thousands of American prisoners are doing time on multiple counts arising from one physical act, victims of the most contorted state court definitions of what constitutes double jeopardy.

Underscoring the identical nature of the charges, at Louis' sentencing the prosecutor was unable to distinguish any unique conduct to differentiate Counts 3, 4, and 5. They're "the same," he admitted, all for the theft of one social security check. Likewise, Counts 6, 7, and 8 were identical, based on Louis obtaining Esther's Xanax. When the pharmacist placed the pill bottle in Louis' hand, Louis earned 3 years for theft of Xanax, 3 years for possession of Xanax (the courts hold that a necessary element of theft is possession, therefore double jeopardy applies), and 3 years for possession of Xanax by misrepresentation (double jeopardy again).

Louis' appropriate charges and sentence are difficult to determine without a true adversarial setting – equally competent attorneys on each side, and an unbiased judge – but if we discount hypokalemia as a "serious" bodily injury, and agree Louis touched Esther "in a rude, insolent, or angry manner" (the statutory definition of battery), and accept Louis' guilt on two Class D felonies for taking her check and her Xanax, the maximum penalty is $3 + 8 + 3 + 3 = 17$ years, not 46.

And then, why should Louis receive the maximum penalty on each count, and why should they run consecutively? Per numerous appellate decisions, the maximum should be reserved for "the worst of the worst," and there's nothing in the facts or in Louis' history suggesting he's the creepiest convict on the block. Had he received the advisory sentence on each felony in the above paragraph, he'd have $1 + 3 + 1 + 1 = 6$ years, do 3. The public defender's ineptitude cost Louis an extra 20 years in prison.

The elder Amalfitano was also screwed, bullied into accepting a 34-year sentence in order to avoid an additional 10 to 30 years for a Class B habitual offender enhancement. Undoubtedly, he'd have gotten the max there too, had he gone to trial, for a 64-year sentence. To put it in perspective, the maximum term for murder in Indiana is 65 years.

Think what you want about the Amalfitanos, the fact is they got 80 years in prison, and will do 40, for locking Esther's door for two weeks, (an action that could be argued was for her own safety), and for stealing approximately $1000 from her, money she probably would have pooled with them anyway. The cost of confining these two will exceed one million dollars, footed by taxpayers. The 1,000-to-1 proportionality of the punishment is something to consider. Esther received no restitution, and the remaining members of the Amalfitano clan became more fractured and destitute. Like most cases, there was no balance, no proportionality, no restoration, and no utilitarian weighing of costs and benefits.

"Louis," I tell him, "your case will be difficult to remedy with a PC petition simply because there are so many errors. A one-issue petition is easy to write, easy for an impatient judge to read, and more likely to obtain relief. A multi-issue petition alleging a laundry list of defects and factual inaccuracies causes a judge's eyes to glaze over."

Diatribe-like PC petitions always fail, and there's a fear that Louis' petition will fall into the diatribe category and be ignored. But Louis decides to delay filing a PC – he wants to go with a Motion to Correct Erroneous Sentence (MCES).

The MCES is the remedy for a sentence "defective on its face," and it is questionable whether Louis' sentencing order qualifies. Yes, statutes were violated when his sentences were run consecutively, and double jeopardy can be argued on the MCES. But the courts are more likely to entertain the merits of an MCES when there is no argument over the facts, and they prefer to hear double jeopardy claims in a PC petition. Nevertheless, it's what Louis wants to do, and I draft the MCES for him. Many prisoners like to file the MCES because they feel it gives them an extra opportunity to get the sentence reduced.

Louis' motion is pending before Judge Pyle when Louis and Luigi are suddenly summoned to pack up for transfer out of Pendleton. I wish Louis luck and accept the last of his stolen kitchen food – he's probably the most brazen and successful kitchen thief Pendleton's ever had. It will be four years before I learn more about his fate.

Next afternoon, an hour before closing, I'm researching cases for Donnie Ware and Michael Daniels when Edgar Lee interrupts. "A guy just came in, needs your help in a hurry. His deadline to file his appellate brief is today."

"Today?"

"Yeah, due today. He had one of the jailhouse lawyers helping him, but he left, and now this guy has no idea what to do."

I give Edgar Lee the you-can't-be-serious look, and he laughs. "So it's a race between me and the One Hour Photo shop next door?"

Edgar Lee laughs again. "Glad I ain't you!"

The young man with the pleading expression, hoping someone will bail him out, is 27-year-old Robert Oldham, aka "Goddie." One hand holds a plastic bag containing a disheveled mass of paper, the other clutches a thin appeal brief I recognize from afar by the blue cover. He drops the bag, fishes through his cluttered pocket, and produces a folded letter from Kevin Smith, Clerk of the Indiana Court of Appeals. It's titled, "Notice of Defect."

Prisoners are renowned for their inability to follow rules, and a court's filing rules are no exception. The court is very specific regarding the format of briefs, and when a submitted document violates a rule, the clerk refuses to accept it. A Notice is sent, which is a form listing all possible defects. The specific defect is checked, and the prisoner has 20 calendar days to remedy the filing. Most defects are easily fixed – line spacing, font size, margins, colored covers, required sections, page numbering, attaching the order being appealed, et cetera – by simply revising the document and mailing it anew.

I discover this is Goddie's fourth Notice of Defect, and I ask who's been helping him. "Petey's been doing this for me," he says, and I automatically know Goddie paid fifty dollars for this mess. "Petey" Peterson was one of our most prolific jailhouse lawyers, until he transferred to Pendleton's Outside Detail (OSD) Unit, a 200-bed minimum-security dorm outside the back gate.

I scan through the brief, a mere five pages, wall-to-wall with misspellings, and the case cite *Marbury v. Madison* catches my eye. Anyone with a good recollection of U.S. history may recall the 1803 case establishing the authority of the Supreme Court to declare a law unconstitutional. Petey wants to use it to declare Goddie's sentence "unconstitutional, erroneous, and a fundamental miscarriage of justice." A full page was devoted to explaining *Marbury* to the court, or rather, explaining Petey's understanding of *Marbury*.

Goddie's appeal is nonsense, but I withhold my opinion – it's not Goddie's fault he was suckered in by a jailhouse lawyer wooing him with spectacular phrases like "fundamental miscarriage of justice," a phrase I see repeated five times in the brief.

The brief lacks a section titled "Summary of Argument." Well, that's easy to draft: "There was a fundamental miscarriage of justice when Robert Oldham was sentenced to 40 years in prison." It's as silly as the contents of the brief, so it fits right in. Besides, the brief's contents can't be changed after a Notice of Defect is sent – the clerk retains the previous filing and will only allow the changes requested on the Notice.

I type a new Table of Contents, and we renumber the pages. A new Certificate of Service is notarized with today's date, to provide a "proof of mailing date," allowing Goddie to meet the filing deadline in compliance with the Indiana "mailbox rule." The mailbox rule allows a prisoner's submission to be considered "filed" on the date it was handed to prison staff for mailing. We make ten copies – nine for the court, one for the Attorney General. It's out with ten minutes to spare, ("God saved me," he says), and I use the remaining time to discuss his case.

"I hope you know," I tell Goddie, firmly, "what we just mailed has absolutely no chance of winning. Zero. Will never happen."

He's confused. "Then why did we mail it?"

"Because you deserve your day in court. And two, I want you to hear the denial from the court, not from me. If you just go around believing what guys tell you here, you'll never get anywhere."

He looks even more confused, so I get to the point.

"Quit listening to those jailhouse lawyers in the cellhouse. They're only out to get your money. If a guy can't follow simple filing rules four times, that oughta tell you he has no idea what he's doing."

"But I hear Petey's got lotsa people out of prison."

"And who told you that? Petey? Petey's buddy? Look, Petey couldn't get an innocent dog out of the animal shelter."

With all the references to Petey, Pete Mitchell has picked up on the conversation. He's often confused with Petey Peterson and bristles every time someone misidentifies Petey's work as his own.

Pete Mitchell adds, "We spend many hours every week trying to fix cases Petey's screwed up. Bring your stuff up here next week and we'll see what we can do for you."

We advise Goddie to pursue a PC petition, not an MCES, and the following week he's back, grinning, toting a bag of jumbled papers twice the size of his last one.

I spend several hours reading Goddie's case, and despite some peculiarities I emerge with the gut feeling he did pretty good to come away with only 40 years. He shot his cousin in the forehead from ten feet away, in the middle of the street with about a dozen witnesses present. Goddie was 20, his cousin a year younger, and they routinely passed their time that summer drinking, using a variety of drugs, and openly playing with guns. On this occasion, Goddie fired a shot in the air, sending the crowd scattering – except for his cousin, who bravely stood his ground and said, "You won't shoot me."

Goddie fired a round over his cousin's head, and his cousin merely folded his arms and cocked his head back defiantly. The next shot put a neat hole in the middle of his forehead, and the 19-year-old dropped dead.

Panic ensued. The cops arrived, arrested Goddie, read him his rights, then searched for the gun. They found it hidden nearby. When they questioned Goddie he professed to not know what he'd done, and he vaguely referenced his desire for an attorney twenty-five times. Unfortunately for the direct appeal that failed, he only said things like, "I think I need an attorney," instead of the declarative statement that would have ended questioning: "I want an attorney."

He was charged with murder, which is "knowingly or intentionally" killing a human being. It carries 45 to 65 years in prison. At first glance, one might presume his conviction would be easily won by the state. Firing a gun, twice, at the victim's head could possibly be construed as an intentional homicide. And in dozens of cases, the courts have held that firing a weapon in the general direction of another person satisfies the "knowingly" element.

Goddie's public defender chose a bench trial – judge only, no jury – a wise move whenever the bare facts will cause the ordinary juror to think, *What the hell's wrong with you?* She argued the killing was accidental, Goddie had no motive to kill (which has no legal significance), and they were both heavily influenced by drugs and alcohol (a statute declares intoxication cannot be used as a defense). She concluded the proper conviction should be Class C reckless homicide, carrying 2 to 8 years.

In cases decided by a jury, the state expends great effort to ensure jurors don't arrive at a compromise verdict, one that convicts on a lesser charge and acquits on the highest felony. In a bench trial, there are no jury instructions. It is presumed the judge knows the law and will apply the proper felony. So I was surprised when the judge convicted Goddie for Class A voluntary manslaughter, a charge neither the state nor the defense presented for consideration.

To convict on vol man in Indiana, the killing had to have been "knowing or intentional" *and* a finding of "sudden heat" existed to cause the killing. Indiana courts affirm that sudden heat "occurs when provocation engenders rage, resentment, or terror sufficient to obscure the reason of an ordinary person, preventing deliberation and premeditation, excluding malice, and rendering a person incapable of cool reflection." Being taunted with fighting words, or being physically provoked, often support a sudden heat finding. Some spousal killings involve sudden heat – circumstances may cause one to "snap" and lose control. Of course, when I see sudden heat used by the judge in Goddie's case, which had no evidentiary support, I think of Donnie Ware, who'd been hit with an egg and taunted with racist language. Ware's jury didn't find sudden heat applicable (if they considered it).

Goddie's verdict was a gift. I explain it to him, then cover his sentencing. The advisory Class A sentence was 30 years, but the judge found two aggravators to raise it to 40. One aggravator was Goddie's habit of engaging in reckless behavior, shooting the gun in the street "all the time." The second aggravator was Goddie's "position of care, custody, or control" over the victim. This aggravator is typically applied to formal caregivers, such as parents, babysitters, teachers, or nurses. I don't see how it could apply to two adult cousins only a year apart. I advise Goddie the only basis for a PC petition is to argue counsel was ineffective by failing to object to the aggravators, and try to get a new sentence.

"But I want to get the conviction thrown out," he pleaded. "You said so yourself, no way I shoulda got convicted of manslaughter."

"That's right," I replied. "You should have been convicted of murder, and if you were to get a new trial, you'd get convicted of murder and probably get 60 years."

He's reluctant to agree. He's got the idea that if he could get a new trial set, the state would just drop the case. I know precisely where he gets that idea, but say nothing. He has several months to consider his options, pending resolution of the MCES appeal. But before he goes, I ask Goddie one more question.

"That first murder case you caught, how'd that end up after you won your appeal?"

There's no mention of his prior murder case in the paperwork he gave me, and gives me a stunned look, wondering how I knew about it.

I add, "I found it on LEXIS. I always check LEXIS for a guy's prior cases."

He's frozen, doesn't know what to say. The whole time, he's been passing himself off as a semi-innocent first offender who just made a drunken mistake. But he's been through the system before. At age 15 he caught a murder charge for the shooting of 18-year-old Benjamin Brownlow. It was late August of 1999 and Brownlow was shot at 2 a.m. near 36th and Kenwood in Indianapolis, by a short, stocky, black male generally fitting Goddie's description. The evidence wasn't strong, though, so the prosecutor gained a conviction by putting "bad character" evidence into the trial and making prejudicial remarks in closing. This prosecutorial misconduct prompted the appellate court to overturn the conviction and 50-year sentence in December 2002, and Goddie was released in early 2003. Less than two years later, and a few blocks away from the Brownlow murder scene, Goddie caught his second homicide, bringing him to the table with me.

He finally finds some words, his mind processing the fact I know more about him than he suspects. "They didn't have any evidence to try me again," he shrugs, "so they had to drop the case."

I know better than to ask if he did it. There's a five-year statute of limitations on felonies in Indiana, but no limitation on a murder case. So I would never ask, and I know he'll never tell.

"As far as that case goes, I'm innocent," he declares, with finality. Then he smiles in a conspiratorial way. "Innocent until proven guilty, right?"

CHAPTER FIVE

The Mercy of the Court

"A life sentence is a hidden death penalty." – Pope Francis, at International Association of Penal Law, October 26, 2014.

One evening I was lamenting the number of unjust practices that combined to make the incarceration rate explode. I covered a laundry list of common complaints, and then posed a question to Mel.

"Mel," I asked, "in your experience, what do you think is the single number one cause of over-incarceration?"

"Sentences," Mel replied. "Excessive sentences. It doesn't get any simpler than that."

The complaint I most frequently heard was not that the trial had been unfair, although that was common, but that the prosecutor had sought a sentence disproportionate to the offense, and that the judge had agreed to it.

Pendleton is a maximum-security prison, so it is mainly the repository of those have gone to trial and lost. A majority of IDOC prisoners did *not* go to trial – they took plea bargains. In fact, 95% of all state cases are adjudicated by plea bargain, a statistic that holds up nationwide. But in America's maximum-security prisons, the statistic is nearly reversed, with close to 90% refusing the plea (or never being offered one). At Pendleton, the refrain, "I was given too much time," is probably over-represented as compared to the mass of state prisoner complaints.

However, Pete Mitchell, who had done time in Indiana's lower security prisons, offered that excessive sentencing was the main objection of those who had pled guilty too. "They plead guilty to an open plea, to a cap of, like, ten years, and the judge gives them the max under the plea agreement, ten years. It's always a sentence near the top end of the range. And these guys pleading guilty, they do so very reluctantly, knowing they'll get whacked hard on the plea, but they fear what will happen when you exercise your right to a trial."

Edgar Lee joined in. "And this aggravator-mitigator crap the judge is supposed to weigh," he interjected, "is all just talk. One aggravator, just one, and the judge will jack that sentence to the top." By design, the judge was bound to begin any sentencing consideration by starting with the advisory sentence, such as four years on a Class C felony, then weigh the aggravators against the mitigators. By case law, a solitary aggravator was sufficient to support the maximum, which was eight years on a Class C. One mitigator could reduce a sentence to the low end, two years on a Class C. When both aggravators and mitigators are present, as is the usual scenario, the judge has broad discretion to put the sentence anywhere within the statutory range. But judge after judge finds that "the aggravators outweigh the mitigators," and the high end is the result.

The judge reaps a personal benefit by sentencing defendants to the high end of the range. The judge gains a reputation for being "tough on crime," pleasing prosecutors, cops, and much of the general public.

"A judge tough on crime is like an umpire being tough on baserunners," was my analogy. "If the runner doesn't beat the throw by three steps, he's out."

A promising addition to my client list was the compelling case of Arturo Gallardo, the Acapulco Drug Lord. If Arturo, a Mexican immigrant, was a big-time drug-dealer, he hid it well. He had lived in Elkhart several years, blending into the community by working 60-hour weeks and raising five kids with his Indiana-born wife, Emily. In almost a decade of labor at three assembly plants he'd advanced from $5.15 to $9.00 an hour, ten times more than he'd made in Acapulco. He drove an old Buick, nothing flashy, and his one vice was hitting the bars on the weekends. Seven times he'd been arrested for public intoxication, and he was jailed once for driving while intoxicated. Fortunately, immigration authorities weren't contacted, or he'd have been deported. Elkhart was an industrial town (RV Capital of the World) that Immigrations and Customs Enforcement (ICE) mostly ignored before 2005, a policy favorable to the many business interests dependent upon unskilled labor, and well-known among Hispanic immigrants in need of sanctuary. To remain in the United States, Arturo thought, all he had to do was keep laboring to bolster corporate America's bottom line, and avoid a felony conviction.

In 2005, avoiding ICE became tougher for immigrants. Operation Streamline, a federal zero-tolerance law mandating prosecution and deportation of all people found without documentation, began targeting Elkhart's factory workers. ICE agents began raiding factory floors, no warrant required (thanks to the Supreme Court), and an ICE bus would appear in town weekly, empty in the morning, loaded as it trekked west on I-80 at night. Families were broken up, devastated. Like many other illegals, Arturo quit his job at a large factory to take a lower-paying job with a smaller company, one off of ICE's radar.

At a bar in May of 2007 Arturo was asked by a new acquaintance named Hector where cocaine could be bought. Arturo told the guy to check around down at "The Hole," a run-down section of old Elkhart a few blocks from the river. He'd tried that, Hector said, and since nobody knew him, nobody would sell to him. He needed Arturo to make an introduction, or buy it for him. Arturo declined to help, but over several weeks Hector was, well, hectoring, so Arturo relented and took Hector to a house where he was pretty sure dope was sold.

Hector gave Arturo the cash, $150, and the pair stood on the porch as Arturo bought an "eight ball," one-eighth of an ounce of powder cocaine. The dealer passed the baggie out the door to Arturo, who passed it to Hector in the car. Arturo received no money for himself from either Hector or the dealer. He was vaguely aware he'd committed a crime, but was sure his role was far less serious than that of the man in the house, who made his living dealing drugs. Hector left Arturo alone after that one purchase.

Arturo thought nothing more about it until five months later, on November 24, 2007, when his Thanksgiving weekend was intruded upon by sheriff's deputies arresting him for a Class A felony, delivery of cocaine.

Hector, of course, was a confidential informant (CI). He'd been caught possessing cocaine, and in exchange for non-prosecution he agreed to help catch three dealers by making undercover drug buys while wearing a wire. Arturo's purchase, entirely in Spanish, had been audio recorded, and the cocaine weighed slightly over three grams, enough to make Arturo eligible for a 20 to 50 year sentence.

Arturo was offered the advisory sentence, 30 years, to plead guilty. After doing 15 of the 30, he'd be deported to Mexico. He turned down the deal, and I asked why.

"I wasn't a drug dealer," Arturo reasoned. "I didn't see why I should go to prison for so long for showing someone where to buy drugs." He anticipated a better deal, lesser charges, but unlike most drug defendants, he had no information with which to bargain. So the Elkhart County Prosecutor held firm on the 30, and a trial ensued.

With a little better defense, Arturo Gallardo might have been found not guilty. His trial transcript was the shortest I'd ever seen, the case balancing almost exclusively on the testimony of Officer Chomer, who had supervised the CI, Hector. Hector did not testify. The jurors sent back one question from the deliberation room, a query requesting a review of Chomer's identification of Gallardo. Judge Terry Shewmaker told them to rely on their memory of Chomer's testimony. Hector had identified Gallardo three days after the sale, after he was shown an old booking photo of Gallardo. Gallardo's photo was not part of a six-photo array, as is normally done, but was a single photo alone on Officer Chomer's desk. Hector signed his name below Gallardo's picture, and fourteen months later, three days before trial, Chomer was given the signed photo and asked if this was the person he'd seen with Hector on the night Hector had purchased cocaine.

Again, with Chomer, it was a one-photo array, a practice scrutinized by the U.S. Supreme Court in *Stovall v. Denno* (1967). The jurors knew nothing about *Stovall*, but they clearly had a problem with the identification procedure. Gallardo's public defender apparently had never heard of *Stovall* either, and had filed no motion in limine to exclude Chomer's questionable identification. Gallardo was convicted. If you hand cocaine to another person you've legally satisfied the definition of "delivery," whether you receive proceeds from the transaction or not. The Indiana legislature had enacted a drug law, the harshest drug law in Indiana's statutes, specifically to include people like Gallardo. You don't have to be a drug dealer to face 50 years in prison, you just have to be associated with one.

On September 4, 2008, Judge Shewmaker sentenced Gallardo to 42 years in prison, citing two aggravating factors to enhance the penalty above the advisory 30 years: Gallardo's criminal history, and his status as an illegal immigrant. The 42 years, which I considered an unusual choice, (why not a round 35 or 40?), happened to be the same sentence given to the drug dealer in the house, who faced three Class A felony charges. Shewmaker's decision to give both of them 42 years suggests the judge believed the two were engaged in an ongoing drug enterprise, something never alleged by police or prosecutors.

I shook my head at Gallardo's prior "crimes." Perhaps to a doctor, psychologist, or Alcoholics Anonymous attendee, alcoholism is a disease; but to a judge it's a crime, as criminal as theft, robbery, or rape. No person had been harmed by Gallardo's drinking, and there were none of the other charges that normally follow – no domestic violence, no car accidents, not even a resisting arrest when all it takes is one word of reluctance and you get whacked on the head and charged with resisting. Gallardo was a peaceful, amiable drunk. But to Shewmaker he was an unrepentant criminal, deserving additional years in prison because of his habitual drunkenness.

The second aggravating factor, Gallardo's illegal status, was puzzling. The Indiana Court of Appeals upholds that type of aggravator, but I've read cases where the defense successfully argued it as a mitigator, and the higher court upheld that as well. Shewmaker clearly found illegal entry into the United States reprehensible, stating on the record: "Every day you were in this country, you were breaking the law." It seemed unfair to use Gallardo's illegal status as an aggravator when Elkhart County had arrested him eight times and let him go every time. If his mere existence in Elkhart was a crime, it was one Elkhart had condoned.

Like the judge, I also wondered if there was a hidden conspiracy tying Gallardo to the dealer. Had Arturo been a "runner" for the dealer, sharing in the profits? I asked Arturo the dealer's name, so I could look up his case, but Arturo couldn't remember it. It had been five years, and he barely knew the guy. He promised to find out, and it took him three weeks to return with the name. His unfamiliarity with the dealer left me no doubt that Arturo's role in delivery of cocaine on June 19, 2007, was a one-time affair. Arturo, called simply "Acapulco" by his soccer teammates, was no drug lord.

Gallardo's direct appeal raised two issues. One was the perfunctory claim under Appellate Rule 7B that his sentence was excessive. The second, to my horror, was ineffective assistance of counsel for trial counsel failing to raise an entrapment defense.

His appellate attorney, in private practice, was clueless, absolutely clueless. Entrapment may apply when a defendant has been unethically coerced into committing a crime, such as being offered a reward or profit far above the amount one would normally make from the criminal act. Had Hector enticed Arturo by offering him $100 to make the buy, there might have been an entrapment argument. But Arturo was offered nothing and received nothing for his role. Being pestered for weeks doesn't qualify as entrapment. I read the attorney's brief and it was clear he had no idea what defined entrapment; in fact, he never cited a case that defined the term.

But even worse was that he'd raised the entrapment issue under the rubric of ineffective assistance of counsel. An ineffectiveness claim must include *all* of counsel's errors – any error not raised is forever waived. A direct appeal should only raise IAC under a very narrow set of circumstances, when the ineffectiveness is blatant and obvious from the trial record. Most IAC claims will involve errors outside the trial record, making them best argued in a post-conviction petition. Gallardo's appellate attorney had blundered enormously, raising the silly entrapment issue under IAC, which precluded Gallardo from raising any other claims against trial counsel, particularly the one issue with a legitimate shot at reversal – the tainted identification procedure. Apparently this appellate attorney had never heard of *Stovall v. Denno* either, and when he read Gallardo's miniature trial record he didn't pick up on the jury's sole concern, Chomer's identification of Gallardo.

The direct appeal, no surprise, was a thudding failure. If one aggravator exists, the judge is free to enhance the sentence. The unpublished opinion also dismissed the entrapment claim in two short paragraphs, undoubtedly teaching the neophyte attorney that entrapment is an affirmative defense highly difficult to win. All the appeal really accomplished was to make it much more difficult for Gallardo to earn post-conviction relief.

All this was hard to explain to Arturo, who also had jailhouse lawyers in his ear, telling him some outlandish ideas for his PC petition. One proposed filing an allegation that all Elkhart cops are corrupt and unreliable, which, even if true, would never be met with agreement by any judge in Indiana. I convinced him his only recourse now was to allege IAC on appellate counsel for not raising the identification issue, a three-hurdle issue at this stage. Gallardo would have to prove ineffectiveness of appellate counsel for failure to include trial counsel's failure to allege a tainted identification procedure as part of the appellate IAC claim, which would have to be proven an unconstitutional procedure with a "reasonable probability" of having affected the trial's outcome. It was complicated, and would be difficult to win, but now, thanks to the public defender and to Gallardo's retained appellate counsel, it was all we had.

I urged Arturo to employ a PC attorney because he'd have no chance, I knew, were he to go to court with this by himself. Besides his handicaps – English as a second language, little education, no familiarity with the law – Elkhart County, and Judge Shewmaker's court in particular, is a venue notorious among prisoners for its bias favoring the prosecution. Prisoner legend has it that Shewmaker once publicly declared his intention to hand out one million years in sentences during his reign on the bench. Bill Woodford, one of our exceptional law clerks who had successfully argued several PC petitions, had two words for me when I pondered Arturo going into court pro se: "Utterly hopeless."

Bill's case was from Elkhart County. He had been a passenger in a stolen truck containing nine $20 rocks of crack cocaine, a whopping 3.21 grams total, and got 70 years from Shewmaker. Despite Bill's legal aptitude he could garner no PC relief for himself. He could relate dozens of cases unique to Elkhart County for its obtuse interpretation of the Indiana statutes, published cases, and court rules. "The only good thing about Shewmaker's court," Bill once told me, "is that he operates so far outside normal interpretations of the law that he's vulnerable to being overturned by the Court of Appeals – *if* you have the right lawyer."

Robert Storey's case emanated from Elkhart County, and had been overturned. "I see you have friends on the Court of Appeals," Shewmaker snidely remarked when Storey arrived for his second trial. Perturbed at the inconvenience of trying Storey a second time for manufacture of methamphetamine, his rulings didn't improve as the new trial progressed. Nearly every witness, Shewmaker agreed with the prosecutor, was an "unavailable witness," allowing the witness's prior testimony to be dispassionately read into the record by courtroom personnel. This prohibited new lines of cross-ex, and gave the second twelve jurors no way to gauge the witness's demeanor or reliability. Storey was convicted again, and Shewmaker took great pleasure in reinstating Storey's 50-year sentence.

But a year later Storey was in front of Shewmaker a third time, conviction and sentence lifted again, because the appellate court determined Shewmaker still hadn't gotten it right. A third panel of twelve heard the case, once again read into the record by staff, with even less enthusiasm. "This was the worst, most unfair trial of all," said Storey, "but Shewmaker managed to dodge all his previous prejudicial mistakes." Either that, or the appellate court was sick of looking at the case, and gave up. For the third time, Shewmaker tagged Storey for the 50-year max, and this time it stuck. Storey's PC petition, filed pro se, was met by Shewmaker with outright hostility, and went nowhere.

Another prisoner, Roger DeLucenay, had just returned from Shewmaker's court after conducting a pro se PC hearing, and described a farcical situation. Roger had been tried *in absentia*, a Medieval practice I ignorantly thought no longer occurred in America – until I came to Indiana. However, if a defendant makes bond and fails to appear for trial, an Indiana court may try the defendant anyway. The various trial rights are deemed "waived" by the defendant's voluntary absence – right to assist counsel in his defense, right to effectively cross-examine witnesses, right to testify on one's own behalf – constitutional protections designed to ensure a fair trial. Most states simply wait until the fugitive is tracked down and arrested (which usually doesn't take long), and then holds the trial. But some counties, like Elkhart, are quick to seize upon the wonderful opportunity to conduct a trial uninterrupted by the nuisance of having the defendant present and engaged in his defense.

Roger's PC hearing had been a travesty. He was kept in shackles throughout the proceeding and wasn't allowed an ink pen to take notes. His neatly arranged legal papers, hundreds of pages, were thrown into a jumble by deputies, and Shewmaker, without pity, pressed DeLucenay for the volume and page number of any case Roger mentioned. Roger had 48 years for drug and weapons possession, which sounds scary until one sees it was a minuscule amount of narcotics along with a nonfunctioning pistol found under the back seat of his car. He'd missed out on a 17-year plea bargain due to skipping bond. One could objectively conclude Roger DeLucenay had 17 years for minor dope possession and 31 years for insulting the court by jumping bond.

Roger wasn't likely to win his PC, and I didn't want Arturo Gallardo to endure the same kinds of obstacles.

Arturo said his family would hire a lawyer for him, so we filed the PC petition. I assured him the attorney would amend the petition, tweak it to his liking, conduct the evidentiary hearing, and file the appeal sure to occur whether he won or lost in county court. His wife scratched together $2500, no easy feat with five kids and one income, and found a South Bend attorney. They were impressed with this attorney, Arturo told me, "because his law office is in one of the tallest buildings in South Bend."

I was a bit skeptical. I searched LEXIS and found no hits on this attorney's name, meaning he'd never been involved in a published appeal. And, at only $2500, I feared he wouldn't put in much of an effort. Perhaps he'd never worked a case in Elkhart County and had no idea that it wasn't really a court but an extension of ultra-conservative law enforcement. Judge Shewmaker reminded me of infamous sheriff Joe Arpaio of Maricopa County, Arizona, in that both were supported by an anti-immigrant white majority in a jurisdiction "threatened" by a large Hispanic infusion. He responded by being exceedingly "tough" on crime, a superpredator in the War on the Poor. If Gallardo's attorney walked into this milieu and prevailed I'd be quite astonished.

Hispanics like Gallardo have been the fastest-growing ethnic group filling America's state and federal prisons since 2000. Hispanic prisoners numbered 206,900 in 2000 and grew to 331,500 by 2011, a 60% increase. During the same period, white prisoners increased by 7%, from 436,500 to 465,100, and the black population declined 3%, from 572,900 to 555,300. Nationwide, 41% of prisoners are black, 34% white, and 24% Hispanic, an oddity when one considers that only 12% of Americans are black and 16% Hispanic. These minorities are grossly over-represented in prison, but then, these minorities are also much more likely to live in poverty.

Law enforcement efforts in places like Elkhart, Indiana, are focused primarily on impoverished minorities, the lowest-hanging fruit on the tree. One mistake and they're at the mercy of the system, unable to marshal the legal resources to keep them from being processed through criminal justice channels. For the Hispanic community, that one mistake may be simply being alive in the United States and without documentation. I see more and more Hispanics coming into prison, with nearly all receiving enhanced sentences, despite good work histories, dependent families, and non-felony criminal records.

Since Gallardo's case was in the hands of a professional attorney, I wished him well and didn't concern myself with it. He updated me on how rapidly his PC was progressing, and besides seeing him dominate on the soccer field, I didn't interact with him for nearly a year.

Back in K-dorm I got to know Dave Fields, a mid-30s white kitchen worker from Cincinnati. He'd done time in Ohio, and subsequently got out and had the misfortune of crossing the state line into Indiana and getting involved with a trio of misfits. His buddy, Michael Green, had a plan for a grand criminal escapade, and Dave was foolish enough to go along with it.

Michael Green knew exactly where he could score some cash – from the rural Dearborn County home of retirees Larry and Judith Pohlgeers. In 2000 Green had broken in, ransacked the rooms, and made off with $850 he'd discovered in a dresser drawer. The burglary had been easy to plan and carry out because the victims were friends of the Green family, giving Michael inside knowledge of the layout of the house, the lack of security, and the Pohlgeers' schedule. Unfortunately for Michael, he'd been caught and prosecuted, receiving probation after the victims declared they didn't want to see the young man they'd trusted sent to prison. Now it was two years later and Michael Green was money hungry again. The Pohlgeers' leniency was forgotten.

Green recruited two teenage friends, Nathan Haas and Bryan Allen, along with 27-year-old David Fields. Fields had priors for robbery, receiving stolen property, and domestic violence, and impressed the other three as someone who would know how to pull off this heist. His only drawback was his incessant drinking, a habit that had cost him jobs and damaged his family life. He had two kids to support, but his criminal record thwarted his ability to find work, and his drinking eventually cost him whatever job he could land, so money was always tight. Green's assurance that the Pohlgeers' house was loaded with cash convinced Fields to buy into the burglary conspiracy.

On Friday night, August 2, 2002, the four rode past the targeted house, plotting a way inside. Cars were in the driveway, so they elected to come back on another night. For the drive-by they'd all be charged with Class A felony conspiracy to commit burglary, carrying 50 years in prison. None of them had any idea how much time they were about to face for their scheme.

They returned on Monday night, parked nearby, and all four crept to the door of the bucolic Pohlgeers house. A television flickered inside, illuminating the couple seated in the living room. Green and Fields donned ski masks and gripped metal pipes wrapped in black electrical tape, while Haas and Allen posted outside as lookouts. The door was yanked open, and the masked pair rushed upon the startled couple. Larry Pohlgeers rose from his chair and Fields cracked him over the head, splitting the skin and unleashing a torrent of blood. The old man would later testify he had permanently lost his hearing in one ear from the blow.

Meanwhile, Green likewise rapped Judith Pohlgeers on the head, a woman he'd known for years. She fell too, and her husband tried to rise to help her. "Stay down, old man," Fields growled, and Larry found himself unable to get up. Green made a beeline for the dresser drawer he'd stolen from before, jerked it open, and found it devoid of cash or valuables. The other drawers of the dresser also held nothing worth taking.

Haas and Allen, horrified by the bloody scene, implored Green and Fields to leave. Violent bravado might have sounded good as an abstract concept when all four were in the car drinking beer, but the bloody reality had them ready to bail out and run. Green told Fields, "Let's go," and they bolted away. They'd been inside less than sixty seconds and gotten nothing, leaving the elderly victims to call 9-1-1 after the assailants were long gone.

That only one dresser was ransacked is what detectives call a clue. Same dresser in which Michael Green had found cash two years before – what a coincidence. They went looking for Green, and soon learned he'd been associating with teens Haas and Allen. The youngsters were located, and both heard authoritative voices read them the Miranda warning. Unsurprisingly, both spilled the story, like fish with their guts sliced open.

When detectives apprehended Michael Green, he, too, had plenty to say. The mastermind, the truly violent criminal the detectives should want, said the trio, was David Fields.

Dave was back in Cincinnati, mind swirling, with a firm intuitive sense that his world was about to crash. A couple phone calls confirmed his hunch, and he knew he was a wanted man. Ten beers into a cold 12-pack he decided to make it easy on himself and surrender. He crossed the state line, gave up, and "did the right thing" – confessed everything.

Confessions tend to make a defense attorney's job a tad difficult. It's hard to win a case at trial, of course, when the defendant's own recorded words will convict him. And it's hard to negotiate a favorable plea bargain when the attorney's one bargaining chip – the threat to go to trial – will be met with, "Go ahead, make my day." It's like playing poker with bad cards, all face up. You can't bluff, and you can't win.

And here there were four confessions, to a violent, bloody crime inflicted upon an innocent, elderly couple, in a small county unaccustomed to such acts. Dearborn County, occupying the southeastern tip of Indiana, demographically resembles affluent Hamilton County: nearly all-white, above average incomes, low crime rate, both voting for the conservative Republican Mitt Romney and against Barack Obama in the 2012 election (Dearborn – 70.2%; Hamilton – 67.4%). But while Hamilton County, on the north edge of Indianapolis, has six times the population of Dearborn County, Dearborn has placed more prisoners into the Indiana DOC. Indy residents generally consider Hamilton County somewhat "tough on crime." If Hamilton is considered tough, Dearborn ought to be considered "insane on crime." Just how insane, Green and Fields were about to find out.

On the face of it, the obvious charge would be a Class A felony, burglary with serious bodily injury. Twenty to fifty years. End of story. But on a case like this, sensationally reported in the small town media, any prosecutor can think up more charges. Throw the book at the defendants. Also filed were: Class A attempted robbery, Class A conspiracy to commit burglary (for planning the robbery), Class B aggravated battery (for hitting Larry Pohlgeers ,with permanent injury), and Class C battery with a weapon (for hitting Judith Pohlgeers, without permanent injury). Fields' public defender told Dave he was facing a maximum of 228 years, 50 + 50 + 50 + 50 + 20 + 8, if the sentences were all consecutive.

Fields' lawyer tried to negotiate a plea, but had to settle for a prosecutorial diktat. The state would drop the B and C felonies, agree that conspiracy to robbery and the robbery itself could be merged, and leave Fields to the mercy of the court on a sentencing range of 20 to 150 years. It was the best deal

Dave was going to see, stressed the attorney, and if it was rejected, he could expect a nightmarish trial and the full 228 years.

While 150 was possible, the attorney could argue that Fields' surrender, confession, and remorse were mitigating factors. A trial was not a serious option, so Dave signed the plea agreement. Green's deal was nearly identical. The two lookouts, Haas and Allen, had private counsel and obtained better deals. Haas initially received 20 years in prison, reduced to 12 by the appellate court. Allen got slightly less.

At Pendleton ten years later I asked Dave to describe his sentencing hearing.

"Man, it was awful," Dave recalled, closing his eyes and shaking his head at the thought of that day. "It was like a trial with no objections, no defense, everything getting worse and worse, and at the end I had to get up on the witness stand." The prosecutor had begun by having the detectives testify, describing the crime, the confessions, and the roles played by all four defendants. Then the Pohlgeers couple and their grown children testified, covering the same ground, each one more livid than the last, and each one concluding with a demand for the maximum sentence. Dave's allocution followed.

"I was ashamed of what I'd done," explained Dave, "and all I knew to do was keep my head down and apologize." He'd used submissive body language to express remorse, in addition to his words, which rang hollow to some. Without question Dave was embarrassed by his crime – his embarrassment was evident a decade later, in a setting where I commonly heard prisoners tick off their offenses totally devoid of remorse.

"I couldn't defend what I did," said Dave. "I didn't even try."

In passing sentence the judge found multiple aggravating factors, including a "complete lack of remorse," siding fully with the state and burying Dave with maximum, 150 years. Then, without explanation, the judge suspended 29 years. (Why suspend any of it? Why the oddball 29 years?) That left Dave with 121 years, do 60 years and 6 months, putting Dave out the prison door at age 88.

Michael Green got slammed too, and both appealed their sentences. The appellate court injected a bit of sanity (not much), declaring the Class A conspiracy to burglary an overcharged offense. Since the plan on the August 2nd drive-by was to commit a nonviolent burglary, not a Class A burglary with injury, the conspiracy should've been a Class B felony. A sentencing statute, I.C. 35-50-1-2, limits consecutive sentences when the nonviolent offenses are part of "one episode of criminal conduct," and since the conspiracy was a nonviolent offense, the Class B combined with the Class A could only total 55 years – but still consecutive to the other, violent Class A felony – meaning the max was 105 years, not 150. Both Green and Fields won new sentencing hearings.

The second round of sentencing went pretty much like the first, except this time the Pohlgeers' demeanor was decidedly lenient toward Green and even more vitriolic toward Fields. Green, they decided, was not as culpable. He lucked out – only 74 years on resentencing, putting him out at age 60. Fields got the max, 105 years. Freedom at age 80. Both appealed again, to no avail. In Fields' second direct appeal I noted Justice Crone's offhand comment that Fields had "received a significant benefit from the plea" by having the class B and C felonies dropped. Other than that benefit, he'd gotten nothing in return for his cooperation.

Fields' second direct appeal became final in 2006, six years before I reviewed his case. In those six years he had shipped his legal work through a gaggle of jailhouse lawyers, all of them flummoxed as to what he could do next. (The last one to have the file, bipolar Big Stan, 6-foot-5 and 290 pounds, received a note from me: "Please send me Dave Fields' legal work immediately." Stan brought it to me in the law library, hot: "Listen, you fucking asshole, if you ever tell me to do something *immediately* again, I'll stab you to fucking death.")

With no trial, the usual long list of potential trial errors was inapplicable. His sentencing issues seemed exhausted by two rounds of appeals. The only thing left was the guilty plea, trying to get it declared constitutionally invalid through a post-conviction petition.

There are two common ways to contest a guilty plea. One is to argue that the defendant's *Boykin* rights were not adequately explained or properly waived (right to a jury trial, to counsel, to cross-examine witnesses, to testify or choose not to testify); the other is to argue that the plea was not "knowing, voluntary, and intelligent" (KVI). Fields' *Boykin* rights had been covered. Had Fields not known all reasonably possible defenses, or been unduly coerced, been incompetent to stand trial, or been unaware of the factual elements of the offenses, he could argue his was a non-KVI plea. But none of that was in the record.

I also considered the "illusory plea" argument, a type of non-KVI plea where the defendant receives the maximum sentence on a guilty plea while obtaining no benefit whatsoever for his plea. But as Justice Crone commented, Fields received the substantial benefit of having two felonies dropped. So I handed back Dave's file, telling him I saw no issues worth pursuing on a PC. Same story he'd heard for six years.

Like any insoluble problem, Dave's case simmered in the back of my mind, fueled by a nagging feeling, one I often get about prisoners' cases, that something about it wasn't quite right. Surrendered. Confessed. Pled guilty. No trial. Clear expression of remorse. Maximum sentence, 105 years. Murder tops out at 65 years, excluding LWOP and the death penalty. Horrible crime, no question. But nobody died. And I've seen much, much worse get much less time.

Three months later, while mindlessly circling the rec yard track, it hit me: Justice Crone was wrong. There was no "substantial benefit" for the guilty plea because the two dropped felonies could not have resulted in more time.

With or without the B and C felonies, Dave's maximum sentence was 105 years. Count 5, the Class B aggravated battery on Larry Pohlgeers, would have been merged under double jeopardy into the Class A attempted robbery of Larry because the Class A felony requires the element of physical injury. A dozen published cases on this point, I would discover through LEXIS, were unanimous and unambiguous – convictions on both counts 1 and 5 would constitute double jeopardy. And then count 6, Class C battery on Judith Pohlgeers, which is not listed under I.C. 35-50-1-2 as a "crime of violence," would have been part of the "single episode of criminal conduct" and had no potential to raise the total sentence above 105 years, just as the Class B conspiracy had been capped after the first appeal. That all of the offenses were one episode had already been established by the court. The perceived "benefit" – dropping two felonies – had no real value, which is the very definition of an illusory plea. Another dozen cases supported my argument. Fields' plea was improperly coerced when the state (and his own attorney) threatened him with a punishment that was not legally permissible. The guilty plea and 105-

year sentence would have to be vacated. I reported this news to Dave, and suddenly he had the best – and worst – thing to have in prison: hope.

"You need an attorney," was my first advisement to Dave, as it is to every prisoner I assist. A professional lawyer always stands a better chance than does a pro se prisoner, and Dave agreed, but he had no resources with which to hire counsel. He had been locked up for ten years, worked in the kitchen for a dollar a day, and was barely able to afford hygiene items. Postage for legal mail severely taxed his budget. Because of his job, he didn't qualify as "indigent" to get free postage or free copies.

We wrote to the public defender who had handled his two appeals, asking for representation on the PC, but their office had done enough for David Fields and had no interest. I was confident, though, that the issue was simple enough that even I could work this case through the county court, where it would be denied, and through the Indiana Court of Appeals, where it would stand a good chance of winning.

His case was fast-tracked in Dearborn County, and in the year it took for Fields' PC to run through its stages we contemplated Dave's future strategy should the PC be granted relief. He would revert to post-arraignment, sentence gone, guilty plea gone, and neither could be mentioned in front of a jury. He could demand a trial, and even with four confessions and three codefendants the state might be challenged to round up the witnesses after so much time had passed. He'd have some slight leverage, enough to negotiate a better deal. Less than 105 was guaranteed, and we theorized ways to argue for lesser culpability than Green, who had chosen the victims, violated their trust twice, and gotten 74 years. A flat 50 or 55 seemed possible (still excessive, in my opinion, when compared to non-Dearborn County cases), which would have Dave about halfway done, his outdate a decade away but at least within sight.

We lost at the county level, as expected. The judge tossed Dave's PC like he was hurling a bag of kittens into the Ohio River. County court judges rarely admit mistakes were made in their jurisdiction, and if you don't like it, appeal it. We did, and I spent several weeks polishing Dave's brief. The Indiana Attorney General submitted a rather dispirited brief, and my hopes for Dave soared. To get a prisoner's century-plus sentence vacated would be a big deal, and I wanted to win both for Dave and for my own ego. Pro se victories of any magnitude are rare, and as we awaited the decision I told Dave, "The only flaw in your brief is that it doesn't have an attorney's name on the cover."

I was familiar with two attorneys who had clerked for appellate court justices, and I discussed the subject of pro se filings with them. Independently, they confirmed that nearly all prisoner filings were atrocious, full of misapplied case cites, poorly written, and a waste of the court's time. The pro se briefs were so bad that the clerks were directed to separate the pro se filings from the professional briefs, whereupon the judge would turn to the "Issues" page of each brief, maybe skim through the "Summary of Argument" section, and tell the clerk, "Write a denial." It was considered a good way for novice legal minds, fresh out of law school, to grasp the art of writing legal opinions. If a truly worthy pro se brief happened to be buried in the sad pile of scatter-brained briefs, the judge was unlikely to be aware of its existence. And once it had received the judge's cursory glance and been consigned to the denial pile, no young clerk ever possessed the temerity to resurrect it.

I knew this, and I always spent extra time carefully perfecting the page the appellate court judge would see – the "Issues" page. A concise, perfectly-worded issue, I hoped, would grab their attention and set it apart from the mass of bad briefs.

When the appellate decision came back I couldn't discern whether a clerk had written *Fields v. State*, or if a judge had taken the time to author it. The response was clever, out on a limb no clerk, I pondered, would venture upon. The opinion was labeled "unpublished", so as not to set a precedent (their excuse) and not to invite public scrutiny (my opinion). It was a denial, but it never stated that Dave's illusory plea argument was wrong. Instead, the judge wrote there was no way to determine whether counts 1 and 5 were double jeopardy "because no trial had taken place." The facts could not be ascertained without a trial, they said. The court saw no way to figure out if the aggravated battery on Larry Pohlgeers was the same conduct used to raise the attempted robbery of Larry Pohlgeers to a class A felony with serious bodily injury. So, lacking the info a trial would expose, the court could not tell whether it was an illusory plea.

Really?? I thought. Not enough information? That's their excuse?

Never in the history of illusory pleas has a court required trial evidence for the appellant to win his argument, namely because an illusory plea can only come from a guilty plea, and never from a trial. The opinion was finely-crafted nonsense. Besides, there was plenty of testimonial evidence, far more than necessary, from both sentencing hearings to establish the facts of the case. Every detective and every witness had testified. I had included their testimony in the Appellant's Appendix (a bound, separate filing the judges, I knew, wouldn't even pick up), and cited this record in Fields' brief. It was all there, no question as to who did what, no factual controversy. Basically, the opinion was telling us, Yes, you're 100% right, but we just don't want to give David Fields any more sentencing relief.

I put it directly to Dave: "If you had had an attorney, you would have won this appeal."

We petitioned for rehearing, accentuating the testimonial record from the sentencing hearings, records overlooked by the court. Rehearing denial was swift, without written explanation, as is done on all rehearing denials. We petitioned the Indiana Supreme Court to accept transfer; this was also denied without commentary. I would have petitioned in U.S. District Court for a writ of habeas corpus, but Dave had long been time-barred by the 1996 Anti-terrorism and Effective Death Penalty Act (AEDPA), which limited the time to petition to one year. Dave's one-year clock had started in 2006, when his last direct appeal became final, and expired in 2007, when no PC petition had been filed in state court.

We tried a successive PC petition, asking the appellate court for permission to raise the illusory plea petition anew and hold an evidentiary hearing in the county court, again, to have all of the witnesses who had testified to testify again, to prove the facts of the case so that the court would be able to make a double-jeopardy ruling. I felt like writing, "Or, you could read the goddamn Appellant's Appendix you previously ignored, you hard-headed ignorant motherfuckers," but it never pays to get mouthy with a judge.

The successive PC request was also denied, also without explanation. And with that, David Fields was dead in the water, hope gone, 38 years old with 42 years left to do in prison. I'd had high hopes for this case, and my confidence had rubbed off on Dave. We both came crashing down.

It was like watching a man reach for a life preserver at the side of the boat, only to have a great white shark snag his ankle and drag him under.

Dave knew as well as I did the crimes committed by some of our neighbors and the sentences they had received – such comparisons are made by every individual who walks into prison. On the day Dave's case became final, Pendleton had 165 men with release dates beyond Dave's 2-9-2057 outdate. Of these 165, 29 had LWOP and 26 had life. All but two of the lifers were in for murder. Nearly all of the other 110 were sentenced for murder in combination with other felonies, such as robbery, rape, or burglary. A few were serial rapists or child molesters, and one, Artez 'Mississippi' Gray, had a string of carjacking convictions arising from one lengthy attempt to elude police in Marion County. Gray's outdate was in 2116. There were over 350 murderers at Pendleton with shorter sentences than Dave's 105 years. Some had murder running consecutive to other violent crimes and still fared better than David Fields.

In comparison to Fields' case, William Moore's incarceration was a prime example of the importance of county jurisdiction coupled with the advantage of private counsel. Moore, a mid-40's computer specialist and Navy veteran, had found another man in bed with his Guamanian wife in their Hamilton County home. He shot both, killing one, and faced murder and attempted murder charges. Multiple victims of violent offenses always supports consecutive sentences (guaranteed when a defendant exercises his right to a trial), and the prosecutor could have asked for sentences above the advisory terms (55 and 30 years) due to Moore's criminal history (a prior for cocaine possession, and a few other minor scrapes with the law, all non-violent). In most counties, with a public defender assigned, the defendant would have anticipated getting 85 to 95 years out of the 65 to 115 range. Bill lucked out – "only" 50 years. The two violent offenses were run concurrently, with the consent of the Hamilton County Prosecutor and the approval of the judge.

Within 20 feet of Dave's bunk in K-1 dorm were two other prisoners whose cases made us question the proportionality of Dave's sentence. Dog Bite (one of several dog-themed nicknames at Pendleton – Dog Biskit, Dog Booty, Dog Breath, Big Dog, Raw Dog) had 50 years for attempted murder out of Marion County, with one of the most bizarre trial records I had ever read. Dog Bite had been, in his words, "trolling for queers" and enticed a gay man to take him home. After some sexual activity the man had fallen asleep.

Dog Bite procured a knife and cut the man's throat. The victim awoke, resisted, and fled into the bathroom, slamming shut the wooden door. Dog Bite tried to break down the door while the victim pleaded for 9-1-1 to be called before he bled out. Dog Bite persisted kicking the door, and the man jumped out the second-story window and ran. Murder thwarted, Dog Bite snatched up the guy's wallet and keys, stole the man's truck, and within an hour was leading police on a high-speed chase that ended in a crash. He elected to go to trial, lost (of course), and got the maximum sentence. Fortunately for him, the prosecutor had not pressed for consecutive sentences on the multiple charges. Had Dog Bite been prosecuted in Elkhart or Dearborn County, he surely would have been stretched out on a string of felonies, and boxcarred to a date exceeding his life expectancy, a de facto LWOP sentence.

Another prisoner, D-Bizzle, had thrown his son, a toddler, into the wall so hard his heart ruptured. Like a discus thrower, he had held the boy by an arm and leg and spun to create a deadly level of centrifugal force. The Marion County Coroner described the injury as equivalent to a fall from a seven-story building. A plea agreement negotiated by private counsel secured a 40-year term for voluntary manslaughter.

Throwing one's self on the mercy of the court with an "open plea" or "blind plea" seldom turns out well. I had tendered such a plea at age 18 in Tazewell County, Illinois, in 1980, on a case where I had stolen change and cassette tapes from five unlocked park cars in the ultra-conservative (and notoriously racist) town of Pekin. The five victims were asked, in writing, to suggest a punishment. One responded, "six months in jail," and the other four had no reply. My ding-dong attorney, who specialized in civil suits and almost never handled criminal matters, suggested we plead guilty and let Judge Ivan Yontz choose a fair sentence. Yontz cared very little about interrupting my college career, and sent me off to prison for a five-year stretch. A few months later he gave a kid named Adolf (last name escapes my memory) six years for beating a man to death with a pool cue. Perhaps the difference was that Adolf's homicide occurred in a bar on the edge of town, while my thefts took place in Yontz's neighborhood, 400 yards from his doorstep.

The true value of an attorney is not his or her ability to win at trial, as some may presume. Sure, we're all impressed when an obviously guilty, high-profile defendant gets off as a result of a clever lawyer muddying the evidence

– the O. J. Simpson trial comes to mind. But few defendants are wealthy, and even fewer go to trial and win. Private counsel's value is in the pretrial stage, dreaming up potential defenses, and generally giving the state's attorney a hard time with multiple filings and motions purposed to bury the other side in paperwork, all to soften up the prosecutor into surrendering a sweet plea agreement.

Public defenders, overloaded with clients, do not have enough time in the day to apply the same pretrial strategy, and the plea offers they negotiate aren't as favorable, in most cases. Money matters. It creates leverage against the state, gains access to the prosecutor, and lessens the eventual penalty. Money, the one thing most defendants don't have, is a critical factor for anyone seeking justice in America, because justice very rarely comes from the simple mercy of the court.

One who created ambivalent feelings in me about the topic of mercy was the case of Michael William Daniels, my former death row client residing in G-cellhouse.

Michael Daniels had been convicted of murder, and on September 14, 1979, Daniels' sentencing order directed that he be executed "in a manner prescribed by law, before sunrise on March 28, 1980." Within an hour of being sentenced he was triple-shackled and in a van on his way to X-Row at Michigan City. He was 21 years old. He had 196 days left to live.

Thirty-three years later I asked him what he thought when that sentence was read in court.

"I didn't get why they had to say *before sunrise*," he said. "What if the sun didn't rise that day? What if it was cloudy all day? How do they know *when* the sun rises? *Before sunrise*? Why even say that? But what I was really stressin' on, yafeelme, was they violated my fundamental due process rights; it was a fundamental – *fundamental*, yadig? – *fundamental* miscarriage of justice, and I shoulda been outahere four years ago, yafeelme? Four years ago. Out. Before sunrise, four years ago…" And off he went on another one of his rants.

Like every conversation we had in G-cellhouse, Daniels didn't stand at his cell door to talk. He remained in bed, facing the wall, a sheet held tightly around his head, face exposed to the yellow wall, his loquaciousness dependent upon how recently he'd taken his psych meds. His sheets, and especially his pillow case, were rust-colored from contact with his skin, like a slip cover on the seat of a 1930s John Deere tractor.

His legal writings were as scatterbrained as his rants. His handwritten brief, where he appealed the county court's denial of his Motion to Correct Erroneous Sentence, was tough to understand – he had a problem with the governor changing his sentence, and I recognized the overuse of every prisoner's favorite phrase: "fundamental miscarriage of justice", as if those magic words will open the prison gates. He used five case cites, every one an incomplete citation. For example, he wrote, "LANE 727 N.E. (2000)" when referring to *Lane v. State,* 727 N.E.2d 454 (Ind. App. 2000). I cleaned those up, organized the brief into the sections required by the court rules, typed it, made copies, applied color binders, and provided pre-addressed envelopes. All he had to do was sign it and mail it.

Two weeks after his brief was mailed he received a Notice of Defect, and I had to prepare the same legal work again. He had scribbled a new argument onto all ten briefs, something incomprehensible, and added notes in the margins. Somehow it was my fault. "You didn't tell me I couldn't do that," he said. The second filing was accepted, and in two months Daniels had a terse denial. While the court professed to "liberally construe" his issues, it took only a few sentences to categorize his argument and reject it.

His case history would have driven almost any person to madness.

Throughout the years since his arrest on January 27, 1978, Daniels' hopes had been raised, then dashed, over and over, as he alternately won release dates, lost them, and endured new execution dates. His future was constantly being reshaped by forces outside of his control, his hopes influenced by professionals who couldn't forecast the future any better than he.

His hopes first rose on November 8, 1978, when the Marion County Prosecutor agreed to allow Daniels to plead guilty in exchange for a 60-year sentence. That plea bargain would have released Daniels in 30 years, in 2008, at age 49. Even the widow of the murder victim agreed to the terms. But five weeks later the judge refused to accept the deal, forcing the parties to go to trial.

At trial, witnesses recounted Daniels' role as the gunman in a mid-blizzard robbery spree. Over a foot of snow fell on Indianapolis on the night of January

16, 1978, and as residents shoveled their driveways, Daniels, Kevin Edmonds and Donald Cox cruised the neighborhoods, looking for victims. Daniels would later be described in court as a "slow learner" and "easily led," factors Cox surely recognized when he put the pistol in Daniels' hand, drove the car, and selected the victims.

At 8:00 p.m. Daniels and Edmonds forced Steve McCloskey to hand over his wallet; McCloskey's mother attacked Daniels with a broom and got punched in the face in return. At 9:30 15-year-old Timothy Streett gave up his wallet, and when Timothy's father, Allen, had no wallet, Daniels shot him. Allen Streett died.

Undeterred by Streett's death, forty minutes later they relieved Jack Beem of his wallet and Mary Ann Beem of her purse. At about 11:00 they happened upon Dr. Robert Barnett, who refused to be robbed. Daniels shot him three times. Dr. Barnett survived and was a particularly convincing witness.

Sentencing Judge Patricia Gifford made note of Daniels' "horrible, chaotic, abusive, violent life," but went on to say that this only explained Daniels' behavior – it didn't excuse it. Daniels got 20 years on each of four counts of robbery, 50 years for shooting Dr. Barnett, and the death penalty for killing Allen Streett. All of it was consecutive – death plus 130 years.

As is done in death penalty cases, a legion of court-appointed lawyers stayed the execution and commenced the appellate and post-conviction process. The direct appeal raised Daniels' hopes – five potential jurors had been excluded because it was questionable whether they could apply the death penalty. (A defendant is entitled to a jury of his peers, but in a capital case only those peers predisposed to support execution may sit in judgment. By contrast, in a non-capital case, the parties are forbidden from telling the jury the range of potential penalties. Jurors might think twice about convicting on weak evidence if they knew the penalty would be extreme.)

The appeal failed in 1983 and Daniels' spirits sagged again. A post-conviction petition was filed in 1984, raising issues of ineffective assistance of counsel, but the county court rejected the claims, and an appeal failed in 1988. But the U.S. Supreme Court tossed out the denial in 1989 and remanded it back to the county court. Such a rare occurrence raised Daniels' hopes again, but those hopes came crashing back down when the county found a new reason for denial and another appeal lost in 1990.

It was around then that Daniels' mind snapped.

There was a long period of mental corrosion culminating with Daniels sitting on the floor against the wall, wrapped in a blanket, incoherent and unresponsive. "Mikey was always kind of a goofy, silly kid," said Stuart 'Jack' Kennedy, a former death row prisoner who witnessed the meltdown. "Not too bright, easily influenced. But one day he just withdrew, and he never really came back."

Perry 'Steve' Miller arrived on X-Row in 1991, and by then Daniels was fully "gone." Managed by meds. No counseling, no programs. It was a chore to even get Daniels to bathe. Observed Miller, "The State didn't care, because they were going to execute him anyway. Why waste resources on a dead man?"

In 1993 another post-conviction petition argued that the judge abused his discretion when he rejected the plea bargain in 1978. In 1994 Marion County Judge James Detamore agreed, imposing the 60-year sentence. Daniels finally had a release date, and he was moved to B-Cellblock in Michigan City's general population.

But not for long. The State wasn't done with Daniels.

Having invested in 16 years of litigation, the State was no longer agreeable to Daniels having the plea bargain that was originally offered. The Attorney General appealed, the new sentence was stayed, and Daniels was returned to death row. In 1997 the State won the appeal, and the death penalty was back in place, more firmly than ever.

Daniels lost another petition in 1998, appealed, and lost the appeal on a narrow 3-2 decision. His attorneys filed a petition for writ of habeas corpus in federal court. All this time, execution dates came and went.

While the habeas petition was pending Daniels got, in his opinion, some very bad news. On January 7, 2005, outgoing Democratic Governor Joseph Kernan commuted Daniels' death sentence to LWOP. Daniels didn't want LWOP, he wanted the 60-year sentence. In one of my last conversations with Daniels, I asked him why he was arguing that the governor lacked authority to commute his sentence.

"He just can't make up a sentence to screw my case up," he said. "He didn't *give me* nuthin.' He just made it so nobody would help me no more, and so I could die in prison. They still killin' me either way, *don't you see that*? LWOP is a death sentence. A hunnid and thutty years is a death sentence. Any time you can't live to see the end of it, it's a death sentence."

Given all the defects in his mental processes, his was a surprisingly rational observation.

By that measure, the state is killing thousands of people, not just the ones on death row. Anyone with a life sentence, or with a release date too far away to reach, can be said to be sentenced to death as well. That death won't come by lethal injection, electrocution or firing squad – it'll come by age, isolation, inactivity, and medical neglect.

These quasi-death-row prisoners won't get attorneys to argue their cases like real death row prisoners get. When Daniels' death sentence was commuted, his federal statutory right to free court-appointed attorneys dried up, and he was left to fight his case on his own, like so many thousands of other prisoners.

Following the commutation, Daniels left death row for good in 2005 and was transferred to Pendleton's population, where I first encountered him in 2006. He stole my bath towel one day, and I had to track him down, wet, and demand it back. He played it off like he took it by accident. Mine was large and yellow, his was small and white; yeah, I can see the mistake. The next time I had to deal with him was in 2011 when he was on administrative segregation in G-cellhouse. He was in seg simply because he was too dysfunctional to get along in general population.

I do wonder what his story would have been had the judge accepted the plea in 1978. He'd have gone off to prison, completed programs and gotten some education. He'd have been released in 2008, maybe as soon as 2004. He probably wouldn't be the mentally ill – no, that's not the word for it – *mentally devastated* person now burdening the state. Thousands of attorney man-hours would never have been spent on him, and fifteen courts wouldn't have had to make additional rulings on his case.

Perhaps he should have been treated better by the prison system, and by the courts, and should have been out years ago; but I also remembered the night of January 16, 1978, the night Daniels shot and killed Alan Streett in the presence of his 15-year-old son, Timothy. On that night I was also 15, and I was also shoveling snow with my dad, in the driveway of our home in Peoria, Illinois. Would thirty years in prison have satisfied me, had it been my own father who had been killed? Or would I have been more content to see Daniels executed by the state? Or would I have enjoyed watching Daniels suffer for a lifetime, his hopes bounced around like a rubber ball for three decades, until he lost his mind?

I shared these questions with Mel, while adding, "If it was my dad he had killed, I could see killing him myself, just plain ol' retaliation. Leave the state out of it, let me have him."

Mel took a long moment to gather his thoughts, and his reply somewhat surprised me. "Your questions are fundamentally the wrong questions to ask," Mel insisted, rather forcefully. "We don't live in bands, tribes or chiefdoms, as we did thousands of years ago. We live in an advanced social unit – a state. Remember the four social structures we learned in Anthropology? We live in a state, so we have surrendered questions of justice to the state."

Not only did anthropologists and philosophers agree with Mel, but Blackstone in 1818 recognized the concept in his *Commentaries on the laws of England*: Law is a contractual obligation that citizens make to each other "in exchange for which every individual has resigned a part of his natural liberty."

"When Daniels killed Timothy's father," Mel continued, "the case was not called, *Streett v. Daniels*; it was titled, *State v. Daniels*. The state is always the plaintiff in a criminal case, not the victim or the victim's family. The aggrieved party, formally, is the state – not the victim. The crime is a crime against the state, against the state statutes, not a crime against any individual personally. One of the main reasons why we have a criminal justice system is to take those decisions about justice, punishment, and restoration, which formerly led to retaliation, overpunishment, and endless feuding, and put those questions into the hands of unbiased people who can be objective and do what's best for everybody."

"So what I would want to happen to Daniels – my desires shouldn't matter?"

"You should be heard," Mel conceded. "But no, the penalty you desire should not matter because you are too close to the situation. You would be biased. The penalty you would choose would probably not be what is in everyone's best interest."

It is a common question one poses to one's self whenever a crime occurs: "If that crime had happened to me, what penalty would I desire?" In every case, one places one's self as the hypothetical victim, and calculates from there. Under that paradigm, Mel argues, the answer obtained will always be wrong, always be emotionally charged, and biased. The way to attack the criminal justice problem was to *never* place one's self as the victim, but to *always* place one's self in the role of society at large.

"There's more than just retribution and punishment for the state to consider," Mel argued. "There's also costs. And not just what costs come with dollar signs attached."

"Yeah," I countered, "but the way an American state operates is to focus on the monetary costs, and let all the collateral damage go unaccounted for. The primary concern in a thoroughly red state like Indiana is the bottom line. Fiscal conservatives run this state."

"True enough. So we'll forget the collateral costs for a minute. On a capital case like Daniels', let's just look at the monetary costs, and see if it makes any sense."

Per state-conducted studies, $1,000,000 is the typical cost for death penalty litigation. Between the attorney general's office, county prosecutors, and public defenders, 32 attorneys had squabbled for three decades over Michael Daniels, producing nothing more than a mountain of paperwork. The initial trial alone cost roughly $450,000, as compared to the $42,000 cost for the average non-capital trial. In all, about $1.5 million was diverted from taxpayers to lawyers for the mere pleasure of trying to execute this man, which ultimately failed.

Then there were the costs of housing Daniels on X-Row, which, due to its increased security, costs much more than the $25,000 per year for the average prisoner. Indiana hasn't parsed out a statistic on X-Row's cost per prisoner, but in California it's $90,000 per prisoner per year. Indiana does everything cheaper, so let's call it $65,000 per year for an X-Row prisoner. The total additional monetary costs for Daniels' odyssey now approach $2.5 million. Nice investment. And the result? He eats, he sleeps, he argues, he rants, he prays; he stares at his TV, he stares at the wall; he writes, he dreams; and the next day, he does it all over again.

"I can think of better things to do with two and a half million dollars," said Mel, and I agreed. Lost opportunity costs, as economists would call it. That money could have built a community swimming pool, a library, or a computer learning center for disadvantaged youth. Instead, it trickled into paying the mortgages on the homes of lawyers surrounding Indianapolis.

Nationwide, prosecutors have learned from cases like Daniels' and have discovered it is much less work, much less expensive, and subject to much less criticism to forego seeking the death penalty, which is why capital punishment has been on the decline in America. Executions rose from zero in 1976, to a peak of 99 in 1999, then steadily declined. In 2011, only 43 prisoners were executed, leaving 3,082 on the nation's 37 death row units, this tiny population burning up seven billion dollars of taxpayers' money.

For those opposed to the death penalty, fewer executions suggest a strong appearance of progress; but the anti-death crowd has no idea of the magnitude of their failure. The appearance of progress on the death penalty hides the fact that the state is sentencing more and more prisoners to die in prison from old age. In the United States, 110,000 have life sentences, with over half of them unlikely to see parole. Another 49,000 have LWOP, and a conservatively estimated 47,000 have outdates past their 70th birthday. Of the 1.56 million inhabiting state and federal prisons, roughly one in ten will die there. Were all those destined to die in prison lined up and shot, the world would be aghast. But when they die one by one, over decades, nobody notices the methodical pace of the state's life-ending machine.

A special irony is that the decline of the death penalty began just a few years after Congress passed legislation designed to increase its use. The Anti-terrorism and Effective Death Penalty Act (AEDPA), enacted April 24, 1996, promised to speed up capital litigation by requiring a prisoner to file for federal habeas corpus in district court within one year of finality of state court proceedings. No more waiting for years for justice – the executions would come fast and furious, the bill's backers promised.

However, as Daniels' case has shown, the AEDPA has had no effect on state capital cases because attorneys have still been able to maintain state court proceedings for many years. The real effect of the AEDPA has been to keep non-capital state prisoners out of federal court with habeas corpus petitions – very few know about the one-year limit, how to calculate it, or how to preserve federal issues while doing state post-conviction work. In other words, the AEDPA's effectiveness has been felt almost exclusively by state prisoners with the "informal" death penalty, estimated at 150,000, and growing.

As for the "Antiterrorism" portion of the AEDPA, the reader may judge from historical events whether the AEDPA did anything to prevent terrorism since 1996.

Daniels' sentence has been converted to the informal death penalty, and he joins the mob of 150,000 entitled to one direct appeal, and thereafter deprived of free legal assistance. For most, no professional will ever do a thorough review for a wrongful conviction issue, not unless a family fortune is available to fritter away on private counsel. Very few have that luxury, so they end up in the prison law library: "I need help. They got me dying in prison over minor drug possession." And there's not much we can do for them.

Melvin Tunstill was dismissive when I talked to him about Michael Daniels' case. "He's just another sociopath," Mel said. "He developed into a sociopath as a coping mechanism. Being a sociopath is an easy way to avoid guilt, to detach yourself from emotions that are uncomfortable. It's a learned behavior, formed as a way to deal with a world that throws too much negativity toward you."

Mel slept fitfully that night, waking us up several times with prolonged coughing attacks. The body-convulsing hacking reminded me of Bud Sosbe, who had disrupted our sleep in K-4 dorm for many nights, until he was finally sent to an outside hospital, where he died four days later. "Pneumonia" was the rumored cause of death for Sosbe, a rumor started by whom, we did not know.

Mel's shortness of breath was becoming noticeable, and it led to him saying less, searching for an economy of words. I asked him what was wrong, and had he been to medical to have it checked out.

"Aaaah," he waved dismissively. "It's not in their interest to find anything wrong with me."

If he had a serious illness, it was either undiagnosed, or something he did not care to discuss. I just wondered if he would be one of the 150,000 to die in prison, or would some miracle, of unforeseeable form and origin, get him released?

A few days later Edgar Lee approached my desk with a short, stocky, middle-aged white guy in tow. "I need you to help my guy Smitty here," he said with a grin I couldn't decipher as a joke or as genuine. "He says *Miller v. Alabama* is supposed to put him out the door."

We had discussed *Miller*, and the confusion it was certain to bring, soon after it was reported in the media. Larry Fowler downloaded the opinion from the Supreme Court's website, so our clerks were ready to field the questions that were sure to come.

In typical media fashion, the reports stated that the "Supreme Court banned sentences of life without parole for juveniles." This line spread like contagion, each host loving the virus, amplifying it, and passing it on to willing and eager recipients. Misinformation is like a plague, whose symptoms are delusion and euphoria.

By reading the *Miller* opinion (a task reporters must find nauseating), one could learn that, post-*Miller*, juveniles could still receive LWOP sentences. What *Miller* stresses is that no state may employ a statutory sentencing scheme requiring LWOP for a crime committed by a juvenile. The judge's hands cannot be tied – he or she must have the option of sentencing the juvenile to a term of years, or to life with the possibility of parole. After weighing the juvenile's potential for rehabilitation, and after considering the imposition of a fixed term, the judge may still hand down an LWOP sentence without violating the Eighth Amendment.

When you are a lowly, ignorant, prison law clerk, and your interpretation of a case differs so far from what everyone else is saying, so far from what everyone wants to hear, you're passed off as some kind of idiot – at least for awhile. The first kid to come in with LWOP heard my take on *Miller*, argued, and finally stormed out, saying, "Y'all motherfucking law clerks is stupid as hell." Indiana had not had a statute requiring an LWOP sentence since 1978, so I knew the only men who could possibly benefit under *Miller* had to have been locked up for at least 34 consecutive years.

Another kid came in, more insistent than the last. "I got this article right here, black and white, point blank and simple, says plain as day: Juveniles!

Under 18! Can't get! Life without parole! Supreme fucking Court! And you tryin' to tell me you know better than the national newspaper, that you right and they wrong. Damn, man! You po-da-be tryin' to help a motherfucker get out! But you tryin' to play me for a stupid, like I can't fucking read!"

I suggested he put the newspaper article aside and read the *Miller* opinion for himself. Then a third guy came in with 150 years for five attempted murders he committed at age 19. "Nineteen's not a juvenile," I said. "It could be," he replied, with typical jailhouse logic. "Depends on what law you look at. You can't drink until you're 21, so under 21 can be a juvenile." Well, good luck arguing that in court, I think. I add, "And 150 years, do 75, is not a life sentence." He was incredulous. "Why ain't it? Can't nobody do 75 years!"

A fourth youngster wanted to argue *Miller* in a sentence modification to try to reduce his 50-year sentence. "Well, you can use the concepts outlined in Miller to argue for a lesser sentence, but be aware that Miller does not have the force of law for you." He also left disgruntled, carrying a copy of *Miller v. Alabama*. I knew each one would highlight phrases they liked while ignoring context and refusing to believe the opinion's narrow application.

And we never broached the most crucial aspect of *Miller* – retroactivity.

So when Edgar Lee dragged Smitty to my desk, I peered over my glasses disapprovingly, as if to say, I just told you to take these dumbasses with their stupid *Miller* case and keep them away from my desk.

Edgar Lee read my look. "No, for real. My guy Smitty's got a case."

David Wayne Smith, #10087, I haltingly learned, did qualify under *Miller*. He was Indiana's oldest juvenile, preserved in amber, ensnared by a calamitous case in 1977, now turned 53 years old, the thinning hair, tooth loss, and crow's feet belying the passage of time. But his demeanor, almost child-like, allowed me to see his teenage personality, transplanted from the 70's. Unlike most teenagers who end up in prison, rebellious and self-centered, Smitty could be described in one word: obedient. He was on the slow side of the mental spectrum, school had proven enormously difficult, and while he didn't test one sigma below normal in intelligence, he was within the test's margin of error for that level. He was a born follower, no personal gyroscope on board. Back in 1977, when a born manipulator came along, and two others were riding with the leader, Smitty trailed like a stray duckling.

"Biggest mistake of my life," Smitty told me, describing his hesitant decision to get in the car with Roger Drollinger, Michael Wright, and Daniel Stonebraker on Sunday night, February 13, 1977. "I had no idea when I got in what was gonna happen."

Turned out, there were three sawed-off shotguns in the car, and a .38-caliber revolver, wielded by Drollinger. Drollinger's pending trial date for drug charges in Montgomery County were at least part of his motivation – a robbery would fund his quest for paid legal representation. While the crime they were about to commit wasn't to get drugs, and wasn't fueled by drugs, one could nonetheless say it was semi-drug-related. Drollinger's other motivation, posited the prosecution later, was to copycat the rural murders described in Truman Capote's book, *In Cold Blood*. On that score, the four would trump Capote.

They drove down two-lane roads in Parke County in northern Indiana, looking for signs of wealth at farmhouses and randomly scattered trailers. At one point, Drollinger slowed to allow a barking watchdog to approach the car. He teased it, then dispatched the dog with a shot to the head. It was a sign of things to come.

At a mobile home anchored near Hollandsburg they saw several newer vehicles and surmised that cash must be inside. Drollinger passed out the shotguns and assured the other three that nobody would be foolish enough to resist four armed men in the middle of the night. "The night seemed to flow," said Smitty, decades later, "like a river you want to get out of, but it's all going too fast."

Those versed in social psychology have observed a phenomenon where individuals within groups cease to act as individuals and adopt the will of the group's leader. Inhibitions and conscientiousness are lost as every member of the group expects someone else to step up and do what's right. Meanwhile, a malevolent leader's misbehavior escalates. Through their quiet acquiescence, the lesser participants unwittingly encourage the will of the primary actor.

When teenagers do something stupid, parents often hear the excuse, "But everybody else was doing it," which in reality is a better excuse than parents will admit. My mother would come back with, "If everybody else jumped off a bridge, would you do it too?" I'd think, Yeah, I probably would. Depends on the height of the bridge and the depth of the water. For Smitty that night, the bridge was high and the water was deep, and everyone else was taking the plunge.

The trailer belonged to Betty Spencer, and the cars belonged to her four stepsons, Ralph, Raymond, and Reeve Spencer, and Gregory Brooks. The robbers crept to the door and gained entry. Just as Drollinger promised, the weaponry convinced all five victims to lay on the floor. The home was shaken down, but not much of value was produced. For reasons unclear (or possibly, for no good reason), Roger decreed that all five should be killed. Leave no witnesses. Drollinger directed each cohort to select a target, and they opened fire on all four of Betty Spencer's stepsons. Then Betty was shot. She was still moving, so Stonebraker was directed to shoot her again. Her hair peeled away from her bloody scalp, and she laid motionless.

Betty Spencer survived. It wasn't her hair that disengaged from her head in a bloody tangle, it was a wig. Spencer identified the four, and like most multiple-assailant crimes, the facts emerged rather effortlessly for investigators. Wright and Stonebraker agreed to testify against Drollinger and Smith. Smith's attorney concocted an insanity defense. The idea that Smitty was less culpable than the other three never gained strong footing in court, though, and all four defendants wound up with identical four-life sentences. Smith's life terms were run concurrent. By Indiana law, multiple lives cannot be granted parole, so it was effectively LWOP. He was 17½ when the murders occurred, and now he had been locked up for 35 years. He was 53 years old, and suddenly, due to *Miller*, he anticipated going home.

Smitty's facts fit the *Miller* opinion perfectly. Under 18, pre-1978 law, life sentence. I'll be damned, I marveled, Edgar Lee hooked a ten-pound bass. This is a big, high-profile case, and it is winnable. I went to work drafting a post-conviction petition, and two days later I called Smitty back in to discuss it.

By Smitty's calculation, his freedom was six months away. It was simple, right? The life bit is unconstitutional, so he petitions the county court. The judge complies with *Miller* and sets a new sentencing date. Smitty will receive a term of years, with the max on any one count being 60 years. His four lives are concurrent, so his four 60's will be concurrent. He would do 30 on 60, and since he's already done 35 he would be released from the courtroom on time served. Everyone he had talked to had figured it the same way. No impediments foreseeable. Simple case. Out by Christmas.

"Not so fast," I cautioned Smitty. "You're looking at two or three years before you get a new sentencing date, and even then you may not get out." Not what he wanted to hear. I was certain, at that moment, he did not believe me. But to his credit, he didn't storm off and find a jailhouse lawyer who would whisper a more alluring tune in his ear.

"Why will it take so long?" asked Smitty. The slug-slide slowness of the legal process, post-conviction, seems out of character for a justice system that steamrolls most people into prison. A person can go from arrest to trial to prison within 70 days (and I have seen less – a former cellmate from Joliet, Robert Dale Conklin, went from arrest to imposition of the death penalty in 46 days down in Georgia), but to reverse the process may take years, sometimes decades.

We would file the petition immediately, but since Smitty had no money he would have to request a public defender, which would take about six months. Once an appearance was filed, the attorney would insist on amending the petition. There will be two issues in the PC, not one, I stressed to Smitty. The first issue, naturally, is whether his case factually qualifies under *Miller*. Obviously, it does. The second issue is whether *Miller* has retroactive effect for cases on collateral review. That question has not been settled, and until it is, no court may apply *Miller* to Smitty's case and have it go unchallenged by the state.

"There will be years of the state and federal courts arguing whether *Miller* will be retroactive," I predicted. "So your county court, being disinclined to release a convicted murderer, will deny your PC petition, saying *Miller* is not retroactive. And even if it did grant the petition, it would be stayed as the state perfected an appeal." Either way, Smitty would not get out.

The PC case, win or loss, would skip over the appellate court and go directly to the Indiana Supreme Court. Their determination, likewise, would be appealed by the losing party on a writ of certiorari to the U.S. Supreme Court. "Add it all up, and it's 2½ years, at best, before you get good news. Three years," I suggested, "is more likely." And then I was afforded the thrill of telling him, that after all that, even with a win he might stay in prison anyway.

Smitty's presumption that the only possible new sentence would be one forcing his release was incorrect. The courts could conclude that the only thing unconstitutional about his sentence was the provision forbidding parole eligibility for multiple lifes. Remedy: allow Smitty to be reviewed by the parole board. Or, he could receive four 60-year sentences, and they could be run consecutively, regardless of the concurrent status on the four lifes he had now. He could end up with 240, do 120, a sentence unimpeachable by *Miller*. And none of this would happen unless the issue of retroactivity was decided in his favor.

Smitty was confused, and questioned why I had to include an argument on retroactivity. "How could it not be retroactive? I don't understand that at all."

Retroactive effect of any Supreme Court ruling is guided by *Teague v. Lane* (1989), and if Smitty doesn't understand it, he's in good company. Some of the best legal minds in the country don't understand *Teague* or how it should be applied. To quote the relevant section, "Justice Harlan's view that new constitutional rules of criminal procedure generally should not be applied retroactively to cases on collateral review is the appropriate approach. Unless..." (and here are two exceptions) "...it places certain kinds of primary, private individual conduct beyond the power of the criminal law-making authority to proscribe," or, "if it requires the observance of those procedures that are 'implicit in the concept of ordered liberty'." Whatever that means. The Court explains that the first exception is not relevant in most cases, while the second, the one causing endless debate, "should be limited in scope to those new procedures without which the likelihood of an accurate conviction is seriously diminished." As if that clears it up.

Many Supreme Court opinions have been issued without the public knowing whether the opinion should be retroactive. A recent example is *Padilla v. Kentucky* (2010), where prisoners attempted to use *Padilla* retroactively for ineffective assistance of counsel claims. *Padilla* held that counsel's failure to correctly advise an alien legal permanent resident that his criminal conviction may cause deportation satisfied the deficient assistance prong of *Strickland*, entitling the prisoner to return to court to argue the prejudice prong of *Strickland*. Could *Padilla* be used retroactively, by prisoners whose cases predated Padilla's filing? The *Padilla* opinion itself didn't say. For three years, post-*Padilla*, lawyers argued and courts disagreed with each other over the meaning of *Teague*. The first case to be granted certiorari by the Supreme Court regarding the retroactivity of *Padilla* was *Chaidez v. United States* (2013), where Chaidez had a favorable (retroactive) ruling from the district court, which was reversed by the Seventh Circuit Court of Appeals. All over the country, state and federal courts disagreed on whether a *Teague* exception applied. In *Chaidez* the Supreme Court held that *Padilla* is not retroactive. Hundreds of *Padilla*-laden cases were thus decided (and discarded).

Yes, the Supreme Court could have said *Padilla* is not retroactive when they issued their opinion in 2010, thereby saving a cackle of lawyers three years' worth of work. But why issue a terse paragraph on retroactivity when it is so much more fun to watch state and federal jurists openly display their ignorance on the *Teague* rule?

So *Miller v. Alabama* was decided in 2012, and as all nine justices surely knew, the debate over the *Teague* rule began anew. Smitty and I began monitoring cases from around the country. Courts in Nebraska, Mississippi, Iowa, and Massachusetts said *Miller* was retroactive; courts in Pennsylvania, Minnesota, Louisiana, and Alabama said no. The Eleventh Circuit Court of Appeals was deluged with cases, many from Florida. Analyses differed around the country. It was as if judges were drawing conclusions first, working backwards from the outcome they would prefer to see, then constructing elaborate frameworks to justify their arguments.

In the petition I originally wrote for Smitty, I argued that *Atkins v. Virginia* (2002), forbidding capital punishment for the mentally retarded, was retroactive, and *Graham v. Florida* (2010), forbidding LWOP for juveniles in non-homicide cases, was retroactive, therefore *Miller* should be retroactive too. When Smitty obtained a public defender my petition was replaced by one with a more erudite argument, discarding my weak reasoning based entirely, I confess, on the judicial system's nemesis, common sense. The new argument contained thoughts one might find published in some law journal. But I don't think it would have mattered what any petitioner or lawyer wrote for or against *Teague*'s application; the nation's judges were left to figure it out for themselves. And in that, they could not form a consensus.

In the end, those who have crowed about getting it right – well, hey, the coin only had two sides.

There's this pervasive idea, fed to us early, that the courts carefully consider weighty issues of constitutional law and arrive at well-reasoned opinions, and case law advances thereby in a steady direction, bearing a slow but irreversible pace. Precedents are set. These precedents shine as landmarks, beacons guiding future opinions. The legal term for this is *stare decisis.* An equable unvarying philosophy pervades through a chain of opinions.

Theoretically, the law progresses almost like science – one riddle solved, providing the basis to solve the next riddle, and so on. The watt leads to the volt which leads to Ohm's Law, and off we go, building to Edison and Tesla. The court's opinions don't waver back and forth – that would be like Newton's Laws of Motion being rephrased every twenty years. The opinions are not susceptible to political pressure or personal bias any more than the Law of Gravity has a Codicil of Notable Gravity Exceptions. The Supreme Court does not flip-flop. Justices are not clouded by personal bias. And if you believe any of that, you are not well-acquainted with our judicial system.

The Supreme Court has reversed precedent dozens of times, a fact giving hope to opponents of controversial opinions, like *Roe v. Wade* (1973) (abortion rights), and *Citizens United v. Federal Election Commission* (2010) (election campaign funding). Time, or "evolving standards," as published in *Trop v. Dulles* (1957), affects the permanence of precedents, as do the personal philosophies of court personnel. The obvious existence of personal bias in judges is why we have the ever-present conservative v. liberal fight over high court nominations.

To illustrate how the Supreme Court can flip-flop in rapid fashion, consider their 1970's opinions on capital punishment. In 1972, a 5-4 majority in *Furman v. Georgia* declared the death penalty in violation of the Eighth Amendment's cruel and unusual punishment prohibition. Justices Douglas, Brennan, Marshall, Stewart, and White were opposed by death penalty advocates Rehnquist, Powell, Burger, and Blackman. Justice Stevens replaced Douglas in 1975. The issue came before the court again in 1976 in *Gregg v. Georgia.* Stevens provided a conservative Republican swing vote, reinstating the death penalty – but this political element is only half the story. Curiously, Stewart and White switched sides, becoming pro-death, while Blackmun and Burger, former death penalty advocates, now dissented against the *Gregg* majority. Four of the eight justices could not agree *with themselves* four years later on whether they had gotten *Furman* right. When 4 of 8 change their mind, it's a result we might expect from coin flips done in chambers.

Capital punishment was constitutional and legal again, thanks to both a political infusion and, apparently, random chance.

Or, for a more familiar political example, one could read *Bush v. Gore* (2001) – (actually read it, and not some reporter's commentary about it) – and conclude that the only good reason to stop the recount in Florida was for political victory, and not to comply with, as the court determined, the Fourteenth Amendment's Equal Protection clause. The 5-4 vote, firmly along party lines, handed the Presidency to Bush. Nothing new – an electoral commission's 8-7 vote, also along party lines, stole the 1876 election from Samuel Tilden and gave it to Republican Rutherford B. Hayes. The apolitical judge is part yeti, part Loch Ness Monster: sightings have yet to be confirmed.

In 1989, *Stanford v. Kentucky* held that it was okay to execute juveniles; in 2005, *Roper v. Simmons* condemned the practice as unconstitutional. Flip flop. The same day *Stanford* was published, *Penry v. Lynaugh* held it acceptable to execute the mentally retarded; in 2002, *Atkins v. Virginia* reversed *Penry*. Flip flop again. Precedents are never firm, and the law is always fluid.

Poor Smitty, he didn't want to know about politically-motivated judges, *Teague*, or retroactivity; he just wanted to go home. By the reasoning embodied in *Miller*, he should. *Miller* extended the rationale outlined in *Roper v. Simmons* (2005), which forbade capital punishment for juveniles, and in *Graham v. Florida* (2010), which ended LWOP for juveniles on non-homicide cases. Juveniles, *Miller* held, have a "lack of maturity," and an "underdeveloped sense of responsibility" that leads to "recklessness, impulsivity, and heedless risk-taking." They are "more vulnerable to negative influences and outside pressures," and they have "limited control over their own environment and lack the ability to extricate themselves from horrific, crime-producing settings." A juvenile's character "is not as well-formed as an adult's" and "his actions are less likely to be evidence of irretrievable depravity." The Supreme Court advised lower courts to consider the "mitigating qualities of youth," especially in cases where the juvenile has exhibited obedience in prison, which would reflect one's capacity for reform.

On every point of *Miller* we could scratch a checkmark for David Smith. He'd been locked up in a rough, maximum-security prison for 35 years, a place where there are roughly 100 serious disciplinary infractions per month. In 420 months Smitty had zero write-ups. Guiness should be notified – this may contend for a world record. The odds of anyone residing at Pendleton that long and by sheer luck never incurring a write-up is 3.8 trillion to one. His immaturity in 1977 and his compliant, obedient nature were just what Roger Drollinger needed when Smitty was persuaded to hop in the car. He had no idea what he was getting into that night, and did not possess the ability to extricate himself from the unfolding series of events. There was no way to abort, no ejection seat once they rolled out.

Smitty was assigned two of the state's best public defenders, and their strategy, a reasonable one, was to wait. Instead of battling through petitions and briefs that would lead to more appeals, all awaiting a high court *Teague* ruling, they held the proceeding in abeyance while other cases advanced toward the Supreme Court.

"You're in for a long wait," I advised Smitty. He was exasperated as 2012 neared a close.

"Yeah, these attorneys tell me just like you said, that it would be two or three more years before we know something."

Well, I thought, what's three more years to a guy who has done thirty-five? The lawyers and the courts probably thought the same way. No sense of urgency, not as long as the deprivation of liberty is an abstract concept, happening to someone else, not you.

"Smitty," I asked, "what happened to all the jailhouse lawyers who said you would be out by Christmas?"

His eyes narrowed and he shook his head in derision. "Those guys had no idea what they were talking about. Everything that's happened, everything the lawyers told me would happen, it all went down just like you said. At first I didn't see how *Teague* had anything to do with my case, and now I see that *Teague* is all that matters. You were the only one here who was right."

I had fished for this answer, and my silly ego absorbed a small dose of satisfaction. Everybody likes to be proven right. But then I came down as I looked through the chain-link fence separating our rec yards and saw the disappointment in Smitty's eyes. I was consistently being proven right about the wrong outcome, always the bearer of bad news. The truth was this: none of us would get out of this prison quickly or easily.

CHAPTER SIX

Technically, They Can't Do That

"Woe unto the defeated, whom history treads into dust."
– Arthur Koestler, *Darkness at Noon* (1941).

At Christopher Turner's 2012 post-conviction hearing, public defender Ben Jewell described Turner as "the worst" client he had ever represented. "Argumentative," said Jewell, "and uncooperative." A real pain in the ass. Turner was the client who had tried his patience the most, out of over 2,000 destitute defendants. They had disagreed on everything about Turner's defense, and Turner's unmet demands had devolved into Turner repeating the litany voiced by thousands, perhaps millions, ever since *Gideon v. Wainwright* (1963) had ensured free counsel for all indigent felony defendants: "My public pretender ain't doin' his job."

Turner had run off the first public defender assigned to his case ("impossible to deal with," she said), but Jewell was resolute, a specialist in "difficult" clients. Armed with stubborn resolve, Jewell firmly explained why Turner's defense ideas were unworkable. "There's no way you can win at trial," he said. "Force a trial, and they'll string you up with more time than you can do." Gradually, between tantrums, Turner agreed. Jail was an atrocious place, and Turner began to anticipate moving on to prison. Jewell outlasted Turner's intransigence, and plea negotiations began.

Two cases were pending. One was a Class D criminal confinement from November 27, 2005. Complainant Tichina Montgomery, Turner's ex-girlfriend, alleged a rage-filled Turner had forcibly prevented her from leaving the house during an argument. The warrant was issued a week later. When Turner learned of the warrant, his mood toward Tichina did not improve. On January 3, 2006, he forced his way into her residence, angry about "the lies she told to get that first case put on me." He yelled at Tichina, smacked her around with an open hand, and punctuated the incident with the threat of more violence if she ever put the cops on him again. She promptly dialed 9-1-1, and the state's charges from the second incident were: Class B's burglary, criminal confinement, and battery, and Class D intimidation. What had begun as a domestic quarrel had escalated into Turner facing some serious time.

Fortunately for Turner (and everyone involved) Indiana had set up an excellent program aimed at reducing domestic violence, a 90-day in-patient facility combining anger management classes with counseling in communication and interpersonal relations. The violent offender – Turner, in this case – is confined, both to cool off and to learn. The victim – Tichina – also attends sessions to improve her relationship skills. Indiana's conservative Republican legislators initially balked at financing the EDV Program ("Ending Domestic Violence"), but women's rights groups persuaded them to change their vote once a long-term savings to the taxpayers could be shown. Turner's case was diverted into the EDV Program, and . . .

. . . Okay, so no such program exists. There might be a diversion program if you're white, wealthy, and have smacked your cheating girlfriend in Beverly Hills, but the poor (of all colors) cannot afford to pay for counselors or for the lawyers who could set up such non-criminal outcomes. Turner's public defender entered plea negotiations with the simple aim of seeing Turner warehoused in a prison for as little time as possible.

That state prosecutors negotiate cases at all, given their 2-to-1 likelihood of winning at trial, must have them believing they are rather benevolent to most defendants and "tough" on only a recalcitrant few. They probably fancy themselves as employing the mule-moving carrot-and-stick approach. Defendants see it differently: not much carrot, and a whole lot of stick. As one crudely put it, "They offer ten inches or twenty inches. You don't want either one, but in the end, you're beat down and bent over, takin' the ten."

In May 2006, the state offered Turner an "open plea," meaning Turner would walk into court with no idea what the judge might do, and take his chances. The maximum penalty, 43 years, was calculated by running the two violent felonies, battery and burglary, consecutively, then tacking on the November criminal confinement case, so 20 + 20 + 3 = 43. Turner had priors, so the prospect of flying into court blind did not appeal to him. He rejected the offer, and both he and Jewell endorsed the written offer sheet as "refused."

On September 6, 2006, the state offered a "reasonable" deal. Fifteen years on the January incident, 1½ on the November charge, consecutive; total sentence 16½ years. Turner appeared in court at 9:00 a.m. that day, but the hearing transcripts made no mention of the state's offer. The offer was docketed at 12:37 p.m., with no endorsement by Turner or Jewell as either refused or accepted. It is plain from the written record that Turner was given no opportunity to consider the 16½ year sentence. He learned about it after he obtained his attorney's client file.

In December 2006, the state's new offer, from a different deputy prosecutor, was 40 years. Turner refused the 40, and he and counsel signed the offer sheet as refused. A few weeks later Turner's resistance crashed, and he signed an open plea, believing Jewell could successfully argue mitigating factors to get a sentence less than 40 years. "He convinced me he would stress the effects of medication I was on, and other stuff," Turner explained. "But he didn't do none of that."

On January 5, 2007, Turner was hit with 43 years. Tichina, who had attended every court proceeding, was jubilant. "My mom said she was dancing a jig in the hallway." Which was in character, given that she had repeatedly pointed and laughed at Turner when he was shackled and wearing the orange jail jumpsuit, and classily signaled him with "the finger" while mouthing the words "fuck you" while court was in session.

Such schadenfreude is rather common when defendant and complainant have had an intimate history, and in those cases the justice system often becomes a mere tool for personal vengeance rather than a mechanism for the just order of society. It's one more tool in the "payback" toolbox. When I heard Turner's description of Tichina's antics I could read in his eyes, he didn't have to say it: *After all this, the bitch has it coming to her now.*

Well, maybe twenty years of sitting in a cage will help him get over it. In the meantime, he had appealed the sentence and lost, filed a PC petition, and amended the petition three times. By the time I got it, he had 17 issues, 16 of them worthless. Every issue his jailhouse lawyers had found were all forms of the same argument: the sentencing hearing was conducted unfairly. This was the sole issue from Turner's direct appeal, and therefore, res judicata. The one thing he had going for him, though, was counsel's failure to advise him of the 16½-year plea deal.

"It's a rock-solid issue," I advised Tuner, "and the way to win this PC is to eliminate all these worthless issues and focus on the one issue where the relief is clear cut. You'd get the 16½-year sentence; no other remedy is possible."

"What about all the other stuff Jewell didn't correct?" asked Turner. "They had false information in the PSI, failed to consider mitigators known to the court, a long list of stuff. Technically, they can't do that."

Like Jewell, I didn't want to get into an itemized description of why all 16 non-issues were a waste of time. "Technically, you're right, they can't do that. But they do. They do it all the time, and the higher courts consistently let them get away with it. It gets chalked up as at the discretion of the court. Those are all loser issues you have there. And if you raise them, you'll get back an appellate opinion that focuses solely on your losers and totally ignores the one issue that has a chance at winning."

Appellate courts have long respected an attorney's narrow focus in an appeal. A seventeen-issue brief is like hunting with a shotgun; a one-issue brief is like hunting with a rifle.

Failure to show a defendant a plea offer was recently declared by the U.S. Supreme Court to be ineffective assistance of counsel, violating due process rights under the Sixth and Fourteenth Amendments. In *Missouri v. Frye* (2012) and *Lafler v. Cooper* (2012) the court set the remedy at re-offering the defendant the plea agreement he never saw. In Indiana, case law predated *Frye* and *Lafler* on the issue. *Lyles v. State* (Ind. 1978) and *Dew v. State* (Ind. 2006) also supported Turner's argument. We had the case law on our side, and more important, we had the facts. Turner had signed every plea offer, as had Jewell, with the exception of the 16½-year offer that had been docketed three hours after Turner left the courtroom.

Turner, one of the most pleasant, rational, and agreeable clients I ever had (so unlike Jewell's experience), asked around for others' advice. He came back satisfied. "Let's do it, just like you say. One issue. It's a winner. Kill all the rest."

I drafted a "Findings of Fact and Conclusions of Law" for the county court judge to consider. If he rejected it (which is likely in all cases, merit or not), we would have solid grounds for an appeal. The brief would be simple, short, and no judge would be able to ignore the solitary, persuasive issue.

"This will cut my release date by 13 years," Turner mused aloud. I saw the wheels turning as he made plans for his release.

Desire and expectation flowed harmoniously together, and out poured hope, the same hope held by Arturo, Donnie, Smitty, and others. All were envisioning a future on the outside. Freedom. The system would work. It had to. The facts and the law were on their side, so the courts would fix this. Intelligent people in high places would ensure that justice would be done – this is what they're there for. This was America, after all, where "liberty and justice for all" is the pledge.

Between trips to the anti-ark and the daily grind of educating confused souls at the law library I found myself answering the same questions over and over. Whenever that happens, it's time to write a book.

Tony Warren-Bey and Pete Mitchell joined me outlining a how-to book, titled, *P.C. Guidebook: The Complete Guide to Post-Conviction Relief for the Pro Se Petitioner, Indiana Edition*. Warren-Bey, rather sick of the law after he fell off the cliff with his case, helped some, then lost interest. Pete agreed to review and edit my writing. There was a facility prohibition on doing non-legal work at the law library, but an instructional book on PC petitions was about as "legal" as it gets, so supervisors Fowler and Serour had no objections to the work.

"Long after I'm gone, dead or whatever, I'll still be answering guys' questions through this book," I told Mel. No longer would every Indiana prisoner have to learn the PC process from scratch. For the first time since the PC rules went into effect in 1969, prisoners could read the instructions. I sent the pages to Samizdat Publishing LLC in Virginia, and a few months later the books began to arrive at the prison mail room.

None of them, however, reached the hands of the prisoners who had ordered them.

While in K-1 dorm I overheard a conversation laden with a frequent prisoner theme: disappointing attorney performance. Dujuan Emerson, saddled with 65 years on a robbery-murder case, complained that, "The court violated my 180-day detainer rights, and all my attorneys let them get away with it." My ears honed in, and some innate drive to find winnable cases kicked on. In federal prison, at FCI-Oxford (Wisconsin) and FCI-Cumberland (Maryland), I had helped dozens with detainer issues. The Interstate Agreement on Detainers Act (IADA), a federal compact between 48 states and the federal government [Mississippi and Louisiana excluded], was a powerful tool in the hands of prisoners wanted for prosecution on untried charges in another state. I had flipped a conviction of my own with it, in Kentucky, in 1997. I dropped my pen and wrangled into the conversation with Emerson.

"You were out of state and requested extradition, demanding trial within 180 days?"

"Yep, I was at FCI-Pekin, in Illinois," he affirmed. "They sent me to Nap [Indianapolis] on the 178th day, and at my arraignment on the 180th day I told the judge I wanted my trial within the 180 days. He set it for five days later, the 185th day."

"Did counsel object to setting the trial date past the 180th day?"

"I didn't have no counsel yet. Counsel was appointed on day number 180."

Beautiful, I thought. Possibly a winnable case. But there were many unknowns, and the evidence would be difficult to marshal after fourteen years had gone by. I asked why no attorney had taken notice of this before (knowing, through experience, that a majority of criminal defense attorneys are unfamiliar with the IADA).

"I told my trial attorney, and he didn't do nothing. Then I wrote to my appeal attorney, and she had other issues to deal with. So I put it in my PC, and my PC attorney had it in there, but when we went to a hearing he orally amended the PC and left it out. So no court ever heard it."

"Okay. So let me ask you this. How was the 180-day clock started? What event triggered the days to start counting?" This was crucial, because courts and defendants often miscalculate, using different starting points.

"The day I gave my request to the superintendent at FCI-Pekin. The court counted from that day."

Thanks to the Supreme Court ruling in *Fex v. Michigan* (1993), this traditional way of starting the 180-day clock was determined to be wrong. Emerson's trial court had read the IAD Act literally, where the law says prosecution must commence within 180 days after the prisoner "shall have caused to be delivered" his request for final disposition. For a couple decades, in every state, the clock began on the day the prisoner signed the request and handed it to his warden. This action "caused" its delivery to the prosecutor. In 1993 Justice Scalia, in his 5-4 majority opinion, got the idea that everyone had misunderstood the statute all these years – that what Congress really meant was to start counting the 180 days *after* the paperwork was delivered to the prosecutor. Justice Souter, dissenting, replied that if Congress had wanted the days to begin ticking off upon delivery, they would have chosen the pellucid language, "upon delivery." Scalia's tortured interpretation kept Mr. Fex in prison, and gave prosecutors a little more time to prepare their cases.

At first glance, one might see Emerson's use of the IAD Act as a perverse attempt to avoid justice. Nobody likes to see some scumbag walking free on a technicality. But the technicality Emerson relied upon had cost him dearly at trial. Believing he had a right to dismissal for failure to timely prosecute his case, Emerson had refused to waive the IAD Act's provisions on day 180. This forced his newly-appointed public defender to defend him on murder and robbery with only five days of preparation – no investigation, no witness depositions, no pretrial motions. The prosecutor, in contrast, had an enormous advantage in preparation. Prosecutors are no dummies – it is common for them to suspend the transfer of a prisoner under the IAD Act until just before the 180 days expires, then put the defendant in the predicament Emerson faced.

For every defendant crying foul over some technicality, there's a party on the other side that benefits from this "technical" violation of the law. The laws are designed, presumably, to ensure that trials are fair, but prosecutors have a real genius for transforming these protective laws into outcome-changing prosecutorial advantage.

I knew the state had *Fex* in their back pocket to screw up anything I tried to do with Emerson's case, but I decided to press on. If Emerson's trial court had admittedly set trial beyond day 180, it was possible the state would not raise *Fex* as a defense.

Emerson's only avenue for relief was to ask the Indiana Court of Appeals to allow a successive PC. We tried that. We were shot down, as is customary, in two weeks, with no specific reason given. Emerson wanted to follow with a petition for writ of habeas corpus in federal court.

"You can't take this to federal court. Habeas does not exist for IAD violations."

Emerson was confused. "Why not? The IAD is a law of the United States, right?"

"Yep, sure is."

"And habeas corpus is for violations of U.S. laws, right?"

"No question about it." It exists for "a violation of the Constitution or laws or treaties of the United States," as stated at 28 USCS 2254.

"So why can't I file for habeas corpus on this?"

Good question. It took several days, using *Carchman v. Nash* (1985) and *Reed v. Farley* (1994), to explain why the court had carved out an exception. The legal reasoning was complicated. "Fundamental defect" standard, and all that. I cut through all the technicalities and laid it out plain and simple for Emerson.

"Mass incarceration has overloaded the courts, so they invented some twisted, nonsensical justification to keep state prisoners out of federal court. Their docket is too full as it is."

This, he understood. But he was still sure the courts were doing it wrong.

"Technically, they can't do that, right?"

"Technically," I replied, "they do whatever they want."

Emerson's last option was a petition for writ of certiorari to the U.S. Supreme Court, complaining that the successive PC process in Indiana does not comport with Fourteenth Amendment due process. I knew it was a 1,000-1 shot, but the machinations afforded Emerson some level of satisfaction. We took it "all the way." To the highest court. He ended up denied at every level, yet his IAD issue had never been ruled upon.

That Emerson had a murder conviction at all rested upon another technicality – the concept of "accomplice liability." Emerson had 65 years for murder. Technically, he was a murderer. But he had never killed anybody, never even tried to.

On July 31, 1996, Dujuan Emerson and Larry Porter interrupted a basketball game at Watkins Park, in Indianapolis, storming the court with pistols drawn. The potential loot was minuscule. Under one basket, Emerson pointed a gun at Anthony Robinson and relieved him of his gold chain. Under the far hoop, Kenneth Mason was resolved to give Porter nothing. Porter shot Mason, killing him. Per Indiana's accomplice liability statute, Emerson was held responsible for Porter's actions, making him "just as guilty as the shooter." Hands tied by the legislature, the jury's only choices were to convict for murder, or enter 'not guilty' on the homicide. There was no opportunity to parse out liability between the conspirators, no way to ensure that a trigger-happy defendant would shoulder more liability.

"I never did know if Porter had it out for Mason," Emerson told me. "Maybe he planned to kill him all along, and never told me."

In most jurisdictions in the United States, an equal level of liability placed upon all conspirators is the norm. As the Supreme Court stated in *Waddington v. Sarausad* (2009), "in for a dime, in for a dollar."

In many accomplice cases, codefendants went into the crime with dissimilar intent. The law ignores intent, focusing instead on whether one defendant's action (murder) was a foreseeable event. Were guns used? Then killing someone was foreseeable. Even a codefendant who had held no gun would be liable for the actions of the shooter.

Not that there's anything wrong with that. It just does not allow for a conviction on a lesser charge, such as a Class B "Assisting a Homicide," a charge that does not exist in Indiana.

Roughly one-fourth of homicide convictions are obtained through accomplice liability instructions. On some of these cases, the homicide victim was one of the criminal perpetrators, shot by a burgled homeowner or robbery victim. The dead man's co-perpetrator graduates from burglar or robber, to murderer.

Christopher Lewis was another case where accomplice liability and a creative definition of murder combined to put a promising young man away for the majority of his adult life. Lewis was a bright and athletic teenager hoping to play college basketball; unfortunately he also had a penchant for smoking marijuana. Lewis and some cohorts hatched a plan to rob a dope dealer. The dealer had contemplated such a possibility as a natural consequence of the business he had chosen. He was armed. One of Lewis's partners was killed by the dope dealer – so Lewis was convicted of his buddy's murder. Under the law, Lewis had caused this foreseeable event. Sentence, 55 years.

Detectives like to get in on the accomplice liability action too. When they have two suspects, they know they can get a murder conviction on both if only one talks. So as I have read in numerous discovery files, the detective tempts the arrestee: "We have an apple, and only one of you gets to take a bite. Do you want him telling on you, or are you going to do the smart thing, and get down first?" In adjacent interrogation rooms, both suspects are oblivious to the fact that a confession gains them nothing and loses everything. When one fingers the other as the shooter, both go down for murder.

"The state gets double the penalty when they convict accomplices," noted Shane Bramley, my cellmate in 2010. "When two guys are convicted of one murder, the murder isn't penalized with 55 years. Instead, the state gets 110 years. The state gets to take *two* lives."

"Yeah," I replied. "It's like the price tag for a crime increases when multiple defendants are held to pay for it. But then, it's not like a broken window, where two guys chipping in $30 each makes perfect restitution for a $60 window."

"So the state can take two lives for one? Why does it have to be that way?"

It doesn't have to be that way – this punishment scheme is one of many options chosen by the state. In some countries, criminal liability is parsed out among accomplices, much the same way civil liability is divided among multiple civil defendants in the United States. For example, a jury may assign 70% liability to one defendant, 20% to another, and let the victim swallow 10% of the blame for 'contributory negligence' or 'assumption of risk.'

Some victims voluntarily assume an enormous amount of risk, "playing with fire." Criminals killing criminals. In quite a few murders, once you learn the circumstances, the resulting homicide is not surprising, but seems to be a perfectly natural, inevitable consequence.

Whether it's a criminal or civil case, a fair division of culpability comes closest to the ideal of proportionality. A balancing of the scales. But as Justice Scalia has often reminded us, proportional punishments are not a right enshrined in the U.S. Constitution. Proportionality was not the Founders' intent. And what is the opposite of proportionality? Imbalance.

"I hear you guys cryin' about how they do things in other countries, and even in other states," CO Red said, blasting into our conversation again one late afternoon in the law library. He adopted a mock whiney voice: "In Ohio, three grams of crack is only a year in prison, here in Indiana it's fifty. In Germany you have your own room and wear your own clothes and can go to school. In France they only lock up people for the most violent crimes, and the sentences are way shorter. Waah, waah, waah," Red cried, brazenly telling us we were all crybabies.

"What you forget, or ignore," Red continued, "is that some other countries woulda killed you already. Murder somebody or sell drugs in Saudi Arabia, see what you get. You get executed! Steal something in Pakistan, you get your hand chopped off. Rape a girl in Thailand, they tie you to the ground, beat you with bamboo, pour honey on you, and let the fire ants tear your ass up. Y'all talk about how it's done in other places. Believe me, you better be glad you're here in America."

Red was addressing a room full of amateur litigators, so he should have expected a logical reply. What did he think we'd say? "Yeah, Red, you're right. God bless America?"

Pete Mitchell countered first. "Those countries you mentioned – Saudi Arabia, Pakistan, Thailand – all of them are still operating with ancient legal systems."

"Pre-Medieval law," I added.

Pete continued. "Those codes were devised before human beings got together with advanced philosophies. Without a better understanding of what makes a society work. This is the twenty-first century, and we need laws that make use of our modern understanding of sociological problems – not laws devised in the seventh century, or 2,000 years ago, or even 200 years ago."

I couldn't resist jumping in. "When we 'cry' about how it's done somewhere else, notice that we're always talking about countries that have *advanced* criminal justice theories, not countries that have ignored hundreds of years of human progress."

"You said 200 years ago," Red shot back. "Are you trying to say the Constitution is too old, like it's outdated? That's the best constitution ever invented!"

Whatley and Edgar Lee came out of their chairs like an electric current had run through them.

"*Best* constitution? What kind of idiot are you?" Edgar Lee already thought Red was a simpleton and this solidified his opinion. "Same document that says I'm three-fifths of a human being? Same paper that says I'm property, not entitled to shit?"

"All that's been amended out. That's what makes the Constitution so great; we can amend it to keep it perfect."

We've amended it twenty-seven times. We've even had to amend the Amendments. Perfect?

"It's hardly perfect," I explained to Red. "How about the Electoral College, the most manipulative set of rules ever devised for choosing a President. Just ask yourself this: If you were to devise a way to elect the President today, would you come up with an Electoral College? Of course not, it's ignorant! And then, there's nothing in the Constitution to stop political parties from gerrymandering Congressional districts, so they can scheme to make minority votes count for less. The Bill of Rights is also ambiguous. The Second Amendment, the right to bear arms? Does that right belong to individual citizens..."

"Individual citizens," Red interjected.

"...or to the militia, which just happens to be mentioned in the Second Amendment as the reason for its existence?"

"Everybody in America is the militia," reasoned Red.

"Every white male property owner, you mean," snapped Warren-Bey. "The Constitution was written by them, for them, to keep them in power."

I piled on. "Not only is what's written into the Constitution imperfect – we argue every day in the courts over what the Constitution really means – but we should also criticize the Constitution for what's been left out." It seemed obvious. "If we were to rewrite the Bill of Rights today, we would have separate amendments ensuring equal rights for women, a right to education, a right to health care..."

"Handouts!" Red yelled. "Handouts! Y'all want more money taken out of my paycheck!"

"What's your problem with taxes?" Pete rejoined the fray. "Taxation is just everybody pooling their money together to create a community we'd all like to live in."

"No it ain't! It's taking money from people who worked for it, and giving it to people too lazy to work." Red possessed the perfect libertarian laissez faire philosophy when it came to personal economics.

I steered the conversation back to the Constitution. "A perfect constitution would also make sure that every adult could vote, no matter what, and that every vote had equal value."

"What do you mean by equal value?"

"I mean nobody can redraw districts to make minority votes count for less. And the only way to do that is with a parliamentary system of representation, not this whack-o republican system we have now."

"A parliament? You mean like in England or France? That's asking for chaos!" Red was sure that democracy had advanced beyond the parliamentary stage. "If a parliament was the best way to do it, the Founders would have put that into the Constitution. But it's not. The system we have now, with a Congress, is the best system."

Perfect tautology. It's the best because it's the best. America's the best country in the world because it's America.

"Listen," I carefully explained to Red, "every democracy in Europe has a parliament. They chose to use the parliament system for democracy *after* seeing the system we devised in the United States in 1787. Many of them chose that system around 1848. And what a parliament does is ensure that *everybody* has a voice in government that is proportional to their population. If we had a parliament, we would have 12% of our country's representatives representing African-American interests, 16% representing Hispanic issues . . ." I could see the horror in Red's eyes as he thought of this inconceivable world. ". . . half of parliament would be composed of women. And," I conceded snidely, "there would even be a few shills left to represent corporations and the super-wealthy one percent."

Edgar Lee giggled at the last line.

"Look," said Red, "what I don't get is why y'all want to blame all this on Republicans all the time, as if they're the ones to blame for people being in prison. They're about freedom! They're the Party of Lincoln! The party that freed the slaves!"

"Party of Lincoln, my ass," I laughed. "Every time a Republican uses that line he's pretending the listener doesn't know that the Republican Party abandoned the civil rights platform in 1877, when they sold out the South to put Rutherford B. Hayes in the White House. They ended Reconstruction in order to advance other Republican incentives. Don't even try that 'Party of Lincoln' crap. They haven't given a shit about blacks or poor people for over a hundred years."

"Yeah," said Edgar Lee, "Party of Lincoln is a coded phrase, meaning, We think y'all stupid and don't know your history."

Red had heard enough, and wasn't moved by our rhetoric. "All these ideas you got – you must live in a dream world, thinking up shit like that all day. You need to get in touch with reality. You live in America! It's a great country, and it doesn't need to change."

"My country, right or wrong? Is that what you're saying, Red?"

"You're damn right! I defend anything this country does. Within reason."

He had no idea the 'My Country, Right or Wrong' slogan came from the gate above the entrance to Buchenwald.

As Red exited toward his desk we heard Rush Limbaugh winding up another radio session.

The international comparisons we had discussed sent me, a numbers aficionado, off to collect data on worldwide incarceration statistics. What caused a country to have a high incarceration rate? It seemed like a silly question, at first. Obviously, a high crime rate would be the most likely suspect. A high crime rate would cause a government to react with the tool at its disposal – the sovereign right to deprive its citizens of their liberty. Imprisonment rates should parallel crime rates everywhere. Countries don't lock up people because they *want* to, but because they *had* to – or so I thought.

I compiled data on international crime rates and incarceration rates and found no pattern, no correlation. High crime countries sometimes had high incarceration rates, and sometimes they had low incarceration rates. Same with low crime countries. There was no cause-effect relationship.

I noticed some countries were economically depressed, and did not have the ability to enforce laws or lock up its citizens. Some were politically dysfunctional, and locked up too many people. Kleptocracies in small African nations didn't invest in law enforcement or in prisons. Corruption ruined the ability of Central American countries to enforce the law – Honduras was the murder capital of the world. Pure authoritarians in North Korea, Cuba, and China locked up their dissidents, enlarging prison populations out of purely political motivations. It seemed impossible to identify any predictors useful to explain mass incarceration in the United States.

An explanation was needed, because at the top of my list of 153 countries, with the highest incarceration rate and a middle-of-the-road crime rate, was the United States.

Mel scanned my lists and saw no way to make sense of it. "These countries are so different, it's like comparing apples and oranges."

"More like apples and aardvarks." At least apples and oranges were both hand fruits.

Then I realized what I had to do. Group countries by region. Create subsets with shared cultural histories. Only then would useful patterns emerge.

I divided the 153 countries into nine world regions and sorted them from highest incarceration rate to lowest. It was like watching a muddy, turbulent river dissolve into a clear, slow-moving stream. An alarming trend became visible, like seeing crocodiles lying on the sandy bottom. In each region, the most oppressive government was also the most right-wing government. [See Appendix 2.]

Leaving the United States out of the equation, the world's median incarceration rate was 132 per 100,000 population, and the average was 127. These were 2011 figures. Central America, including the Caribbean, had the highest incarceration rate, at 288, with Cuba the most oppressive, at 510. The former USSR region ran second, at 243, and their worst was Mother Russia, at 470. East Asia was third, lopsided by North Korea's estimated 600 rate. All three of these regions were led by communists, so there was no real surprise that their incarceration rates would be high.

On down the list, Uruguay's Marxist government was South America's incarceration leader, at 289. Iran led the Islamic nations with a 284 rate. Iran – their government was notoriously conservative, proud of eradicating social ills like pornography and homosexuality. Rightists in Slovakia led Eastern Europe; rightist "Red Shirts" in Thailand caused a prison population explosion disproportionate to its neighbors; and in poverty-ridden sub-Saharan Africa, a militaristic government in Rwanda used prisons to deal with ethnic Tutsi-Hutu conflict. In Western Europe, with a regional incarceration rate of only 95, conservative England stood out as the most prison-happy, at 148.

INCARCERATION RATES BY REGION
(Prisoners per 100,000 population)

REGION	Ave	Highest	Rate
Central America	288	Cuba	510
Former USSR	243	Russia	470
East Asia	226	North Korea	600 +/-
South America	215	Uruguay	289
Islamic	137	Iran	284
Eastern Europe	136	Slovakia	188
Southeast Asia	118	Thailand	435
SubSaharan Africa	95	Rwanda	492
Western Europe	95	England	148

The most confounding figure of all was that, atop this list of oppressive misfits composed of communists, right-wing extremists, clerics, racists, and dictators, was the United States. A whopping 707 people incarcerated per 100,000 – 5.57 times the non-USA world average.

Are we worse than communists like Kim Jong-Un? Can American freedom only flourish by means of prisons and jails? Do our people have worse character than people living in Russia and Rwanda? Why are we more oppressive than Castro and Putin? What explains this?

"Maybe it has something to do with guns," Pete Mitchell proposed. "More guns, more violent crime, more prisons." Nice theory, but gun crimes are a tiny slice of the crime problem, and crime does not strongly correlate to incarceration rate anyway.

As the regional breakdown shows, it's not crime – it's politics. The political will of a country's leaders dictate the country's incarceration rate. High incarceration is a choice – and it is politically motivated.

"But America isn't run by communists or right-wing extremists," Mel offered, "so what gives?"

I told Mel, we might be more extremist than we think. Taking America's two political parties – Democrats and Republicans – and comparing them to the left/right spectrum in other democracies, you emerge with the realization that there is no true "left" wing in America. We haven't had a viable Socialist Party since 1920, when Eugene V. Debs garnered a respectable number of votes for President – ironically, running from his federal prison cell, which is an indicator of how mainstream political forces feel about socialism in this country. When have no true "liberals" as found elsewhere in the world. In other countries, the political extremes range from socialism on the left to ultraconservatism on the right. The USA really only ranges from centrist to rightist. The Democratic Party isn't liberal at all when compared to the world's left-wingers.

Then, of America's two parties, which one has striven for hegemony in the law-and-order sphere? Which one called for massive prison construction in the 1920's, to go along with their ill-fated Prohibition Era? Which one called for the War on Drugs? Which one has made "tough on crime" a central tenet of its platform every year since 1968?

The Republican Party has infused itself into every position of authority in the American criminal justice system – to define crimes, prosecute defendants, escalate the sentencing ranges, and hand down the sentences. They have been particularly pervasive on the local level. Their anti-crime movement has employed the only tool they believed would work – incarceration.

It may not be "politically correct" in polite society to assign responsibility for mass incarceration to the Republican Party, but it is "historically correct," so it is a discussion Republicans are going to have to live with. They created a system that now holds more prisoners than Stalin's gulags held at their height. There are more Americans in prisons now than there were slaves in the South in 1820. Technically, America has the most oppressive due process system in world history. And this system is not about crime, it's about economic hegemony and social stratification – class warfare, the lifeblood of every plutocracy.

And they're correct, in one respect – all this is certainly *not* "politically correct."

+ + +

When it came to legal technicalities, habitual offenders were my most interesting class of prisoners. They had a knack for finding slivers of hope in the most mountainous haystacks, desperately concocting ways to question the methods used to append their enhanced sentences.

Robert Luetke's case was typical in that he had found a procedural error he thought would negate the habitual enhancement to his burglary conviction; yet atypical in that he also claimed he was innocent of the burglary. "I know you won't believe me, nobody does, but for real, I wasn't there to do no burglary."

An alarm had been triggered at a hardware outfit on the edge of Columbus, Indiana, and at around 3 a.m. Luetke and a codefendant were found hiding in a soybean field nearby. Neither had a word to say when they were arrested. Someone had gained entry to the store and run away when the alarm sounded. Luetke made a pretty good suspect, to say the least, and his four prior burglary convictions left the prosecutor with a pretty good hunch that Luetke was the burglar. Again.

"I swear to you, man, I swear," the chrome-domed Luetke persuaded me, "I wasn't there for no burglary. We went there to steal a tank of anhydrous ammonia parked out back. It was worth $2000."

Anhydrous ammonia, used in agriculture, is also an ingredient treasured by rural methamphetamine manufacturers. (It's also a component for explosives, ala Timothy McVeigh's 1995 bombing in Oklahoma City; but meth is it's most common illicit use.)

"Oh, so you're guilty of attempted felony theft, but not burglary?"

"Exactly. I know I can't prove that, but I can prove that the way they amended the charge to add the habitual was illegal. They amended it way past the omnibus date, and technically, they can't do that."

He was speaking of *Attebury v. State* (Ind. App. 1998), and I had heard it over a hundred times.

Attebury was a perfect interpretation of a state law, enforcing the edict of Indiana Code 35-34-1-5(e): "An amendment of an indictment or information to include a habitual offender charge must be made not later than ten (10) days after the omnibus date. However, upon a showing of good cause, the court may permit the filing of a habitual offender charge at any time before the commencement of trial."

Pretty simple. The omnibus date is normally set for 70 days past the arraignment date, and its purpose is to have both parties on notice of what charges will be presented, and what defenses will be raised.

In *Attebury*, the prosecutor ignored the statute and amended the charge far past the omnibus date. There was no hearing held to "show cause," and the court sat idly by, also ignoring the statute. The Court of Appeals reversed Attebury's habitual enhancement.

Some time between *Attebury*'s publication and subsequent high court rulings, some judges must have approached those who had written *Attebury* and asked, "What the hell were you thinking? You can't interpret a statute by merely applying it as it reads!"

A year later, in *Mitchell v. State*, the Indiana Supreme Court pointed out some things the *Attebury* court had overlooked. Did counsel object to amendment past the omnibus date? Did counsel seek a continuance? If not, the issue was waived. Effectively, *Attebury* was reversed. But no prisoner reading *Attebury* would know that unless they researched to see how *Attebury* was used in subsequent opinions.

Unfortunately, most prisoners stop digging once they see a gleam of gold in their pan.

Even when apprised of the *Mitchell* case, you can't blame them if they still like *Attebury* and think *Mitchell* is nonsense, because *Attebury* is the one that rationally interprets the law. There's a law. It's simple, spelled out by the legislature as a requirement, not as a suggestion. The state cannot amend the charge, without a good cause showing, more than ten days past the omnibus date. The court's function is to impartially follow the law. The statute is unambiguous – there are no ifs, unless this, or did someone object? Yet the courts decide they do *not* have to follow the law as it is written, or discern the plain intent of the legislature; but rather, they can exercise their unchecked judicial authority to invent exceptions to the law.

My frustration with habitual offenders and their incessant reliance upon *Attebury* had passed its breaking point, and I had given up trying to set men straight with the *Mitchell* opinion. When Luetke displayed assurance about his habitual filing, I said, "There's more to it than that. You'll find it's more complex than you think." Luetke intended to hire an attorney, so he would learn about the issue from a professional, someone more persuasive than me.

"I think your best way of getting a reversal, though," I advised him, "is to press the *Doyle* violation."

Luetke and his codefendant had exercised their Fifth Amendment right to remain silent – at arrest, in the months before trial, and all the way through trial until the state rested its case. When it was the defense's turn, they testified. "We both explained why we were hiding in the soybean field. We had heard about the anhydrous tank and went there to steal it. Somebody else happened to be burglarizing the place at the same time."

They were cross-examined relentlessly, with the questioning focused on why, if they weren't doing a burglary, they didn't say that when arrested? Why this story *now*? Why didn't they talk earlier? The state's closing argument centered on a common sense plea to the jury – if the defendants' testimonies were true, they'd have made these exculpatory statements before trial.

The facts and the law fell perfectly in line with the U.S. Supreme Court case, *Doyle v. Ohio* (1976). Doyle had used the same strategy as Luetke, waiting until trial to tell his story, and Doyle's prosecutors used this lapse against him. The court held that "it would be fundamentally unfair and a deprivation of due process to allow the arrested person's silence to be used to impeach an explanation subsequently offered at trial." Or else, what's a Miranda warning's value, if the right to remain silent can be used against you? A new trial was required.

Luetke liked the *Doyle* issue I had found, but he was more certain about the tardy habitual filing. He hired an attorney, and later told me, "My lawyer says I've got a good chance getting the habitual knocked off. He says your *Doyle* issue is good too," and by the way he said it, I could tell his law jockey would ride the *Attebury* case to its inevitable conclusion and relegate the *Doyle* violation to also-ran status. "All I need to go home," said Luetke, hopefully, "is to get the habitual taken off."

I doubted he would get any relief, but I remembered Serour's advisement, and held my tongue. Luetke had hope, and I wasn't going to pull that from beneath him.

Mel-T voiced a common opinion regarding habitual offender statutes. "They're all really double jeopardy. You're being punished a second time for offenses you've already served time on."

That argument is why the state calls the habitual offender sentence an "enhancement."

"Enhancement, my ass," said Edgar Lee. "Put it in monetary terms so that the average person can understand. It's like if you were late paying your $800 rent, and the third time that happened they hit you with a $2000 late fee."

"It's much worse than that," said Mel. "It's flat out against the Constitution to be twice put in jeopardy for the same offense. Trouble is, the courts made up some excuse to let it slide." Habitual enhancements could be declared double jeopardy tomorrow if the Supreme Court so desired. "If they wanted drug dealing to carry a 20-to-80 year range they should have made it that in the first place."

"Well," I offered in the state's defense, "80 years might be a little steep, unless it was your third time doing it."

"That's just it," Edgar Lee shot back, "it could be your first drug conviction and your two priors were theft and burglary – you still get the enhancement on the Class A dealing conviction, like you're a habitual drug dealer, when you ain't!"

"Habitual *offender*," I stressed, "not habitual drug dealer."

"But the sentence is enhanced for drug dealing, which is an extra 30 years, even though you've never dealt drugs but one time. If you had picked up the felonies in reverse order – dealing, burglary, and then theft – you'd get an extra 2-to-6 years, not thirty."

Which proves the defendant is not being punished for being a habitual *offender*, but being punished for the current *offense*. The courts are dead wrong: double jeopardy should apply.

"What I really object to about the habitual," noted Mel, "is the pretext that we should be punished more severely because we 'didn't learn' from being in prison the first time." Actually, habitual statutes don't require the defendant to have done prison time before – two terms of felony probation are sufficient.

"Didn't learn?" Edgar Lee was likewise incredulous. "What the fuck were we supposed to learn? What were we taught? We sat in a warehouse, counting off one fucked up day after another. We learned to survive in a fucked up environment. We learned that the state would pay millions of dollars to keep us locked up, but wouldn't pay shit to give us education or vocational training. We learned that a release plan was a hundred dollars and a bus ticket back to the same fucked up neighborhood we came from. We learned street game, and how to make connections in the criminal world, because that's all that was being taught in prison." Edgar Lee came to his summation. "Didn't learn? Oh, we learned alright."

"And we're penalized more severely because we didn't learn. Learn?" asked Mel. "Man, everybody learns in prison. Just not what people want them to learn."

"True dat!" Edgar Lee nodded like this was the commonest knowledge.

"Prisoners learn that nobody gives a fuck about them," Mel continued. "Free world people comment all the time about how easy they think we got it in here, that it's supposed to be bad, and should be worse. So we learn that society is against us, now and forever." Mel saw a clear division, a caste of untouchable ex-convicts that society refused to hire, refused to rent to, refused to accept. "Sometimes I wonder why any ex-prisoner would even want to assimilate back into society. Fuck them. They treat us like shit, they finance these places and turn their heads away – they deserve whatever naturally happens from this system they built."

Another voice chimed in. "They thought I was bad when they put me in prison. I was just doing what I had to do out there to get by. I wasn't trying to 'Get Rich or Die Tryin'," he said, alluding to the title of a popular CD by rapper 50 Cent. "I was just trying to survive. They think I was bad then, just wait 'til I get out."

"Like mistreating a dog in a cage. You let him out and then act surprised when he bites you."

"The dog didn't learn!" Laughter.

"Hit him with a stick! Pepper spray that dog! Lock him back up and see if he learns the second time."

"Aw, shit, he's biting us again! Lock that dog up for life!"

We laughed, but there were 944 five-by-ten cages housing humans in our facility, and 240 eight-by-ten two-man cages. A paltry few received any meaningful education – education is not a constitutional right. Virtually none of the prisoners – only 2% statewide – receive substance abuse treatment, even though 81% come in with substance abuse issues. Rehabilitation is not a constitutional right either. The only right in play was the state's right to confine its citizens.

Mel had spent decades arguing these same points, and he was running out of air – figuratively, and literally. He lapsed into another coughing fit, and departed with a final thought. "You ask me, the state is the habitual offender. They keep doing the same stupid shit over and over, and they don't learn."

The quest for rescue by technicality is pursued in every prison in America, every day. In G-cellhouse I listened to a guy tell me that when he testified at trial he was impeached by felony convictions that were more than ten years old. "Evidence Rule 609 says they can't bring up any conviction more then ten years old, and when I testified in 2008 they used my 1993 burglary conviction because I'd been locked up for 6 of the 15 years since 1993. The state says the 6 years don't count because I was locked up, but I got all these federal cases saying the opposite. The feds say it doesn't matter whether you've been locked up or not, ten years is ten years."

"The feds interpret Rule 609 exactly as it reads; the State of Indiana does not. The state courts have their own definition of what ten years is."

"But the state rule is exactly the same as the federal rule! The state copied the rule from the feds!"

"Doesn't matter," I explained, with no way to justify the state court rulings with anything approaching common sense. "Federal rules only apply to federal cases. The state rules, although identical, word-for-word, apply only to state cases, and are interpreted only by state courts. Whatever a federal court says about Rule 609 does not apply to you."

"That don't make no sense! The two rules are exactly alike. How can the feds say it means one thing, and Indiana say it means something else?"

State sovereignty. That's just the way it is.

At least he was trying. Quite a few men get into seg units and their behavior regresses to a juvenile stage. Lunch trays were being passed out near me, and in the process a piece of white cake hit the floor behind me.

"Where'd that cake come from?" Two cells down, some goofball was eyeballing the filthy hunk of cake.

"I don't know," said his neighbor. "It musta fell outa somebody's ass."

"Hey, law clerk," giggled the first. "You got cake falling out your ass!"

A female counselor came down the range, and they turned their focus to her. She stopped at a cell to confer with a prisoner, and as she did so the guy I was talking to stopped mid-sentence and began to stare, like a dog waiting for a meatball to roll off the table.

"Hey, how 'bout I get back to you later?" His eyes were fixed on the woman's outline.

"Yeaaaaah, later...." Eyes glazed over, his hand was traveling into his pants as I stepped away.

Back in the law library, I eavesdropped on a trio strategizing to end the IDOC's practice of taking away visiting privileges when prisoners received disciplinary write-ups. "Technically, man," said one, "the law's pretty clear. The statute says they can't fucking do that, no matter what our dumbass Court of Appeals says." They were referring to *Malone v. Butts* (Ind. 2012), and technically, they were right.

Indiana Code 11-11-3-9 states that visits can only be restricted when the visit "would threaten the security of the facility, or program, or safety of individuals," and I.C. 11-11-5-4 states that disciplinary punishments may not include "restrictions on visitation." So what the IDOC does to get around the law is to wait a week after a prisoner is found guilty of a disciplinary infraction, and take away visiting privileges as an "administrative action."

Caught with a cell phone? No visits, six months. Caught with hooch? Visits gone, one year. The "administrative actions" escalate, and some lose their visits permanently, for infractions having no conceivable nexus to the visiting room. The administration doesn't even pretend the visits can be classified as a "threat" under the Indiana Code; it's simply an administrative decision, and unappealable.

Dozens of Indiana prisoners have butted up against *Malone v. Butts* and gotten nowhere. The Indiana courts have the IDOC's back.

I prepared Donnie Ware for his PC hearing by drafting long sets of questions he could use to query his attorneys on their performance. I also tried to teach him how to conduct himself, and how and when to make objections. It was like a miniature trial, and he had to go it alone since his family's promised few thousand dollars for a PC attorney never materialized.

"I'm never going to get this stuff," Donnie confessed one afternoon. "I know when I get in there, they're gonna run all over me."

"You can handle it, Donnie," I said. "Believe me, it won't be so bad. Just stick to the script, no matter what they do."

I sent him off to Marion County, and a week later he came back, unsure if he had done well or not.

"I did like you said. Even when they objected to my questions, I just kept on, reading from the list you gave me." The tactic worked – eventually they quit objecting and soldiered through Donnie's questions.

He did great. At the end of the hearing he presented the court with a written request for a transcript of the PC hearing, something (oddly) a petitioner has no constitutional right to have until an appeal is filed. The cordial request worked (it has worked every time, in my experience), and I read that Donnie had successfully entered exhibits into the record, persevered through numerous objections, and gotten the replies we needed to prove ineffective assistance. The issues he had raised regarding jury instructions and double jeopardy – the attorneys proved themselves unacquainted with these particular issues and their supporting case law.

"You did good, Donnie," I congratulated. "Way better than most. Most cases, the guy comes back and I've got nothing useful to work with." In Donnie's case the deputy prosecutor actually remarked about the confounding jury instruction, "That's the way murder works. If they find the defendant guilty of murder, they [the jurors] don't have to consider the lesser included offenses."

It was gold. Sure, the whole issue was a mere technicality, the use of a confusing jury instruction that forced a murder conviction when voluntary manslaughter or reckless homicide was the correct charge, but it was the kind of technicality that mattered, the kind that would change a guilty finding to a not guilty finding. It would not be harmless error.

"And technically, they can't do that, right?" Donnie was catching on.

"Technically, that's right."

What's a technicality, anyway? It's a violation of a rule. The rules to any game are arbitrary. The law is nothing but technicalities, made-up rules for a made-up game.

CHAPTER SEVEN

The Margins of Society

"Individuals are forced to make choices in an environment they did not choose. They would surely prefer to have a broader array of good opportunities. The question we should be asking . . . is whether denizens of the ghetto are entitled to a better set of options, and if so, whose responsibility it is to provide them."
– Tommie Shelby, political theorist

CO Red jangled into the law library one quiet afternoon, a half hour before closing, to deliver another unsolicited opinion. "This prison was built on drugs and alcohol," he proclaimed.

We were unimpressed. That most prisoners had substance abuse problems was no revelation, so we offered no reply. Where was he going with this?

"That's right," Red continued, taking our silence as agreement. "Alcohol's prohibition built this prison in 1923, and the crack epidemic caused the expansion in 1986." He was referring to the 1980's construction of five dorms comprising I-Complex. Each dorm held 48 single cells, but they were converted to double-bunk housing for 480 men in short order as the prison population swelled. "Those two things," Red said, in educator mode, "drugs and alcohol, cause most of the crime in this country, and that's why we have places like this."

Red's analysis, probably parroted from the conservative talk radio program he had just heard, had the allure of being easy to comprehend in a world where the simple explanation is most likely the best explanation. Perfect causality – mass incarceration is a result of crime, crime is a result of bad actions, bad acts flow naturally from the use of drugs and alcohol. Bad people shoulder the blame because they made bad choices – mainly, the choice to use drugs. The solution? Also simple. Lock up the bad people, crack down on drugs, and crime will go down. It's a question of public safety, and the logic appears unassailable.

Mel-T had come over at 3 p.m. to discuss some legal work I was doing for him. Mel passed Red's post daily on his way to his job as a chaplain's clerk, and he held a simmering contempt for Red. They were ideologically polar opposites.

"Red, you fucking dumbass." I rarely heard Mel use foul language. He reserved it to stress certain points in an argument, or to provocatively offend someone. "Lemme ask you this. Do you think the incarceration rate is driven by the crime rate?"

Red wasn't offended, only challenged. He had picked the fight, so there was no backing out now. He gave Mel a sour look, as if it was ludicrous to suggest that crime is not the proximate cause of incarceration.

"Of course it is. How could anybody think otherwise?"

"You're saying, the more crime there is, the more the state has to put people in prison? You say that's what's goin' on here?"

"Sure. More crime, more people to lock up. And there's more crime because there's more drugs."

Mel turned to me. "Show him the numbers you showed me the other night."

I had built a spreadsheet over several months, collecting a wide range of data on state rankings in various categories. In column one was each state's incarceration rate. Subsequent headings ranked the states by crime rate, violent crime rate, murder rate, poverty, high school dropout rate, and ethnicity. Minorities were listed in individual columns, and collectively. I was searching for the strongest correlation to incarceration.

Far right on the spreadsheet were categories seemingly unrelated to incarceration, something of a control group of data. Population, geographical area, population density. Health statistics. Obesity, mortality rates, drug overdoses, Cesarean delivery rates (Louisiana #1). Percent of population without health insurance (Texas #1, Massachusetts #50). Divorce rates (Nevada #1, of course, followed by Arkansas, Oklahoma, West Virginia). Personal income.

Crude oil production. Party affiliation in state legislatures. Voting patterns in presidential elections. Motor vehicle registration per capita. You name it, if it had the 50 states ranked, I added it to my database. You will never discover hidden causalities or surprising indicators if you don't look.

The formula to correlate paired data sets is fairly simple, and well-known to anyone who remembers taking statistics in college. Each column in my research was compared to the incarceration rate, and a number between +1 and -1 was the result. A +1 indicated perfect correlation, and a -1 meant perfect negative, or inverse, correlation. A zero indicated no correlation at all, perfect randomness. I applied the formula to all 88 columns, and sorted them left to right by their divergence from zero.

I took a sheet of paper out of my portfolio, a copy of the data I had shown Mel. On it were the columns of data most presume would have the greatest effect on incarceration – violent crime, ethnicity, et cetera. I briefly explained to Red what I had done, and the sources of my data. [See Appendix 3.]

"You'll see here in the second column, Red, that the greatest correlation to the incarceration rate is not the crime rate. It's the poverty rate. The crime rate," I said, moving my finger far right, "whether it's violent crime, property crime, murder, or whatever, has a much lower correlation."

There was much to learn from this relatively simple data. "Notice that the second highest correlation is with education. First is poverty, second is the high school dropout rate." Which were, in themselves, connected. Dropouts earn less.

Red took a minute to scan through the numbers and seized on the most obvious – a geographic connection to high incarceration rates. Most of the states with extremely high imprisonment numbers were in the South. Louisiana was number one, Mississippi was number two.

"Doesn't this prove," Red asked, "that states with high percentages of black population – no offense," he said to Mel, who waved the comment aside, "have the highest incarceration rates?"

I led him to the column showing state rankings in black population and minorities in general. "We looked at that hard, and while there is some correlation, a stronger correlation than crime rates, it's still not as strong as the two biggest factors – poverty and education."

STATES' CORRELATIONS TO INCARCERATION RATE
50 U.S. States (2010)

INC – Poverty Rate	.634
INC – Dropout Rate	.553
INC – Black Population	.539
INC – Republican voting, President, 2012	.528
INC – Property Crime Rate	.496
INC – Violent Crime Rate	.494
INC – Minority Population	.489
INC – Land Area	.147
INC – Population Density	-.020

Red thought for a moment. "Well, this isn't really surprising. I can see the connection. Makes sense. Poverty leads to crime, crime leads to incarceration."

"Wrong!" I scolded Red. "You are misreading the data. If poverty caused crime, and crime caused incarceration, then the correlation between crime and incarceration would be *higher* than the correlation between poverty and incarceration." I placed my finger on the poverty column. "Poverty has the highest correlation to incarceration, not crime. Which tells us the criminal justice system is driving more people into prison simply because poor people can't defend themselves against this system."

Red fished around for a response. "You can't get arrested for being poor," he said. "You get arrested for committing a crime. I still say crime causes incarceration."

"I'm not saying it doesn't take a crime to get a person put in prison. I'm saying if you take two states, or even two counties in Indiana, and they have the *same* crime rates, for some reason one jurisdiction is filling the prison at a rate five or six times higher then the other jurisdiction. And the reason for this, if you look at the data, is a conservative Republican set of local prosecutors and judges preying upon people in poverty who cannot defend themselves."

Mel jumped in. "Two states, same crime rate, they should have about the same incarceration rate, right?"

Red shrugged. "Pretty much."

"But they don't. The state with the higher poverty rate, that'll be the state with the higher incarceration rate. Not because the poor committed more crimes," Mel reasoned, "but because the poor are getting shafted in court."

"What sets it off the worst," I added, "is when conservative types are making the law enforcement decisions – who to target. And the prosecutorial decisions – who to imprison. And the sentencing decisions – how long to imprison them. The poor in a conservative political environment is the perfect storm for mass incarceration."

The four o'clock bell was imminent, and Red trudged out with the data sheet. I hoped he understood that this undermined the first plank of his logic, that the incarceration rate was solely a function of crime. Sure, crime mattered – one person breaking the law was the first step in that person's journey to jail. Every person caught breaking a serious law, rich or poor, went to jail, at least temporarily. But the factor most determinative of whether they went to prison, and for how long, was poverty.

Then, if you entertained the idea of remedying the poverty-incarceration connection, column two provided the solution. Education. Nothing reduces poverty like education, because it increases earning potential. Educate the poor to lift them out of poverty, and as a collateral consequence, see a drop in the incarceration rate.

Spend money on schools, or spend money on prisons.

"I like what you did with Red," Mel told me later. Mel had moved to another dorm, so we didn't get to talk as often. We made Fridays at lunch our designated half hour for discussions. "But I gotta tell ya, as a black man, your numbers don't explain why blacks are locked up at a rate six times higher than whites. Only a racist criminal justice system explains that."

I was loathe to contradict Mel on issues of race, having never been black and therefore unqualified to speak experientially on being black in America. Mel's sensors were surely more finely tuned to detect racism, something whites are rarely forced to think about. I once joked with Mel, "Do you ever get to take a vacation from racism?" "No," he said, shaking his head wearily, "it's all day every day, for life." Nevertheless, I thought my data could illuminate how racism affects the astoundingly high rate of incarceration of black Americans.

"Since poverty is the number one predictor of incarceration, ask yourself, who lives in poverty?"

"Blacks. Minorities."

"Exactly." I used a World Almanac to show Mel some poverty statistics. "The poverty rate hit its lowest point in 2000, after eight years of Clinton being in office – 11.3%. By 2012 it had crept up to 15.0%. But for blacks, no surprise, it's still 27.1%, while for whites it's 12.7%. Blacks are more than twice as likely to live in poverty."

"Okay," said Mel, "but that doesn't match the six times rate of blacks getting arrested and incarcerated."

I turned the page. "You're right. What *really* explains it is the number of single-parent female households living in poverty. You have kids growing up with little adult supervision, coupled with poverty." In 2012 there were 4,793,000 such households – 2,774,000 white, 1,624,000 black, and 395,000 other. "Check out the percentages," I said. "It's 57.9% white, 33.9% black, 8.2% other. Since blacks make up 12.2% of the U.S. population . . ."

". . . then blacks are almost three times more likely to come from a lone female parent household living in poverty."

"Wrong. You fell into a common math misconception. It's closer to *four* times more likely." I showed him how if 12.2% of the population has a 33.9% rate, and whites at 74.6% account for 57.9% of those with an impoverished single female parent, the math is: (33.9/12.2) divided by (57.9/74.6), which equals a 3.58 times higher rate. About three and a half times as likely to come from a type of home life that is a serious recipe for trouble.

Statisticians Steven Levitt and Stephen J. Dubner, in their book, *Freakonomics*, likewise found that "...childhood poverty and a single-parent household are among the strongest predictors that a child will have a criminal future." Curiously, they also correlated abortion rates to crime rates, albeit with an 18-year lag between the two. Fewer abortions, more crime eighteen years later. (If you're anti-abortion, you are, by default, pro-crime.)

"Still," argued Mel, "that doesn't match the six times higher rate of blacks getting arrested and incarcerated. You've explained a little bit of the problem, but I think the rest of the problem is explained purely by racism in this country."

I wasn't done with the numbers. There was one more criminogenic factor to take into account.

"Geography is to blame for a higher rate of black involvement in crime and in the incarceration that results. Blacks are over-represented as a portion of the urban population, wouldn't you agree?"

"That's pretty obvious. Not many blacks living out in the sticks."

The numbers I showed Mel bore out what we presumed. I had the U.S. Census data from the top 100 cities, with their racial compositions. In these big cities, 57.0% were white, 21.7% black, 21.3% other. In Indiana, 68% of the black population lived in the three largest urban areas. "Since 21.7% in the cities are black, and 12.2% of the U.S. population is black, blacks are over-represented in cities by a factor of 1.78." (21.7/12.2) = 1.78.

Why would urban environment matter? Why would it be more conducive to high incarceration rates? The answer is a function of geography – closer contact with other human beings means more interactions, more opportunities for crime. It's also easier for police to find people to arrest in a densely-populated area. They target impoverished neighborhoods. A racially-motivated philosophy toward policing has been thoroughly documented by Michelle Alexander in *The New Jim Crow.*

Mel and I talked about the neighborhoods with which we were familiar. I told him about all-white towns where the kids are all "bored to death," with nothing to do. Not a lot of temptation around. He told me about "the hood" in Indianapolis, Chicago, Detroit. When bored, kids brave enough to venture outside in an impoverished environment could find plenty of things going on, most of them bad. Not pick-up games of baseball like I experienced in my youth.

"Here's where the data really gets interesting," I told Mel. "We know from Department of Justice data that blacks are imprisoned at a rate of 3,023 per 100,000 population, and for whites it's 478 per 100,0000. By comparison, blacks are 6.32 times more likely to get locked up."

"That's what I've been saying, six times more likely."

"You take the higher likelihood of living in poverty in a single female household – 3.58 times more likely – and compound that by the 1.78 times more likely rate of living in a large city. Multiply the two, 3.58 times 1.78, and you get 6.37 times more likely to live in what statisticians consider the most crime-predictive environment in America."

Mel was surprised by this data, as was I when I discovered it. The 6.37 predictive number was less than 1% off the actual 6.32 number.

"So what we really need to ask," said Mel, "is how racism causes all this."

We had learned the history of racism during our studies in the Anthropology and Sociology classes we had taken together at Ball State University. We had both read numerous books on the subject, and I proposed to Mel that there are two kinds of racism: passive racism and active racism. Passive racism involves holding prejudicial beliefs. Active racism is acting on those beliefs to unfairly deny resources.

"In my opinion," I told Mel, "active racism comes into play, causing all these problems for the black community, as a result of power-holding white leaders denying blacks equal access to jobs, housing, and education. This is done mainly by government officials and business owners, the ones who control the resources."

Schools are not funded equally. To spend government education funds equally would require allocating the money on a basis of dollars per student. Instead, school districts are funded by levying taxes based on property values – wealthy areas can afford to provide good schools, poor areas cannot.

Jobs are not equally available, due to discriminatory hiring practices and the relocation of jobs far from black residential areas. As 71-year-old former Gary, Indiana, resident Leo Dent, Sr., told me one day, "Back in my day, we [blacks] all had manufacturing jobs. Now those jobs are gone. No industry exists for this new generation." And sometimes jobs are not available because of the first factor, education. It is difficult for a business owner to hire any person who does not have the education or training to do the job.

Globalism, a force curtailing American job opportunities, also brought interesting sources of our commissary items. We bought salmon from China, beef from Brazil, and corn from Thailand. Corn! We were surrounded by thousands of square miles of corn, yet it was cheaper to buy corn grown in Asia and shipped 9,000 miles.

The other factor affecting criminal futures, single parent households, seems like a cultural choice until one considers the feedback loop involved. Sending more men to prison causes more kids to grow up in a single parent setting. For every adult in prison, there are 1.8 children without a parent. For the black community, the number is higher because while 19.7% of the white population is under 18 years old, 26.6% of the black population is under 18. Black kids bear the brunt of the government's high incarceration rate of black men.

"You want to see a statistic that'll blow your mind, Mel, check this out." I opened the World Almanac to a section titled *Living Arrangements of Children in the U.S. by Parental Presence*. "Kids with two-parent households: Whites, 74%; Hispanics, 66%; Blacks, 38%. For black kids, the 'normal' household situation is a one-parent home. And those one-parent households are also the ones overwhelmingly more likely to live in poverty. One income, from one parent, who usually is not home."

"That's a lot of kids running the streets with little to no supervision," noted Mel. No kidding, I thought. With nearly a million black adults in prison, nearly two million black children were left to cope with an imprisoned parent. One in four black kids will have a parent in prison at some time during their childhood.

"I'd say most of the guys who come in here, who establish a so-called 'criminal career', first come in when they're under 25 years old."

Mel agreed. "They come to prison and get nothing. No guidance, no education, no vocations, no counseling, no nothing." Mel had seen thousands come and go. He would tell every kid he cared about, "Try to leave this place better than when you came in." Most did not. Or they applied that advice in the wrong way – getting physically stronger, or more cunning, or more well-connected to the wrong people. What else was there?

"What your data also proves," Mel concluded, "is that blacks are not any more criminally prone than any other group. Put any group in the same kind of situation – poverty, broken families, bad schools, no jobs – and then put conservatives in charge of the local criminal justice system, and high incarceration rates will be the result."

Ned McConnell would have disagreed.

"These people are pretty much like I figured," Ned snickered dismissively as he alluded to our fellow prisoners on the yard. "A bunch of incorrigibles. Damn near all of them are exactly where they're supposed to be." Ned had only been at Pendleton a few months when he sidled up to me with this comment. Like anyone voicing a conclusory opinion, he presumed he was entertaining a like-minded audience.

"Some definitely belong here," I replied, noncommittally. Ned interpreted this as agreement, and forged ahead.

"I never lived around 'em before," Ned continued, "but the stereotypes are true. Blacks are lazy and violent. No morals. Hispanics are simple and illiterate, most of 'em fit for nothing but manual labor. Then there's the white trailer trash, a bunch of drunks and dopers. I was going to get a job as a tutor, but then I looked around me and said, What's the point? They're too stupid to learn."

I was just getting acquainted with Ned at that time. We had only spoken a few times, mostly about golf. He had considered becoming a golf instructor, then fell into the more lucrative occupation of selling pharmaceuticals for a large drug company. He was a "drug dealer," but of the legal kind. Pushing Oxycontin to pharmacists.

We were a distinct minority behind Pendleton's gray walls, two white guys sans tattoos, college-educated, former homeowners who had enjoyed steady employment. I had owned a land surveying business, employing six people, specializing in residential surveys. Ned and I both pulled down close to six figures per year. He was recently divorced at the time of his arrest; I was about to be married. He lived in an upscale all-white subdivision north of Indianapolis; I lived on Indy's east side, in the Warren Park enclave, an older and less trendy neighborhood, but one demographically similar to Ned's location in Boone County. From all our commonalities Ned presumed we held similar social attitudes, a presumption I frequently received from conservative Republican types (how Ned described his political affiliation). I listened to him quietly, almost stealthily, searching for the tenor of a response that would elicit more of his worldview.

"A lot of them got behind in school early and couldn't catch up," I offered. "Some had bad schools, and some simply never understood the value of an education."

"Well, it's not my fault they fell behind. All I know is, I'm not going to waste my time with 'em."

After hearing Ned, I thought, This is a guy who needs to read some green sheets.

A "green sheet" is a prisoner's pre-sentence investigation (PSI) report. A PSI is compiled by the county probation office prior to a convicted person's sentencing, to provide the court a profile of the defendant before an appropriate sentence is determined. Along with the defendant's criminal history, both adult and juvenile, the PSI summarizes the person's home life, education, employment history, physical health, mental health, financial status, and any commentary the defendant has given to the interviewer. Since it contains confidential information, it is printed on light green paper to foil reproduction via most copy machines.

Sometimes the PSI is so highly personal, or embarrassing, prisoners won't give it to me when I ask to see their legal papers. When they exclude it I say nothing, unless we are exploring a sentencing issue where the judge allegedly failed to consider potential mitigating circumstances. In those cases, the green sheets are necessary.

A few weeks after Ned offered his remarks, he visited the library while I was working on Martin Blair's case. Martin was Ned's age, but on every other detail he was the opposite of Ned. Martin was black, had grown up excruciatingly poor, and was in contact with the criminal justice system at a very young age. This was Martin's third stretch in prison, and this time he had 50 years – 20 for criminal confinement, 30 more for being a habitual offender.

A white couple had approached Martin to buy crack. Martin, burned once before, suspected they were informants trying to make an undercover buy. Ever cautious, Martin led them to a concealed area down an alley, held both at gunpoint, and had them lift their shirts and consent to a pat down to make sure they weren't wearing a wire. When one "substantially interferes with the liberty of a person," criminal confinement has occurred, regardless of the duration or purpose of the detention.

The cops got involved when they spied the out-of-place duo, post-purchase, and presumed they were on a drug-buying mission in Martin's impoverished neighborhood. They pulled the two over, feigned omniscience, and the girl immediately cooperated, hurriedly telling them about the black drug dealer in the alley with a gun.

A back-up unit sped through the alleys, and its searchlight fell on Martin, who ran. It was a long foot chase, and by the time Martin was handcuffed he had stripped himself of dope, gun, and money. "You got nothing on me," Martin hollered from the back of the patrol car. Running from the police is only a misdemeanor.

Martin's arresting officer rolled over to his partner's squad car, had the girl get out, and she identified Martin as the person who had held her at gunpoint. The white guy, who had been to prison before, was an intentionally poor witness, not sure if it was Martin they'd dealt with or not. But the girl was 100% certain about a lot of things – that Martin Blair sold crack, that he pointed a gun at her, and that she never wanted to smoke crack or get arrested again. She just wanted to return to the safety of her suburban lifestyle where there were no alleys and no armed black drug dealers. She said in her official statement, "I promise you, I'm going back to church starting on Sunday."

Ned had selected some books and was in a lounge chair waiting for pass line movement at the top of the hour. I plopped down beside him with Martin's green sheets. "Check this out." It was the only time I violated a prisoner's confidence by showing his PSI to another person.

Ned read fast, then slowed perceptibly as Martin's home life was described. He re-read some sections, and his proclamations (Damn! Jeeesh!) grew quieter as he absorbed more info about the Blair household. "Damn," he said as he finished. "That's pretty messed up."

"Ned, I see this stuff all the time."

Martin Blair was born in 1975, the fifth of his mother's seven children. She had never married, and her seven kids had three fathers. The first man in her life had been murdered, assailant unknown. The next two didn't stick around long – both were alcoholics, abusive to her and to the kids.

Martin's father exited Martin's life bound for prison when Martin was a toddler. The family frequently changed residences in Muncie, in and out of public housing due to evictions, forced out onto the streets at times. They squatted in abandoned houses, rigging extension cords from other houses to get electricity, and toting water from any open spigot they could find. School was hit-and-miss for all seven kids, and child protective services were constantly involved in their lives.

Martin was placed in foster care and treated for malnutrition when he was six – that's also the first time he saw the inside of a school. He experienced three foster homes in a year, then the family was reunited in a small cinderblock apartment in a public housing unit. These were the Reagan years, when the cost of living was rising and the outrage over "welfare queens" prompted cuts to social safety nets like welfare and food stamps. Like his siblings, Martin was picked up for shoplifting so many times that he was informally banned from every grocery store and convenience store within walking distance.

Two older brothers fell into the neighborhood's default industry, drug dealing, the low-level distribution end of the multi-billion dollar drug trade so feared by the government. When crack revolutionized the cocaine market, enabling dealers to sell twenty dollar amounts instead of more expensive powder quantities, Martin's brothers were swept up in the law-and-order backlash, and were soon consigned to careers in prison. Martin became the "little man" of the family in 1988, at age 13.

Far behind his peers in school from day one, Martin was twice held back a grade. At 14, school was over. He was sent to juvenile detention for burglary. Released a year later, he found his mother addicted to crack and his neighborhood a raging battlefield in the War on Drugs. A gun was necessary for survival. In April of 1992 Martin was handling an acquaintance's handgun and accidentally – it was indisputably an accident – shot and killed a man.

Martin, at 17, was charged with murder in adult court. Or rather, overcharged with murder. Martin's confession, the eyewitness statements, and the physical evidence clearly framed the shooting as an accident, but the prosecutor chose the highest level felony in order to obtain a stiffer plea agreement on Martin's actual offense, a Class C reckless homicide.

Martin agreed to the maximum sentence, eight years. The maximum term is supposed to be reserved for the "worst of the worst," so say the appellate courts, but this principle can be circumvented when a defendant expressly agrees to the max on a lower level felony and receives the benefit of getting a more onerous charge dismissed.

Despite being a juvenile, Martin was sent directly to adult prison. He received little incentive to participate in education or programs, and at his age he often fought and spent lengthy periods in solitary confinement. His mental health assessment shows professional concerns about paranoia and delusions in 1995 and 1996, just prior to his release. Of course, there was no treatment.

Once he got out he was in no better position to function in society than when he went in. He returned to prison within a year, a stint at Westville, his time spent learning new ways to buck authority and tolerate solitary confinement.

At his sentencing on his current charge I noted with irony the judge's statement that Martin had "failed to learn" from prior IDOC commitments. On the 16-to-50 range, Martin was declared totally incorrigible, deserving the 50-year max.

Failed to learn? Oh, he'd learned alright. He'd learned from his experiences since he was in diapers. He had learned that the world was a sad place, filled with poverty, hunger, and violence. Through Martin's eyes the world must have appeared as Jack London described in *White Fang*:

> "...he might have epitomized life as a voracious appetite, and the world as a place wherein ranged a multitude of appetites, pursuing and being pursued, hunting and being hunted, eating and being eaten, all in blindness and confusion, with violence and disorder, a chaos of gluttony and slaughter, ruled over by chance, merciless, pitiless, endless."

Martin learned to steal to eat, he learned to fight to survive, he learned to carry a gun for protection, he learned cheap drugs could relieve his mind from the world around him. He learned that nobody, absolutely nobody, could be trusted. I'm not sure he learned that anybody cared.

Weeks before, after I had read Martin's PSI and we sat down to discuss his case, I felt compelled to say something about his personal history. It was hard to select the right words.

"Martin," I began, "I read your PSI. And I want to tell you, I'm sorry. I'm sorry you had to grow up the way you did." Our eyes met and I could see that nobody had ever said anything like this to him before. "I'm sure your parents loved you. And it's not their fault. They did what they could. But no child." Long pause. "In America." Long pause. "Should have to go through all the difficulties you faced. This country . . . is supposed to be better than that." Martin stared unblinkingly into my face, and nodded almost imperceptibly. "And I'm sorry you had to go through all that."

The adage, "It takes a village to raise a child," has a corollary. It takes a village to ruin a child, too.

Not every detail about Martin's life was listed in the PSI, so I filled in Ned on other info Martin had given me. "And Ned," I added, "you wanna know what's really messed up? This guy is actually quite intelligent. Unschooled, but smart. Some time in the past fifteen years he discovered books and figured out there's more to the world than stealing and drug dealing. I talk to him about the law and give him cases to read, and he understands the legal concepts perfectly."

Ned just listened.

"He's not stupid; he's above average."

Ned had no response.

"He could have grown up to be anything he wanted, but when he was put into that environment," I said, nodding toward the green sheets, "what else would you really expect of him?"

"Yeah, it's messed up. He never had a chance."

"And I see this in case after case. Kids beat on, abused, truant, sexually abused, raised by one parent or by a grandparent. Or raised by the state. Nothing around them but negative role models, living in run-down housing projects or trailer parks where they encounter violence the moment they step out the door. Mostly black. But then, most of the whites and Hispanics I see in prison have similar backgrounds. By 'most' I mean around 90% come from poverty. It is by far the most common denominator of the people around us."

"Yeah, yeah, yeah," Ned spat, perking up. "I get why you're showing me this. But still, it all comes down to personal choices. You can choose to break the law, or choose not to break the law. They're here in prison because they broke the law, not because they're black or poor or anything else."

Here it was, the functionalist perspective of sociology, citing individual responsibility as determinative of a person's lot in life.

"Sure, it's about choices," I began, placidly. "But what poverty does is alter the range of available choices. In a poor neighborhood you've got fewer choices, and more bad options, making you more likely to make a bad choice.

What money does," I explained to Ned, "is expand the range of good choices while eliminating the bad."

I was familiar with the subdivision where Ned grew up. A child there could play golf or tennis, go swimming, or ride his bike on the street. There were well-coached, well-funded sports leagues. A kid there could stay home amid a subfranchise of Toys-R-Us and never be bothered. They had computers, X-Box, skateboards, and Barbie dolls. They wore brand-name clothes and never gave a thought to stealing someone else's sneakers, and they never got hungry enough to make shoplifting a pack of baloney seem tempting. They didn't see crack being peddled on the street corner, and didn't see women furtively ducking into strange vehicles. The prospect of becoming a drug dealer isn't within the imagination of most ten-year-old kids in a wealthy subdivision.

A kid in a wealthy neighborhood has hundreds of choices, and has to look hard to find a bad one. A kid in "the hood," no matter his color, has very few choices, many of them bad. That bad choices are made should not surprise us.

The culture of poverty effectuates a shift in morals. Morals, after all, are based on a social group's norms of behavior – not, as commonly thought, on religious codes, written rules, or laws. There are circumstances to justify stealing, just as there are circumstances to justify killing. One should not have to think too hard to conceive of situations where "good" people steal or kill.

In some communities, dealing drugs and carrying a gun can be rationalized in a way that negates evil intent. "Just trying to get by" is an expression I often heard from convicted drug dealers. They weren't aspiring to be drug kingpins. They didn't have visions of being the next Tony Montana. They were trying to survive in a world where their skill sets, collectively, did not match the few jobs available.

"I was getting' it the only way I knew how" is another well-worn excuse. At Pendleton I met dozens of drug dealers and only encountered two who were caught with more dope than could be concealed in the palm of one hand. The drug weights were almost exclusively less than five grams, the weight of a sugar packet, and if they went to trial the sentences were between 40 and 80 years, do half. Only the poorest of the poor would engage in an enterprise so obviously fraught with peril, and then only when it was the best option from a range of bad options.

"It's not that the poor lack morals," I told Ned, referring to his earlier opinion, "it's that they have developed a moral code adapted to their situation. It's a moral code very different from yours. And if we were to transplant your two kids into public housing, or one of the worst trailer parks, they would emerge with a similar set of morals, no matter what you tried to teach them."

"Yeah, I'll grant you that. I wouldn't want to try to raise my kids in the ghetto."

"Of course not. That's why, as a parent, one of the first things you consider when buying a house is, *Will my kid be safe?* And then, *Is it a good school district?* You do that because you know environment matters. *Environment matters*. A kid can't reach his full potential living in a bad environment."

"Yeah, environment matters," Ned conceded, "but not every poor black kid attending a bad school ends up in prison. Some rise above it and become doctors and lawyers and entrepreneurs. How do you explain *that*?"

Easy analogy. "Ned, it's like the link between cigarettes and cancer. Not everyone who smokes will get cancer, but those who do, without question, suffer a much greater risk of developing cancer. Same with a poor neighborhood – it doesn't guarantee a kid will go to prison, but it creates an environment conducive to crime and prison. Which is why you don't want your kid growing up there, if you can avoid it."

Ned was constitutionally resistant to empathizing with the world of poverty. How do you expect a man who's rich to understand a man who's poor?

We talked more about kids, the places we had lived, and the people we had encountered growing up. He had had it pretty good, Ned confessed, especially when compared to the little pocket of a dozen houses forming the nameless neighborhood where I had grown up. I had spent my formative years surrounded by a steel mill, a mental hospital, a truck lot, a tavern, and railroad tracks. My sister described my nephew's reaction when they turned off Route 24 to see the old neighborhood: "Why are we going to a dump?" I was twelve before I realized the creek I played in, catching crawdads, was actually an open sewer taking overflow from a dozen septic tanks.

"The culture of poverty is the same no matter where you live in America," I declared to Ned. It was almost time for him to go, so I retrieved from my desk copies of two essays, written by Jeremy Gross and Dujuan Emerson. Their essays were two of several testimonies I had collected for a booklet to be titled, *Prison is For Real*, a publication aimed at the 16 to 24 age group. Ned lived in O-dorm with Jeremy and knew Jeremy to be a very sharp, very intelligent, and industrious individual who had earned Associate's and Bachelor's degrees in prison, graduating with honors. Jeremy wrote:

> As a teen, I never thought I'd die in prison, but that's my reality now.
>
> The environment I came from wasn't the best. My parents both drank and fought a lot, which sometimes led to hospital visits for both. It ended in divorce after I watched my mom set my dad on fire while he slept. I was six then, and until age 18 I had little contact with my dad. He drank and spent most of his time in prison. My sister and I lived with our mom after her release from jail for arson. Mom drank, used drugs, and prostituted to support her habits. When mom disappeared for a few days, a neighbor alerted police, and we were placed in foster care. After a year we were returned to our mom, who had remarried and gained some stability but continued to drink and smoke weed. I still had no positive role models.
>
> I began drinking, smoking weed, fighting and stealing. At 15 I broke into a house and stole a gun, which I later used to rob a store. I was quickly arrested, and I spent two years in Boys' School. When I got out, I did all the same stuff and started using harder drugs. Then I got another gun. I figured that getting arrested couldn't result in anything worse than Boys' School.
>
> By this time I was 18, and Boys' School was no longer the punishment. I knew nothing about the law or the consequences I faced as an adult. Again wanting easy money, I robbed a convenience store. This time I shot and killed the clerk. Within hours I was arrested for murder and robbery. The prosecutor sought the death penalty. I never thought that the same robbery that got me two years in Boys' School would now result in me murdering a man and have me facing a death sentence.

> I was convicted and got life in prison without parole. In Indiana this means you are in prison until you die. I've spent more than half my life behind bars. At age 35, I probably have a long time before I die, and I know every moment will be spent in prison. I never knew that prison was for real, but it is.

Ned read Jeremy's passage silently, and offered only one comment: "He needed someone to give him some discipline when he was a kid." I semi-agreed, saying Jeremy sure lacked guidance, then asked Ned what he meant by "discipline."

"Someone to smack him up side the head," Ned jokingly replied. "He needed to know he would be punished when he did wrong."

"So punishment is the answer?"

"It's like touching a hot stove. It's how you learn. You can't change their behavior without it."

Between age 18 and age 35 Jeremy's behavior had changed quite a bit, and the evidence revealed punishment had little to do with it. His first few years in prison were rough, of course – imagine being a teenager in one of the worst prisons, serving life without parole. Most would ask themselves, *What's the difference whether I behave or not? What's the point in acquiring an education I can never use?* Jeremy went through that stage, then his natural intelligence and curiosity led him to enroll in college classes. With college as an incentive he cleaned up his act (a disciplinary write-up would cause expulsion). He learned, for the first time; and he came to value himself as a sentient, rational human being, also for the first time. He became a Christian, but kept his faith somewhat private – it was an aspect of his character he did not shoehorn into conversations, in contrast to other Christian prisoners who wear their faith on their sleeve. The rabidly faith-centered are referred to as the "God Squad," and Jeremy wasn't one of those. In all, threats and punishments had nothing to do with Jeremy's behavioral transformation.

I once asked Jeremy what kept him straight now. Why didn't he use drugs or alcohol any more? Why is he so careful to avoid trouble?

"I'm better than that," he said. It was such a simple, beautiful answer. "It's not who I want to be."

He could be released tomorrow and the only impact on the community would be one less job vacancy because of how fast he would find employment. And in time, given his skills, he would probably establish an enterprise that would *create* jobs.

I laid another essay on Ned, this one penned by Dujuan Emerson.

"Who's this guy?" asked Ned.

"Swanny. Black guy up in the PLUS program right now."

"No idea who that is." Ned didn't socialize much.

"I'd say Swanny is typical of thousands of black kids from the hood." Emerson's own words were these:

> I grew up in a very violent community. I felt I had to maintain a certain image in order to survive. I'm sure there are young men out there now who feel exactly the way I did twenty years ago.
>
> My mother had five other kids besides me, and we were poor and living in the projects, hungry and afraid at times from being exposed to a lot of drinking and violence. I went to school to have a good time instead of learning. My mother struggled to keep me in school. My father was a drug addict and an alcoholic. I thought I had to grow up fast, so I started hanging out with the wrong crowd. I began skipping school, selling marijuana, drinking, and carrying guns. By age 16, I was addicted to crack and was arrested often. I had many chances to change my life, but I didn't want to change.
>
> I had been in many fights and shootings, and I got stabbed when I was 17. I got shot on two different occasions, but that didn't slow me down. I was motivated by being a person that people would fear, so that I could have my way. I never stopped and identified who I had become.
>
> I became convicted of robbery and accomplice to murder, and the day I was sentenced my life changed forever. My future was gone. I didn't care about anything. I felt empty inside. Reality started to sink in – all the people I thought would be there for me had forgotten about me. When you're in prison, you're on your own.

> I gambled to make ends meet, and began doing things that I knew could get me in trouble. I had to almost lose my life before I realized that I had to change. My mother and the Lord helped me get through many stressful days. I asked God for forgiveness. I enrolled in the PLUS program. I learned that there are rules, and I had to follow them. Now my life has changed, dramatically for the better. I am now proud of who I have become, and I have my family's pride and respect. My pursuit in life is to live in a productive and loving way, helping others to find happiness in their life's journey.
>
> Will your journey be like mine? Or will you walk away from the wrong things you are doing, and be a man? The choice is staring you in the face right now. I say to everyone, don't rob yourself of your youth and your freedom.

"Another kid with no discipline," concluded Ned.

"So what do you think turned his life around?" I asked.

"Time, probably." Ned considered confinement the panacea. "Lots of time to sit and think about what a piece of shit he was."

The simple salve of time was not the solution for most prisoners. For every Jeremy there were ten other prisoners who had faced the same "hopeless" situation and had not changed a bit. For them, prison became a continuation of their street life – still selling drugs, gang-banging, robbing, stealing, getting high, gambling, making wine. "I'm a hustler," said one, echoing many. "This is what I do best. Ya gotta hustle to survive in prison. That's just the way it is." A day-to-day, hand-to-mouth existence.

Poverty's effects didn't end once a man graduated from defendant to prisoner. The same hierarchy of human needs identified by Maslow still applied, and the state only fulfilled the most basic needs – food, clothing, and shelter, and nominally, safety. In providing these needs, the state fell short in quantity and quality, and those prisoners who could afford to do so made up the difference with their own money. The "hustling" going on provided a profit margin sufficient to compensate for unprovided basic needs. A pillow? Four dollars. Sounds inexpensive to a free-world person, but at Pendleton it represents sixteen hours of state labor. Old clothes are free, new ones cost money. Double thick mattress? It'll cost plenty. Shoes, same deal. And who can survive every day without coffee, a snack, or a self-prepared meal to substitute for the 'savory stroganoff' that keeps reappearing on the Aramark menu? The solution, for nearly every prisoner, is to engage in some kind of hustle.

There are clean hustles and there are dirty hustles. The latter are more likely to get the hustler placed in the hole. Clean hustles don't violate major facility rules – such as Donnie washing clothes separately. Dirty hustles are dirty work – dope dealing, running gambling tickets, stealing from Aramark. Those hustlers take risks. Examine any poor community in the world and you will find the same kind of economic activity and the same acceptance of risk.

Mel and I were curious whether the states' poverty-incarceration rate correlation held up in years other than 2010. We also wondered if we could find a similar correlation on the county level. We pored through old World Almanacs and dozens of textbooks, creating spreadsheets for the years 1990 and 2000. We compared each state's ranking in various crime categories to the incarceration rate, looking for major differences from the correlations found in our study for the year 2010. There were none. Poverty again came first, most strongly correlated to the incarceration rate, followed by the high school dropout rate.

County comparisons within Indiana proved more challenging. The data we desired was almost exclusively acquired from Internet sources, thanks to the patient assistance of family members who found the data, printed it, and mailed it in. Over several months we accrued the most relevant numbers – incarceration rate by county (obtained from the IDOC), poverty rates, crime rates, black and minority populations, and a measure of political conservatism, derived from voters' 2012 preferences between President Obama and Republican candidate Mitt Romney.

We culled our data to Indiana's fifty largest counties. Forty-two smaller counties, under 30,000 population, often had no numbers to report, and their rates fluctuated wildly due to the small raw numbers tallied. The top fifty still gave us plenty of small, rural counties to counterbalance urban centers. Seventeen were over 100,000 population, thirty-three under 100,000.

We anticipated that large urban areas would have high crime rates with correspondingly high incarceration rates, and that a clear link between minorities and incarceration rates would appear. "I'll bet," said Mel, "the blacker a county is, the higher the incarceration rate." Many have the perception that crime is primarily a black problem, and many blacks perceive that they are over-prosecuted and over-sentenced due to a racist criminal justice system. After all, it is undeniable that blacks are locked up at a rate over six times higher than whites. Any positive correlation we could find between black population and a county's incarceration rate would help to substantiate these perceptions.

Mel-T would have lost his bet. Our preconceived notions about county-level racism in the criminal justice system were wrong. There was no correlation – almost a perfect zero – between percentage of black population and a county's incarceration rate. You could get the same level of correlation by comparing two lists of randomly generated numbers. Even when we combined all minorities into one column the result was an insignificantly low correlation factor.

The only strong link at the county level was, once again, poverty to incarceration rate. When compared to other measures, poverty was overwhelmingly most determinative of a county's incarceration rate. [See Appendix 4.]

INDIANA COUNTIES' CORRELATION TO INCARCERATION RATE
50 Largest Indiana Counties (2013)

INC – Poverty Rate	.513
INC – Violent Crime Rate	.262
INC – Minority Population	.136
INC – Net Population	-.017
INC – Black Population	-.018
INC – Republican voting, President, 2012	-.104

We were a bit stunned. Mel had me run the numbers again, searching for an input error. There was no error. How could there be no correlation between black population and incarceration rates when blacks make up 9.5% of Indiana's population but 33.6% of Indiana's prisoners? How could we explain this?

The only explanation supported by the data was that blacks in Indiana are over-represented in poverty (and in the number of single parent households) and as a portion of large urban populations. Poverty and geography – the same factors seen on the state level as most determinative of high incarceration rates. Indiana had 625,000 black citizens, with 68.2% of them living in Indiana's three largest counties, putting them in the environment most conducive to crime. All three large counties harbored low-income black neighborhoods. Those 'hoods were targeted by police as "high-crime" districts. More cops on the streets means more arrests, more convictions, more prisoners.

On closer examination, what really surprised us was the political correlation to a county's high incarceration rate. Research into local politics – the party affiliations of county prosecutors and judges – revealed that the top eight counties in incarceration rate were all dominated by Republicans. A sharp contrast existed between the two largest urban centers, Marion County (Indianapolis) and Lake County (Gary). Demographically, the two had little differences, but Marion County, governed locally by Republicans, had an incarceration rate 2.64 times higher than the Democratic-controlled Lake County. Everything else was similar between the two, so the frequency and lengths of sentences were entirely a political choice.

Rural counties demonstrated the same political bias in action. Huntington County, with a population, crime rate, and ethnic diversity no different from 40 miles north in LaGrange County, had an incarceration rate 6.43 times higher. Dearborn County (David Fields' unfortunate venue) was nearly demographically identical to Warrick County but had an incarceration rate 8.63 times higher. In each comparison, the difference was solely the political philosophy of those controlling the county's criminal justice system. They faced similar levels of crime, applied the same state statutes, and wound up with bizarrely disparate levels of incarceration. Political affiliation was the only difference.

To put these small, overwhelmingly Republican counties into an international perspective, they were more totalitarian than any Communist or any dictator in history. And this is going on all across America.

"There is no defensible reason," I said to Mel, "why Madison County, population 130,000, should have an incarceration rate of 869 per 100,000 residents, when Clark County, population 112,000, has an incarceration rate of 214 per 100,000. The two counties are similar in every respect. Sentences are four times worse in the city of Anderson *only* due to their rabidly conservative

Republican judges and prosecutors." The Amalfitanos already knew this. Their Madison County judge had been an Indiana State Trooper and was later promoted to the Indiana Court of Appeals, another body overwhelmingly Republican, bent to uphold the state's draconian sentences.

I thought I had made a good case for Mel to grasp. Active racism by those with economic power pushes more blacks and Hispanics into poverty. Those living in poverty (of all colors) have more contact with the police and the criminal justice system. Those under the glare of politically-motivated prosecutors and judges suffered from harsh sentencing practices. Those were the elements that caused mass incarceration in Indiana, and in America.

"That poverty matters more than crime, more than race, in determining a state or county's incarceration rate," observed Mel, "seems right, but still kinda makes my mind flop around. Does anybody else know about all this?" Mel was wondering why he had never heard anybody blame poverty-geography-politics as the problem.

"Actually, Mel, I think it's old news. You remember LBJ and the War on Poverty?"

"Yeah, and it only took a few years of that before there was a white backlash, and they put Nixon in office, and the War on Poverty was replaced with a War on Crime and a War on Drugs. All under the law-and-order banner."

"Exactly. And Martin Luther King, if you listened to one of his main themes, saw poverty as the main obstacle undermining the civil rights movement." King wasn't exclusively a champion of equal rights for minorities. He also directed listeners to repair the nation's high level of poverty, regardless of race.

Mel thought back to the 60's and early 70's. "The Black Panthers were saying the same thing, basically, stressing economic independence as a solution to poverty in the black community. Eliminating poverty would have solved most of our problems."

Still would, I thought. Do it through education and training. But fifty years after the 1960's struggles, where were the black-owned industries? Where were the black-owned banks? Many now argue that black neighborhoods are economically worse off now than they were fifty years ago. Black joblessness has soared. Industries have moved away from places like Gary, Ft. Wayne, and Indianapolis. Whites would have to return to the Depression Era to appreciate the financial struggle taking place in America's poorest neighborhoods today.

As we discussed race, poverty, politics, and incarceration at our lunch table, young Mr. Goddie ambled past Mel and set his tray down two tables away. I watched Mel's eyes slither along Goddie's trail, and Mel caught me watching him watch Goddie.

"That kid don't even try," Mel said, contemptuously. "Makes us all look bad."

I had related to Mel the occasion when I had surprised Goddie with my knowledge of Goddie's first homicide, the one Goddie thought I wouldn't find out about. A LEXIS search of "Robert Oldham" had hit on Goddie's overturned murder conviction. What I didn't tip to Goddie then, or to Mel, was another case with Oldham's name in it. Goddie's uncle had stabbed an Evansville man to death in the presence of his nine-year-old nephew. The uncle's appeal centered on his attorney's failure to call Robert Oldham as a witness.

"Even effort is learned behavior, Mel."

We like to think of effort as entirely the product of intrinsic forces, total self-motivation, but it's not. Weightlifting partners can attest they push more weight when they have someone encouraging them. Even in the realm of effort, environment matters. Effort is acquired, from the people around you.

If Goddie never gave his best effort, was it his fault, or did his upbringing have something to do with it? I'm sure a fatal knife attack was just one of dozens of crimes Goddie witnessed growing up. I doubt that people "doing the right thing" were his role models.

I sat silent for awhile, considering Goddie and several others in the prison lunch room who were making no progress.

"Maybe somebody needs to teach him *how* to try."

Mel rolled his eyes and shook his head. "Waste of time," Mel stated. He saw potential in almost everybody, but some were too far gone for even Mel to believe in.

Donnie Ware's collection to hire a PC attorney never reached four digits, so he was forced to appeal the county court's denial of his PC petition pro se.

The court's denial was typical – a cut-n-paste job from the attorney general's electronically filed proposed findings. Our filing, submitted on paper, was ignored. A person adept with MS Word could have transformed our opponent's file into a purportedly court-written document in less than ten minutes.

We filed a Notice of Appeal, and four months later our three-issue brief was before the Indiana Court of Appeals. The state's brief addressed the first two issues – obliquely, the same way the county court had handled them. They pretended not to know how *Sanders v. Cotton* applied to Ware's mangled jury instruction on murder and its lesser included offenses. The constitutional double jeopardy claim was countered as is usual, under the dictates of *Richardson v. State*. But Donnie's third issue, a common law argument for double jeopardy, was not addressed at all. A failure to address an issue in a post-conviction setting doesn't spell automatic victory for the plaintiff, as it would in a direct appeal, but the state's silence heightened the prospect of victory for Donnie on the two Class D felonies.

"If you win on the common law issue, that's four years off your seventy," I told Donnie. Not life-changing, but it was something. "And their argument on the jury instruction issue is not very impressive. It's a winnable case for you. The trouble is, Donnie, you don't have an attorney's name on the cover of the brief."

He knew what that meant for how his appellant's brief would be processed, but there was nothing he could do about it. Teresa and Adela could barely get by as it was, and they couldn't afford a PC attorney for Donnie. Shortly after Donnie's arrest, Teresa was unable to keep up the house payments, and she was forced to move into a trailer park. Adela was having problems adjusting to the trailer park culture, and this bothered Donnie much more than the fact that he could not afford an attorney.

A few weeks later, the appellate court affirmed the lower court, and confirmed my prediction on how they would sloppily dispatch Donnie's brief. The attorney general had ignored Donnie's third issue, and the court ignored it as well. Not a word was written about it. It was as if the judge didn't even read the headings in Donnie's brief. I wanted to tell Donnie, "Technically, they can't do that," but I was tired of following that line up with, "but in reality, the courts do whatever they want." They don't have to follow statutes, or the constitution, or their own court rules. Exceptions, excuses, and double-talk were endless. It was all a farce.

A petition for rehearing was filed, and denied without commentary. Same story on Donnie's petition to transfer to the Indiana Supreme Court.

"The good news, Donnie, is that this involves a federal issue, so now we can take it to federal court." The U.S. district court, I hoped, would not so cavalierly gloss over *Sanders v. Cotton*, which was issued by the Seventh Circuit Court of Appeals. The *Sanders* decision had reversed an Indiana murder conviction based on a confusing jury instruction practically identical to Donnie's. I drafted Donnie's petition for writ of habeas corpus and we mailed it in, along with the five dollar filing fee.

"At least it doesn't cost much to file it," Donnie said, writing out a remittance slip that represented twenty hours of his labor in the prison laundry.

Of course it doesn't cost much, I thought. The court's fee schedule is commensurate with the average prisoner's ability to pay. They know their clientele: the poor. People who possess virtually nothing. Nothing but their lives. Their liberty and their property are gone.

CHAPTER EIGHT

Ten Years Per Gram

"Imprisonment . . . now creates far more crime than it prevents, by ripping apart fragile social networks, destroying families, and creating a permanent class of unemployables. Although it is common to think of poverty and joblessness as leading to crime and imprisonment, this research suggests that the War on Drugs is a major cause of poverty, chronic unemployment, broken families, and crime today."
– Michelle Alexander, *The New Jim Crow*, p. 230.

One of Mel-T's favorite books, *The New Jim Crow*, by Michelle Alexander, contends the War on Drugs is responsible for mass incarceration. CO Red, who never picked up a copy of *The New Jim Crow*, made a similar claim – that a crusade against alcohol built Pendleton in 1923, and that the War on Drugs caused an expansion of 600+ beds in the 1980's. Many hypothesize that an end to the drug war would relieve prison overcrowding. However, if we were to release all 331,700 imprisoned drug offenders tomorrow, the United States would still have the world's highest incarceration rate. Drug offenders are "only" 21% of the nation's prisoners. There must be more to the mass incarceration problem than just drug crimes.

"You have to factor in all the other crimes," advised Mike Lindsey, "like the murders, robberies, thefts, burglaries, weapons possession, et cetera, that are related to the drug trade. There are a lot of people in here who aren't in for drugs, but wouldn't be here if not for the drug war."

If we could determine the percentage of crimes that were drug-related, we could accurately assess the impact of the War on Drugs' contribution to mass incarceration.

We had plenty of murderers around us, so we began our inquiries with them. They were pretty free with their motivations for killing. Well, most of them were – Kenny Allen fixed me with a dead-eye stare for an uncomfortable moment, and said flatly, "It wasn't drug-related." A few others claimed no motivation, protesting innocence on the murder charge with an admission of guilt on manslaughter. But most were forthcoming, and the circumstances were clear. A solid 30% of the murders were in some significant way connected to drugs.

Applying the 30% figure to the nation's 166,700 prisoners doing time for murder yields 50,000 drug-related murder convictions. That's a lot of murders, and those are just the ones that got caught. Only 60% of homicides get solved. Given that the United States experienced 636,000 homicides from 1981 through 2014, a 30% rate suggests 190,000 citizens have died from drug-related violence.

The death toll makes the War on Drugs a "war" in a very literal sense. It is four times the number of battle deaths in Vietnam, and despite the War on Drugs' longer duration, the drug-related deaths have came at a faster daily rate than in Vietnam.

I uncovered a 1990's study by the Department of Justice also concluding that 30% of America's crimes were drug-related. Mel and I turned to other crime categories, applying the 30% rate to everything except sex offenses (sex offenders account for 13.4% of the prison population in Indiana). If 21% of U.S. prisoners are in for drug convictions, and 30% of the other 65.6% imprisoned for non-sex, non-drug crimes are in for drug-related activity, then 40.7% of America's incarceration is attributable to drugs and drug-related crime.

Since it would take a release of 80% of America's prisoners to get the incarceration rate back to "normal," drugs and drug-related crimes account for half of the mass incarceration problem.

Drug convictions made up one-fourth of Indiana's prisoners, but they generated little post-conviction work for us, due to the extremely slim chances of finding a winnable issue. Our experience as law clerks told us not to invest much time with drug cases, even though most drug offenders thought they had many appealable issues.

The top complaint voiced by prisoners in on drug possession is illegal search and seizure in violation of the Fourth Amendment. The layperson's conception of what constitutes an illegal search and the U.S. Supreme Court's rulings on the issue over the last 40 years are so far apart that prisoners routinely refuse to believe anything we tell them about modern interpretations of the Fourth Amendment. It's like they all obtained their legal savvy from watching episodes of *Law and Order*, where any whiff of a search's impropriety tosses the evidence out of court and sends the detectives into a dejected little snit.

In the real world, most cops go their entire career without getting seized evidence thrown out of court. Nevertheless, prisoners still believe the Fourth Amendment establishes a rule of "the game" that will be enforced. ("The police can't just go into your car / glove box / trunk / suitcase / apartment / mother's house / locked safe / sealed mail / tool shed / tool box / desk / gym locker / school locker / medicine cabinet / locked briefcase / cell phone / computer / pocket / underwear / shoe / fake shaving cream can / baby's diaper without probable cause or without a warrant!") And once upon a time, mainly before *Terry v. Ohio* (1968), it was true that cops couldn't go poking around on a "fishing expedition," exploring on a mere hunch or because a person fit a certain profile. But 40 years of ultra-conservative interpretation of the Fourth Amendment, anchored on the nebulous word "unreasonable" in the amendment's text, has stripped the Founders' intended right to privacy from the Bill of Rights. Today, cops can dig into almost anything, for any articulable excuse. The Fourth Amendment text reads:

> The right of the people to be secure in their persons, houses, papers, and effects, against unreasonable searches and seizures, shall not be violated, and no Warrants shall issue, but upon probable cause, supported by Oath or affirmation, and particularly describing the place to be searched, and the persons or things to be seized.

Unfortunately, the word "unreasonable" invites broad interpretation. The Supreme Court has progressively redefined it to the government's liking, mainly in an effort to support prosecutors in the War on Drugs. Since 1981, the government has been the plaintiff in over 95% of Supreme Court cases on Fourth Amendment issues, and they have won nearly every time. Justice Stevens, dissenting in *California v. Acevedo* (1991), observed that "this Court has become a loyal foot soldier in the Executive's fight against crime." That even the highest court is biased in favor of the government should surprise no one familiar with criminal justice – the lower courts are much worse, and more open about it.

Search and seizure law, in practice, has devolved into this standard of review: if drugs were found, the search was reasonable; and if drugs were not found, well, then, we're not in court and there's nothing to rule upon.

The "unreasonable" search barely exists any more. Evidence exclusion is reserved for defendants with the highest priced attorneys. The pretrial window, even for the wealthy, is the only real opportunity to get evidence stricken under the Fourth Amendment, and the chance of victory in that early stage is also slim. By the time the ordinary prisoner gets to a prison law library, the search and seizure issue has long dried up.

Further closing the door on Fourth Amendment claims is the Supreme Court's ruling in *Stone v. Powell* (1976), prohibiting any state prisoner from raising the issue in a federal writ of habeas corpus. The Fourth Amendment, wrote the *Stone* majority, is not "incorporated" under the Fourteenth Amendment to apply to state due process in the way the First, Third, Fifth, Sixth, and Eighth Amendments have been incorporated. A good question is, Why not? The Court's answer is that a search does not implicate the "ultimate question of guilt or innocence," and, more telling, there would be "substantial societal costs of applying the rule." Rephrased: it would make a lot of work for the courts.

The "incorporation doctrine" continues to evolve, and the Supreme Court has reversed its course on a multitude of issues over the years, so *Stone v. Powell* may be eradicated some day. The Second Amendment right to bear arms wasn't incorporated until 2013, in *McDonald v. City of Chicago*. Once incarceration rates return to levels predating the War on Drugs, the high court might find their federal courts, with 80% fewer criminal cases, once again able to field habeas corpus petitions, and the Founders' original Fourth Amendment intent may reappear.

Several other perceived defects in their drug convictions commonly wind up in drug defendants' pro se PC petitions. "They enticed me to make the sale within 1,000 feet of a school." I hear that one in almost every Class A felony case. "I didn't know somebody put drugs in my car." Doesn't matter, it's your car, you're responsible for everything found in it. "It was entrapment." Most don't know the meaning of the word, thinking every buy-bust sting was a "trap," therefore "entrapment." Even lawyers (like Arturo Gallardo's) screw this up. "My 3.5 grams of cocaine was only 10% purity – shouldn't that be 0.35 grams of cocaine?" No, drug weights include any substance mixed with the drug. One gram of cocaine with 453 grams of baking soda equals one pound of cocaine. And then there are the myriads of technicalities these defendants devise, indicators of the hopelessness of their cases. "They lacked jurisdiction." "They used an unregistered informant." "Their radio frequency wasn't licensed by the FCC." Their petitions often end up looking like they were written, well, by a person on drugs.

Drug defendants, generally, are also a curiously independent group when it comes to legal work, seldom asking for advice. And if the advice given does not match what they have already written, it is ignored. They don't believe what they're told about the law, and when they're shown case law they don't believe the plain interpretation on the page, instead favoring some fantastic (and erroneous) interpretation in some other case. Dividing the prisoner population by offense, drug defendants are both the most unmovable and least successful of all post-conviction plaintiffs.

I have only worked on one drug case at Pendleton where I thought the guy had a reasonable shot at getting a conviction overturned, and my role in his case was small. It was also on a direct appeal, not a PC case. Christopher McCaster, nicknamed P-Town, in reference to his home town of Peoria, Illinois, had convictions out of Tippecanoe County for possessing cocaine and conspiracy to deal cocaine. Both amounts were under three grams – pebbles of rock cocaine – but the crimes were within 1,000 feet of a "family housing complex," and were run consecutive, giving him 70 years, do 35. On direct appeal his public defender argued that the two convictions were double jeopardy, a reasonable assertion backed by recent Indiana appellate decisions.

Despite solid supporting case law, the Indiana Court of Appeals ruled against McCaster in an unpublished opinion that didn't make much sense to me, or to McCaster. Days after the denial, McCaster received a letter from the public defender saying he was done with the case, and he wouldn't attempt a petition to transfer to the Indiana Supreme Court. Good luck to you, nice knowin' ya.

Giving up was not what P-Town wanted to hear. He learned he had 30 days to petition to transfer on his own, and 17 days had already expired. No deadline extension was possible for any reason, by appellate rule. There was no possible way for him to research, write, type, and copy a petition in 13 days, given his cellblock housing, and lack of familiarity with the law. He brought it to me.

It took me two hours to research it, write it, proof it, format it, and make all the necessary copies. Like most "good" issues, it was a simple argument, easy to make clear for the court.

We also filed a pro se appearance form and sent the petition to the Indiana Supreme Court. Oddly, the clerk did not file it. Instead, McCaster received another letter from the public defender, this time saying McCaster had a pretty good issue for transfer after all, and that the attorney would be filing a petition to replace the pro se one that had been submitted.

Indiana's Supreme Court receives about 3,000 petitions to transfer jurisdiction every year, and around 200 are granted. One in fifteen. The decision on granting transfer is usually by a 5-0 vote, for or against transfer, with some 4-1 votes along party lines thrown in there, the one dissenter being the "liberal" justice opposed by four conservatives. Hardly ever is a transfer vote split 3-2.

We were mailed the petition McCaster's public defender wrote, and it mirrored mine substantially, but some confusing gobbledygook was added that made absolutely no sense to me. Well, I chalked that up to me being not so smart, and to my wrongheaded proclivity for always trying to make "sense" out of the law.

The court's ruling came back a month later, a stunner, 3 to 2. Against transfer. A loss; his appeal was dead. We commiserated over such a close loss, and ironically, on a case his attorney initially felt was not worth the effort.

McCaster's case was one of hundreds whose drug-dealing charges were raised to a higher felony due to the 1,000-foot rule. I had always believed, based on the cases I had seen, that the colorblind 1,000-foot rule affected blacks more than whites, and research confirmed my hunch. Data from the IDOC showed 2,505 prisoners whose primary conviction was dealing cocaine, and of those, 1,076 had been enhanced to a Class A felony – 43%. For dealing in meth, an activity almost exclusively the province of white defendants, there were 1,480 convicted, with 289 enhanced to a Class A – only 20%. The meth and cocaine statutes were word-for-word identical on the 1,000-foot rule. The amounts of cocaine and meth commonly used and commonly dealt are indistinguishable. The only differences between the two are race and geography – black/urban vs. white/rural.

In urban areas, the defendant is much more likely to unknowingly be within 1,000 feet of a "school property, public park, family housing complex, or youth program center," as stated in Indiana Code 35-48-4-6 and 6.1. Since an overtly racist statute focused on blacks' criminal activity would expose legislators' biases, geography was cleverly employed as an excuse to accomplish the trick. The 1,000-foot rule worked to send black defendants to prison for longer sentences than whites for the same behavior, but to the uninitiated the statute read like a colorblind attempt to protect juveniles from drugs.

Sure, a few whites get enhanced sentences too – an unintended consequence of lawmakers' 1,000-foot strategy. This is the type of "collateral damage" to which Michelle Alexander referred when she wrote that the laws have been written with the intent of oppressing the black population while accepting that whites – poor whites, I must add – will become victims of the harsh sentencing scheme as well.

Instead of a 1,000-foot rule to protect juveniles from drugs, why not a more precise law, as in, selling to a juvenile qualifies for a higher level felony?

The 1,000-foot issue seemed ripe for an argument under the Fourteenth Amendment's equal protection clause, but I never pursued it because I knew the courts would apply a "strict scrutiny" standard of review, meaning I would have to prove purely racist intent. The legislature's true intent was well-disguised, and no court in today's political climate would ever declare the 1,000-foot rule overtly racist.

The Indiana legislature eventually took action to reduce drug penalties. Following the lead of Congress, which reduced crack cocaine federal sentencing guidelines in 2007 and 2010, Indiana passed an overhaul of their sentencing schemes, effective July 1, 2014. The "new law" cast away the A-B-C-D level felony levels, replacing them with levels 1 through 6. "Truth in sentencing" principles were invoked, meaning prisoners would no longer serve half their term, but 75% for most crimes, and 85% (6/7ths, precisely) for violent crimes and sex offenses.

Sentences for drug crimes were most radically affected by the 2014 revisions. The 3-gram threshold for cocaine and meth was increased to 5 grams. The highest possible felony was no longer Class A, but a Class 2. Because so many drug defendants were caught with the quantum eight-ball unit (3.5 grams), or less, most of them would have qualified for a Class 3 felony under the 2014 law. A Class 2 felony is 10 to 30 years; a Class 3 felony is 3 to 16 years. The habitual offender enhancement, formerly a flat 30 on a Class A, became 6 to 20 years on felony levels 1 through 4. Even though drug offenders must do 75% of their sentence under the new law, the aggregate time is much less because the imposed sentences are much shorter.

The new, more lenient drug law is something Kenneth Elmore wished he would have faced in 1993. Elmore's case is a classic example of a defendant getting, effectively, a life sentence for dealing a minuscule amount of cocaine. On September 24, 1993, Elmore sold a single $20 rock to undercover informant John McGavock. The Indianapolis Police Department swooped in, nabbing Elmore with 16 baggies containing a combined weight of 3.1793 grams. (At .16 grams each they were really $10 rock size, not $20, indicating he may have been selling light to stretch his profit.) He was charged with a Class A felony, 20 to 50 years, with a flat 30 to be added for the habitual offender enhancement.

Elmore had five young children to support, a fact glossed over by the sentencing judge, who buried Elmore with a 75-year sentence. Do 37 years and 6 months. On his direct appeal, one Indiana Supreme Court justice noted, "given 50 is the presumptive for murder, a 75-year sentence for dealing in cocaine appears quite high." But no relief was granted. (Indiana's reviewing courts have the right under Appellate Rule 7B to revise any sentence.) The appeal died in 1995; his PC petition went belly up in 2003. It wasn't until Elmore was in year 21 of his prison stay that the sentencing law on his offense changed, drastically reducing the penalty he would have faced had the new law come a generation sooner.

Under the 2014 law, Elmore's 3.1793 grams would have been a Class 3 felony, 3 to 16 years, with a 6 to 20 for the habitual. Net range, 9 to 36 years, do 75%. Even getting the 36-year max, he would do 27 instead of 37 and a half.

So the solution was easy, right? Petition for resentencing under the new law.

Unfortunately, unlike the federal sentencing guidelines revised in 2010, Indiana's revisions were not made retroactive. The new law did nothing for Elmore. Or for the 2,500 people similarly situated.

The common-sense way to get around the lack of a retroactivity clause is to either ask for executive clemency or petition for a sentence modification from the county court. Clemency petitions are hardly worth the effort – dropping them in the mailbox is like dropping them down a dry well. Governors like Indiana's Mike Pence are politically risk-averse, letting the courts run the criminal justice system unimpeded by checks and balances from the executive. If a pardon is granted, it comes near the end of their term, and never prior to another election. Political considerations are paramount. No governor wants to run for office in the future and have to face the Willie Horton-type ads Michael Dukakis had to endure when he ran for President in 1988.

Elmore put in for a sentence modification, incorporating the argument that Indiana's legislature has reconsidered what is a "fair" sentence for Elmore's conduct. To be fair to Elmore, his 75-year sentence should be reduced to no more than 54, allowing him to do 27, which would be the most severe sentence for his offense under the new law. The court, however, never ruled on Elmore's motion. The Marion County Prosecutor, exercising his gatekeeper's function under the sentence modification statute, refused to allow the motion to be heard by the court.

Some state prisoners have difficulty understanding why the federal government cannot intervene in state sentencing decisions. Douglas Anderson was one of those prisoners.

"Can't I ask Obama to commute my sentence? I saw on TV he might let a bunch of drug offenders get out." Anderson had a Class A conviction for dealing in cocaine, from Tippecanoe County, and thought the President had the power to free him.

"The President has no power over state sentences," I told him. "Only over federal sentences. Governor Mike Pence is the only one who can commute your sentence."

"And that ain't happening," Blakemore chimed in, "because Pence is a Republican." American politics are actually pretty easy to understand. Blakemore, Mongoose's codefendant, stayed current on the law and on politics.

Anderson had little education but he was cognizant of the difference between Democrats and Republicans. With a Democrat as governor, there was a slim chance of executive clemency; with a Republican as governor, there was no chance.

Anderson asked a good question: "Why can't we get a Democrat to run this state?"

+++

Why no Democrats? The simple answer is that Republicans run Indiana because voters have elected Republicans. The longer answer explores the interesting history that created the state's modern political and cultural environment.

Indiana Territory's earliest settlers were not primarily Northerners migrating west, as some may presume from the map, but Southerners from Kentucky traveling north as Indian lands were acquired by various treaties. Achieving statehood in 1816, Indiana attracted Southerners in search of fresh farmland with clear title, giving the state an early history infused with the attitudes and values of the upper American South. Even today, locals consider Indiana as having two cultural halves, one "south of 40" and one "north of 40," referring to a dividing line on U.S. Route 40 cutting across the state at Indianapolis.

Abraham Lincoln, transplanted from Kentucky, spent his formative years in Southern Indiana, 1816-1830, before moving on to Illinois at age 21.

Hoosiers revised their state constitution in 1851, mainly to address three large concerns. One new constitutional article assured fiscal conservatism as a permanent feature of the state. In the 1840's, legislators had sunk the state coffers into enormous debt with a harebrained scheme to build a canal connecting the Great Lakes with the Ohio River. The new constitution contained a preventive remedy: the state may not go into debt, for any reason.

Another article addressed a problem recently arising in Eastern states – gerrymandering. Indiana decided no county could be subdivided to create political districts for state or national office. There would be no "rigging" a geographical area to ensure that the party in office would maintain political control.

Third was the notorious (in historical hindsight) Article 13. This article, ratified separately by popular vote, made it illegal for any "person of color" to enter the state "for any purpose." Persons of color already residing in the state could stay. Article 13 passed with 89% of the vote in a referendum. They were anti-slavery, like all Northern states, but they were obviously not too keen on the idea of freed slaves crossing the river and relocating on white-dominated Indiana soil.

Article 13 was such a novel, wonderful idea that three other states – Illinois, Iowa, and Oregon – placed similar provisions in their constitutions between 1851 and 1858. Indiana, being the first, was already on its way to becoming a land of little ethnic diversity.

The post-Civil War passage of the Reconstruction Amendments forced Indiana legislators to quietly repeal Article 13, but by then the ban on "coloreds" had prevented blacks from securing any major foothold in the state. Black enclaves grew much slower in Indiana than in neighboring states.

Around 1916, Indiana's overwhelming whiteness made it fertile ground for the rebirth of America's most infamous racist organization, the Ku Klux Klan. D.W. Griffith's Klan-glorifying silent film, *The Birth of a Nation,* appeared in theaters in December 1915, and nowhere were viewers more enthralled than in Indianapolis. A new edition of the Klan was incorporated, placing its national headquarters in central Indiana. The Hoosier State became ground zero for the national Klan membership explosion. Of Indiana's 1,080,000 adult males in 1924, 350,000 were bona fide Klan members.

Indiana adopted a Klan-themed state flag in 1917, an adaptation of the Confederate Bonnie Blue Flag (gold star on a field of blue), using the color scheme to show a torch held up against a night sky's field of stars – every black man's nightmare. Flag designer Paul Hadley, from Mooresville, lived in what is still the whitest county in Indiana (Morgan County) – curiously little ethnic diversity despite its proximity adjacent to Indianapolis. While the Stars-and-Bars Confederate battle flags no longer fly over the capitols of some Southern states, the 1917 Indiana flag still flies over the Hoosier State, commemorating an age of terror.

While the origin of the word "Hoosier" is still debated, many blacks today consider it an epithet for a white person. Perhaps that has to do with Indiana's history as a state seeking racial purity.

Indiana's Klan allied itself from the start with the Republican Party. In 1924, head Klansman David Curtis Stephenson hand-picked the entire Republican slate for state offices. The Klan controlled the state legislature. Governor Jackson and the Indianapolis mayor owed their positions to the Klan, as did minor office holders across Indiana – particularly judges and prosecutors. Republicans won by landslides in the 1920's.

Klan fervor became a national phenomenon in the Roaring Twenties. Four million joined the "Invisible Empire," a significant figure when one considers that only 29 million votes were cast for President in 1924. Republican Calvin Coolidge got 2.5 million more votes then his two opponents. Shortly after Coolidge was inaugurated, this "empire" made its presence known by marching on Washington on August 8, 1925, massing the largest Klan rally in history.

Indiana's D.C. Stephenson, however, missed the rally. He had raped and murdered Madge Oberholzer on a train rolling between Indy and Hammond in March of 1925. In November of that year he was convicted and sentenced to life in prison. Stephenson and Dillinger shared a cellblock at Pendleton – Dillinger was a nobody at that time, just another common thief being schooled by older cons in the art of bank robbery; Stephenson was both famous and infamous.

With Stephenson's conviction the Indiana Klan slowly unraveled. Indiana's popular pastime of lynching young blacks accused of crimes came swinging to a halt after the national media published photos of a dead black teenager accused of rape in Marion, Indiana, in 1930. The youngster was suspended under a tree limb as a gay crowd of white onlookers laughed and partied beneath him. The photo still appears in American History textbooks depicting the Klan era. By the late 1930's it was no longer publicly acceptable to align with the Klan. But the Republican Party was not damaged by its close ties with the KKK. It was still okay to be a Republican.

Indiana's populist shift toward the Democratic Party in the 1960's was countered cunningly by Republicans. The GOP found ways to gerrymander state elective districts despite the state constitutional prohibition, and in 1974, when challenged on their practices, they led the successful movement to amend the inconvenient Section 6 of Article 4. The Democratic vote was diluted, and black townships lost 75% of their representation. In the 1982 elections in Marion and Allen Counties (Indy and Ft. Wayne), Dems got 46.6% of the vote, but only 3 of 21 seats in the Indiana House. Overall, in 1982 the voters cast 52% of their votes for Democrats but won only 43% of the House seats, thanks to a clever 1981 Republican redistricting plan. As has happened across America, the U.S. Supreme Court condoned the politically motivated redrawing of voting districts. In *Davis v. Bandemer* (1986) they ensured that white majority rule would not be undermined by the prattle of minority voices.

To those outside the United States, our system of democracy must look like a cleverly crafted arrangement more interested in securing the interests of the wealthy and corporate class than in protecting the rights and satisfying the needs of society. To some *inside* the United States it looks like this.

American democracy contrasts with the world's other democracies in a fundamental, structural way. Nearly all democracies in the world have chosen parliamentary systems of government, where, for example, a party winning 52% of the vote gets 52% of the seats in the legislature. This method ensures that minority parties will have a proportional voice in government. It also evolves to destroy the two-party system, giving rise to multiple parties seeking to protect the diverse interests of the people. There is no gerrymandering possible when there is a parliament. There is no "red state, blue state" talk. There is no overbearing dominance by any one party, reigning imperiously under the guise of "majority rule."

When a two-party system develops one-party domination, the state functions as if only one party exists. No checks, no balances. No need to tolerate arguments from the minority set. One doesn't need many examples from around the world and throughout history to appreciate the fact that one-party rule is not such a good thing for the people.

Indiana today no longer has a Klan-centric government, but its offices are overwhelmingly occupied by Republicans. By a percentage of voters, Indiana barely leans Republican – Obama won the state in 2008 – but a small voting edge can translate into complete dominance. Indiana has a Republican governor, Mike Pence. Eight of eleven in Congress are Republicans. The legislative branches are super-majority Republican, 74% in the Senate, 60% in the House. Four of five Supreme Court justices are Republican, as is 75% of the Court of Appeals. Laws get made their way, interpreted their way, and implemented their way.

They may no longer be Klansmen, but the Klan pedigree explains why their philosophy and tactics have changed little over a century.

Sadly, a Republican stranglehold on the criminal justice system is the norm in a majority of U.S. states, because voters are often attracted to the Republican "law and order" platform when it comes to electing judges, prosecutors, sheriffs, and police chiefs. Nixon, Rockefeller, and Reagan adopted "law and order" as a fundamental Republican value in 1968, and the GOP never let go of the law-and-order franchise, upping their "toughness" on crime every time a Democrat tried to invade their criminal justice territory. In this "arms race," nobody could out-tough the tough-on-crime Republicans, and from 1968 onward, all state laws became tougher, and sentences became more severe.

The structure of American democracy, combined with an undercurrent of anti-black racism hidden in the core of the Republican Party, practically guaranteed that mass incarceration would occur.

I could count on Mike Lindsey to succinctly characterize the law-and-order movement's history.

"It's dementia! It's a form of dementia. Look it up."

I did. Merriam Webster's Collegiate Dictionary defines dementia as a "usually progressive condition marked by deteriorated cognitive functioning often with emotional apathy."

"Well, that hits it on the head," I said, admiring how neatly the definition of dementia fit the history of mass incarceration. "It *is* a progressive condition. It *does* involve deteriorated cognitive functioning. And emotional apathy is mandatory."

"It's all there," Mike said.

"But this is a special kind of dementia," I added. "It requires an authoritarian perspective." We looked up the definition of authoritarian: "1. of, relating to, or favoring blind submission to authority. 2. of, relating to, or favoring a concentration of power in a leader or an elite not constitutionally responsible to the people."

"That's almost too perfect," Mike laughed. "Not constitutionally responsible is exactly what's going on here."

"Then it's settled." I laughed along with Mike. "We've found the disease, and given it a label: Authoritarian Dementia."

Authoritarian Personality Disorder might be a better label. As long ago as 1950, psychologists studied the genesis and idiosyncracies of the authoritarian personality, and how it blinds the afflicted on the subject of human equality. Adorno and colleagues examined the authoritarian personality to provide answers on how factions in Europe's population developed racist and genocidal features, concluding that every human rights abuse in history has been rooted in authoritarianism.

+ + +

I wanted to help Mel-T get out of prison, before it killed him. But like most drug cases, there was little I could do. He had pled guilty with some misunderstanding as to the correct sentencing range, but won no relief on direct appeal or on his pro se PC petition. In 2012 we asked the Marion County prosecutor to agree to a sentence modification, proposing to reduce Mel's sentence from 60 to 50 years. Our proposal highlighted Mel's prison accomplishments over 16 years: Associate's and Bachelor's Degrees from Ball State University, various programs completed, a nearly spotless disciplinary record, active in the American Legion, years of service in the Chaplain's Office. We argued that under the federal sentencing guidelines (which are considered too severe by a majority of observers), Mel's six grams and his criminal history would have fixed Mel with about ten years, do eight. At the time of our motion Mel was 59 years old and had done twice the amount of time he would have had to serve under the federal system. No longer a "danger to society," we argued he had paid his debt.

Didn't matter. It was like putting a message in a bottle only to watch the bottle sink out of sight. Apparently there was no dodging the ancient grudge that had targeted Mel for imprisonment in the first place. No prosecutor would agree to allow Mel an audience with the court. There was probably a red sticker placed on his file, a code spoken to whomever may work in the prosecutor's office, meaning: Let Him Die In Prison.

When the 2014 laws went into effect I asked Mel if he would like to give it another try, making the same argument and adding a new one based on the lower drug sentences in Indiana. He did not seem too enthused about it.

"I like the idea, but I know I need an attorney to get it done." He wasn't knocking my advocacy, just stating a fact. To be successful at a sentence mod, a prisoner had to have professional counsel working face-to-face with the prosecutor.

"I could draft one for you. Wouldn't take long," I offered. Having all the facts outlined in draft form would make it easier for his attorney.

"Naaah," Mel dismissed with a flick of his wrist. "I'm not on that right now. I've got other things to deal with. But thanks."

We were on the walk outside the chow hall, where the sidewalk splits. We parted, he ambling off to his dorm, head upright, always holding a regal bearing, me shuffling off to my dorm, turning to look back at Mel several times. I wanted to ask him, *What is more important than trying to get out of prison?* It would have been rude to ask him that, so I didn't. Something else was on his mind, and despite our friendship, he wanted to keep it to himself.

For roughly three hundred library-frequenting prisoners at Pendleton, nothing was more important than trying to get out of prison. Tyson wrote passes for the same subset of men every week, with another hundred making irregular visits to see if anything new and useful had occurred in the legal world. Some of the most dedicated patrons, newly embarked on their post-conviction journeys, ordered copies of the *P.C. Guidebook: Indiana Edition*. None of them received their books, though, because the Pendleton mail room supervisor decided the book should be banned. The reason? Because it was written by a Pendleton inmate.

There are valid reasons to ban publications from prisons, and all of them are based on "legitimate security concerns." The Supreme Court in *Turner v. Safley* (1987) and *Thornburgh v. Abbott* (1989) established criteria for rejecting publications without transgressing the First Amendment rights of the sender or recipient. Prisons may, with great deference from the courts, ban things like pornography, gang-related literature, and escape-related topics. No books on locksmithing. No MacGyver-themed tomes on organic chemistry. *Guns-n-Ammo* magazine can't get in. The prison only has to show a rational nexus between the publication and a concern for the "safety and security" of the facility. A how-to manual on pro se legal work could not legally be banned by any prison, regardless of the identity of the author. So naturally, we sued.

Three of us became plaintiffs in concurrent lawsuits in U.S. district court. For several months we heard staff snidely comment that our suit was "silly" and a "waste of time," not to mention that we had each wasted $400 for the filing fees. Then an ACLU attorney, Gavin Rose, noticed our filings and agreed to become counsel on one of the complaints. The ACLU has a good track record, taking on winners and earning attorney fees on top of whatever the complainants are awarded. The snide comments from staff dried up, replaced by sideways glances and open loathing.

In an attorney visit, Rose was taken aback by the staff's conduct. "They banned it without reading it?" Yep, banned it because I wrote it. "Nothing objectionable in it?" Not a thing. All the cases used for sample filings had pseudonyms so as not to expose personal legal affairs to other prisoners. "Well, that's not the way to ban a book." We know, we know.

Most of the prisoners felt the ban was just another tactic by the state to keep us in prison. They can't physically deny us access to the courts, so they try to deny us the resources that would help us intelligently access the courts, which can be just as effective. "They hate to see guys trying to get out," said Otha Hamilton, one of the plaintiffs.

Prison staff also may not, legally, take retaliatory action when a prisoner exercises his right to file grievances and civil suits. But in practice, when certain factions feel their authority is being challenged, they respond, as authoritarians do, by trying to make a prisoner's life difficult. The trick is to dodge a retaliation claim (no surprise here) by disguising the retaliatory action as "normal" disciplinary procedure. As expected, Pete Mitchell and I began receiving an increased level of scrutiny by the authoritarian faction at Pendleton.

The ACLU was negotiating a settlement when I was ushered into a small room by my dorm counselor. "What did you do," she asked, "to piss off the entire administration? You were the main topic of conversation at the last staff meeting." I told her about the book. I was about to win the case, so they were offended all the more. "Did you write something personal about them?" No, staff wasn't mentioned. "Well, you better watch what you do," she confided. "They're watching your every move." Bogey number one on the IDOC radar.

I appreciated the heads up, but I was already alert. The head of the recreation department, Melissa Nash, had lobbied for my firing from the law library. Fowler and Serour were present when she pressed her case.

"You were not authorized to write a book," Nash asserted. "It's misuse of state property to use our computers for personal gain when you should have been working."

Nash and I had developed an acrimonious relationship since 2010, when her failure to schedule the summer softball league prompted us to organize an independent ten team league. When she learned of our activities, she placed a notice on the institutional TV channel on July 9, "banning" our softball league. Four teams folded, including the Supernovas. On July 27 the Supernovas were scheduled to play the Diamond Killaz, but the players from both teams were in their dorms. Supernovas' second baseman Eric Pointer, who had led the league in hitting, was in his room on July 27, doing heroin. He overdosed and died. I insinuated that Nash was tangentially responsible for Pointer's death, saying, "Rec activities exist for a reason. Banning a softball league makes no sense." My words, certainly embellished in the retelling, had gotten back to Nash. She had retaliated over the years, employing a series of passive-aggressive slights, and now she was poised to take my job.

"First," I told her, "I don't have to be authorized to write a book, or to publish it." I knew where I stood, legally. "Prisoners don't lose their First Amendment rights. Second, I didn't use *your* computers, I used *our* computers. The computers were paid for by us, the prisoners."

"They're state property."

"Whatever. And third, I didn't write the book on my work time, I wrote it on my own time, when we were working half-time shifts. I came in on my days off to write it."

"You shouldn't have wrote it," she snapped.

"...shouldn't *have written* it, you mean." My correcting her grammar didn't help any. She was notoriously self-conscious about her lack of education. In a quirk of organizational chart madness, the IDOC seemed unimpressed by educational achievement. The commissioner, Bruce Lemmon, had only a Bachelor's degree from Indiana State University in 1969. Department heads were often high school grads in charge of college grads like Fowler and Serour. Seventy-year-old, Egyptian-born Kamil Serour had taught agricultural science at a university in Brazil for twenty years before coming to America at age 50 to do the same at an Indiana university. Life's bumpy road upset that career, and Serour landed in the IDOC, with its dependable medical benefits. Now he took orders from a woman who probably thought malathion was a villain in a video game.

Slighted again, Nash turned from pasty pale to red to purple in two heartbeats.

"You should lose your job because . . . because . . ."

"Yeah, find a reason."

"...because you had to enter into a contract to get your book published. That's unauthorized business activity." She was alluding to IDOC disciplinary code 346, "Unauthorized participation in any business activity."

I was prepared for these allegations prior to writing the book. "There are no contracts for the book," I replied. "I don't even get royalties. I donated it." I had a letter from the publisher confirming all this.

In the end, all she could do was give me a direct order: No more writing books on the law library computers.

Days later, CO Red ushered me into the hallway in a conspiratorial way.

"You're good with civil suits, right?"

I upnodded slightly.

"Let me tell you what they did to me, and you tell me if I've got a case. You familiar with labor law?"

"Little bit," I replied. I felt like tossing out a smart-ass comment, like, *Yeah, I scored 98% on the labor law section of the bar exam.*

"Okay," Red went on, "here's the deal. I was getting off my shift last week, and they said they were short of staff, so me and a few others were forced to stay and work a double shift. I was about to fall off to sleep every five minutes."

"What does your union say about that?" I knew damn well there was no correctional officers union in Indiana. It's a "right to work" state, anti-union.

"We don't have no union . . ."

"Oh yeah, that's right, my bad. I forgot." I pretended to think hard. "What you describe is probably a violation of the Fair Labor and Standards Act. Go to the U.S. Department of Labor website, find the Wage and Hour division, and file a complaint. You also have to exhaust administrative remedy by filing an employee grievance with the IDOC before you can take them to court."

Red now had a plan of action.

As I returned to my work station I wondered if Red would begin to see the need for unions and government agencies to stand as watchdogs over the abusive ways large businesses and organizations exploit labor. Perhaps he would sense a crack in the free market economic philosophy and realize that every institution, particularly large ones, needed to be held accountable. Live and learn.

My discussions with those on opposite ends of the political spectrum helped me figure out why Americans were so divided on issues like the War on Drugs. The fundamental difference, the key to understanding the split between rightists and leftists, is how they classify issues – as either an economic issue, or as a moral issue.

If the problem is an economic issue, conservatives default to the libertarian "free market" philosophy. Hands off, no government interference, no taxes or regulations, let market forces naturally arrive at distributive justice. The liberal wing differs, contending that market forces must be kept in check to ensure economic justice, and the state's purpose is to ensure that the most good is done for the most people.

If the problem is classified as a moral issue, conservatives apply dictates of right and wrong – authoritarianism – based on personal moral standards they wish to be made universal. Liberals differ, asking whose moral standards we should use when we all have different value systems. Issues like abortion, gun control, and gay rights are fought on this ground, as is the War on Drugs.

The War on Drugs is a conservative Republican creation, and has been fought as a moral imperative. To them, drug use is a personal choice, a weakness, a behavior that can be changed. Blame is assigned to those who transgress the anti-drug moral code. Zero tolerance is their mantra, as it is in all moral crusades. A sober look at the costs and benefits of the drug war is impossible when we're fighting any issue on moral grounds.

Mel-T, on the far left, thought the nation's drug problem was misclassified back in 1968, erroneously framed as a moral issue when it was more easily defeated by treating it as an economic activity. Had far-sighted strategists used an economic approach, the War on Drugs would have been won many years ago.

"But the thing is," said Mel at our lunch table, "it's not really a war to stop drug use. It's a war on the black community, disguised, using colorblind, race-neutral terms, as a War on Drugs. Since the true goal has been to destroy the black community, the War on Drugs hasn't been a failure – it's been successful. Just look around you. About half the men in here are black, and most of them are in here for drugs, or drug-related crime."

Pendleton was 43% black, and the IDOC population was 38% black, disproportionate to Indiana's 9% free-world black population.

Edgar Lee spouted a line told over and over by the imprisoned black community: "The CIA invented crack in 1985 to fund arms for the contras in Nicaragua. There was a movie about it. It's true."

"I think it's more like some CIA types found a subversive way to make a profit to fund their arms deals," I replied, "and the business model of selling crack in the ghetto happened to be one that took off. It's true, the CIA sold dope in Oakland and L.A., but they didn't keep on selling it. There are hundreds of cities where crack is sold now and the CIA has nothing to do with any of it."

Mel steered us back from conspiracy theories to our current drug situation. "Now, if you really want to end the violence, and the murders, and all the crime associated with drugs," Mel continued, "the way to win the War on Drugs is two-dollar crack."

I had to laugh. "Two-dollar crack rocks?"

"You got that right. Two-dollar crack."

"And what else? Free weed? Over the counter Oxycontin?" If cheap drugs flooded the market, I postulated, we would have people stoned in public all day every day.

Mel was patient. He had thought this out, and had a strong argument. "Listen, man," he said as Mongoose joined our table. "You see people filling this prison because of weed or Oxycontin? No! You know the numbers – almost everyone in here with a long sentence for drug dealing was dealing crack. Some meth, some powder, some heroin, but not nearly as much as crack." It was true – crack dealers outnumbered all other drug dealers at Pendleton by a 5-to-1 ratio. "Weed, meth, and Oxy – those are white people's drugs, sold by white drug dealers." Technically, he could have included crack as a white man's drug, because 65% of crack users are white. But 88% of crack sellers are black, only 5% white, so the perception that crack is a black man's drug is fueled by the evidence of who's dealing it.

"White people with drug problems get treated differently than black people," Mel claimed. "Rush Limbaugh, he abused prescription painkillers. Did he go to jail?"

"Hell, no!" answered Edgar Lee.

"Even now, with heroin killing more and more white people every day, is there any big crackdown on heroin users or heroin dealers, like there was when crack hit the scene in 1985?"

"Not hardly," laughed Edgar Lee. "When there's drugs in the black neighborhood, the solution is to lock everybody up. When dope is out in the sticks, all of a sudden it's a *health* problem, not a crime problem."

To Mel-T, Edgar Lee, and Mongoose, there was no more clearer evidence of the racist intent of the legislature than in the way the state prosecuted drug offenders.

"But back to economics," I replied. "Tell me how two-dollar crack solves the problem."

"Assuming the problem is to stop drug dealing and the violence associated with drugs," Mel peered over his wire-rim glasses, indicating he didn't believe this was the government's goal, "you have to make dope so cheap it ain't worth selling and it ain't worth fighting over. So cheap that nobody has to rob or steal to get it."

"... to get it," Edgar Lee repeated. "I know *that's* right."

We looked at the business model of the crack cocaine industry. Before 1985, cocaine was only sold in powder form, and it was a white-dominated recreational drug, moderately expensive. The smallest quantum unit sold was the $100 gram, a sticker price out of reach of the poor. The market was restricted primarily to the yuppie class.

As every business student knows, one way to increase profits is to innovate and expand into new markets. The poor didn't have much money, but if the quantum sales unit could be reduced from $100 to $20, a large number of $20 sales would still generate a lot of cash. A few simple modifications to the powder product were invented, and the crack rock was born.

Crack rocks were easy to make, nothing high-tech like a *Breaking Bad* meth lab. Just a skillet and a stove, some powder cocaine, and a whole lot of baking soda. "Doesn't take a genius," observed Mel. "It's so easy, even stupid people can do it."

The distribution part of the business model, though, required a special kind of environment. At $20 per sale, it takes a lot of small sales to make crack dealing worth the time spent doing it. One sociologist, Phillipe Bourgois, studied the crack industry in New York City and determined that most crack dealers, on average, made less than minimum wage. The only people willing to sell crack would be those who are extremely poor and who have no other job prospects, and the best environment in which to sell crack would be places where population density was high and foot traffic common. Geographically, the inner city was the only location where repeated $20 sales could pay off in enough gross sales to make it profitable.

Poverty and geography explained why crack took root in black neighborhoods. The crack business model only worked there. It wasn't a CIA conspiracy that kept the crack industry alive for thirty years.

My conclusory opinion received no pushback: "I think the business of low-dollar dope wouldn't work anywhere else except in the black community."

"Now, to kill the dope game," Mel insisted, "make cocaine cheap, and turn that $20 rock into a $2 rock. All of a sudden, nobody wants to sell it. They barely get by as it is, selling for $20 and making about $10 profit per rock. If they only made a dollar a piece, they'd be better off picking up pop bottles."

"And just like that," Mongoose agreed, "there would be no more robbing or killing over dope or dope money."

"Well," I countered, "I can see two problems with two-dollar crack. Obviously, cocaine happens to be worth its weight in gold. And then, if crack was cheap, wouldn't more people be using it?"

"Look here," Mel responded. "The drug market doesn't work that way. Most people out there don't use crack, and their decision has nothing to do with the price of crack. If crack dropped from $20 to $2, would *you* start using it?"

"Not hardly. You could hand me free samples and I still wouldn't use it." I had told him this before.

"See? All non-users would say the same. Lowering the price of crack does not broaden the market. Current drug users are the market." He was describing a fairly stable subset of the human population. Users use whatever is available, and all price does is move them from one drug to another.

"White people are starting to figure that out," added Edgar Lee. "When they can't get their Oxycontin they move to heroin. When heroin's price goes up, they mix what heroin they can find with fentanyl." The fentanyl tranquilizer, mixed into heroin at ratios between 8 and 16 parts fentanyl to one part heroin, was responsible for an enormous number of overdoses and deaths.

"So get how stupid the government is with the War on Drugs," Mel continued, through another coughing fit. "These dumbasses are trying to cut off the supply of certain drugs with the intention of making demand dry up. Makes no sense at all with the illegal drug market, because a lack of supply in any one drug just moves users to other drugs."

Cocaine was a classic example. Tons of powder were speedboated or flown into Florida in the 70's and 80's, courtesy of Colombians who had yet to ally with Mexicans to create overland smuggling routes. Federal interdiction squeezed the cocaine supply, so dealers adapted, making cocaine stretch a long way through the watered-down crack cocaine market. Others, serving a dope-hungry crowd, turned to meth manufacture to fill the market void. All interdiction really did was to drive drug prices up, which increased the associated violence, and drove drug users to use more dangerous drugs.

More recently, synthetic drugs "spice" and "toon" have been supplanting marijuana use, and heroin has been the default option after painkiller prescriptions have gotten harder to obtain. What hasn't changed a bit is that small, persistent percentage of the population that seeks mood-altering substances.

Mel concluded that the only way to slash the street price of cocaine would be to legalize it. "Legalize *all* drugs," Mel proposed, "and treat addiction as a health problem. Treat drugs, more or less, the same way we treat alcohol."

Legalization would extract, at a minimum, 95% of cocaine's value. In 1989, Jorge Alvarez described for me cocaine's journey from Colombia to the United States. In Colombia, Jorge bought freshly processed cocaine for $1000 per kilogram. He considered that rather expensive, but its price in Colombia was due to its illegality there as well. He would invest another $4000 per kilo in transportation costs, flying it from a ranchland airstrip in Colombia to Norman's Cay, in the Bahamas. There, he would store it at the house of his high school pal from the Colombian city of Armenia, Carlos Lehder. Another pilot would wait for the right weather conditions and hop the load over to Florida, where the kilo's value jumped to $20,000. Just moving it from Colombia to the U.S. increased its value by a multiplier of 20.

The true value of cocaine, in a free market unencumbered by governments declaring it illegal, would be on par with similar agricultural products. Cocaine should cost the same as cocoa, vanilla, or coffee. "Legalizing cocaine turns it back into farm produce," Mel explained. "Just another tropical plant processed into powder. Your $20 rock would cost less than a dollar," Mel said as he peered over his glasses, "and believe me, nobody's doin' no robbin', stealin', or killin' over a handful of one dollar bills."

Mel had sixty years for dealing six grams of cocaine. Ten years per gram. Had cocaine offenses been classified the same as most alcohol offenses, as misdemeanors, his six grams may have warranted 60 days in jail – if he had been dealing at all.

I imagined legalization's effect on the prison system. In Indiana, 24.9% were imprisoned for drug offenses, consuming $180 million of the state's $720 million IDOC budget. Nationwide, 21% of prisoners were in for drugs – nearly half a million prisoners in federal and state prisons and jails. Legalization, if retroactive, would set them all free.

Using the thumbnail estimate that 30% of all other non-sex crimes were drug-related, the long term effect of legalization in the Unted States would reduce imprisonment by 41%, from 2.3 million to 1.4 million. Also gone would be millions of crimes committed every year – burglaries, thefts, robberies, murders – in exchange for society tolerating drug abuse the same way they tolerate alcohol abuse.

Seemed like a good trade-off to me.

CHAPTER NINE

One of Them Cases

"The risk of recidivism posed by sex offenders is 'frightening and high'."
– *Wallace v. State* (Ind. 2009); quoting *McKune v. Lile* (2002).

On a Tuesday morning I awoke to find an 8 o'clock pass on my locker, marked, "Mandatory, D.V. class, Room 201." D.V. class? My neighbors had no clue what it could be. I left my post in the law library at 8 a.m. and merged into the crowd entering Room 201 in the Education Building. As I entered the classroom, formerly used for Ball State University classes, I saw about twenty prisoners self-segregated into two groups. Blacks at the far end, whites closer to the door. I sat next to Donnie, and the mystery of our summons was spelled out on the chalkboard: Domestic Violence Class.

I was familiar with Donnie's criminal history, and I did not recall any arrests for domestic violence. Puzzled, I asked him, "You got any domestic charges I don't know about?"

Donnie was equally confused as to why he had been selected for this class. "No, I've never had anything like that." Besides the egging incident, there was nothing in his record to suggest he had anger issues. "How about you?" he asked.

I had an attempted murder conviction, but it had nothing to do with domestic violence. "No, me neither. I've had a few girlfriends beat on *me*," I joked, "but I never hit 'em back. What are we doing here?"

Others were perplexed, but nobody asked the instructor how we were selected. Our teacher was Ms. Billups, a rotund, forty-something black woman employed as an IDOC psychologist. She gave each of us a six-page handout on resolving conflicts in the home. Her first question to the class set the tone for the next three hours.

"Who here has ever hit a woman?"

Silence. Not a hand went up.

"When is it okay to hit a woman?"

"Never!" A series of voices repeated the word.

Wow, I thought. Ms. Billups had randomly selected twenty prisoners from the most violent prison in Indiana, and none had ever hit a woman, and none ever would. What are the odds?

On Donnie's right was Darrell, who had over 100 years for the rape and attempted murder of his girlfriend, and the same convictions for assaulting her ten-year-old daughter. A fireplug shaped black guy across the room, Marcus, had ten years for battery for strangling his girlfriend. She was begging for help from the 9-1-1 dispatcher as Marcus choked her with the phone cord and exclaimed, "Die, bitch, die!" I had seen his green sheet, and he had about a dozen domestic violence arrests, yet he was the first to holler, Never! In this classroom setting, I did not expect much truthfulness to be displayed.

Ms. Billups went on with her curriculum, ignoring the deceit. Marcus, like a kid hopped up on sugar, was the first to answer every question she threw out. His responses were so fast, it was like he was playing a word-association game. Ms. Billups: "What are the topics you and your woman would argue about?" Marcus: Kids! Money! Where we gonna eat tonight! Ms. Billups: "How often should a man and woman have sexual relations?" Marcus: Every day! Twice a day! There was general agreement from those sitting near 30-year-old Marcus.

"Hold on," I spoke up. "Sex every day? Isn't that a bit much? Wouldn't it be better, more enjoyable for both of you, if you laid off for a day or two and made it more special? You know – delayed gratification?"

"You're supposed to want sex every day! That's what's natural! You get the urge," Marcus reasoned, "and that's what you got a woman for."

"Okay, I understand *you* want sex every day, but what about her?"

"Erry day!! *My* woman, she wants sex as much as I do."

I was a tad skeptical. "Don't you think she would like it more if it wasn't every day? Look, it's like this," I said. "I love fried chicken. But I can't eat fried chicken every day. Fried chicken is better if I have it, at most, every other day."

Marcus whooped uncontrollably, hopped in his chair, and one arm went flying loosely over his head. "You can't compare sex to fried chicken!!" I had sinned against his religion, mixing two sacraments. White boy was out of his mind.

"Well, sure you can," I pressed on. "You're talking about two appetites. And if you can control your urges, you might find out sex becomes better for both of you."

I must have been wrong, because I didn't get any support for my opinion, not even from Ms. Billups. For three hours we listened to Ms. Billups cover the written material, interrupted by Marcus' proclamations, followed by murmurs of assent from those around him. Donnie never said a word. At the end, we were told we would all be getting certificates placed in our IDOC file for completing the class.

I turned to Donnie. "This is the prison system's idea of rehabilitation, I suppose?"

Donnie shrugged, bewildered. I had a hunch Ms. Billups would go back to Psychological Services and check off one of the duties associated with her job description.

Returning to the law library, I was greeted by an unusually cheery crowd.

"There he is! Congratulations!" A couple guys clapped, and my confusion showed.

"What did I do?" Completing the domestic violence class couldn't have brought this on.

"You don't know? You got Ziegler's life sentence overturned! For the first time in twenty years, he's got an out date. He'll be out in ten more years."

My, how legal stories get mangled in the retelling. Zig's life sentence out of Kentucky had not been overturned; in fact, we hadn't filed any paperwork with the Kentucky court where he had been sentenced to life in the early 1990's.

It took several minutes to explain what Ziegler and I had accomplished, and as I detailed our work I expected my audience's enthusiasm would wane, but it didn't. Zig had life, but was eligible for parole after 12 years. He had sixty years in Indiana, running concurrent to his Kentucky sentence. Indiana kept a Kentucky detainer on Zig for when Zig finished the sixty. What I had done was research Kentucky's parole laws and write to Kentucky to get the detainer lifted. I argued that Zig should have been paroled years ago, and that if he ever did get transferred to Kentucky they would have to grant his parole immediately. Technically, they had failed to hold a parole hearing for Zig, and I insinuated some due process rights were implicated in their oversight. It was all mumbo jumbo, really, just nicely worded letters with the thinly veiled threat of habeas corpus action and a ton of legal work for somebody down there.

It worked. We didn't have to file anything in court. Kentucky sent the IDOC a confirmation letter, removing the detainer. Now Zig could transfer to a lower level facility with the certainty that his Indiana outdate was real.

Nobody cared that battle-hardened "lawyer work" didn't produce Zig's victory, or that no conviction or sentence had been overturned. They were starved for good news, and this would do. "You got him out," Mike Lindsey told me. "That's all that matters."

A few days after Zig's victory I was pounding away on my keyboard when Edgar Lee stationed himself next to my computer screen. He wore the half-smile about to turn giggle, and said, "I got a guy over there needs to see you." I looked at him as if to say, Why doesn't he come over here?

"Needs to see you privately," Edgar Lee elaborated. "He's got one of them cases."

Code words. Sex offender. They are hesitant to walk into a room and announce what kind of help they're looking for, and quite a few law clerks won't help them. Most jailhouse lawyers refuse to sully their hands on a sex case, not unless the money is really, really good. Several of us in the law library will look at their cases, though, because experience has taught us that, of all crime classifications, sex offenders are the ones most likely to be truly innocent.

I ushered Yasmani Salazar to a back room. He was a native of Mexico, could barely speak English, and I saw from the front page of his legal work that he was imprisoned for two counts of Class A felony child molesting, and two counts of Class D child solicitation. Marion County.

"*Mi abogado*, she do nothing," Yasmani explained.

"How many years did you get?" A blank stare. I would have to break out what little Spanish I knew. "*Cuantos anos tiene?*"

"*Tiene veinte cinco anos.*"

Aw, shoot, I just asked him how old he is. He's twenty five. So I thought, and tried again.

"*Y su sentencia, cuanto anos desde la corte?*"

"*Setenta. Setenta anos.*"

"Seventy years?" Just checking my translation.

"*Si.* Se-ven-ty years."

Understood. Now, what kind of help did he want? An appeal? A PC? A sentence mod?

"*Que como ayuda tu quieres?*"

Yasmani launched into way more fluent Spanish than I could understand, and I was lost. "*Despacio, despacio,*" I pleaded. "Slow down. *No comprendo Espanol rapido!*"

He shifted to one-quarter speed and we settled into a Sesame Street vocabulary, half Spanish, half English. His *abogado* – lawyer – was *muy malo* – very bad. His appeal had recently failed. He had two thirty-five year sentences and he thought they should be *concurrente, no consecutivo. Mismo victima.* Same victim in both cases. He needed a post-conviction petition done, alleging ineffective assistance of counsel.

He left his legal work with me – yet another twenty pound bag to carry to my dorm for the weekend. I told him I would see him *proxima semana*, and his *peticion* would be *listo* then.

"*Uno semana?*"

Yep, one week.

"*Gracias! Gracias!*" He had one more question on his mind. "*Y cuanto cuesta?*"

I waved my hand about the cost. "*Nada. Sin precio. Es gratis.*"

On Sunday afternoon most of the dorm cleared out to go to rec while I stayed inside with Yasmani's legal work piled across my bed. I was absorbed in reading his trial transcript and scribbling notes when I became aware of two individuals standing at the end of my bunk.

"What the fuck are you doing?" It was Brian Hixon, a guy I had helped get out of seg when IA had put an "active STG" tag on him. He was a "retired" AB – Aryan Brotherhood. Not gang-banging any more, not calling the shots. He had not covered up his blood red AB patch, though – the tattoo was earned by shedding the blood of another race, a prerequisite to full membership. This failure to cover the patch got him placed in seg, indefinitely, and I had argued for him that covering his tat now would be a violation of the disciplinary code on tattooing. They can't ask a prisoner to violate an IDOC rule as a condition of getting out of segregation.

I didn't know the other guy with Hixon. He was an AB, new to Pendleton, who worked out on the weight machines with Hixon.

"I'm, uh . . . doing legal work." Stating the obvious.

"Who for?"

"Uh . . . little Mexican kid, in J-cellhouse." I knew the ABs didn't like to see whites helping anybody but whites.

"Uh huh." Hixon was noncommital about me helping nonwhite prisoners – all the law clerks at Pendleton helped others without regard to race, and no gang objected. Indiana's racial culture wasn't like out west. In California, prisoners strictly followed codes of racial segregation.

Hixon's partner picked up one of Yasmani's papers from my bed. He pretended to read the paper, but his eyes didn't move back and forth. Hixon was also disconcertingly still.

"What's this Mexican in prison for?" The question was asked by Hixon's sidekick in a way that told me he already knew. He just wanted to hear me say it. Hixon, head down, rolled his eyes to the side to watch his partner.

"He's got a, uh, a child molesting conviction." So this was their point of contention.

There's no CO going to rescue you in a situation like this. The CO for K-dorm can't see into the bed area. There's a security camera mounted above the bathroom entrance, but those intent on doing violence don't give a shit about being recorded. If they do care, they just commit the assault in the bathroom, where the camera doesn't see.

An unsettling several seconds passed. The two exchanged glances, and I knew a decision was being made. By Hixon, I was sure. The other guy needed the 'go' signal. The Crystal Bic pen in my hand wouldn't do me much good. Probably just piss him off if I tried to stick him in the eye.

Hixon picked up the page I had been reading. "How much you charging this chomo?"

"Uh . . . nothing. He came into the law library, he's broke, and I ain't charging him nothing."

"Look," Hixon said, slowly. "I know you. I know you like to look out for people. You helped me out of a jam one time." I think he said this for his buddy's benefit. "The thing is, you can't be helping out no chomos unless they pay. You got that?"

"Yeah. Sure. He doesn't have any money, though, so . . ."

Hixon cut me off. "He's got *something*. These chomos don't get a free ride. You got that? So you get *something* from him."

"I already gave my word I would help him for free," I said, falling back on the convict code. You give your word, you have to come through. Every prisoner knew that.

Hixon's buddy laid his page back on the bed, folded his arms, and glared. I was "using" the code to defy their wishes.

Hixon processed the dilemma. "Yeah... I hear you. But this is different. He's a chomo, so the convict code don't apply to him. You get something from him, or we're gonna get something from you."

Strange, the thoughts that enter your head when you're confronted like this. I admired the way Hixon delivered a threat – quietly, calmly, a nonspecific threat, open-ended in its possibilities. He was an excellent, skilled threatener. And we still seemed to be on good terms.

"Yeah, man," I said. "I can see your point." Keeping chomos in line was part of the prison's cultural fabric. Yasmani would have to do me a favor. He already felt obligated, so it would be easy to suggest that he show his appreciation. "He'll come up with something."

Yasmani's case raised several questions, but none of those questions doubted Yasmani's guilt. Class A felony child molesting occurs when a person age 21 or over has sexual intercourse or performs "deviate sexual conduct" on a child under age 14. Yasmani was 23, and his victim, a family friend, was 10. The specifics on what occurred in every sex case are always difficult to read – imagine how jurors squirm when they hear the allegations in a courtroom. Yasmani had digitally penetrated the girl, per her testimony, something no physician could confirm. The girl told her mother, who promptly reported it to the police, who arrested Yasmani. The prosecutor charged him with one Class A felony and one Class D felony, and somehow – despite Yasmani being an illegal immigrant – he was released on bond, with a no-contact order (NCO) prohibiting Yasmani from seeing the girl or her family again.

A few months after making bond, Yasmani violated the NCO. The girl's family decided to trust Yasmani, and he slept in their house. He snuggled up to the girl a second time, same story, and was arrested again. No bond this time. (See? The prosecutor's office isn't as stupid as you thought.)

When convicted, entirely on the weight of the child's testimony, the judge treated the two acts as completely separate offenses, not as a single course of conduct. Committing the second molestation while on bond was an aggravating circumstance. Yasmani got 35 years on each Class A felony, consecutive, for a 70-year term. Under the gain time statute in effect at the time he committed the offenses, he would get one day off his sentence for every six days served – 85% of his sentence. Six-sevenths, to be exact, which is 85.7%.

The direct appeal contained something I had never seen before – a deliberate attempt by the public defender to make things worse.

The attorney raised two issues – insufficient evidence, and excessive sentencing. Insufficient evidence, under the standard of *Jackson v. Virginia* (1979), had no chance of winning because courts have repeatedly held that the uncorroborated testimony of a victim is sufficient to find guilt "beyond a reasonable doubt." To overturn a conviction under *Jackson*, the record must be "wholly devoid of any relevant evidence." The public defender had to be willfully ignorant to try the insufficient evidence argument.

Worse, though, was the excessive sentencing argument. The attorney went through all the motions, comparing Yasmani's 70 to the max on murder, 65, and noted Yasmani's lack of any criminal history. She then decried the 85% mandate, writing that Yasmani would have to do 60 years on the 70. At the end of that line in the appellant's brief she appended a footnote. The footnote read: "The IDOC website lists Yasmani Salazar's EPRD as 9-1-2045."

I was jaw-droppingly appalled. This is what prisoners refer to as "dry snitching," giving information to authorities in an indirect manner. If Yasmani got 70, do 60, his outdate should have been in 2070. A 2045 date indicated the IDOC had miscalculated Yasmani's time under the old 2-do-1 standard, 35 on the 70. The attorney was telling the court, and the Indiana Attorney General, that they needed to contact the IDOC and get Yasmani's release date moved by 25 years.

I guess being freed at age 58 and being deported to Mexico wasn't good enough, in the public defender's eyes. Death by mildew on the taxpayers' dime was better.

So much for the adversarial system of justice.

There wasn't much I could do for Yasmani. I wrote up two PC issues under ineffective assistance of trial counsel – failure to investigate, and failure to adequately cross-examine the girl and her family members. Perhaps these issues would elicit some new, usable information through PC hearings. I was curious as to why, if they believed the girl was truthful in the first instance, they had allowed the molester back in their home.

We checked the box requesting appointment of a public defender (like feeding his carcass to a second wave of vultures), and I told Yasmani his petition would receive a "merit review" within two years. In the meantime, he needed to find "new evidence," of what kind, I had no idea. I could not imagine any evidence, short of the girl's full recantation, that would do Yasmani any good.

He gave me his thanks, and offered to pay me, again, which made it unnecessary for me to bring it up. "*Quince sopas,*" I replied. Fifteen Ramen noodle soups. Five dollars value.

My word that I would work *gratis* was ignored by Yasmani. Within his cultural code he felt obligated to pay. I asked for soups because they were bulky, and I knew the AB's would be watching to see me receive a bag of items.

A few days later I carried the soups to the dorm in a clear plastic bag and tossed them on my bed. They laid there about an hour while I attended to my post-work routine.

Brian Hixon never asked what Salazar paid me.

I had reviewed a total of twenty child molestation cases since 2006, and most of them followed an evidentiary pattern similar to Yasmani's. In all but four there was no physical evidence of any kind, no evidence of physical trauma to the victim. Sixteen cases stood on victim testimony alone, although supported by the testimonies of others verifying circumstantial details. Prosecutors danced around the fine line separating eyewitness testimony from hearsay. The convictions hinged on whether the jurors, or the judge in a bench trial, believed the child.

It would take a rare, disturbed child to single-handedly concoct stories of sexual abuse out of thin air, and even a brilliantly crafted tale would probably wither under effective cross-ex. In nearly every trial record I saw persuasive signs of authenticity. Kids who testified were frightened, ashamed, hesitant – yet gave detailed accounts, with good memories of time and place and circumstance. Their answers did not seem coached, but spontaneous. Emotional scars were visible, and it was sad to know they would take years to recover, if ever.

Then again, if they were well-coached, or if they innocently believed their own false stories, how would I know?

The children were tragic figures before the defense attorney delivered his or her first question, and the lawyers had to tread carefully to avoid inflaming the jury against their client, the accused monster. The nonconfrontational tone of cross-ex invariably annoyed those who wound up convicted of child molesting. "My attorney," said one, "acted like she was this kid's best friend." These prisoners could think of dozens of sharp questions their attorneys failed to ask. Failure to adequately cross-ex, under *Davis v. Alaska* (1974), was an issue raised in nearly every sex offender's PC petition.

The four cases I read that were supported by physical evidence were like a different genre of the offense – horrifying. The magnitude of harm and the duration of the repeated conduct evinced a depravity beyond my understanding. "You thought you could get away with this?" A shrug of one shoulder, no eye contact. "There's nothing I can do about this case." No technicalities? Can't you get my confession thrown out? "No, I can't. You've dug yourself too deep."

Of the twenty child molesting cases, there were two where the testimony raised many questions. The circumstances surrounding both cases were not quite right either, and both prisoners claimed they were innocent.

Chad Kimbrough was probably innocent, as far as I could tell. He was a scrawny, dark-haired guy with oversized glasses, about 30 when he was arrested in 2005. His eight-year-old daughter accused him of molesting her, one incident only. He was charged with a Class A felony, 20-to-50 years, do half, as was the law at that time. The prosecutor offered him a plea deal, 4-do-2, indicating she felt the evidence was not strong. Chad rejected the deal, hired private counsel, and took his chances at trial.

"I didn't want to plead guilty to something I didn't do," Chad explained. "I would lose custody of my daughter and have to register as a sex offender."

I tried to explain to Chad the mathematical logic of accepting or rejecting a plea deal. "If you're threatened with fifty, and they offer you four, you should take the deal unless you have a 92% chance of winning at trial. You're risking an extra forty-six years to win back the four you would lose taking the deal." I also showed Chad the statistical evidence, that about 30% of defendants are acquitted in Marion County. "Why would you risk 46 to win 4, when there is only a 3-in-10 chance that you'll win?"

Chad shook his head and tossed my numbers aside with a flick of his left hand. "I wouldn't have pled guilty even if they would have given me probation." (Quite often, they do offer probation, so as to get a prior offense on the conviction sheet to use for a habitual enhancement later.) "I didn't do it, so I wasn't going to plead guilty to it. Simple as that."

Turning down a plea deal, to the prosecutor, is a worse offense than the crime itself. I gathered data from prisoners who had been offered deals, and compared the offered sentences to the sentences they ultimately received. Like Kimbrough, offered 4 but got 50; like DeLucenay, offered 17 got 48. A survey of 52 prisoners yielded plea offers totaling 621.5 years, and sentences totaling 2090 years. Turning down a plea increases the penalty by a multiplier of 3.36. A rejected twelve-year offer became a forty-year sentence.

Chad's paid attorney did an outstanding job for him at trial. His daughter's testimony differed from her pretrial statements in material ways, and when I compared the two accounts the second one seemed to be an attempt to remember what she had said in the first account. The jurors didn't know this, though; they aren't given the pretrial statements.

On several details, the girl was confused. Were the lights on or off? Can't remember. Was your mother home at the time? Not sure. Why did you wait several months to tell somebody? I didn't. A lot of things didn't quite add up. But the detail that stood out, to me, was the girl's description of Chad's genitalia. She said his penis was black.

Chad was white. It's possible, though, that the only penis this girl had ever seen was black. When Chad left for work, his wife, he learned, was prostituting herself to several black men in the neighborhood, in part to finance her drug habit. Chad got to know more about this after he had been arrested and forced to move out.

Another detail barely touched on at trial was the long-running custody dispute over their daughter, coupled with potential divorce proceedings. Both wanted custody, and both alleged the other spouse was unfit. Chad had several misdemeanor arrests – no drugs, no violence, no sex offenses – and one misdemeanor conviction, for theft, pled down from a Class D felony. His father-in-law, a Marion County Sheriff's Deputy, "hated" him, Chad said. "He was always trying to get me locked up so she could keep my daughter and not let me have visitation rights."

A coincidence left out of the trial record was the daughter's friendship with another girl her age who had been molested. After this friend had testified in her own case, she had gotten to go to a summer camp for abused children. "This other girl got to ride horses at camp, and my daughter had always wanted to go horse-back riding. She loved horses." A bedroom photo of the girl's room showed a dozen toy ponies.

There was so much the jury did not know – this is overwhelmingly true in every case heard by a jury. Three voted to convict Chad. Nine voted for acquittal. They were given an *Allen* instruction and sent back to the jury room to hammer out their differences.

Hours later, they returned to the courtroom, frazzled. No change in the vote. Hung jury.

Now, common sense might tell you that since the standard of proof is "beyond a reasonable doubt," and nine of the twelve found reasonable doubt, it would be reasonable to conclude that reasonable doubt exists. Either that, or

75% of the jurors are illogical, unreasonable people. Perhaps a directed verdict by the court would be appropriate – there is a Trial Rule 50 covering directed verdicts, where the jury's verdict can be tossed aside by the judge for a variety of reasons. But Trial Rule 50 is rarely employed, and it was not mentioned in Chad's proceedings.

The prosecutor opted to retry the case.

Chad's second trial was a shadow of the first one. The girl's direct examination flowed like they were reading a script, and the extraneous information about custody disputes, adultery, and summer camps was nonexistent. Cross-ex was only a few scant pages, no "black" penis mentioned this time, no shaky circumstantial details questioned. It was as if Chad's attorney had no knowledge of the questions asked at his first trial.

Chad, dirt poor to begin with, had run out of money for attorney fees. "I still owe my attorney from the first trial," he told me. "She wouldn't do the second trial unless I paid her up front." He had to claim pauper status, and was appointed a public defender.

"The jury came back in less than an hour. Guilty. I saw Judge Altice's face as he read the verdict form, and even he seemed surprised."

Chad recalled the verdict being read. "I couldn't believe my ears. I thought they were reading it wrong. It hits you so hard, you literally can't speak. You can't form words. Stunned."

Judge Robert Altice slammed Chad with the 50-year max, twenty years above the presumptive sentence, based on aggravating factors. Chad had "violated a position of trust," he had a lengthy misdemeanor arrest record, and he had a prior Class D felony conviction. The felony had actually been dismissed, pled down to a misdemeanor, but the public defender overlooked it. Minor detail. Off to prison Chad went, outdate June 3, 2031.

I had become familiar with Chad's case in 2009, and passed it off to Bill Woodford because my schedule, with a full class load at Ball State, did not permit me to give Chad's legal work the attention Bill could provide. Chad's PC bumped along for a few years while Chad spent his days working in the Chaplain's Office. He had a voracious appetite for self-help religious books, the kind hawked by televangelists. He holed up in his cell and read, avoiding the rec yard like it was the valley of death, which, for many convicted child molesters, it may be. He lived every day *scared*, terrified of others, especially the unpredictable Tom Cat. Chad would skip meals to avoid being in the same building with the brash Mr. Cat. In 2009, another child molester, Kent McDonald, was beaten to death by his cellmate in E-dorm, and the IDOC instituted a policy of only celling sex offenders with other sex offenders. This relieved Chad of some pressure – he had been exploited financially by every cellmate he had had for over three years. Life was not good for Chad, and then his PC petition was denied.

"God's putting me through this for a reason," Chad said, "but I have no idea what that reason could be."

Chad Kimbrough's last hope for getting his conviction overturned rested on the possibility of his daughter recanting her trial testimony. He could not contact her directly, due to a no contact order, but he hoped she would one day figure out what she had done, appreciate the wrongfulness of it, and come forward with the truth. Whatever her excuse would be, "I was mistaken," or "I was pressured to tell a false story," or "I truly believed it at the time, but I have since figured out it was not true," or "I exaggerated," it would be good enough for the court to reverse his conviction and set him free. Or so he thought.

I didn't have the heart to tell him, recantations are almost *never* accepted by the court.

The county court judge in a PC hearing listens to the recantation, declares it "not worthy of credit," and the appellate court defers to the county court's judgment, because the county judge was in the best position to rule on the witness's credibility. One might think a recantation would be an overwhelmingly good reason to put the case before a new jury, since the standard of relief on a PC under *Strickland* is for the petitioner to show only a "reasonable probability" of a different outcome at trial. But the courts have created a way to bypass *Strickland* and any further juror examination by declaring the new evidence or new testimony to have zero value. Would twelve jurors all value a recantation as having zero persuasive value? Doubtful. A recantation should open up due process nearly every time. But the courts are more interested in preserving the "finality" of judgments than in pursuing justice. They have even codified "finality" as the prime motivation for post-conviction processes, in the federal habeas statutes, 28 USC 2254 and 2255.

It's the law: post-conviction procedures do not exist to ensure justice. They exist to prove that the courts seldom, if ever, make mistakes.

David Scott was a Pendleton prisoner who ran through the "not worthy of credit" declaration yet prevailed in the end, winning his release. In 1984, at age 16, he learned of the death of an 89-year-old woman, for whom he had done yard work. She had been murdered in her home. David was a loose-talking braggart type, a tad mentally ill, and he liked the attention his tall tales would garner. He told a few people he had done the killing, and he enjoyed their appalled reactions.

One of these people told the cops, and the cops put a wire on this informant. David was enticed to confess on tape. Wiring up an informant is a handy practice for detectives – they get to interview a suspect through their agent without having to comply with those silly constitutional protections, like warning a suspect of his right to remain silent or his right to have an attorney. They don't have to warn the suspect, *Hey, you're not really entertaining your friend Joe with a tall tale, you're talking directly to the police.*

An "agent" of any business in a civil case would be liable for the agent's actions, but in a criminal case the courts pretend there is no connection whatsoever, and no need to exclude the clandestinely obtained statements.

David Scott's "confession" got him convicted, and sentenced to 30 years for burglary and 50 years for murder. His direct appeal focused on the confession, trying to get it excluded because David was a mentally ill juvenile. The appeal failed.

David moved on to a PC petition, raising "newly discovered evidence." Others could be placed at the murder scene, and one admitted culpability. The PC court judge declared all this to be "not worthy of credit," so no jury was allowed to consider it. His PC appeal failed – the appellate court would not substitute their judgment for the county court's judgment.

David Scott lingered in prison for 24 years, spinning yarns about trimming trees with a helicopter, and any other fanciful tale that would enthrall his listeners, who would laugh at him behind his back. He picked up the nickname "Whiskey." He was a nut job, untreated, and fit right in with the mentally ill faction running chaotically around Pendleton. Just the kind of guy, we figured, who would kill an 89-year-old woman and not have the sense to shut up about it.

In 2008 a murderer in Kentucky got his blood drawn, and his DNA was placed into the CODIS database. His DNA matched DNA left at the scene in David Scott's murder case. The Kentucky prisoner confessed.

An attorney helped David file a successive PC, and no court could fall back on the "not worthy of credit" excuse this time. In short order, David Scott was released. He had less than a year to do until he maxed out his original sentence.

DNA rescued David Scott, but even DNA testing can be held by the court to be inferior to testimonial evidence. In the case of Jerry Watkins, the Indiana courts favored the testimony of a jailhouse informant over blood evidence, in order to keep Watkins locked up.

Watkins was convicted of the November 12, 1984, murder of 11-year-old Margaret Sue Altes in Hancock County. The case-clinching evidence was the testimony of Dennis Ackeret, a cellmate of Watkins. Ackeret testified that Watkins confessed to the murder, and to molesting the girl twice. Another inmate, Paul Frozzitta, testified that Ackeret was making up the confession story to curry favor with prosecutors, but the jury convicted Watkins anyway.

Within thirty days of Watkins' conviction, inmates Bruce Jones and Paul Rork came forward with testimony also discrediting Ackeret, but the court found these two "not worthy of credit." Watkins' direct appeal raised several issues, including an argument based on the "inconclusive" blood tests that did not match Watkins back in this pre-DNA era. The direct appeal lost, and Watkins settled in at Pendleton to endure an ignominious existence as a pedophile child murderer.

Along came DNA testing. The blood evidence left on the victim was tested, and it did not match Watkins. He got released, right?

Wrong. The county court judge on Watkins' PC declared the non-match of the DNA was essentially no different from the non-match of the blood type test done in 1984. The DNA wasn't "new" evidence, it was "cumulative" evidence. Ackeret was still worthy of credit, the others were not, so there was no "reasonable probability" of a different outcome at trial.

What all these post-conviction proceedings come down to is a judge declaring his opinion trumps the opinion of a hypothetical set of twelve jurors. The "reasonable probability" standard of *Strickland* is ignored.

The Indiana Court of Appeals upheld the county court, with identical reasoning, in 1998. Jailhouse snitch – credible. DNA evidence – ignorable.

Since it was a newly discovered evidence claim, as well as a *Brady* claim for the prosecutor failing to disclose exculpatory evidence, and because it raised an "actual innocence" claim, the federal court permitted Watkins to file a petition for writ of habeas corpus. Judge David Hamilton granted the writ, in April 2000, calling the Indiana court rulings a "clear misunderstanding of the DNA evidence." The Indiana Attorney General appealed, trying to keep Watkins locked up. The appeal was denied, and Watkins was released on July 21, 2000, after spending over 15 years in prison for a horrible crime he did not commit.

Neither David Scott nor Jerry Watkins received compensation for their wrongful convictions. Indiana has no law to compensate innocent people for their time wrongfully spent in prison.

"Believing a jailhouse snitch," I analogized to Mike Lindsey, "is like eating out of a garbage can. It's true there might be something edible in the dumpster, but do you really want to risk it?"

"If only jurors would look at it like that," he replied, "a lot of innocent people wouldn't be here."

Every trial court is authorized by law to be the gatekeeper for trial evidence. The judge can declare evidence inadmissible for a number of reasons; however, testimonial evidence does not have to run through any pretrial gauntlet. There is no "Motion to Exclude Witness Testimony" based on the witness's alleged lack of credibility. Felons may testify, as well as the mentally ill (with no warning to the jury that this witness is fresh out of a mental institution, using my own case as an example). Jailhouse rats hoping to receive favorable treatment from prosecutors may testify, while the prosecutor assures the jury no actual deal to secure this testimony has taken place *at the time of the trial*. Rewards may come later, of course, and if the convicted defendant finds out about it, the prosecutor disclaims any connection between the lying rat's trial testimony and the 34 felony convictions that resulted in probation for the rat (using my own case as an example).

There was a time, before 1840, when felons were not allowed to testify because they were inherently unworthy of belief. If a felon was the sole witness to a crime, the prosecution had a big problem, and the defendant would likely go free.

Everyone thinks they have a keen ability to flesh out the truth and determine, through paralinguistic evidence, whether a witness is lying or not. Surely, thirty minutes on a witness stand under the fire of professional cross-examination will reveal the credibility of the witness, even if the witness is a person the jurors have never met before. In reality, the idea that anyone can state with certainty that a stranger is lying to them or telling the truth is patently absurd.

We all get lied to every day, and we scarcely know it. People we know well, people we trust – we're sure we know when they're lying – get away with their lies on a regular basis. You think you know, but you don't. *You don't.* As human lie detectors, we fail miserably.

Spouses cheat, and it can go undetected for years, while an avalanche of lies cascade day after day. Kids lie to their parents constantly, and only because they successfully get away with lying. Anything involving financial gain puts our antennae up, ready to detect lies, yet we strain to figure out the truth.

Some liars do a pretty convincing job. If you can be fooled over and over by the person closest to you, how can you believe an unfamiliar trial witness "beyond a reasonable doubt," especially one with an incentive to lie?

Recreation supervisor Melissa Nash claimed she received a snitch note from a prisoner, informing her I had "non-legal" information on my law library computer. The staff member who told me this also confided to me, "It's bullshit. There was no note. Not unless she wrote it herself." Rats write to IA, not to a rec supervisor.

Nash called IA, and an obnoxious IA clown seized my computer and sent me back to my dorm. I was allowed to return a few days later and continue my work, aided by the back-up files we kept. Six weeks later, my computer was returned. Nothing but legal work on it. No write-up possible.

Two months later, the IDOC agreed to settle the civil suit regarding their ban of the *P.C. Guidebook*. It was settled on my terms – ban lifted, and the IDOC paid all costs. What the Pendleton mail room had done was unconstitutional, and indefensible. The books were delivered to the prisoners, and word of our victory spread like all gossip does in prison – quickly, wildly, with little regard for the facts. Some thought we had "gotten rich" over it. Not even close.

Two days after the settlement was signed, IA ordered my immediate removal from the law library, no reason given. No rules violations were alleged. No poor work performance was graded by my supervisor. No "threat to the safety and security of the facility," the catch-all excuse, was voiced. Just go.

So I went. And filed another civil suit, alleging retaliation for the successful exercise of my First Amendment rights. In the meantime I was out of a job. Within a month I was also out of my dorm, placed in a solitary cell in J-cellhouse, as a consequence of raising safety concerns about K-dorm's new double bunks.

A dorm counselor intercepted me on a walkway days later. "Watch your stuff," he shiftily warned me. "People here have talked about going into your cell and taking all of your legal work in order to keep you out of court."

Prison staff did not behave like street cops, never crossing the thin blue line and betraying one of their own. They were as backstabbing as the convicts.

"Right on," I replied. I knew not to linger with this guy or to ask follow-up questions. "I'll take precautions."

Within a day, my files were farmed out to a dozen locations.

Moving to J-cellhouse, I had the fortune to be celled next to Wally Lockhart, a congenial guy, three years my junior, a fellow Cubs fan. He had recently been initiated into the world of pro se legal work. He had been "framed" on a series of child molesting charges and sentenced to 80 years in prison. The appellate court knocked it down to 70 years, two 35's running wild, with some lesser Class C felonies running concurrent. "I'm innocent on the two Class A convictions," he told me, pleading for my help.

My law library time had been throttled from 45 hours a week to 5 hours a week, and I also recalled the admonition from Hixon and the AB's. I had to throw off my persona as a law library clerk and become a jailhouse lawyer – and be paid. Lockhart could afford my services. He had been in the U.S. Army and Virginia National Guard prior to working for a private security firm in Iraq and Afghanistan. He had put some money aside and diligently compensated me for my time at a dollar an hour.

There were some rather peculiar facts in his story, and I wasn't sure if he was wrongfully accused or just very good at persuasively raising doubt.

Wally's accuser, J.R. (initials are used in the record on sex cases), went to law enforcement rather late in the game, at age 20. Wally was in Iraq at the time J.R. reported the sex offenses, and what set off her decision was Wally's refusal to re-up a year's rent for J.R. at the Valle Vista Arms in Greenwood. Before he left for the Middle East he had paid a year's lease in advance. Wally had, admittedly, maintained a sexual relationship with J.R. from 2003 to 2008, beginning when J.R. was 14 and Wally was 38. The lease expired in July 2009, and the landlord took J.R. to court and evicted her when she (and Wally) failed to renew for year two. The landlord testified for Wally, saying J.R. was angry when Wally didn't send more money. Next day, J.R. went to the Indianapolis police.

It was an easy case for J.R. to make because she knew Wally possessed evidence to prove some of her allegations. They had made a sex video when she was 14. A search warrant produced Wally's copy. It proved the Class C felony of deviate sexual conduct with a minor, but it did not suffice to prove the pivotal charges, Class A felony child molesting, because for those counts the victim had to be under age 14.

She claimed Wally had sex with her when she was 13, and when she was 9. She could not prove these, but through her tears on the witness stand she provided enough detail to be believed. Why had she failed to say anything about these incidents until she was 20? She "loved" Wally, she testified, and "wanted to keep getting things" from him.

The centerpiece of the prosecution was movie time. They dimmed the lights and put on the short video of Wally and J.R. in a motel room. The jury, Wally told me, cringed, and "was giving me this look like they wanted to kill me." Exactly the reaction the prosecutor hoped for.

Wally's defense counsel had tried to prevent the video from being shown, agreeing in pretrial proceedings to "stipulate" that Wally had intercourse with

J.R. when she was 14, as the video itself proved through circumstantial evidence. The state refused to so stipulate, alleging the video showed J.R. at age 13. (In J.R.'s deposition she stated she was 14 in the video, and she mentioned it during the filming.) In the state's closing argument, however, the state agreed J.R. was 14 in the video. Had the state agreed with this fact before trial, the judge would have excluded the video – which was enormously prejudicial to deciding the Class A felony charges. The prosecutor played stupid at pretrial in order to show the video to the jury and elicit the loathing necessary to win a conviction.

Were it not for the video, Wally may have walked on the Class A's and suffered much lesser penalties for the Class C felonies. The state, in closing, conceded the Class A's rested solely on J.R.'s word. "If you believe her, there is enough to convict." And she should be believed "because she cried," and because "she told you honestly" about what happened. The prosecutor also implied there was other molestation evidence, other victims not mentioned: "These are not the actions of someone who has done this for the first time with a child."

Wally's counselors did not object to the video's admission at trial (waiving the issue for direct appeal), and did not object to prosecutorial misconduct when the prosecutor "vouched" for J.R.'s credibility and unfairly alluded to prejudicial evidence outside the trial record.

They were a confused pair of attorneys, barely familiar with the facts, probably because they had only seven days to prepare. Wally's original attorney had withdrawn, a public defender was appointed, then Wally hired new attorneys a week before his trial opened. The judge refused a continuance.

Wally testified in his own defense, but his denials didn't bolster his quest for a not guilty finding. He quibbled over her age on the video, saying she wasn't 14, she was 14-and-a-half. As if that made any difference. He was probably nervous, and unable to look at the jurors after they had just viewed the sex video. "I was uncomfortable up there, and they probably read that as deception."

The whole trial, video included, was about two hours long. State's case: 108 pages. Defense case: 70 pages. Pathetically short. Many sex cases are like that – brief, just believe the accuser. The accuser usually *is* telling the truth. But not always. The jurors might better know how to judge credibility in these cases if they were to know all the facts surrounding the case, not just the facts that survive the pretrial motion-in-limine gauntlet.

What Wally's jury did not know was that this was not J.R.'s first time as a child molestation victim. She had made the same allegations against another man when she was eight, and he went to prison for it when she was eleven. Wally had a letter from J.R., written when she was 12, threatening to send Wally to prison the same way if Wally didn't buy her what she wanted.

Then there were the attempts by J.R. and her mother to extort Wally after charges were filed. Wally had money. The two wanted $100,000 to make the charges go away, revised down to $20,000 later. They made inquiries through Wally's first attorney, and when Wally recorded the calls between him and his attorney and gave them to the judge, the attorney withdrew from Wally's defense.

After all that, I didn't know if Wally had sex with a pre-fourteen J.R. or not. Probably had. Maybe he hadn't. Impossible to know for sure. But that's what the jury had to determine – *for sure*. Guilty beyond a reasonable doubt.

The reasonable doubt instruction has been contentiously defined and redefined for over 200 years, and many versions are employed across America. They all say, in different ways, you better be pretty darn sure the defendant is guilty. Before one settles on a definition of reasonable doubt, though, one may ask, *Why is this the standard of guilt in the United States?*

The standard's proponents may argue that finding guilt "beyond a reasonable doubt" is what makes the American system superior to systems in other countries. Taking one's liberty is a grave act, and the state should only be allowed to do so when it is certain the punishment is deserved. Any doubt, and the defendant should not be punished.

Perhaps there is a better reason why the reasonable doubt standard should be used. It is this: *Because the jury does not know everything*. They only get half the story. Jurors should listen to the evidence, then listen for what evidence is *not* there but that may exist. Jurors should weigh testimonial evidence by asking themselves, *Am I sure I can trust myself to know when a stranger is lying to me?* If jurors approached their task like this, more reasonable doubt would be found.

How often do juries get it wrong? Turns out, this is easy to estimate. As related in *Surviving Justice*, Ohio State University researchers surveyed 188 judges, prosecutors, police chiefs, sheriffs, and public defenders in Ohio, and 41 state attorneys general, asking them to estimate the percentage of U.S. convictions that were in error. Only 9% of the 229 polled were public defenders, so this was a survey of the "tough on crime" crowd, those least likely to find fault in the criminal justice system. The survey showed a conservative average of a 0.5% wrongful conviction rate. Given that 95% of convictions are obtained from a guilty plea, it is safe to presume the conservative crowd is not resting their 0.5% estimate on coerced pleas, but on jury trial outcomes. The 0.5% should be weighed against the 5% of defendants who went to trial and lost. The jury got it wrong, convicting an innocent defendant, 0.5 out 5 times, or at 10% of the jury trials.

It's also logical to presume that juries err the other way just as often, allowing a guilty person to wrongfully go free 10% of the time. Compiling the two error rates, one concludes juries figure out the truth 80% of the time, and 20% of the time they have no idea. And that's because it is so easy for witnesses to testify to a long string of lies and never get tripped up.

"*Anybody* can be accused of a sex crime," Wally noted. "*Anybody* can be convicted, solely on the word of the accuser."

Professional research, as reported in the acclaimed film, *The Hunting Ground*, suggests convicted sex offenders have the highest rate of actual innocence. Five studies were cited, finding false allegations 2% to 8% of the time, with an average of 5% for the studies. One in twenty. Of America's state prisoners, 160,800 are sex offenders, and 5% of them equals 8,040 prisoners doing time – lengthy terms – for sex crimes they did not commit.

Pendleton had 236 convicted child molesters. By the odds, probably 12 were innocent. I was pretty sure Chad Kimbrough was one of them, and I was also pretty sure he would not get out until he had served his full 50-year term. Wally Lockhart might have been another innocent man – innocent of the Class A felonies, but guilty on the Class C charges. There were likely 10 more at Pendleton, unable to prove their innocence in a post-conviction system expressly designed to protect the finality of convictions, not designed to search for justice. And every one of those men lived every day with the fear of being beaten to death.

"I used to beat on chomos every chance I got," Mike Shannon once told me. "Take their stuff. Give 'em hell. Then one day I decided it's not my job to do that."

Mike, with LWOP for killing an Indy cop on September 17, 2001, ("suppression fire," he told me), had struck fear in many child molesters at Pendleton. After several years of victimizing them he left the pursuit to others, of whom there was a never-ending supply.

"Well," I granted, "when you pounded on them, you were punishing a guilty man nineteen times out of twenty."

"It's the one in twenty I regret," admitted Mike. "I'm sure I put the hurt on someone who was innocent, and that's not me. I couldn't keep doing that."

Child molesters often asked me why they were so reviled. "I get beat up by a guy who's in for murder, as if I'm worse than he is. He's got no room to talk – he took a life, and that's gotta be worse than a sex crime. Would you rather be the victim of a sex offense, or be murdered? How is it we're the worst people in the prison system? Why are our sentences longer than sentences for murder?"

What they didn't appreciate was the difference in the identities of the victims. Most murders occur for a reason. Maybe not a *good* reason, but murderers usually have clear motivations, understandable to a third party. Murder victims, a majority of the time, *did something* to precipitate the events that culminated in murder. The Public Safety Director in Indianapolis once aired a report stating 70% of Indy's murder victims in 2010 had criminal records (followed by 80% and 90% in 2011 and 2012). Not to say that a criminal record is cause for a justifiable homicide, but it indicates these victims just might have been messing around with something or somebody they should have avoided.

Child molesters' victims, by contrast, are children. Vulnerable, innocent victims. No child "asks" to be molested, and even those under 14 who behave promiscuously (some do exist) should not be taken advantage of by an adult preying on the child's inability to form intelligent legal consent. In the prison swamp of low morals, does a murderer stand on higher moral ground than a child molester? Probably so. But morally, neither is above the eye level of an alligator.

Most think it's a good thing that sex offenders get long sentences and face violence daily. I would be flying against the wishes of nearly the entire prison culture were I to suggest violence against them should stop. This very natural impulse to make sure chomos endure a miserable existence, though, has collateral consequences for those in the free world.

Christopher M. Stevens went to jail for molesting a boy, took a plea deal for a low-level felony, and did his short time being bullied daily. Apparently young Mr. Stevens was incurable, and knew it. A fellow child molester said he thought Christopher would be back in jail within 60 days of release, and Christopher replied, "No, I won't. Next time, I'll kill him." Guys make all kinds of tough guy boasts while behind bars, and scrawny Christopher's vow was mocked, but not forgotten.

Fifty-six days after his release, Stevens molested a boy again. The thought of being terrorized by other prisoners for decades did not stop him from reoffending. The disincentive of a brutal prison term did nothing. What the threat of extreme punishment did was to give him an incentive to hide his crime.

Stevens killed ten-year-old Zachary Snider.

He was no more adept at hiding a murder than he was at hiding a molestation, and he was quickly arrested, convicted, and sentenced to death. After a series of appeals on par with Michael Daniels' legal journey, Stevens' death penalty was overturned and replaced with LWOP.

Sex offenders are a different breed of criminals, and they belong in separate facilities where they can get treatment for what is properly classified as mental illness. Indiana has taken a step in that direction, placing 1,800 child sex offenders in the 3,000-bed New Castle Correctional Facility. Treatment is provided there. Pendleton has 236 child molesters, Michigan City has 259, and Wabash Valley has 277. In those facilities, there is no treatment, and no guarantee any of them will be alive for the next count time.

The U.S. Supreme Court, in *McKune v. Lile* (2002), noted that 80% of untreated sex offenders recidivate. With treatment, only 15% get re-arrested on new charges within three years of release. These numbers, gleaned from U.S. Department of Justice figures, suggest great potential for curing these offenders.

"There's only one problem with that," Mike Lindsey pointed out. "Even if a treated chomo has only a 15% chance of molesting again . . . would you trust him to be around your kid?"

CHAPTER TEN

Thorazine and Monster Mix

"It's an awful thing, solitary. . . . It crushes your spirit and weakens your resistance more effectively then any other form of punishment." – Senator John McCain

At 6:15 a.m. I was making coffee in my cell, 11 on 4F in J-cellhouse, and heard the range gate open, followed by two pairs of boots striding purposefully down the range. A prisoner yelled, "Shakedown crew on four hundred!" and a chorus repeated the warning. The shrieking echoed through the cellhouse, like treetop animals announcing the presence of a tiger lurking below.

The boots stopped at my door, and a pair of handcuffs tapped on my tray slot.

"Cuff up."

Grim faces. Black uniforms over shank-proof vests. I put my hands behind my back and stuck them through the slot. Click-click-click. Clack-clack-clack.

"Roll eleven!"

The sergeant held my cuffs and pulled me onto the range. Waiting at the control box was an IA officer. I was escorted wordlessly past him and placed in one of the stainless steel shower stalls, 32 inches square. Locked in, cuffs still on, door slot snapped shut. The air did not move through the pepperhole grate. Sweat immediately began to trickle down my ribcage.

Shakedowns usually take five minutes, fifteen if they think you're hiding something. A super-thorough cell toss can be an hour, like the one Shane Bramley and I endured in August 2010. We were in week two of a facility-wide six-month lockdown, the one that was an attempt to rid Pendleton of drugs and cellphones. Fifty-one of 266 security staff members quit or got fired. When Shane and I returned to our formerly impeccably squared-away abode it was like returning to the inexplicable tricks played by a tornado – mini-van in an oak tree, but the bobblehead still attached to the dash. My peanut butter had traveled from the jar to the air vent, my last bag of coffee contained half my black pepper, papers were turned into tickertape, but a toothpaste tube was still balanced on its cap, just as I left it.

This shakedown took an hour and forty-five minutes. I was escorted back to my cell, a pound lighter. I saw the effects of tornado, blender, and wood chipper. Mattress inside out, a storm of commissary opened and on the floor, but . . . no tickertape of papers. My twelve-inch cubical cardboard box labeled "Legal Work" was sitting upright on the bed frame, and still contained a dozen yellow file folders, each one bearing the label of a prisoner's case I was currently working on. Each folder had a single piece of white paper inside. On each paper was written the same message, in bold, black marker: GO FUCK YOURSELF.

It was exactly as I had left it.

The doors rolled for the 10 a.m. lunch line, and wild-eyed Ben Steinberg in cell 6 straggled, waiting for me. "I thought they were coming for me," he said, with his typical paranoia. "Man, what did they want you for?"

"Practicing law without a license."

"Really?? They find anything?"

I kept the joke to myself. "Nothing they liked. Nothing to get in a twist about."

Prison Rule Number One: Always be ready for a shakedown.

Steinberg, an Indiana University student at the time of his arrest in 2005, was nominally a client of mine. He had 65 years for murder, and I had done research for him, trying to find a way to overturn his rock-solid conviction. The evidence at trial left me no doubt as to his guilt – he had driven parallel to a pick-up truck heading south on State Route 41, aimed a rifle out his passenger side window, and shot the driver of the pick-up in the head. A trucker heading north saw the shot and watched the pick-up veer off the road and crash. Ben realized he had been seen, and despite the post-midnight darkness, could probably be identified. In his mind he exaggerated the ability of the trucker witness. Returning to his roommates, he was in a full panic. He said too much, and fled Bloomington. They saw the news the next day, put the facts together, and called the police.

Ben was arrested in southern Indiana and further implicated himself on a recorded jail phone as he spilled an unlikely tale to his disbelieving mother. His intricate denial involved masked strangers taking his car, cell phone, and rifle, as part of a conspiracy to steal his nanotechnology secrets. These mysterious figures had set him up to take the fall for murder.

"Oh, Ben, you need help," his mother pleaded with anguish. A year before, she had lobbied to have Ben placed in a mental health facility, but the state could not force his commitment because he was not considered "dangerous."

Ben's involvement with the mental health system was one of the few commitment cases that was public record. A probate court had found Steinberg to be dangerous, and had him involuntarily committed. Ben had pointed an unloaded gun at a group of people, engaged in "risky" behavior, and psychologists declared him "delusional" with a preliminary diagnosis of schizophrenia. Dangerousness is defined by Indiana Code 12-7-2 as constituting a "substantial risk of harm to himself or others."

Ben hired an attorney (he made thousands weekly through on-line poker) and challenged his involuntary commitment. The Indiana Court of Appeals sided with Ben, writing, "This is not a case where anyone was murdered or even harmed by Steinberg's conduct." Ben wasn't dangerous under the legal definition, and in October 2004 their opinion set 24-year-old Ben Steinberg free. A few months later he committed the murder that led him to Pendleton.

Indiana has an insanity defense, Indiana Code 35-41-3-6, but it is only useful to defendants who were "unable to appreciate the wrongfulness of the conduct at the time of the offense." Alternately, a less mentally ill defendant can plead Guilty But Mentally Ill (GBMI), which subjects the defendant to the same range of criminal penalties, appended by the requirement of the IDOC to give the prisoner mental health assistance. We have a few of those in G-cellhouse, and the psych doc drifts by once a week, asking, "How you doing today?" So a GBMI plea was useless to Ben, both before trial and now, at the PC stage.

The most promising issue I could find for Steinberg centered on his refusal to accept a 12-year plea deal. Such a proposal for an overwhelmingly guilty man was astonishing, and I joked to Ben, "You'd have to be *crazy* to turn down a deal like that!" It was only part joke – there was a real issue there. How can a defendant make a "knowing, voluntary, and intelligent" decision on whether to accept or decline a guilty plea if the defendant has been declared "delusional" and schizophrenic?

"Why didn't you take the 12-year plea?" I asked Ben.

"I just couldn't take it," he explained mysteriously. "I had things to do, stuff was going on, and I had to be out. I couldn't go to prison for any amount of time, or everything would have fallen apart." He went on to allude to his nanotechnology research and a glow stick he had patented in 2002 – but he wouldn't reveal much detail, afraid I would run off with his secrets.

"But now you've got 65 years. So . . . things fell apart anyway."

"I know. Sixty-five is worse. But I just couldn't take the twelve."

Refusing the deal must have exasperated Ben's high-dollar retained counsel. How many mentally ill murder defendants get a shot at a 12-do-6?

With the help of LEXIS, I scoured the nation's published decisions looking for a case where the courts declared a person too mentally ill to intelligently refuse a plea bargain. There were dozens of cases where the decision to accept a guilty plea was tossed due to the defendant's cognitive deficiencies, but only one case where a reviewing court had a set of facts similar to Steinberg's, turning down a beneficial plea bargain due to mental illness. In that one, a U.S. district court in California allowed the convicted man a second shot at the lesser plea he had refused while still delusional. If only we could duplicate the argument and get Ben the same kind of ruling. Problem was, the decision had been harshly overturned by the Ninth Circuit Court of Appeals, and the U.S. Supreme Court had nailed it shut with *cert denied.* The issue was a dead end.

"It's alright," he consoled me. He was disappointed, but resilient. "I've got other things I'm working on now. It'll all work out in the end." His next idea was for a combination greeting card lottery ticket.

Sure, I thought. You'll spend thirty-some years here, being ignored by psychologists, and get out when you're fifty-seven. Brilliant mind, the way a Swiss watch is a beautiful timepiece. But drop some sand in the gears and this is what you get – a dysfunctional object that sits on a shelf.

I had been shoehorned in with a motley cast of characters in J-cellhouse. On one side of me was Wally Lockhart, single-celled due to the PTSD he suffered from overseas deployment. On the other side was a bearded black guy from Gary who had raped and murdered a teenage boy. During lockdowns an overwhelming smell of unflushed fecal matter came crawling out of his cell. Cell 1 held a former military officer, neatly squared away, all surfaces polished to a gleam, who had killed three family members. Polite, cordial, but not someone I wanted to befriend. Cell 5 had a kid from Huntington County, the most incarceration-loving county in the state, locked up on a 4-do-2 for typical teenage misbehavior in the county jail that was construed as an escape attempt.

We had an AB on my range, and a couple SK's – Saxon Knights – an Indiana-based organization that could hardly be described as a "gang," but was labeled as a Security Threat Group by the IDOC. I had never seen them do violence to anyone other than their own, for infractions of their charter's code. A few BGD's were sprinkled in – Black Gangster Disciples – but none of them, or any other group, went around terrorizing or extorting others. Their numbers were too small at Pendleton, and victims of organized abuse had a habit of ratting on their tormentors.

At the end of my range was Pizza Man, Byron Morse, assigned to clean the range. His ability to roam the cellhouse during lockdowns afforded him the opportunity to "hustle," moving items from cell to cell, running gambling tickets, and providing a "store" of commissary items on credit. Most range detail jobs are taken precisely for this reason. Every transaction was squeezed for a few drops of profit, and he was generally despised, both for his business and his character. It was no surprise that somebody, apparently, dropped a dime on him and sent the shakedown crew to his door.

Pizza Man had violated Prison Rule Number One.

He would not cuff up. The CO wouldn't leave the cell door, and back-up was called: the Cell Extraction Response Team (CERT). They softened his resistance with a blast of pepper spray – we all got a taste – then barreled in. He fought back, taking his shit-covered right hand out of his pants to grab and claw at his attackers. Cuffed, he was dragged down to a shakedown booth on 2-range where he hollered for two hours about his constitutional rights.

At some point, a female CO noticed Pizza Man was having a hard time keeping his cell phone in his ass, and a second cell extraction began.

My annual review took place in the counselor's office twenty feet from screaming, shit-covered Pizza Man. Ms. Scaife asked me, "You ready to move out of J-cellhouse?" I didn't fit in with the characters around me, and she knew I had only been placed there in retaliation for being successfully litigious. "How 'bout we move you to O-dorm?"

O-dorm once had a reputation as a zoo / jungle / dungeon, but had improved a bit since its pre-2010 violence-ridden heyday. All of Pendleton's open dorms were gladiator schools back then, and the bigger the dorm, the more problems there were. In 2007 a melee broke out in 50-bed K5 dorm. Fires were set, and suspected rats were beaten up. One, a mouthy wanna-be tough kid named Marco, was beaten, cut, and escaped with his life by squeezing out of a second-floor window.

The basement of O-dorm held 38 prisoners in O-1, and 39 in O-2. Each had 13 upper bunks, meaning 52 were sardined into tiny double-bunked spaces, feet dangling in faces, farts and halitosis fouling the close atmosphere. No particular classification system was used to place prisoners in the open dorms, so the cozy quarters contained some who did not particularly play well with others.

Pendleton had a superintendent who was open to suggestions, Brent Mize, and I sent him a paper explaining in mathematical terms how overcrowding amplified violence, and what could be done about it. Dorm size, irrespective of the characters (n) occupying the dorm, exponentially increased violence because the number of relationships (R) in the dorm increased exponentially. $R = n(n-1) / 2$. For example, if you have five prisoners in a room, they maintain ten separate one-to-one relationships. If you have ten men in a room, they have 45 relationships. For every "bad" relationship in the smaller room, there will be 4.5 bad relationships in the larger room, and 4.5 times more violence. Breaking a ten-man room into two five-man rooms reduces the total number of relationships from 45 to 20, resulting in a 56% drop in altercations. Clearly, an architectural arrangement with multiple rooms containing small numbers of men per room is the ideal setting. Large dorms should be avoided. A 50-man dorm has to maintain 1,225 relationships every day, but five 10-man dorms involve only 225 relationships. I stressed to Mize the enormous potential to reduce violence, if the dorms could be subdivided.

Of course, there was no money in the budget to reconfigure the dormitories, so I proposed another strategy. Since it was vital to have less friction between prisoners within the dorms, those occupying the dorms should be selected for their proven ability to behave. Prisoners behave best when they have incentives – jobs, programs, recreation, other perks. I concluded that the largest dorms should be used for those who are in the rehabilitative PLUS program, followed by using the smaller dorms for individuals holding similar jobs (maintenance workers, laundry workers, etc.), and individuals age 40 and over. Calmer, more mature people in the dorms would reduce the likelihood of bad relationships that often had chain-reaction effects, like what had happened in K5.

Mize never acknowledged my contribution, but the PLUS program soon moved from E-dorm's two-man rooms to K5 and K6, and K3 and K4 were converted to 40-and-over. K1, O-1, and O-2 were turned into workers' dorms. Mize instituted other reforms, offering more incentives and curtailing disciplinary punishments, and within a year he was being lauded for the most remarkable drop in violence in Pendleton's history, highlighted by a cessation of the once or twice monthly assaults on staff.

A few months after I moved into O-2 dorm, Scottie McLean moved into the bunk across from me. Black, sporting a rough beard and unruly hair, pushing 40, and a little overweight, Scottie did not socialize much. Instead of talking to others, he talked to himself. Working out his problems, he added hand gestures to the points he made, shook his head to discard a thought, and nodded as he picked up another thought. Occasionally he would sit on a blanket on the floor between his bunk and his locker and rearrange the squalor of papers and property that was his life. Sometimes he would fall asleep on the floor, to the quiet amusement of his neighbors.

"Motherfucker's crazy," Bini-Wan observed.

Maybe so. But I had a different theory. Scottie's autoconversant nature indicated he had been in solitary confinement a long time. I had encountered conduct like his in the seg units for years. If he was mentally ill, it was probably an environmental effect, not a neurological deformity. Crazy? In a way, yes. But crazy – unreachable? I doubted it. Nobody else would talk to him, so I gave it a try.

Small talk. Baby steps. As I suspected, Scottie had spent most of his last 20 years in solitary, so I cautiously avoided overloading his circuit-breakers. After a few weeks of trust-building he told me his story.

"I remember the exact words the yard officer said that made me go off," Scottie recalled. He was at Wabash Valley in 1994, twenty years old, with a fresh 190-year sentence. "The CO said, *Give me the bandanna, and quit acting like a bitch.*"

Scottie wasn't going to let *anyone* call him a bitch, especially not in front of his homeboys. Fighting words. In a flash he was on the officer, and as his fists drew blood he urged his buddies to join in. Some did, and in the end multiple officers had hit the ground, one with a broken jaw.

The most common denominator in most prisoner assaults on staff is that the staff member has said something offensive to the prisoner. "Bitch" will provoke a fight nearly every time.

Of those in the melee, McLean garnered the most punishment – four years in segregation for the assault, three more years for inciting a riot.

Assaulting prison staff is the least-tolerated offense within a prison. Officers are generally blasé about the crime that landed a man in prison – they'll treat someone who raped and murdered a child the same way they treat a Walmart thief. But bang up one of their own and the retribution will be incessant.

"They first whupped my ass," said Scottie. "Then they put me in the hole on the all-white range. Last cell, by the door to rec. I had to walk handcuffed past all white faces, and they were really yelling."

Don't bring no nigger in here!

Get that nigger off our range!

He remembered the nozzle end of a shampoo bottle being pointed at him from a food slot at waist level, but saw it too late. An explosion of monster mix, brown and sticky, covered him. The officer behind, who saw it coming, only laughed.

Monster mix is mostly shit, weaponized by the admixture of liquids like milk, lotion, shampoo and urine. Shaken, not stirred, it's made to be foul and adhesive and capable of being squirted several feet.

A request for a shower was granted: "Yeah, we'll get you a shower on shower day." That was 48 hours away.

The guy across from McLean told him there was only one way to respond to getting shitted down. "You gotta fight back. Do the same thing to them that they do to you." Reluctant at first, Scottie saw there was no other way.

And so the shit wars began.

"Back then I responded to everything the only way I knew how. Shit for shit. Violence for violence." Tit-for-tat, eye for an eye.

When the white guys passed Scottie's cell to go to the rec cages, Scottie "gunned 'em down" the same way they had humiliated him. Always physically separated, monster mix was the only weapon available. Sometimes the officers got gunned down too, which only added to his segregation sentence.

Seg time was monotonous. Two religious books and a radio were allowed, but there were no TVs, no other books, and no commissary. The prisoners passed the time, as they do in seg units all across America, taunting each other, taunting the officers, and inventing ways to cause trouble. Though they were not socially or politically conscious, they followed a line from George Jackson in *Soledad Brother*: "A man can never be so oppressed that he cannot, in some way, resist."

A couple years into his seg term, McLean started getting some unwanted attention from psychological services. Scottie told me what that was like, the type of scene I had witnessed many times in other prisons.

"A Korean psych doctor came to my door, saying, *You need to calm down! You need medication!* I wouldn't take anything. Then one day, after I'd stuck a CO in the arm with a spoon handle, the psych doc came back. *You been bad! You been bad!* The guards put me in four-point [chained to the bunk] and the doctor hit me with about a foot-long needle, in the ass. I was out for two or three days. That was my first shot of Thorazine."

Thorazine is the trade name for chlorpromazine, a tranquilizer developed in 1952 to treat psychosis. Trouble is, it doesn't "treat" any psychological condition; it only masks it. The Thorazine recipient is rendered quiet, dull, malleable. Manageable is the key word. When physical isolation, beatings, and humiliations have all failed, chemical isolation is often the next step.

The U.S. Supreme Court ruled in *Washington v. Harper* (1990) that prisoners have no due process right to refuse psychotropic medication. Prisoners nationwide can be drugged against their will.

Some states have emplaced procedural safeguards whereupon a prisoner may refuse medication, request a hearing, present evidence and witnesses, and appeal the decision to the superintendent – but I've never seen a drugged-up prisoner who was aware of his rights. Most believed that when they came at you five deep holding a syringe, your right of refusal consisted only in your physical ability to fight them off. There's no Miranda warning for Thorazine.

Scottie's Thorazine shots became routine, every two weeks. If Scottie resisted, which he did at first, he'd get beaten up, four-pointed, and still get the shot. At some point he decided to save himself all the trouble, and when they showed up with the goon squad and the needle-toting nurse, he learned to roll over and accept it.

"Even when I rolled over for it, I was still being *forced* to take the shot. They brought force; they just didn't have to use it." A person with a gun to his head complies the same way. "I let them do it, but it *wasn't* voluntary."

He awakened from his first drug stupor "hearing voices."

"Tell me about the voices," I asked, masking skepticism with concern. "Where did they come from? What did they say? How could you tell they weren't actual voices?"

Scottie explained that it took him about ten years to realize that the voices weren't real but were inside his head. The voices were always "...negative, negative, negative, telling me to act out, to do the worst things." He put his right hand behind his ear to show me where the voices seemed to come from. "They seemed real."

By 1996 Scottie McLean's psychiatric status had been downgraded to Level D, justifying virtually any recourse the psych department deemed necessary. Five years earlier, when arrested for participating in the robbery-gone-wrong of a drug dealer, he'd had no history of mental health issues. Now he lumbered along doing the "Thorazine shuffle," dodging shit missiles, and stuffing his ears to drown out hate-filled voices, both real and imagined. Life was a never-ending cycle of teasing, assaults, tranquilizers, and write-ups, with no end in sight.

Fourteen years like that. That's over 5,000 days. Lights on all day and all night. Head in the toilet to get relief from mace and pepper spray. Being shot with riot guns, stuck with needles, four-pointed for a week at a time, waiting for a nurse to clean the urine and feces from around his body. Attacked by dogs when he really caused a ruckus. Beaten while handcuffed, while someone yelled, "*Stop resisting! Stop resisting!*" Five thousand days waking up, literally, in a world of shit.

In 2008 McLean was transferred to the psych unit at New Castle Correctional Facility. He was a wiry 17-year-old kid when he was arrested; now he was a heavier, bearded 34-year-old man with long, unkempt hair and eyes that warily scanned his surroundings. A cautious officer put a belly-chain and two sets of shackles on Scottie and shuffled him into the plush office of Dr. John Moore. A clock ticked in the dead air, a level of quiet that was in itself alarming. The doctor told the guard to take the restraints off, which was done, then he told the guard to leave the room. Eyebrow raised, the guard hesitated, but left. Scottie suddenly had more freedom of movement than he'd had at any time since 1994, and he was alone, unbound, unwatched, in the office of an elderly white man who had no means of protecting himself.

"He wasn't scared," Scottie marveled. "I had no cuffs on, and he wasn't scared."

Dr. Moore rose, went over to Scottie, and hugged him. "You've had a hard time," he said, gently. "But everything's gonna be alright."

Scottie admitted this made him cry. His eyes welled up as he told me this.

At first a bit suspicious of Dr. Moore, Scottie came to know him as "Papa John," which was also a play on the weekly treat the doctor provided – Papa John's pizza, popcorn, and soda.

In his new environment, the officers were "…nice, respectful. They treated us like humans, not like dogs." There was TV. There were books. Personal hygiene was possible again. Classes re-engaged his mind. One called Cognitive Thinking helped him re-learn how to socialize. "I have a conscience now. I've learned to say, *Thank you*. I know I'm not the only person in the world now."

"Solitude is hell," he concluded. "It's the worst thing you can do to a person."

As he told me all this I thought of the long-abused wolf-dog in Jack London's classic, *White Fang,* being brought into the house at the end of the parable, to sleep by the civilized man's fire. "Blessed wolf," wrote London.

I described *The Call of the Wild* and *White Fang* to Scottie and encouraged him to check out London's books from the library. "You'll like them," I promised. "It's *your* story, but played by a dog turned wolf turned dog. Jack London was really writing about people, and how they change, depending on how they're treated."

Scottie liked to read. Years without books must have been excruciating. "Sounds like a cool story."

"It is. Take note, at the end of the story, the only person who doesn't believe the dog has really changed from being a wolf is . . . the county judge."

Fortunately for Scottie, he was not particularly religious. One of the worst things to do to a mentally ill person is to give him a Bible.

Jeffery Hofstedter was our prime example of schizophrenia augmented by religiosity. White, late thirties, anorexically thin, he balanced a supersize pair of bifocal chominators to laboriously read his Bible aloud, one disconnected word at a time. He had been booted out of pre-GED class enough times that they didn't want him back. His last expulsion came after he accused half the class of demonic possession, stood at the door with hands raised and eyes closed, chanting "Blood of Jesus" over and over until COs forcibly removed him. He landed in G-cellhouse often, one time telling me (accurately), "The Ten Commandments don't say nothing about not busting someone in the mouth." Nobody could drift into a conversation with him without the flow spilling into his favorite oxbow – the certainty that "God knows what's in my heart and he's gonna see to it that I'm released, sooner than anyone thinks." He had over 40 years left to do.

On one seg visit, I noticed he was particularly upset about something.

"If I ever meet Jesus, I'm gonna fucking kill him. Making me suffer like this!"

Like many of the mentally ill, his family had all but abandoned him. He used to get a money order from a relative at Christmas, but since the IDOC went exclusively to a JPay electronic funds transfer system, he got nothing. "They can't figure out how it works, or they don't have a credit card." He didn't miss a meal – one of the few always out the door for breakfast at the insanely early 3 a.m. hour, a time selected to discourage eating and save Aramark money. He ate everything put before him, but didn't gain weight. No prisoner can gain weight without help from the outside. Or a kitchen job.

Friction, for Jeffery, came from clashing his faith and ideology with the heretics around him. Muslims were his most hated group – "They worship a false prophet. They worship a rock. They're demons, and don't realize it!" Mormons were next – "made-up scripture" – followed by Catholics, Baptists and any other denomination raising a point of doctrine with which he disagreed. His arguments wreaked of Bronze Age deity rivalry, Yahweh versus Baal, my god versus your god. He charged into god battles, covered with evangelical word vomit. He ended up with his own personal church, a sect of one.

"What it boils down to is this," Jeffery explained. "God knows everything. He knows the future and He knows the past. He knows what you'll do before you do it. Anything that is going to happen is going to happen because it's God's will; and anything that has happened has happened because it was God's will. God's in charge of everything."

I gave him a questioning look, eyebrow raised.

"Except . . . evil. God doesn't have anything to do with evil. He can't even look at it."

"So, the two murders you committed, were those God's will, or did He not know those would happen, or what?"

He tossed his head back to examine the ceiling while his hands caressed an invisible sphere, like he was miming a clairvoyant. "God knew . . . I would do it . . . but He didn't want me to do it . . . and He didn't see it . . . so He didn't will it to happen. I free-willed it. But Jesus forgave me for that. You see? It's all God's plan. And I don't believe that New Testament verse that says no murderer has everlasting life in him. They messed up that translation, ya know? But what I'm learning from prison is patience. Don't you think you learn patience here?"

"I'm learning it right now."

"Yeah! That's what I'm talking about. Hey, what's your favorite Bible verse?"

"*They shall dig through the wall and carry out thereby*," I said. "Ezekiel 12:12. It's about an escape."

"Mine's Joel 1:5. *Wake up ye drunkards and weep!* I say it to these winos here all the time."

Another day, Jeffery was in an escalating, contentious argument about dinosaurs. His adversary, also narrowly interested in Christianity, insisted dinosaurs were mentioned in Genesis, part of the Creation story. "The creatures described, those are dinosaurs. The Bible doesn't say dinosaurs, but that's what they are."

"I read that dinosaur bones were put there by Satan," Jeffery countered, "to confuse the unbelievers."

Wow, I thought, he had read something from the 19th century.

"No, man," his opponent proclaimed. "They found dinosaur bones and human bones *together*. Them people that dig stuff up, they proved it. Dinosaurs and people lived at the same time." He fished through his clutter and produced a pamphlet with a crudely drawn tyrannosaurus on the cover.

The pamphlet did the trick, quieting Jeffery, sending him trodding off to lip-read the dinosaur theory. He was hung up on dinosaurs for weeks, until one day he was gone. I woke up to see COs packing his trash into clear plastic bags. Out of the blue, he had told a rookie female CO at breakfast he could see Satan in her blue eyes, and that she could repent, or die. He stood tall in front of her, staring expectantly into her face, waiting for her to choose door number one or door number two. She chose door number three, keying her radio, and Jeffery was escorted back into the anti-ark. There, the demons were real.

CHAPTER ELEVEN

Deliberate Indifference

"While many criticize the federal courts for 'mass incarceration,' surely this phrase is a hyperbole, or at least a poor shorthand for the problem being addressed; there is no 'mass incarceration' - - each defendant was separately convicted and sentenced, one at a time."
– U.S. district court judge James O. Browning, in *U.S. v. Tarango*, (D. N.Mx. 2015).

Mel-T left me – suddenly and unceremoniously. In late August 2014, I met him on the walk as he stopped to battle another respiratory attack. He carried a thick book by Henry Louis Gates in his right hand, and held a white washcloth in his left, covering his mouth as he coughed. Dry cough, wheeze for air, cough, cough, cough, wheeze again. His eyes told of sleep deprivation. Whatever ailed his lungs, he fought it like the Russians at Tannenburg – dug in, resisting, but ammunition sparse, and his resolve weakening.

"They're sending me out to see a respiratory therapist," he squeaked.

"Good!" I exclaimed. "It's about time." He should have seen a specialist long ago.

"Be gone a day or two." Mel looked past me, searching for someone, probably a recipient for the Gates book.

"Alright. Well . . . see you when you get back." I walked away, unconcerned.

Mel's hospital visit was a minor event, and none of us gave it much thought. He would get to see the free world, through van windows, and get some hospital food, the fare free-world people complain about but us prisoners consider a treat. Soft bed, clean sheets. Pretty nurses – not the kind that snap, "What's *your* problem today?" A vacation. Lucky guy.

Another local news event eclipsed Mel's story. William Moore, our computer guru in the Education Department, got busted with a rather large collection of porn on his computer. Kiddie porn, some said, but then I had heard others accuse him of being a child molester several times over the years, which was also false. They saw white guy, fifties, no tattoos, and assumed "chomo." Bill was in for murder and attempted murder, 50 years. Nevertheless, the porn bust refueled the chomo rumors. Bill was placed in seg pending resolution of IA's investigation. The boldest rumors had Bill catching a federal case for child pornography.

The discovery sent IA prying into every office where prisoners had computer access. The law library was closed for three days. The chaplain's clerks were kept inside a day. Any room with a monitor and keyboard got searched. No other suspects went to the hole, although the Education supervisor was barred from the front gate, a move the rumor mongers interpreted as Bill snitching on his boss. The rabble didn't need evidence in order to draw conclusions, and they ignored the fact that it was Bill's supervisor who had caught him and turned him in.

Everyone was focused on the juicy Bill Moore porn saga. Four days after the library was searched, and thirteen days after I last met Mel on the walk, we got the surprising news: Melvin Tunstill was dead.

Mel was either in worse shape than he let on, and withheld this from us, or he had no idea the gravity of his condition. It was probably the latter, because Corizon, the contracted private medical provider, had not aggressively treated him prior to his final two weeks of life. Was it lung cancer? Emphysema? Byssinosis? None of us knew. We only knew that he was gone. Age 61, his last 18 years spent in prison.

A memorial service for Mel was held in the American Legion room. The old-timers confirmed it was the only such gathering in Pendleton's remembered history. Most prisoner deaths are greeted with a shrug and a head shake. "Damn! Another one didn't make it out. How long he have left? Fifteen years? Well, at least he cheated the state out of that." But the news of Mel's death was received by every man with a sense of personal loss. Something unique had been taken from us.

A long list of potential memorial service attendees had to be culled – space was limited – and I did not make the cut. I was told a packed room recalled Mel's many kindnesses, and his oft-repeated directive: "Leave here better than when you came in."

Pendleton's mortality rate was high enough to raise an alarm with the American Correctional Association (ACA) at their triennial review in April 2012. The facility experienced 21 deaths during the three-year accreditation cycle. Seven deaths per year, out of an average daily population of 1878, average age 37, age range 19 to 74, worked out to a mortality rate about triple for the same demographic on the outside. If this mortality rate existed for the USA's entire prison population, it would amount to 9,000 deaths per year. The ACA wrote: "There have been numerous homicides and deaths by drug overdose. . . . The amount of deaths and circumstances were of concern to the visiting committee."

The 21 deaths, however, had zero effect on the ACA's final grade for the prison. The ACA standards require "policies and procedures" to be in place – these allow a prison to win accreditation regardless of the actual conditions of confinement. The audit is nothing more than a beauty pageant, with a high entry fee, where everyone goes home with a trophy no matter how ugly they may be. The ACA graded snaggletoothed Pendleton 100% compliant in all mandatory standards (55 of 55, plus 6 "waived" requirements), and 98.6% in all non-mandatory standards (437 of 443, plus 25 waivers). Of the aggregate 529 ACA standards, not one asks if the prison happens to be needlessly allowing people to die.

The 21 deaths were classified as: 6 drug overdoses, 5 natural causes, 3 homicide by stabbing (lucky me, I witnessed 2), 3 suicides by hanging, 1 aspiration of gastric content (nobody rolled him over), 1 died at surgery from notriptyline (anti-depressant) toxicity (oops!), 1 accidental drug overdose (no blame assigned), and 2 under investigation. Yes, that's actually 22 deaths, but the ACA added it up as 21.

In June 2011 the IDOC contracted with Corizon for medical services – a flat $100 million per year – roughly $288 per prisoner per month. In 2013 I counted 7 deaths at Pendleton, and in 2014 I personally knew another 7 who died.

March 6, 2014: Michael Akens fell from his top bunk in B-dorm, his ribs hitting the metal table. The nurse on duty surmised Akens was "faking" and sent him back untreated. He bled out internally and died. June 5: Clayton 'Tater' Bayne, who moved to H-cellhouse to avoid K4's new double-bunking, was beyond anyone's view when he died. Age 73, it may have been natural causes (surely the IDOC's take), or it may have been related to his diabetes. July 24: Robert 'Big Bob' Stewart, long sentence, attempted suicide three days earlier, slicing his wrists. After 72 hours in a strip-cell he promised to be good. He was placed back in cell 1 on 2R, promptly secured a handful of razor blades, and literally gutted himself. A cross-abdomen slash spilled his intestines and decorated the white walls with gallons of blood.

July 26: Russell Yerden, in 6 on 6C in G-cellhouse, died of a drug overdose. The movie *Heaven is for Real* was playing on the institutional DVD channel when they found him. Yerden's death probably made an impression on his neighbor, Philip Littler in cell 5. Littler, with a fresh 45 for murder, chipped a hole in his wall, broke open a roof vent ala the escape from Alcatraz, and was spotted on the roof of the Admin Building in the wee hours of August 20, trying to find a way to negotiate a 35-foot drop as a thunderstorm raged overhead. Desperate times.

September 8: Melvin Tunstill died. December 20: Larry Kuhn, a notoriously slow and ineffective jailhouse lawyer, checked out by heroin overdose. About two dozen guys lost their legal work when Kuhn's cell was cleaned out. Larry's dope buddy, Leo Underwood, who often boasted about his days working on the Alaska Pipeline in 1964, also overdosed, but lived. (Oil wasn't discovered in Prudhoe Bay until 1969.) December 26: Old school Kenny Fulmer died in J-cellhouse from eating Moore's Pies. Kenny caught his life sentence in 1963, two weeks before Kennedy was assassinated, and probably would have been paroled long ago had he not taken hostages and attempted to escape from Michigan City in 1971. He was diabetic, so his death could have been classified as suicide-by-pie.

Those were the deaths I knew about in 2014. Some deaths are unremarkable and go unnoticed.

On paper, Corizon provided wonderfully adequate health care. In a typical year, they fielded over 20,000 health care requests from 1,900 prisoners, seeing every one within 72 hours. They dealt with 250 people with medically-treated psychiatric disorders, 156 with Hepatitis C, 146 with hypertension, 35 with diabetes, 13 with HIV, and in 2014 had an outbreak in R-cellhouse where 61 contracted tuberculosis. Over 4,200 dental visits occurred, tooth extraction the modal result. There were 297 specialty consults – outside experts. The IDOC fielded 122 medical grievances, and all 122 were found in favor of Corizon. Yet, for some odd reason, we had prisoners able to extract a steady income from suing Corizon.

Bobby Holleman was our king of medical litigation. To Bobby, it was pretty simple: "Document everything. Make sure you put 'PAIN' on your medical requests. Exhaust administrative remedies. Whenever they're deliberately indifferent to serious medical needs, you've got a case."

Bobby, with a life sentence, had enriched his trust fund account multiple times with his civil suits. He had recently won $15,000 at trial in district court over untreated kidney stones, lowered by the judge's demurrer to $10,000. Previously, a dietary problem caused a 50-pound weight loss and earned him five figures. He was working on a new complaint, and was besieged by others desiring the same lucrative outcomes.

"They have no idea how much legal work is involved," Bobby lamented, fending off requests. "It's David versus Goliath every time you go up against Corizon's attorneys."

An apt analogy, I thought. Only the Philistines thought David would lose to Goliath. Those in the tribe of Judah knew David had already slain a lion and a bear with his deadly sling – so the smart money had Goliath dropping in the first round. As a prison litigator, Bobby Holleman had a sling like David.

The "deliberate indifference" standard began with *Estelle v. Gamble* (1976), and involves three major elements. The "deliberate" modifier means medical staff must be aware of the serious risk of harm. Second, "indifference" means to do nothing and does not include treatment attempts that failed.

Failure is medical malpractice, a civil tort. Third, the ailment must be "serious," not some pedestrian malady like the flu. Fortunately, lower courts have contended with *Estelle* claims for 40 years and carved out a shortcut: if a doctor prescribes a treatment, and the medical provider does not accommodate that plan, the prisoner has solid grounds for relief.

I could have prosecuted a medical civil suit every two weeks at Pendleton, and won them all, based on the ACA report noting 26 specialty consults per year were denied by Corizon's upper management. I didn't take on these cases because I valued getting men out of prison as more important. I got hooked into one exception, though, when I gave Charles Durham a blank check one day, after he had done me a favor in H-cellhouse. I was moving from H to K, and I left an enormous bag of commissary items behind. Durham, good Samaritan, seized the bag and sought me out.

"If you ever need legal work done," I promised him, "come see me. I got you, no matter what it is." I figured he might need help on a sentence mod or appealing a disciplinary write-up, a few hours' work at the most. "Big C" had been locked up over 10 years and didn't have much left to do in court.

Big C's inquiries into suing Corizon began in 2012, when some undiagnosed skin affliction erupted on his scalp and spread to his forehead. The itching, apparently a creeping feeling below the dermis, sent him into near-bipolar rages of frustration. "Ya gotta help me sue these people," he pleaded. Early on, a nurse recommended a dermatologist, but Corizon's regional director nixed the request.

"We can't sue until a *doctor* recommends a dermatologist," I advised. It was not what Big C wanted to hear.

Big C suffered a few more months. Creams and medications failed. Doctor Michael Person gave up, and recommended a dermatologist. Regional director Michael Mitcheff fielded Dr. Person's email request and shot back a refusal in less than 30 minutes.

We were in business. We filed the complaint in district court under 42 U.S.C. 1983. In the meantime, Big C continued to suffer.

I took a lot of flak in the nearly three years I worked on Big C's medical case. He was not well-liked – most considered him brutish, and stupid. He read at a fifth grade level, and had made little progress toward his GED, despite nearly a decade in class. He loansharked, and was petty about being paid in full – if a man owed $20.00, he expected $20.00, not $19.84. Or you'd get a mop-ringer over the head. At times, when I would argue with him on how to best prosecute his case, he would poke me in the shoulder with his meaty finger, warning me, "Slow your roll, before I get mad." Like Spock, he could find that nerve and send pain zipping down my arm, slowing my roll.

"We're gonna win this case," Big C insisted. "You just gotta be more positive."

I was telling him, "There's a case exactly like yours, same affliction, same treatment, up in Michigan City, and Dr. Mitcheff was defendant there too. Corizon won the case by arguing that the head rash was not a 'serious' medical condition." Nobody with a mere skin rash survived summary judgment in our circuit.

"But this is serious – just look at it."

He was so dark-complected, it was difficult to see the extent of the rash. "I know to you it's serious, I'm just saying, the court did not consider it serious. But the one thing we have going for us this other guy didn't is that you have a *doctor* recommending a dermatologist."

"That's how I know you'll win!"

"Look," I cautioned, "even if you win summary judgment, you also have to win at trial. The magistrate judge will warn you, like he warned me, only 3% win at trial in Indiana."

They could stack the deck with Republican jurors, anti-prisoner, pro-state. A federal civil jury was eight. Both sides got three peremptory strikes. You take the first 14 on the jury panel, figure they would vote 9-5 Republican, then strike 3 from each side, and you got a 6-2 Republican jury. A tad of bad luck on the pool and it would be 7-1 or 8-0. Striking jurors *always* amplified the edge, whichever majority existed at the beginning.

"I still think we're gonna win. You say it's a hundred-to-one shot," Big C argued, "and I say there's no way we can lose."

The litigation history of prisoner rashes said otherwise, but there was no dissuading Big C. *How would he act when we lost?* That was the most likely outcome, and I prepared him for a loss.

Meanwhile, I learned a few things about people like Big C. While his reading skills were below par, he seemed to grasp concepts easily when I presented them to him orally. He wasn't dumb, as many supposed, but had some cognitive disability that prevented him from learning through written communications. His abilities seemed to be on par with those of "Big Mike," the protagonist football player outlined in Michael Lewis' book, *The Blind Side*. I developed a strong belief that if the GED was proctored to Big C as an oral exam, he would probably pass on his first try. About 20% of state prisoners are like Big C, with some kind of learning disability that goes unaddressed.

Bobby Holleman's side project was trying to make a case out of the prison's overall living conditions. Problem was, thanks to the 1998 Prison Litigation Reform Act (PLRA), winning was all but impossible.

The PLRA put an end to prisoner-litigated class action suits, allowing only licensed attorneys to file such claims. Prisoners, like Holleman, had to present an evidence-supported list of grievances, then get an organization like the ACLU to take the case. The PLRA's aim was to get the federal courts further removed from state prison oversight, and in this it was enormously successful, ending hundreds of existing settlement decrees across the country, including the *French v. Owens* decree from 1985 that had banned double bunks at Pendleton. The double bunks returned in 2000 – they weren't a "constitutional" infringement, just a safety hazard. (The late Mike Akens could vouch for this.)

"This place doesn't follow the ACA standards," Bobby complained, "and it doesn't follow state law on things like fire codes, space, lighting, or water quality."

"ACA standards have no force of law, and state laws," I reminded Bobby, "do not form a basis for constitutional violations."

"Yeah, I dig that," Bobby allowed, in his typical easy manner. "I'm just saying, they violate everything that tells them how to run a prison, and they get away with it."

No smoke detectors, no fire extinguishers, overcrowded spaces – all waived under the ACA if the building was constructed before 1993. In other words, if you have a decrepit old prison, do what you want. Leaking roofs, backed up sewage – no demerits. Water bottles were recommended for all staff and visitors, so said a sign at the front gate. We drank sink water through calcified pipes laid down when Babe Ruth was still considered a base-stealing threat. "We test our well every month," explained our superintendent. "Your water is safe." Yeah, if we drank water directly from the well, I'm sure it would be. Try putting your lips on the same faucet where Dillinger quenched his thirst.

"Bobby, you should try getting us our money back from the gym we built." In 1993 the Offender Trust Fund was deprived of $700,000 to build a new gym with several offices and rec rooms. It was almost immediately repurposed into a chapel – fine, that worked for us too. Then, in 2013, the IDOC needed more beds to accommodate the beds lost when dorms A through E were stripped down to single bunks for the INSIGHT program. Our gym/chapel was converted into a 100-bed dormitory. Would the prisoner rec fund be compensated? Not hardly.

The INSIGHT program (Intent on Shaping Individual Growth with Holistic Treatment – the witty acronyms never cease) resulted from a class-action suit to provide better housing for mentally ill prisoners who had been in segregation. They had been hanging themselves at a rate three times higher than other prisoners (also not a problem for the ACA accreditation). District court judge Tanya Walton Pratt found "cruel and unusual punishment" existed, forcing the settlement. The ripple effect – double bunks in K-dorm, the conversion of the chapel into L-dorm and double bunking there – did not raise constitutional concerns, even though those double bunks would have violated the *French v. Owens* decree. The PLRA was to blame for all of the dangerous conditions re-emerging, and the deaths that resulted.

Occasionally we heard from inmates who wanted to sue for a "failure to protect" claim. Sure, if staff is alerted to a likely physical attack, a constitutional duty to prevent harm exists. Typically, we would listen to their stories, toss them their forms, and be done with it. No help at all. I overheard Warren-Bey tell one, "If you weren't snitching all the damn time, they wouldn't have jumped on you in the first place, now, would they?"

In 2007, Pendleton installed a surveillance system, with funds provided by the federal Prison Rape Elimination Act (PREA), at a cost of $250,000. The digital cameras became a tool for disciplinary enforcement – catching fights on camera, for example – but not much of a tool for eliminating rape. The cameras were mounted along the cellhouse ranges, where they could conceivably gather evidence of a rape, if the victim told staff when his cell was invaded. Other cameras were less effective at rape prevention – mounted outside, facing the walkways, in the rec yard, in the medical building, at the kitchen loading dock – not your traditional rapist-favored venues. PREA's quarter-million probably did more to deter chicken patty theft than it did to prevent involuntary poundtown sessions.

Another contingent of Pendleton litigators focused on First Amendment rights, primarily the right to practice one's religion. Nearly all religious grievances involved dietary issues. The IDOC did not want to spend money on religious diets, like kosher or halal food, while prisoners (often with no sincere religious motivation), sought better quality food, to avoid the slop ladeled out by Aramark. Since there was no litmus test for gauging the sincerity of a religious belief, prisoners could adopt any religion they desired – historically, at Pendleton, whichever religion had the best meal plan.

Following a settlement in an ACLU suit, *Willis v. IDOC*, Jewish prisoners began receiving kosher microwavable dinners that soon attracted the noses of neighboring goulash-eaters. "Smells good. So, how do I become Jewish?" Turned out, it wasn't hard. Just say you're Jewish and kosher, and the IDOC had to provide kosher meals. Spaghetti, chicken, meatloaf – all pretty good. Soon the IDOC was feeding hundreds of Jewish converts, while trying to thwart halal demands from the Muslim population.

Don Klinzman summed it up best: "I'm a J-O-O Jew. Joo-ish. Come for the food, stay for the feeling of persecution."

To keep costs down, the IDOC began erecting hurdles to prisoners keeping their diet cards. Prisoners had to show up for 75% of meals, including breakfast, strategically served between 3 and 4 a.m. to deter people who valued sleep over food. Then the IDOC went to a one-size-fits-all plan, arguing that a vegan diet satisfied every religious diet on earth. The vegan trays were even less palatable than the regular Aramark trays – nothing but an obnoxious rotation of peanut butter, faux cheese, and soy "meat" – compelling most to return to the heathen meal plan.

Lifelong Jews, supported by the ACLU filing under the Religious Land Use and Institutionalized Persons Act (RLUIPA), made some gains against the IDOC strategies, and some splinter groups (like Hebrew Israelites) obtained a few food concessions; but for the most part, a religious diet request is still met with a vegan diet plan.

"They're so lucky they haven't been sued by any Modern Taoists," I mentioned to Stuart Kennedy, who replaced Bill Woodford in the law library. "A Modern Taoist's diet cannot be vegan. They require real meat every day, organic food only, an egg daily, and green tea daily." Prepackaged organic meals would send food costs soaring from $2.37 to at least $15.00 a day. And, they would have to give Modern Taoists two hours of recreation *outdoors* every day, which would make a mess of their 23 / 7 solitary confinement strategy.

Kennedy was familiar with many religions, a product of being well-read. He graduated from Ball State with a 4.00 GPA, a remarkable accomplishment for a man who started his time on death row.

"Give it time," Kennedy predicted. "Once prisoners in America find out about Modern Taoism, and more important, how it demands that human beings be treated like human beings, there will be a huge number of converts. They'll force Aramark out of the prison food business."

In the cat-and-mouse game of prisoner civil litigation, it was easy to assign all of the blame, conniving, and manipulation, on the prisoners. Malcontents who had broken the law, suddenly righteous with the First and Eighth Amendments, demanding to be treated better than they, deplorable convicts, had treated others. They were targets for loathing by staff, and by some prisoners who felt they should "man up" and deal with it. Crybabies causing trouble.

On the other hand, the state was playing the game too. The state contracted services to private corporations (bribes and kickbacks sometimes involved) to avoid responsibility for those services. The corporate business model was to provide a lower quality product in order to create high profit margins.

The profit margin, in simple terms, was derived from denying prisoners the services they formerly received. A surge of prisoner complaints and a flurry of lawsuits were tolerated, also as part of the business model. Nobody measured the effects of the corporate services – the ACA auditing was done on input mechanisms, like policies and procedures, not on output. Lacking output measurements, there was no true accountability. Metal staples in the rotini was okay, as long as there was a policy against it. In the end, thanks to privatization, the quality of food suffered, health declined, and mortality rates rose.

"The average person on the street hears about poor prison conditions," remarked Bobby Holleman, "and says, *GOOD. I don't want my tax dollars making prisoners comfortable.* What they don't understand, though, is that by treating prisoners as less than human, they get less than human behavior in return."

I had heard versions of this argument for years. A neglectful prison environment only taught one to devalue humanity.

"What I really wish I could do," Bobby went on, "is sue under international human rights law, not under the U.S. Constitution. Maybe then people would understand that we're litigating in order to *stay alive*, in order to be treated like humans." He leaned back in his chair, arms spread wide, and gestured at the busy law library. "That's all we're really trying to do here."

CHAPTER TWELVE

Mod Mania

"Justice is at best one of those words that make us look away or turn up our coat collars, and justice-without-mercy must easily be the bleakest, coldest combination of words in the language."
– J. D. Salinger, New York Post, Dec. 9, 1959, p.49; arguing against sentences of life without parole.

"Prison often turns first-time offenders into repeat criminals and, thus, can actually harm public safety. Research suggests smart policing, treatment, alternatives to prison, and educational programs are what work to bring down crime."
– Former police chiefs Garry McCarthy (Chicago) and Ronald Serpas (New Orleans), Law Enforcement Leaders to Reduce Crime & Incarceration, in *Prison Rates Fail to Make Us Safer*, USA Today, October 22, 2015, 7A.

When all else fails, when a prisoner has lost at trial, on appeal, and on all post-conviction relief, there remains one sliver of hope: a sentence modification.

Judging by the number of B-1 forms passed out by our law library every year – Motion for Modification of Sentence – over half of Pendleton's prisoners explore the possibility of getting their sentence reduced by the county court. The B-1 is by far the most requested form, it's popularity undiminished by the minuscule likelihood of success. When filed pro se, as most destitute prisoners must do, the exercise is akin to buying a lottery ticket. Invest in come copies, buy a couple stamps, mail it off, and hope you're the Powerball winner. "Yaneverknow," said one contestant, "I might get lucky. Can't hurt to try."

"Realize who you're dealing with, and what incentives they have," I often told these hopeful prisoners. After all, the judge and prosecutor were the ones who worked to put the prisoner behind bars in the first place, and the B-1 motion asks them to undo their labor, alter their previously reasoned judgments, and allow the felon to roam among the public at an earlier date. Phrased another way, they are being asked to risk their professional careers that this felon will not get out and quickly commit another crime. Given the uncertainty inherent in predicting human behavior, it should not be surprising that nearly all sentence modification motions fail.

Some of the pro se sentence mod motions are fairly elaborate, the contents rather compelling. The movant lists his prison accomplishments – education, vocations, programs, disciplinary record – and outlines his post-release plan. Most have jobs and residences lined up, with letters of support from family members, employers, and community leaders. A reasonable motion requests a portion of the sentence to be eradicated, or converted to a term of probation (best strategy); an unreasonable motion asks for the minimum sentence or immediate release (never happens). Prisoners often attach a letter to the judge, a plea, and if they have listened to any law clerk it will be a letter accepting responsibility for the crime, not mitigating culpability by trying to explain half-cocked justifications for committing the offense. When the well-drafted motions are mailed there's real hope, despite the odds, that they'll be granted a hearing.

Unfortunately, many prisoners cannot accept responsibility for their crime in a way that would please the state, because the prosecutor often demands that the prisoner accept the narrative that the state used to convict the man at trial – and that narrative is simply false, a conglomeration of lies and half-truths. In those cases, the prisoner is in a quandary – kowtow to the lies, and get released, or hold fast to the truth and stay in prison? One thinks the solution is easy – get out of prison at any cost – but what if getting out entailed admitting something horrible that you did not do?

I have also had the liberty of reading mod motions filed by retained counsel that were in all respects identical to well-drafted pro se motions. Guys will bring them in and ask, "Whaddya think? Did she do a good job?" They're looking for affirmation, to inflate their ever-swelling optimism, and I have no problem giving them that affirmation. "Every mod motion filed by an attorney is a good mod." This isn't because of superior content or writing style, but because an attorney's signature and bar number is on the final page. The signature magically opens the courthouse door, like a password in a fraternity. By my informal count over two years, mod motions filed by attorneys are 400 times more likely to be granted a hearing.

A private attorney equates to access to the prosecutor, first, and then access to the court. In Indiana, after 365 days have elapsed from the original sentencing date, the county prosecutor becomes the court's bouncer on sentence mods – nobody gets in the door without the prosecutor's written consent. In most states, the sentencing court retains autonomous jurisdiction to modify any sentence, and no party may interfere with the court's control over the sentence, probably because an arrangement like Indiana's creates potential for corruption.

Prosecutors deliver one of three levels of mod cooperation: no hearing allowed; hearing allowed, but the prosecutor will argue against a reduction; or hearing allowed, with the prosecutor agreeing to the reduction. A pro se prisoner writing from his prison cell stands no real chance of persuading the prosecutor to even allow a hearing; those letters never garner a reply. And we have tried contacting the county public defender's office to obtain free counsel for a mod, but they're too busy, and mods aren't part of their duty. It takes an attorney the prosecutor sees on a regular basis – he or she may be able to lobby the prosecutor, get a hearing, or better yet, persuade the prosecutor to agree to a new sentence.

So money plays into the equation for freedom, and not just a little bit. The more money invested in a mod, the higher the likelihood of success.

Modification attorneys offer three levels of service, clustered around three fees: $1,500 - $10,000 - $25,000. The low-end attorneys, I infer, are charging $150 an hour for ten hours' work, and they guarantee a hearing will be held. Looking at their clientele, I perceive they will accept $1,500 from *any* prisoner, no matter his prison record, regardless of the prisoner's inarguable case for relief. Certain losers.

One such prisoner was one of my neighbors in O-2 dorm, Jelani, who had done 20 years on an 80-year sentence. Jelani had a Class A felony for selling crack, 50 years, with 30 for the habitual. Jelani had completed two programs at Pendleton: Thinking For A Change, and Inside Out Dad. The first stretches over a few months and is pretty much taught and run by prisoners, trying to get other prisoners to think about consequences before they act. The second teaches parenting skills. Fine idea, but not exactly life-changing. In Jelani's case, all four kids were grown and gone. He had not accomplished anything else – no GED, no vocations. He had accumulated 23 disciplinary reports in 20 years, "but none in the last two years," he pointed out. I drafted a mod motion for Jelani, which he sent to an attorney I had never heard of, along with the $1,500 fee.

I sense the low-end mod attorneys may be a little shady, given how little real "service" they provide, and based on the low $1,500 fee, an amount so common it appears to be a price-fixing scam by the lower order of the guild.

"Where'd you find this attorney?" I asked Jelani.

"My cousin knows him. He used to own a buy-here pay-here lot on East Washington."

How fitting, I think. He went from selling used cars that aren't worth a damn to providing legal services that aren't worth a damn.

Jelani's attorney leapt over hurdle one, successfully getting the prosecutor to agree to a hearing. I can imagine the deputy prosecutor smirking or rolling his eyes as he ended that phone call. At the hearing, Jelani related, the deputy prosecutor's only argument was, "The State's position is that this defendant is not a good candidate for release." It was a mild way to tell the judge, *No way do you let this guy out,* as if the judge couldn't arrive at the same obvious conclusion. By not being demonstratively opposed to the motion, the prosecutor allowed Jelani's attorney to argue on Jelani's behalf in a manner that sold Jelani on the belief that his buy-here pay-here attorney worked harder than the state. Jelani was satisfied with the effort.

Two months went by before Jelani got the court's decision in the mail. During that two months Jelani made several batches of wine, lost a cell phone to a shakedown (they couldn't pin it on him for a write-up), and robbed another prisoner of his phone at knifepoint in the middle of the night. The robbery occurred in the bunk next to me – I awoke to the altercation, realized what was happening, and put in industrial earplugs and covered my ears with my headphones, drowning out everything. I was asleep in minutes, my last drowsy thought being, "You've kept a clean record for two years, Jelani, you stupid fuck, only out of sheer dumb luck." The judge, of course, denied Jelani's mod.

Mid-level mod attorneys, stationed around the $10,000 fee, make a serious effort toward winning relief. They will actually try to persuade the prosecutor into agreeing to the mod, and months may pass as they work on eroding the prosecutor's resolve prior to filing the mod motion. The relationship between the attorney and the prosecutor is the key factor – I advise prisoners to hire an attorney known to get along well with the state's attorney. Former deputy prosecutors make good mod attorneys. It's a tremendous advantage, practically essential, to have the prosecutor agree to the mod before the hearing is held, as it allows the judge to have someone to blame if the prisoner gets out and commits another crime. "Both parties agree to a lower sentence? Fine," thinks the judge. "Then it's not my problem. Whatever."

Roy Martin's sentence mod went according to plan, thanks to Roy's prison record and the $10,000 attorney fee. Roy was arrested for murder May 5, 2001, in an Indiana county across the river from Louisville, went to trial, was found guilty, and got the 55-year advisory sentence, in the middle of the 45-to-65 range. The victim had borrowed Roy's car without permission (the state's story), or to quote Roy, "He stole my car." Their differences were not worked out, and Roy shot the man. Roy had no prior criminal record. The murder victim – plenty of criminal record; and his dirty dealing, while not justifying his murder, went a long way in explaining why it happened.

So Roy went off to prison and did all the right things. He stayed out of trouble, much like he did on the outside. He took college classes, earning associate's and bachelor's degrees from Grace College. He completed the PLUS program and its wide variety of rehabilitative courses. The IDOC knocked 3½ years off his release date – six months for PLUS, one year for the associate's, and two years for the bachelor's. He was a model prisoner with nothing left to accomplish in prison, and in his fourteenth year he became my bunkmate in O-2 dorm.

Roy's family scratched together ten large to hire one of his county's best attorneys. The attorney pled Roy's case for early release to the county prosecutor and the victim's family. Both agreed to some leniency. A hearing was held November 18, 2014, and all went well. Supportive family members came in to verify Roy's release plan. In front of the judge was a request to reduce Roy's sentence to 45 years, with 10 of that suspended to probation; 35 years executed in the IDOC, serve 17½. Applying Roy's 3½ years of time cuts, he would do 14 years in prison. The judge took it "under advisement" for two months, and on January 21, 2015, it was approved.

"You'll get out a lot sooner than you think," Roy told me, as he detailed his journey. Our prison records were similar, and I was doing time for attempted murder, not murder. At trial the state accused me under two theories – as the perpetrator, or maybe as the accomplice. I had argued for years that I was an accomplice to nothing more than an assault.

"Nobody died in your case, did they? Anybody even go to the hospital?" No and no. Roy saw this lack of harm as a persuasive factor. "Trust me," Roy said, "you'll be out in a few more years."

He was released a few minutes after midnight on May 4, 2015.

Spending 10K on an attorney, though, doesn't guarantee results. Tom Cat, an obnoxious youngster in for drug dealing, plunked down $20,000 for a top-shelf Indianapolis attorney, saying, "Money talks. I'll buy my way out of this place." His record was hardly any better than Jelani's, and his mod was denied. Twenty grand down a rat hole (if that's truly what he paid).

Leif O'Connell also hired a good attorney, who did the preparatory footwork and got the county prosecutor to agree to a major sentence reduction, from 175 years to 55 years. Leif had gone on a rampage in St. Joseph's County in 1997, acting as vigilante after gangsters shot and killed his girlfriend, Annie. He and co-defendant Jerred Kahlenbeck went on the hunt. According to jailers, they were doing a good job of shooting the right people. Leif's 175 years represented one murder and five attempted murders, the sentences running wild. Jerred, less culpable, had 55 years. The modification agreement proposed to shave 60 years off Leif's 8-31-2083 release date, but the judge, for reasons unexpressed, declined to approve the deal.

If $1,500 employs the buy-here pay-here attorney, and $10,000 gets you in the door of a reputable dealership, the $25,000 and up fee puts you in the plush office of a luxury car dealer. I only met one guy at Pendleton with money long enough to employ such an attorney, and he did so with supreme confidence that his sentence would be slashed – and it was.

Jason Davidson, 40, was quite well-to-do when he caught his homicide case in Kosciusko County in 2009. He was cagey about the details, but it was a run-of-the-mill killing over marital infidelity, with his emotions blamed on prescription medications, Ambien and Zoloft. Murder got cleverly worked by his appellate attorney, Janet Myerson, into a voluntary manslaughter conviction, 30 years, do 15. Jason told me he had a "combination" PC motion and sentence mod pending, and was "very confident" he would be relieved from doing the entire 15 years in prison.

There's no such thing as a combination PC/sentence mod, but I understood the general concept. The PC attorney uses the PC issues to get the prosecutor to "settle" the PC by agreeing to a modified sentence.

"What did you spend on all this?" I asked Jason. "Twenty grand? Twenty-five?" His expression told me I wasn't close. No poker face.

"I really don't want to get into that," he replied. But whatever he spent, he was cocksure of a wonderful result.

A few months after my inquiries were deflected, he was packing out, on his way to a lower-security prison. I discovered, years later, he had done 5 years, 6 months, and 9 days in custody for his homicide. Pretty sweet.

Corrupt bargains occur in the luxury lawyer category, but these arrangements do not come to light very often. A smart, corrupt public official is careful not to get caught. Take cash only, never a check. Have the cash handed to a third party. Avoid any kind of recording – no emails, no phone calls, no video. Only accept a cash bribe from someone equally unethical and with incentive to remain quiet. Bribery is pretty simple. It's been going on for centuries, so you would have to be pretty stupid or pretty careless to get caught.

One such stupid, careless prosecutor was David Wyser. Wyser was a highly-regarded deputy prosecutor in Marion County, a close ally of the elected Republican prosecutor, Carl Brizzi. Wyser handled some high-profile cases in Indianapolis and was frequently on television, commenting on cases on behalf of the prosecutor's office. An example of untrustworthy squared (lawyer = untrustworthy, politician = untrustworthy; put the two together and you have a county prosecutor), he was a lawyer with political ambition, gearing up for a run for Hamilton County Prosecutor. Today, he's a boat inspector in Reno, Nevada. The Paula Willoughby case was his undoing.

In 2009, Paula Willoughby was 17 years into a 70-year sentence for murder, and her wealthy father, Harrison Epperly, hired Janet Myerson to champion Paula's modification effort. She had already won a reduction from 110 years to 70 years thanks to direct appeal proceedings. David Wyser was assigned to her case, and Myerson exchanged numerous emails with Wyser under the subject line, "Free Paula." Which is exactly what a vigorous defense attorney should do – work on the prosecutor, break down his resistance. Wyser made clear his resistance would be broken down faster if he received some personal incentive. "What will Paula do to make me feel warm and fuzzy?" he wrote in one email. "You should convince him [Epperly] to write me a check on behalf of the whales," Wyser wrote in another, referencing the *Free Willy* movie.

During a phone call with Myerson on May 29, 2009, Wyser instructed Myerson to tell Epperly to contribute to Wyser's campaign fund. Campaign funds, as every politician knows, are slush funds for doing clandestinely with money what you can't do openly. Epperly contributed immediately, endorsing a $2,500 check. Wyser cashed the check on June 22, 2009, and filed a sentence modification agreement in favor of Paula Willoughby the next day. Her murder sentence was reduced from 70 to 40 years, and she was released on July 2, 2011, having served 19 years.

After the mod was finalized, Wyser received another $2,500 campaign contribution from Epperly, and in Wyser's own words in federal court, "corruptly accepted it as a reward." All of these facts emerged collateral to a federal probe investigating Carl Brizzi's alleged public corruption cases. Wyser pled guilty to bribery, voluntary surrendered his law license to a five-year suspension, and was sentenced to federal probation by district judge Sarah Evans Barker on November 25, 2013. (Despite his federal felony conviction,

Wyser wasn't disbarred from the practice of law in Indiana. Apparently it takes more than mere public corruption to be asked to find another profession.)

Brizzi was the primary target of the federal investigation, but he was a fish they just couldn't hook. Epperly and Myerson met Brizzi on multiple occasions, and Epperly also contributed $25,000 to Brizzi's re-election fund, but nobody would testify to any quid-pro-quo arrangement.

Timothy Durham, Brizzi's campaign manager, accepted the $25,000 check. Brizzi's hands were clean, and once the investigation was under way, Brizzi directed Durham to do the right thing and return Epperly's money. It might have been the only ethical thing Tim Durham ever did – he's now serving a 50-year federal sentence for securities fraud and wire fraud, after his Fair Finance corporation was exposed as a Ponzi scheme, bilking hundreds of investors out of $200 million. (Call it a hunch, but I'll bet Brizzi's personal finances weren't invested in a Fair Finance portfolio.) The federal bribery cases on Brizzi – there were published accusations that Brizzi was the beneficiary of $48,300 for modifying Joseph Mobarecki's sentence too – were circumstantial, so federal prosecutor Joseph Hogsett declined to prosecute.

Which is a shame, because "Carl Brizzi, Assistant Boat Inspector" would look so good on a business card.

To be clear, Carl Brizzi was never charged with a crime and never brought up for ethics violations for the Willoughby or Mobarecki sentence modifications. He was not implicated in any of Tim Durham's shady dealings. He is an attorney in good standing with the bar, and is in private practice.

Despite winning her release through bribery, Paula Willoughby kept her modified sentence and remained free, where she has lived a law-abiding life. Harrison Epperly and attorney Janet Myerson cooperated with the feds and were not charged.

The world of luxury lawyers and bribery was beyond the reach of the modification hopefuls that stood before me every day, flat broke, wishing for a chance to go home too. I advised them, gave them the forms, and generally pushed them away, because my time and effort was wasted messing with a pro se sentence mod. "See Pete Mitchell," I often said, when they insisted they couldn't do it alone. Pete would hook them up, doing a good job for $15. There were a few exceptions to my 'no mod' policy, and one of those exceptions was Travis Roberson.

Travis came in wanting me to find a post-conviction issue to overturn his conviction. I came up blank, but I saw an opportunity for a unique sentence mod argument.

In January 2007, Jennings County Court sentenced Travis to 38 years, 3 suspended, leaving 35 years executed in the IDOC, do half. At age 16 Travis had attacked another boy in the high school cafeteria, cutting the victim's throat, the culmination of a dispute over a girl. While the rest of the school coped with their shock, Travis sat in an administrator's office and angrily admitted his intent was to see the other boy die. Travis had been seeing a psychiatrist, and been prescribed anti-depressant medication, but Travis neglected to take his meds for several days as he stewed over lost love. A bloody mess was the result. He was charged with attempted murder, jailed, and the case was transferred to adult court. The facts were clear enough to gain a conviction, and attorney efforts to mitigate the sentence due to Travis' mental issues were weak. Travis pled guilty and was sent behind the wall at Pendleton, at age 17.

I was aware of a rarely-used statute, I.C. 11-10-2-10(3), stating: "...no [juvenile delinquent] offender may be transferred to the Indiana State Prison or the Pendleton Correctional Facility." The IDOC ignores this law and sends teenagers to both Michigan City and Pendleton on a regular basis. But I used this to prepare a sentence mod for Travis, and attached a "Certificate of Lay Advocacy" with a brief comment:

> ". . . Put simply, Mr Roberson does not belong behind the wall here at Pendleton with the worst of the worst offenders. This facility has removed nearly all rehabilitative programs that were formerly offered. Mr Roberson belongs in a facility that will provide him opportunities for positive adjustment and prepare him for his eventual release. It should be mentioned that the Court at sentenc-

> ing noted the need for counseling for Mr Roberson. Currently he is untreated. At a lower-level facility he can obtain the full attention of the psychological services department. In his current facility there is a good chance that his lack of access to counseling will have a detrimental effect."

I was concerned that Pendleton's harsh environment would harm Travis far more than it would help him. A rough prison experience, one might presume, would have a strong deterrent effect, but that theory is based on an enormous misunderstanding of what guides human behavior. From behavioral psychology to human economic behavior, people are consistently driven by incentives, not by fear. A horrible prison environment is something humans can learn to adapt to; and when a person does adapt, he or she is forever made unafraid of the only deterrent the state possesses.

As Jimmy Croom, an O-dorm neighbor, neatly expressed one day, "Treating us bad just teaches us it's okay to treat people bad. It teaches us to have no respect for other people." Punishment doesn't develop any inner desire to do what's right; it merely fosters resentment. It teaches that obedience is required only when force is present to deter. For the majority who obey the law, they obey not out of fear, but for personal incentives – to maintain a good reputation, to garner respect, to create a safe society for themselves and others. Nothing about Pendleton had the capacity to do anything for Travis but turn him into a criminal. Prisons do that exceedingly well in America, as if that is their explicitly designed function. Prisons turn fucked up kids like Travis into full-time menaces to society. The system's dull-witted response to crime – incarceration – has the unintended effect of creating more crime than it prevents.

We specifically asked the court to modify Travis' sentence to 38 years with 10 years suspended, 28 executed, in order to reduce Travis' release date from 11½ years away to 8 years away, which would cause Travis' custody score to drop, forcing the IDOC to transfer him to a lower-level prison where vocations, education, and counseling would be available. This seemed like a reasonable request, and we sent the prosecutor a letter asking his permission to hold a hearing. As we mailed it, Travis asked what his chances were. "Four hundred to one," I replied. "But since it's me doing this," I joked, "knock that down to only two hundred to one." As if my work was twice as good as anyone else's.

A poker player can calculate the odds of being dealt pocket aces at 220 to 1. Lucky Travis sat down at the table and was dealt bullets off the top of the deck. He received a reply from the Jennings County Prosecutor, agreeing to a new sentencing hearing, and the prosecutor had set up a court date. The kid had this miracle letter a week before he bothered telling me about it.

"Get an attorney!" I hollered at him, once I got over my surprise. "If you go in there by yourself, it'll be a disaster." Gangly kid, awkward social skills, no gift for the tricks and delusions of oratory.

His family hired a former prosecutor from Johnson County. Excellent choice. The hearing date was re-set, and the attorney arranged for supportive witnesses to attend. Travis went out Pendleton's back gate, happily shackled, giddy over the prospect of getting 3½ years of freedom restored.

It looked good, but there was still one major hurdle to overcome, besides the judge's approval. The victim had a constitutional right to be heard.

Under Article I, Section 13(b) of the Indiana Constitution, "victims of crime" had the right "to be treated with fairness, dignity, and respect," and "to be informed of and present during public hearings and to confer with the prosecution." In practical usage this meant no sentencing hearing could be conducted without notifying the victim. In Travis' case, his high school nemesis, who had suffered a knife slash millimeters from his jugular vein, would attend the sentence mod hearing.

When Travis returned from court he told me how everybody, including the judge, thought a sentence reduction would be the best thing. It was all set to go. And then the victim spoke, angrily expressing his opinion that Travis should have been slammed with the maximum 50 years in the first place, and still deserved 50 years. The judge wasn't bound by the victim's desires, but he was spineless and wasn't going against the victim's wishes either. Travis' sentence remained unchanged.

"Every victim asks for the maximum," I consoled Travis. I had read hundreds of sentencing hearings and in almost every one, no matter the circumstances, the victim wants as much retribution as the law will allow. The max. They want the max as certainly as eyewitnesses are always "100% sure" about their identification. What do you expect them to say?

It would take a very self-actualized, philosophical, and rational crime victim to rise above the injury and set ego aside when asked to suggest a punishment: "For this offense and this offender, I cannot form an unbiased opinion. If you follow *my* suggestion, there is no point in having a criminal justice system. Abolish your offices, return my tax dollars, and hand the criminal over to me. It is solely the state's job to determine a fair sentence, not mine, so do your job."

The state, however, is barely more rational than the average crime victim when selecting punishments. Authoritarian personality disorder takes over. Legislators have not used an objective approach in creating sentencing guidelines, relying instead on subjective, emotional, non-scientific, gut reactions to crime. The sentencing ranges enacted into law have been picked out of thin air, or worse, selected as "tougher" than those in neighboring states, a type of out-of-control sentencing arms race.

A scientific study has never been employed to determine what sentence would be proportional to any class of offense. There have been gains in "victims rights," but the principle of restorative justice has been ignored. *An unrestored, uncompensated victim remains a victim.* If nothing is done to make the victim whole again, the scales remain unbalanced.

Travis Roberson's inability to invest his twenties in education and job training is typical for prisoners throughout the United States. To the incessant frustration of prisoners, the system seems unwilling to fund rehabilitative programs proven to drastically curtail recidivism.

In 2010 a number of legislative budget cuts to the IDOC tore into all education programs at Pendleton. Fiscal conservatives sought to save taxpayers' money, a ripple effect from the 2008 housing crisis and recession. The statewide IDOC education budget was ripped from $25 million to $8.9 million, leaving it at 1.24% of the IDOC budget. That's roughly $308 per prisoner per year (28,900 prisoners at the time) for the "corrections" part of the organization's title. Aramark's $25 million contract to provide meals amounted to $865 per prisoner per year ($2.37 per man per day), and medical services, contracted to Corizon at $100 million, worked out to $3460 per prisoner per year. Ivy Tech now provides the bulk of education services – when they made their proposal they promised "more programs" for "less money." They were half right. The effect at Pendleton was the loss of all three meaningful vocations – carpentry, welding, and auto body. Now there are none.

The state legislature also killed the most highly-sought, most effective educational program, college, by rescinding prisoner eligibility for the O'Bannon Grant. For 30 years, this state grant had allowed prisoners to take classes offered by Ball State University and Grace College. Professors entered the prison and taught a slate of 40 to 60 courses every semester, to an enrollment of 150 to 250 students. Indiana had been one of the few states still providing college to prisoners – other states suffered college funding shutdowns in 1994 when Congress rescinded prisoner eligibility for the Pell Grant as part of the Violent Crime Control and Law Enforcement Act (VCCLEA).

The demise of Indiana's O'Bannon Grant for prisoners was accomplished almost exactly the way the Pell Grant was curtailed nationally, a curious tale of deception in itself. Beginning in 1992, Congressman Bart Gordon (R-TN) told Congress that 100,000 prisoners were receiving Pell grants, taking funds away from good, law-abiding students. He cited the case of a police officer's child who had "lost" his grant eligibility due to funds going to prisoners. Another Southerner long known to be hopelessly infected with Authoritarian Personality Disorder, Senator Jesse Helms (R-NC), backed Gordon's argument. Never mind that Gordon's claims were absolutely false, or that the Government Accounting Office and U.S. Department of Education presented the true numbers to Congress – the restriction passed anyway, and President Clinton (cleverly poaching on Republicans' tough-on-crime territory) signed it into law. In truth, only 23,000 of 4,000,000 Pell Grant recipients were prisoners (0.6%); they received $34.6 million, an average of $1,500 each; and no free-world person had ever been denied funding due to a prisoner qualifying for a grant. The cop cited by Representative Gordon earned far too much for his child to qualify for need-based financial aid.

Indiana's legislature voiced the same deceptive reasoning when they curtailed the O'Bannon Grant. They claimed law-abiding students were being denied grants because Indiana prisoners were getting them. In truth, no qualifying student in the history of the O'Bannon Grant had ever been denied. Nevertheless, the Indiana General Assembly decided they would no longer invest in human capital or develop human resources when those humans were prisoners. Republican Governor Mitch Daniels (now at Purdue University) signed the grant restriction into law.

College was, without question, the most effective of all rehabilitative programs. Indiana cites a recidivism rate of 43% returning to prison within 3 years. The Bureau of Justice Statistics reports a higher rate, claiming 67.8% nationwide are re-arrested within 3 years. However, these 3-year recidivism rates plummet in correlation to educational achievement: with vocational training only 20% return to prison; an associate's degree, 13.7%; bachelor's degree, 5.6%; master's degree, less than 1%. As reported in *Prison Legal News*, numerous studies support these figures. A study by the RAND Corporation concluded that every dollar spent on prisoner education saved $4.55 to $5.26 in future incarceration costs. And with on-line distance education, college could be provided to prisoners more cheaply than ever. Fiscal conservatives, if they had any sense, should be clamoring to reinstate Pell Grant eligibility for prisoners – but this would first entail analyzing prisoner issues in the economic realm, not as a moral crusade.

"Republicans are against prisoner rehabilitation because they consider us less than human," Mel-T had noted to me many years ago. We had clipped an article from the *Indy Star* in 2006 concerning overcrowding in the Marion County Jail, where Prosecutor Carl Brizzi referred to the people being released daily as "human sewage." The labeling of other groups in less-than-human terms ('vermin' in Nazi Germany; 'cockroaches' in Rwanda; et. al.) is one step in every genocidal movement. "They project their personal morals upon others, and they're divisive in everything they do."

To make it appear that programs still exist at Pendleton, many ordinary jobs have been rechristened as vocations. The U.S Department of Labor is complicit in the scheme, awarding certification for those who complete 1,000 to 4,000 hours of labor and pass some written quizzes over six months. Clerks manning various desks (like me) became graduates of the USDOL Clerk Apprenticeship program, and guys collecting trash became USDOL Sanitation Apprenticeship grads. The quizzes are none too tough – achieving uninterrupted attendance is the only real obstacle to completion.

Most American prisons adopt the "labor as vocation" strategy without the USDOL's help, pretending every working prisoner is engaged in instructional learning. But to get these jobs, say as an electrician or as a plumber, they'll only hire people who already know how to do the work. Nothing is taught. When a prison's website claims a long list of vocational programs, don't believe it. Prisons everywhere employ the same ruse to fool the public.

One of the few surviving rehabilitative programs in the IDOC is the PLUS program. "PLUS" is yet another tortured acronym, for "Purposeful Living Units Serve." It should be called what it is, a Faith and Character Based Residential Rehabilitative Program, but "FACBRRP" doesn't have the cachet of an acronym like PLUS.

PLUS is an 18-to-24-month program, heavily structured, requiring participants to deal with their personal defects and errors in thinking openly and honestly – a requirement that weeds out recalcitrant prisoners every week. Three out of four who enroll get tossed out. A perfect disciplinary record while in the program is a must. Coupled with being disciplinary-free for one year before entry, a PLUS graduate must show an ability to abide by the rules for roughly three years, an accomplishment itself strongly correlated with lower recidivism.

Some joke that PLUS stands for "People Living Under Stress," or "Please Let Us Survive," indicative of the pressures inherent in the program, but for those who have completed it, there was little real stress. Prisoners either went into the program with an honest, mature attitude, or they failed. The program downplays the significance of any environmental factors, and instead challenges prisoners to ignore their upbringing and take personal responsibility for every decision that contributed to their incarceration. It employs the functionalist perspective of sociology, to a degree that denies the existence of sociological factors as even a remote cause for incarceration. If you are in prison, it is your fault alone, and you cannot compare your start in life to those who were more well-off.

Those graduating from PLUS are much less likely to return to prison – only 9.25%. To get a perspective on that number, it represents 28 out of 300 coming back to prison instead of 129 out of 300 – and the IDOC releases 300 prisoners per week.

PLUS is the only anti-recidivism program left in the IDOC, but whether a court would recognize its efficacy and grant a sentence mod because of it was a legal crap shoot that depended on the quality of the prisoner's legal representation. At every turn in this system, it comes down to money.

What's missing from the prisoner-release system, all across America, is hard data that would help render an intelligent decision on which prisoners to release. Sentencing hearings, sentence mods, and parole boards, for the most part, are out of touch with modern, scientific, analytical tools (or they lack the personnel with the fortitude to use those tools). The same way sports teams use analytics to position their players, corrections departments could use analytics to thin the overpopulated herds within their prisons.

You could walk into any prison in America year after year and select 8 to 10 percent who are ready for immediate release.

Risk assessment indicators can inform courts, parole boards, and governors on what works and what doesn't work to curb recidivism. A well-prepared defense attorney might include the statistics mentioned above, and conclude the argument with this:

> "If this court believes the purpose of the Department of Corrections is to provide correctional services, then the court should release those prisoners who have demonstrated an ability to follow the rules, who have improved themselves through education and training, and who have

been identified by corrections experts as having the lowest risk to re-offend."

I have read hundreds of sentence modification motions, and none included any figures quantifying the statistical significance of the prisoners' accomplishments. But then, like most things before the court, the focus isn't on what works best, or what makes sense. The focus seems to be on an altogether different question: Has the guild of legal professionals been adequately compensated in exchange for this prisoner's release?

A more callous way to put it: Does he have money? Is he one of us?

It takes an exemplary record *and* money to get a sentence modification. A good prison record alone won't do it, and money alone won't do it. And a little bit of luck helps too – like the good fortune of having a deputy prosecutor willing to risk becoming the next boat inspector.

CHAPTER THIRTEEN

Degrees of Innocence

"As somebody who's been sent to prison, who's never had a formal legal education, just being able to have an intelligent legal exchange with judges and lawyers makes them irate."
– James Newsome, exonoree, in *Surviving Justice: America's Wrongfully Convicted and Exonerated,* p. 117.

Exonerations are rare, but when one happens, it reassures the public that "the system works," as if the criminal justice system's only problem is the slim fraction under 1% where guilt has been improperly assigned. "Yeah, it's unfortunate that Mr. X had to spend a decade in prison for a crime he did not commit," a pro-government pundit might declare when a prisoner is set free by the court, "but the outcome reminds us that our system is still very close to perfect. And when it does fail, it still has the capacity to get it right in the end." Prisoners define innocence in many ways, but to the public, there is only one kind of innocence – actual innocence.

We only lost two residents to actual innocence during my ten years at Pendleton: David 'Whiskey' Scott, the confused teenager who confessed to a murder he did not do, and exonerated by DNA 24 years later; and David Camm, the Indiana State Trooper twice convicted of shooting his wife and two children in New Albany.

When Camm's third jury, in upscale Boone County northwest of Indianapolis, unanimously found him 'not guilty,' you may have pictured a supportive cheer erupting in the law library and in the cellhouses, but that was not the case. Camm's freedom enthralled no prisoner at Pendleton. It wasn't because he was a cop, or because some still thought he was responsible for the three murders, or because allegations of child molestation had been made. It was because he wasn't "one of us" – he hadn't faced the same hurdles as the rest of us.

Camm had chosen to do his time in solitary, under protective custody. Not all former cops choose to "check in" at Pendleton, and they fare quite normally. Camm hadn't been in our law library, and he hadn't fought anything in court on his own, like the rest of us had to do. He had good lawyers, arguably the best in the state. He had won two direct appeals, when hardly any of us could win one. The higher courts had combed through his appellate issues with great care, probably with deference to his former occupation, and in fine detail published decisions five times longer than the average appellate decision. Camm had been locked up thirteen years, most of that time wasted in R-cellhouse, where none of us got to know him. His victory, while justified, didn't portend anything for the other prisoners at Pendleton. In fact, it did just the opposite.

"Just goes to show," Warren-Bey commented, "it takes money to get justice." One news article estimated taxpayers doled out over $3 million for Camm's prosecution and defense.

"What it shows," said Pete Mitchell, "is that cops get special treatment from the courts. Nobody else wins on the issues Camm had in his two appeals."

Camm's second appeal was a 4-1 decision by the Indiana Supreme Court, declaring prosecutorial misconduct occurred when the state theorized Camm was motivated to kill his family to cover up the molestation of his daughter. Speculative evidence supported the state's theory, so the high court reversed Camm's second conviction. On the day Camm was found not guilty by jury number three, the five-member Supreme Court learned of Camm's acquittal as they exited a session held on the IUPUI campus. A person I know was on the campus and overheard one justice indignantly comment: *"This* jury didn't know Camm had molested his daughter."

The state's failure in Camm's third trial was blamed on the prosecutorial tactic of having Charles Boney, Camm's alleged co-conspirator, testify. Boney had not testified before. The all-white jury saw this enormous black guy, steely-eyed and ominous, coldly laying out his long, involved story of premeditation. They had no problem excluding Camm from the tale and assigning all of the evil to Boney alone. "A huge mistake by the state, putting Boney on the stand," one interested observer stated. "But there was no doubt, no way David Camm was guilty." She was familiar with the New Albany area and had followed Camm's case closely. "No way!"

Ned McConnell seemed gleeful that a Boone County jury had acquitted David Camm. "I knew they'd find him not guilty," Ned beamed. "They're not gonna convict a white cop for murder when it's obvious a black guy was involved in the crime. Not in *my* county!"

Indiana's court rules on change of venue ignored county demographics and unwittingly pushed high-profile trials to more conservative, whiter counties. This worked well for prosecutors in most cases, but backfired when the defendant's race and class matched the new jurisdiction. Whites benefited from the venue rules, and minorities were harmed. This favored David Camm.

"What are you saying, Ned? Camm was acquitted in Boone County because he was white and Boney was black?"

"No, no, it's not like that," Ned backpedalled. "I'm just sayin', in Boone County you get treated fair. If you didn't do it, they'll find you not guilty, like they're supposed to."

"You think they treated *you* fair in Boone County?" Ned had 42 years for voluntary manslaughter, obtained through a plea dropping a murder charge.

"Well . . . pretty much. I think I got more time than I should have, but I had Jim Voyles, and it was the best he could do." Voyles was widely considered the best attorney in Indianapolis, the Big Bertha of attorney artillery. Expensive, but effective. He had defended heavyweight champion Mike Tyson on a rape case in 1992. People who bring up Voyles' defense of Tyson rarely mention he lost that case, and Tyson did three years on six.

"Yeah, forty-two's not bad for a homicide on your ex-wife," I remarked. "A lot of guys here wish they had that sentence." I switched to a sympathetic tone. "But the crime itself, Ned, there's also the fact that you have to live with what you did. You must feel *awful* about it. You know, hittin' her in the head with a hammer?"

Ned's face fell, and he fixed me with a glare that said, *You prying son-of-a-bitch, nobody's supposed to know the details about what I did.* His case wasn't reported on LEXIS because he had not filed an appeal. He didn't talk about the circumstances of his case, to anyone, ever. His brain worked fast to register that I knew he had beaten his ex-wife to death with a hammer, and I could have known this only from Internet sources, and I had the audacity to confront him with it. *You must feel awful about it,* I had offered. No, in fact, Ned didn't feel awful about it at all.

"She attacked me first." His glare didn't waver. I suddenly felt lucky this hot-tempered yuppie didn't have a hammer within reach.

"Oh! Well, that makes for a different situation." He implied it was self-defense, as if his ex-wife, a nurse, sprang upon him with potentially deadly force while their two children, ages 5 and 3, were in the house. Sure, perhaps she attacked Ned while he was innocently engaged in building a birdhouse, and his hammer blows were reflexive, the only way to fend her off and save his own life. His flashpoint temper and sense of entitlement suggested otherwise. Had it really been self-defense, Voyles would have gotten him off scot-free.

"Yeah, nobody knows how it really was. Just me." Ned's statement contained a warning: *Don't go around telling people I'm some kind of cold-blooded murderer.*

And a second message, implied: *We're not friends any more, motherfucker.*

That was the last time I talked to Ned.

A few days after my tete-a-tete with Ned, Arturo Gallardo sought me out, wanting to know what he could do now that he had lost his PC petition in Elkhart County and lost in the Indiana Court of Appeals. Like Ned, he had 42 years. Unlike Ned, he hadn't bashed anyone in the head with a hammer. He had only told someone where to buy dope. I gathered Arturo's legal work again, wanting to know how his PC had gone wrong, and could hardly believe what I read.

The $2500 attorney in the impressive South Bend high-rise had amended Gallardo's PC petition, dropping my IAC claim against appellate counsel, the only ineffectiveness claim available, and substituted an IAC claim on trial counsel. Judge Shewmaker correctly ruled the claim prohibited by *res judicata* doctrine because IAC on trial counsel had already been raised by Gallardo's first idiot attorney on direct appeal. Shewmaker's ruling was a terse, three-paragraph denial. The appellate court smacked it down the same way, disdainfully, as if they wanted to ask Gallardo's counsel, *Just how stupid are you? How did you ever pass the bar exam?*

The attorney would never have to answer for his ineptitude, because he was protected by *Pennsylvania v. Finley* (1987), which classifies PC proceedings as "quasi-civil," not criminal proceedings, so no constitutional right to counsel attaches. And since there is no constitutional right to PC counsel, there can be no such thing as "ineffective" PC counsel. All PC counsel has to do is show up for the proceedings. In Indiana, it's known as the *Baum* standard.

The demise of Arturo's PC proceedings put me in the position of explaining and defending what I had tried to do, while also convincing Arturo he had employed three professional attorneys – at trial, on direct appeal, and on a PC – who 3-for-3 had no idea what they were doing. It was a tough argument, and I encouraged him to show his case to other reputable law clerks. About a month later he had heard several concurring opinions and was back, asking, "What do I do now?"

"Keep a clean disciplinary record," I told him. "Complete all the programs you can. Someday you can file for a sentence mod, hopefully after Shewmaker retires." I made it clear this was his only hope.

I wanted to file for executive clemency for Arturo and ask Governor Mike Pence to commute his sentence, and deport him to Mexico, but there was no sense getting his hopes up. It would make sense, suspending half his sentence and sending him out of the country, and telling him he would serve the remainder if he stuck a toe north of the Rio Grande. In fact, that might be good policy for all of the 142,000 non-citizens in U.S. jails and prisons. However, our Republican governor with enormous political ambition wasn't about to let anyone out of prison early, and certainly not a "drug-dealing" illegal immigrant.

A hundred years ago, governors routinely commuted sentences as part of the system of checks and balances against the legislative and judicial branches, but a sense of political self-preservation has removed the executive branch from the criminal justice system. Was Arturo a serious political risk? Certainly not. But as every politician knows, zero risk is the best risk of all.

I asked Arturo how Emily and the kids were doing, and he winced, like it was too painful to think about. "She's mad at that attorney about the $2500," he said. "He won't give any of the money back." He lamented that they had been fooled by the extravagance of the attorney's office.

"You can't judge a book by its cover," I told him, "and you can't judge an attorney by the size of his building."

"So how do you know if an attorney is any good?"

He posed a great question. Amazon has book reviews, Travelocity rates hotels, and Angie's List can recommend a good plumber, but there's no website that can assure you an attorney knows what he's doing. (If one existed, an attorney would probably sue it for defamation.)

The bar association will simply tell you they are all professionals, all equally competent. I've never seen it, but I suspect their bar exam is none too tough. The kind where you put the right answer down and wonder if the examiner will be smart enough to know it's right. I'm reminded of Frank Abagnale, the con man played by Leonardo DiCaprio in *Catch Me If You Can*, who posed as a district attorney in Louisiana – he studied for two weeks and passed the bar exam. Then he got into a courtroom and showed he was clueless.

I used the medical profession to analogize for Arturo. "You know an attorney is good," I proposed, "the same way you know a surgeon is good. If you're not dead after surgery, maybe he knows what he's doing."

Arturo considered this, then extended the analogy. "They killed me three times," he said.

Yep, I thought, and I couldn't save you either.

He'll get out in 2028, when he's pushing fifty, and his children will be in their thirties. I hope they'll visit him wherever he ends up. In the meantime, he'll burn up another $325,000 in taxpayers' money, and they'll have nothing to show for it.

Donald Ware's case finally progressed to the point where we had always predicted he stood the best chance of relief – federal court. His issues were good, but once again I told him the major defect in his petition was the absence of an attorney's name on the cover.

Donnie priced some attorneys for his habeas corpus, but they were $8,000 and up, about half of Teresa's annual income. He couldn't get professional legal help, but I was determined to give him the next best thing – an argument incorporating an attorney's winning brief, almost word for word. His jury instruction issue depended on *Sanders v. Cotton*, so I burned up a favor and had an attorney get me the briefs filed by Sanders' attorney. I polished Ware's brief to perfection.

Donnie's habe was a beauty, I thought, and federal court was the venue we had been waiting for. The state courts had ignored *Sanders*, as expected, but we were very hopeful that the feds would see it differently. Either that, or the *Sanders* decision was written solely for the benefit of Sanders, and maybe to show the unbelievers that the courts could set somebody free once in awhile. The district court held Donnie's petition an inordinately long time, well past the ordinary six-week rejection schedule. This only built suspense, and buoyed Donnie's hope.

Each day, as we anticipated a ruling in *Ware v. Zatecky*, our optimism swelled. At noon one day, I saw Donnie's name posted on the counselor's door: LEGAL MAIL – WARE 981444. He got off work at the laundry at 1:45 p.m., and I found an excuse to venture upstairs and hover outside the office when Donnie signed for the court's ruling.

We opened it together. Freedom or despair – which was inside?

Cover letter – saying nothing. Here's your decision.

Eight stapled pages came next. Donnie began scanning the first page, left to right, left to right, and I wanted to tell him, the decision is on the last page, just turn to that.

"I don't know what this means," Donnie said. "It's all legal argument and stuff." He tried to hand it to me.

"Flip to the end."

My eyes hit the two words that mattered two seconds before his eyes discovered them, so I had time to move from the page to his face and see his expression change. His mind comprehended, and his face went slack, like the whole world was no longer intelligible. This was where hope, that pernicious emotion, met reality.

"Writ denied?"

It was like seeing a man reach for a life preserver, miss, and slowly sink out of sight.

There was another two-page court document, a declaration by the same judge declaring that no reasonable jurist could find merit in Donnie's petition, therefore no certificate of appealability would be issued. No appeal would be allowed.

A prisoner bringing a civil suit over cold toilet seats had a right to appeal the district court's decision, but a prisoner petitioning under 28 USC 2254 on a criminal matter had no absolute right to an appeal. The same judge that ruled on the petition also ruled on whether or not any other judge could possibly disagree with the petition's denial. This meant Donnie would be barred from the Seventh Circuit Court of Appeals, the same court that had issued the *Sanders* opinion in 2005.

"The judge says your issue has no merit whatsoever," I translated to Donnie. "Like we're fucking idiots for even inventing this argument."

"But that's not right," Donnie pleaded. "I don't know the law, but I know what you wrote was good. It made sense. It's the same thing that won for the other guy!"

Yeah, sure. Made sense. What good was that? The other guy, Sanders, had an attorney, so maybe that was the only real difference.

Or maybe my approach was all wrong, and I really had no idea what I was doing. I was as lost as the expression on Donnie's face.

"We'll still fight this," I promised. "The judge, she's a transplant from Marion County, extreme conservative Republican, typical authoritarian, and we can ask a multi-judge panel in Chicago to review her denial of the COA." If we were granted a COA by the Seventh Circuit, we'd be back in business. "It's bad, Donnie, but we're not done yet. Not by a long shot. I'll get right on this."

Three weeks later, we had filed the request for a COA and were on the rec yard, talking about future proceedings. Donnie still had options if the COA was denied.

"If that happens," I said, "you can still petition the U.S. Supreme Court for a writ of certiorari. One in 900 are granted, so don't get your hopes up. Really, though, what you'll have left is a sentence mod. Or a PC-2, if you happen upon newly discovered evidence showing you didn't commit the crime."

He raised an eyebrow, and it was then I decided to come clean about what I had figured out about the 2005 homicide.

"Look, I know you did it, Donnie. And I know how it happened." His eyes didn't waver from the ground. "The young man laying by the storm drain, dead – the storm drain was the clue to this case. That storm drain helped me figure it all out."

Donnie didn't say a word, so I continued.

"The drain behind the Public Storage building told me the kids were running down a slope. Rainwater was directed away from the main road to storm sewers in the easement behind the building." My former career as a land surveyor guided my understanding of the area's physical layout. I had also run a level-loop in front of the scene in 2001, so I knew something about the gradual local elevation changes.

"You were 200 feet away from four running kids. It was dark. The corridor between the buildings was even darker. You aimed low, to shoot near their feet, but you didn't know they were running slightly downhill, and you shot the first kid in the leg. The rifle recoiled, the barrel raised a bit, and the kids traveled farther down that gently declining corridor. A one-degree shift in your barrel's aim at 200 feet raises the bullet's trajectory by 42 inches." Simple trigonometry. "He ran further down slope, your barrel was raised, but you still thought you were firing at foot level. Your second shot hit Brandon Dunson in the back, cutting into his heart. He ran around the corner and fell, white shirt still in his pocket. He died next to the storm drain, and you never knew you shot him."

Donnie flicked his head back, pained by the memory, and stared at the treetops poking over the distant gray wall. He processed my theory in silence. I let him think; I'm sure he was recalling that awful July night in 2005.

"I *did* aim low, I remember that. And when the news said someone was killed, I didn't believe it. I truly did not believe it. Or, I thought, maybe someone else had shot at them too, after I had left. But yeah, I aimed low, I remember that, and the only way to explain how that boy got killed is like you say. I didn't know they were running onto lower ground."

It was a textbook definition of reckless homicide. Not aiming to kill. No intent to kill. Not "knowingly" killing. Rage, taunting, gun available. Overreaction, shots fired, the death accidental. It wasn't a murder, but only the two of us knew that. No court would agree with us, because the time for explaining the incident was at his trial, ten years ago. Whatever level of innocence Donnie possessed, it didn't matter any more. He had ten years in, and twenty-five to go.

He was now in a position where nobody had to listen to him.

CHAPTER FOURTEEN

Illusions

"If we lived in a dictatorship, the revolution would be much easier." – Melvin Tunstill (2014).

My horizons were twenty-five feet above ground, where the crest of Pendleton's gray wall met blue sky. I missed seeing the sun's full journey every day – no sunrises, no sunsets – and the sun fading into an orange glow was a distant memory. Prison is an artificial place. Doors, walls, wire. Cages. Concrete above and below. Cells like coffins. Rough steel bars eroded by decades of palm sweat – *How many hands for how many years will it take to wear this steel away?* Some days, depending on where they've put you, sun, sky, and air are gone, and you believe a day has gone by only because footsteps routinely passed your door and meals were delivered. One unproductive, meaningless day rolls by, then another, and the calendar flips, and you ask yourself, *What have I accomplished here? Can there be a purpose?* I exist. But my existence is artificial, like everything around me. Unnatural. Like I ceased being human and have transformed into a new species, *Homo incarceratus*. Darwin could explain why I am here. If I have survived, it is because I have adapted to my island environment. But that means I'm not me any more.

After ten years at Pendleton I was on my way out, but I kept this news to myself. I began to feel detached from the community, like an observer passing through, a tourist on a strange holiday. I was distantly attentive, rather than personally invested, in the tribulations consuming the lives around me. I hadn't sent anybody out the front door, but I still had a couple good lottery tickets in my pocket, undecided cases that had hope. Removed from the daily struggle, I began to broaden my view, and reflect on my work history. Was it worth my effort? Why had I fought so many unwinnable cases?

Bobby Holleman framed his legal work in the context of a human rights struggle, and the more I thought about it, the more I realized I had been engaged in the right endeavor, but absolutely for the wrong reasons.

A selfish incentive had propelled me into legal work. At some time during my campaign of mostly losing battles, however, my incentive had changed, and the need to gratify my ego had dissolved. I truly did not care about taking credit for any measure of victory, and it did not matter if I got a guy out of prison or not – a win would not prove a thing. It would send one solitary man home, like liberating one mink from the fur factory, or one porpoise from the tuna net. A hundred losses proved more than one win. My mission was shifting from one battlefront to another.

My neighbors continued to resist the legal system. I listened, but had little to say. In 2015 we began receiving prisoners sentenced under the new law, who had caught their cases after July 1, 2014. They had either 75% or 85% to do on their sentences, and were not particularly motivated to participate in programs or comply with the disciplinary rules. The guy who moved into Jeffery Hofstedter's open bunk was one of them.

"How the fuck is this 85% law fair? I got 70 years for murder and a bullshit Class B felony, and I know a guy upstairs who's got 70 years for the same charges, and he gets out in 35 years, and I have to do 60. Just because he killed somebody in 2005, and I caught my case in August 2014? How can they do that?"

The guy upstairs to whom he was referring was Donnie Ware, and this was the first time I heard someone insinuate Donnie was getting off easy. New perspective. Here was the flip side of the new sentencing ranges – drug defendants argued for retroactive sentencing, while almost everyone else coming in with a fresh conviction argued for a return to the pre-2014 law.

"The legislature can set the punishments for crimes at anything they want," I told the new fish. I couldn't begin to care about his intricate set of personal problems, so I never bothered to learn his name. "Every sentence in every jurisdiction in the world is somebody's totally arbitrary idea of what a sentence should be."

"Yeah, but what they've done to me is basically give me life without parole." He was mid-30's, so he'd get out in his mid-90's. With our facility's triple mortality rate, I hadn't seen anybody make it past age 75.

"Yeah, pretty much," I agreed. "But the legislature has the right to do that."

The fish put his mind to work on ways to shorten his time in prison. "What about time cuts? You know how that works? How can I do programs and stuff to cut down my release date?"

A couple listeners nearby smirked and shook their heads at the new fish's ignorance. The IDOC was not a goal-oriented system.

"You're thinking of the educational time cuts we had for convictions prior to 2014," I explained. "We could get up to four years in time cuts, or one-third off, whichever was less, for completing college, vocations, and drug abuse classes. But for you new guys, all those awards have been cut down to two years, and the award gets applied to your imposed sentence, not the time you have left to do."

"Back end, not front end?"

"Exactly. Since I earned four years off, I do 31½ on 71 instead of 35½. You – you can earn 2 years off your 70, but it's not applied to the 60 you do, it's applied to the 70. So instead of dropping you to 58 years to do, it lets you do 85% of 68. So you'd do 58 years, 3 months, and some-odd days."

"But tell him the good part," Natti chimed in. "How there ain't no more college."

"Oh, yeah. They ended college grants in 2011, and took all the vocations away from Pendleton, and there's no drug counseling here either."

"So how the fuck am I supposed to earn any time off?"

We shrugged.

"What reason do I have to do anything around here? What's stopping me from knocking one of these smart-ass COs in the mouth?"

"Well, they got G-cellhouse for you if you do that. But incentives? There are none."

Indiana was a late-comer to the Truth-in-Sentencing table, a movement designed to appease anyone who was victimized by a former prisoner who had been released before serving his "full" term. Like the Christopher M. Stevens case – molester Stevens had 4 years, 3 suspended, and did 6 months. Less than two months later he was molesting and murdering a child. (Legislators: "If only he had done 100%, or 85%, this never would have happened.")

The United States Congress was responsible for the truth-in-sentencing scheme, as part of the 1994 Violent Crime Control and Law Enforcement Act. The VCCLEA incentivized the 85% law, giving grants to states that changed their sentencing and parole laws to 85% mandates. Congress also explicitly incentivized higher incarceration rates, again tying grant money to imprisonment rates. No longer would the public have to endure the scourge of monsters like Stevens, being released far too early and committing horrible crimes. Truth-in-sentencing would protect the public.

And if you believe truth-in-sentencing is a good idea, find a mirror and get a glimpse of what an idiot looks like. Stevens did not get out "early." He got out exactly when the prosecutor and judge thought he would get out, in six months. Had they wanted him locked up for four years, they'd have sentenced him to eight years.

No prosecutor and no judge has ever put a person in prison and not known, to a high degree of certainty, when the prisoner would be released. If a prisoner got out a little ahead of schedule, it was because the prisoner *earned* it, and the prosecutor and judge knew this earnable mechanism existed. They didn't get fooled; they're not stupid; if they act shocked, they're faking it. Whether it's a 50% mandate to release, or 85%, or 75%, or 10%, the judge is aware of it at the time of sentencing, and the defendant is sentenced accordingly. Released early? No such thing.

What truth-in-sentencing really does is remove incentives for prisoners to reform, and make prisons more difficult to manage. Prisoners need incentives – they're kinda like all humans on earth in that respect. Incentives drive human behavior far more strongly than do punishments or disincentives. A state could set the initial time-to-do rate at 50% or 40% or even 75%, and then allow earned incentives to take it down, allowing the prisoner to earn his or her release based on the likelihood to re-offend factored by the seriousness of a subsequent offense. Apply modern analytics to corrections the same as is done in other fields. Risk management, in other words. And in this Information Age, we have the risk assessment tools at hand to do just that.

The amount of time to do on a sentence needs to be a percentage that balances the need to control prisoners' behavior while still offering incentives for achievements. A 60-do-6 sentence (10%) gives prison administrators too much control over prisoners' behavior – COs could thwart a prisoner's release through petty infractions; a 7-do-6 (85%) gives them too little control; a 12-do-6 (50%) hits that balance between behavioral control and providing opportunities to earn a release through achievements.

The best solution to relieve overcrowding is new legislation that would provide release mechanisms through executive branch authority. Sentence review boards, or sentence modification boards, under the authority of the state governor's office, could review prisoners' files and intelligently select the best candidates for release. Time served or time left to do would have little to do with the assessments. What matters most would be the potential for harm to the community.

The ultimate question is, *Why keep a person locked up when his or her negative impact on the community is likely to be minimal, or zero?* In every prison system in America, one can easily identify a tenth of the population qualified for immediate release. They're easy to spot, and they are not necessarily short-timers. They stayed out of trouble (if you can follow petty prison rules, you can follow the law), have employable skills (a strong indicator of post-release success), have attained high educational levels (by far the best predictor of success), and have put substance abuse problems behind them (if they had any). They work, they study, they learn, and they have proven an ability to conform.

In every other industrialized country, these positive attributes mark a prisoner for release and represent the purpose of the correctional system – to correct anti-social behavior. The way American states do it now, the thug who hasn't learned a thing gets out just as fast as a person who has no business being locked up. In a backhanded way, 85% truth-in-sentencing, with no way to earn release far below that percentage, is a reward system for those with the worst behavior.

As I left O-dorm on a pass for my once-weekly law library visit, I noticed sewage bubbling up out of the floor drain in the basement hallway. The water pipes leading into our dorm were calcified from ninety years of use, and the pipes leading out were crammed with plastic bags, orange peels, and other slow-to-dissolve obstructions. A major sewage back-up occurs regularly in every old prison in America.

Returning an hour later, the sewage had spread from the hallway to the sleeping areas, where 77 prisoners wrapped deodorant-laden towels around their faces to filter the odor. Fecal boluses floated everywhere. Staff did nothing, and tempers began to rise. The officers slunk out the door like a pack of raccoons, leaving the mess for the 6 o'clock shift. By then, some prisoners were stifling a desire to lash out.

I did some rough calcs, and put the sewage overflow at 900 to 1,200 gallons.

A lieutenant came wading in at 6:20, greeted by a chorus of yells.

"What the fuck!? Y'all have had us in this shit for three hours! Get us the fuck out of here!"

"Y'all gotta be patient!"

"Be patient?! What the fuck you think we been doing?"

Minutes later, the order came for us to grab our mattresses and property boxes and move to the gym. Relief! None of us could move fast enough. First to get to the exit door upstairs was Scottie McLean, traveling light with one plastic bag of necessities and his mattress perched on his shoulder. When the door opened, Scottie began to step outside – and was forcefully shoved back inside by the lieutenant.

"I didn't say go yet, you fucking idiot!" Scottie staggered backwards.

Oh, here we go, I thought. *Scottie's gonna beat this lieutenant half to death.* If he had fought over being called a bitch, he'd probably kill over being called a "fucking idiot" and shoved at the same time.

Scottie straightened himself up, and stuck his chin out. Unperturbed, he said, "Tell me when you're ready, L-T."

Not one trace of hostility.

We spent one night on the floor of F-gym, and my over-riding thought was, *Papa John at New Castle damn sure earned his money.* Violence averted.

Spring eased into summer in 2015, and legal questions still descended upon me despite my clear signals of disinterest. Wally Lockhart wanted to make an issue out of how he was returned to Indiana from Iraq, with no extradition process. "Basically they kidnapped me and brought me back." Well, Wally, they can do that. The U.S. Supreme Court, in *United States v. Alvarez-Machain* (1992) declared that if U.S. agents violate the laws of another country when apprehending a suspect, the suspect has grounds for a claim in that country, but not in the United States. "Forcible abduction does not impair a court's jurisdiction to try a person for a crime." Extradition treaties are no longer the only means to return a wanted person to U.S. soil.

"So, if I was to get out and move to Laos, which has no extradition treaty with the United States, it wouldn't matter? They could still come and get me anyway?" You got that right, Wally. There's no place left to hide. Our government doesn't just ignore its own law, it ignores international law as well.

An ear-hustler nearby broke in: "As an ex-con, you can't leave the country anyway. You can't get a passport, and no country will let you in."

This line of crap had been passed around for decades. "You're wrong on both counts," I shot back. "A passport is an identification document, and anybody can get one. I've gotten three while holding a felony conviction. And other countries will issue a tourist visa to anyone who's not on a terrorist watch list." Mr. Dippin-in-Business disappeared.

No matter what I told Wally, he was intent on barraging his PC court with multiple weak issues, an all-too-common pro se practice that would doom his petition. He had also filed a civil suit against his trial attorney, alleging professional malpractice, which gave the attorney a clear incentive to derail Wally's PC petition. Wally's actions guaranteed he would be opposed by the entire legal community. Wally had maybe two winnable issues, but they would be buried under stinking layers of nonsense.

Larry Rowe tried to get me to find an issue for him, on a three-county burglary spree that netted him 40 years. The first two counties agreed to concurrent sentences, but the third, Huntington County, tacked their twenty on the end, consecutive. "When I did the burglary, I didn't even know I was in Huntington County," he pleaded. He had burglarized rural domiciles in the winter, when pristine snowfall clued him to vacant homes. He crossed the unmarked county line, entering a jurisdiction so bent on severe sentencing, that if it were an independent principality, it's incarceration rate would be number one in the world, double the rate of the runner-up. Authoritarian dementia reigned there without oversight.

"Nothing I can do for you, Larry." Three guilty pleas, no hope.

"Sentence modification?"

"From Huntington County? Forget about it. Maybe if you've got twenty grand to spend; otherwise, no way. You've got 40-do-20, so if they bring back programs and college, maybe you can work it down to 16."

Like Dave Fields, Louis Amalfitano, and Arturo Gallardo, Larry Rowe's problem wasn't what he did, but where he did it. Counties run by characters afflicted with Authoritarian Personality Disorder were sentencing quagmires, fiefdoms of insanity on the Indiana county map.

One prisoner pleased with the 2014 law changes was Mike Cavinder, whose professional career centered on shoplifting big-ticket items. Previously, under Indiana law, all thefts were felonies regardless of the item's value; but now the stolen goods had to amount to $700 to rise to a Level 6 felony. "The max you can get now, Mike, is one year in county jail, on a misdemeanor. Just keep it under $700 and don't punch the store dick on your way out – violence would make it a felony assault." Mike was elated. He was doing time for jaw-jacking a store's security guard.

"So now," Mike asked, "I just let them arrest me?"

"Yeah. It's a strategic decision. Do the one year instead of risking a 16-do-12 or more," I told him. "And there's a bonus – there's no habitual possible on a misdemeanor."

The new law made Cavinder very happy. He could go back to being a non-violent thief, resigned to having his livelihood interrupted by the mere nuisance of short stints in the county jail. I could picture him trolling through Best Buy with soap and shower shoes in his back pocket, ready for the county lock-up.

In June, another mentally ill prisoner hung himself in the INSIGHT unit, a black mark on a program designed to deter suicides. None of us were surprised. Their new dorm set-up was oppressive, with not enough time out of their single cells, and their windows were welded over with pepperhole grates.

Air didn't flow, and sunlight barely trickled inside. They were better off than in G-cellhouse, but not by much.

Six days after the hanging, we experienced another death. A prisoner killed CO Red, but not in a way any of us could have anticipated.

We caught the story on TV on a Friday night. IDOC officer Terry Riggs was at a stoplight on Post Road on Indy's east side, just north of the I-70 exit. An escapee from a juvenile facility in Central Illinois drove a stolen van at triple-digit speed into Red's truck, causing a head injury that sent Red into a vegetative state. His organs were harvested and donated the next day.

All it meant at Pendleton was that a new guy would be manning the desk at the Education Building, checking passes and listening to the radio. There was no shutdown for staff to attend his memorial services, and none appeared to be moved by Red's death. I recalled how Red and Mel-T had argued about severe sentences at a law library table less than a year ago, and now both were gone. The "bad guy" at the table, oddly, left a far more lasting impression.

The man still holding five matching lottery numbers, waiting for the Powerball to drop, was Smitty. His public defender anticipated a Supreme Court ruling on the retroactivity of *Miller v. Alabama* to be published in early 2015. *Toca v. Louisiana* was the case, but it unexpectedly reached a settlement, taking it off the court's docket. Smitty's PC petition in Jasper County was ruled upon by Judge John Potter in July, without the benefit of the long-awaited retroactivity determination. Judge Potter, of course, ruled *Miller* was not retroactive. Smitty's attorneys filed an appeal, waiting for another case, *Montgomery v. Louisiana*, to reverse Potter's findings.

I wrangled a final meeting with Smitty in August, talking to him through the fence separating our rec yards.

"It's been three years since we first filed the petition," Smitty recalled, "and here I am, still waiting for something to happen."

I assured him it would work out. "You're in good hands with the public defenders you have, Smitty. They're the best in the public defender's office. You just have to be patient." My words sounded silly as soon as I spoke them. He had waited 38 years.

"Can you guess how much longer it'll be?"

Hard to know for sure. "Maybe six months for *Montgomery* to be decided, three months after that to decide your appeal, then three months until a new sentencing hearing. That's if it all goes your way."

"So another year?" His pleading look showed me that no matter how many years he had lost to the state, losing one more still hurt.

"Yeah, afraid so. At least a year." I gave him my mother's address, in case we got separated, and asked him to write and tell me how his case progressed.

In February of 2016, shortly after *Montgomery* made *Miller* retroactive, I heard from Smitty again. I expected him to be overwhelmingly pleased with the *Montgomery* ruling, as this would propel his case forward. But he wasn't happy, and he enclosed these lines excerpted from his attorney's letter:

> As I told you on our January 20, 2016, meeting, there is a strong possibility the relief in your case will be life with parole. The appellate court could find the statute that forbids parole for those serving multiple life sentences unconstitutional as applied to you. As I told you, we will try to get you a new sentencing hearing, but please don't be hopeful.

So, despite victory, it looked like Smitty would not be resentenced. Instead, his case would flip from LWOP to Life, and a parole hearing would be set. He knew denial of parole was the norm, without regard for his 39-year spotless record. Common sense told me the proper remedy had to be a new sentencing hearing, to fully comply with the precepts outlined in *Miller*, but what did I know? His attorneys had a different idea. I hoped his attorneys were wrong, and that a better outcome would occur, but I could see Smitty's optimism had been shredded. Even when you win, you lose.

The Seventh Circuit did not grant Donald Ware a certificate of appealability, concurring with the denial of the COA by the district court judge. A rehearing on the COA was denied. I laboriously assembled a petition for certiorari to the U.S. Supreme Court, and it came back *cert denied*. That nailed Donnie's coffin shut.

We sat on a picnic table in the rec yard, as had become our custom since I moved to O-dorm, talking about the futility of fighting cases in court. A flawless blue sky was painted above us as August flowed into September.

"How do you know," Donnie asked, "that the courts are screwing everybody on their criminal cases, and it's not just you misunderstanding the law?" He wasn't being accusatory, just posing a fair question, one I had often asked myself. Could all of us law library clerks and jailhouse lawyers be under the delusion that we understood the law, when really, we didn't?

"I know it's the courts being unfair for a couple reasons," I explained to Donnie. "For one, even when I use the same arguments that won for attorneys, reprint them word for word, and have the same (or better) facts, we get denied. Two, I've had my work reviewed by attorneys who specialize in appeals, and been told my work is as good as theirs. But three," I stressed, "the way I know for sure the court is unfair is that I consistently win civil cases and consistently lose criminal cases."

My won-loss record spoke volumes. On civil litigation, where the standards of review and the issues were just as complicated as in criminal cases, I had "won" ten of eleven cases. A win, I asserted, was any positive outcome. In criminal cases, out of nearly 150 where I had filed something in court, I had won seven. And none of the seven were significant victories, just small measures of relief.

"I win 91% of civil cases, and 5% of criminal cases. Realistically, I felt I should have won about 30% of the criminal cases, if the courts had followed the law."

"But the law is whatever they decide it should be," Donnie concluded. "They don't have to follow any precedents. They just do what they want."

Yeah, that's pretty much it.

We talked for an hour, and I told Donnie about my imminent departure from Pendleton. Some things had worked out for me in court. He was glad to see me go, but it didn't do anything for him, left behind to do laundry for the next 25 years.

Donnie had received a visit over the weekend, and showed me a picture of Adela, now age 13. "She's growing up fast," he said, remembering the last time he saw her at home, when she was three. "She's becoming independent." He told me Adela had figured out how to use Teresa's credit card, and she had downloaded over $500 worth of music. "Teresa told her that was both her birthday and Christmas put together this year." We laughed, but the poor girl was flirting with trouble more and more. Incidents in the trailer park that would have sent a dad after some malevolent boys, if dad had been in the house. Declining grades. Emotions rising to the surface. She needed her father at home.

There are over four million kids in America in precisely Adela's position, with a parent cast away in prison or jail. If mass incarceration has cost American adults an unnecessary 50,000,000 years in prison, it has cost America's children an unnecessary 90,000,000 years without a parent at home. So, who's being hurt the most?

"Adela's got the phones and the Internet figured out," Donnie related, "and now she's way ahead of me on all that." Technology was leaving Donnie behind. "Like, a 'hashtag'. I've heard about hashtags, but what's a hashtag for?"

I had grown just as computer-ignorant in the past decade. In the age of online distance learning, one would think the first places to get wired in to distance education would be prisoners, but that has not been the case.

"Beats me what a hashtag is for," I said. "All I know is, it used to be called a pound sign, or a number sign, or a tic-tac-toe sign. Now they call it a hashtag, and they put words next to it, and it has something to do with Twitter."

"That's something else I don't understand," said Donnie. "Why would anyone care what another person is thinking or doing 24 hours a day? They gotta twitter about stuff all day long, like I should care."

We were in a backwater far off the information superhighway, disconnected from the social network, disengaged from the world, alone on our island. Our existence in prison was made less real for society because we weren't active players in the world's daily discourse.

At one time, the salient phrase was, *cogito, ergo sum* – I think, therefore I exist. Now it's *scribo, ergo sum* – I write, therefore I exist. And the writing has to be posted on the world wide web.

Arturo Gallardo dribbled past us with a soccer ball, headed inside, signaling that rec would soon be over. I told Donnie about some of the cases I had worked on that I still thought would win. Big C had summary judgment pending on his skin rash civil suit, which would probably win, because my brief was a thing of beauty. (He did win, a month later. A Shelbyville attorney then glommed onto the case, to pick up easy attorney fees from Durham's eventual settlement.) Smitty had some relief coming, we didn't know yet exactly what. It was still possible he could walk out the front door. Luetke had a shot, but I felt he had the worst kind of representation – a low-dollar attorney was worse than a public defender. The effectiveness hierarchy was: high-dollar attorney, then public defender, then lowball attorney – although it was impossible to get prisoners to believe this.

Louis Amalfitano, with his 46 years, had all kinds of good issues, but he was at another prison, and I saw his release date had not moved in four years, so apparently he had not made any progress. Dave Fields was working his way through the PLUS program. Christopher Turner lost his PC and his appeal, with the courts ignoring some pretty unambiguous evidence. Michael Daniels, mentally tortured for nearly 40 years, had moved on to New Castle.

"It seems like every case you've worked on," Donnie noted, "has been a guilty person! You didn't get any cases where the guy was stone cold innocent. Just guilty people." Not a classic protagonist in the bunch.

I thought about that, and about all the people I had tried to help in court over the years. I thought back to Solzhenitsyn's criticisms of Stalin's criminal justice system, and how similar their system really was to what was going on around me. Political motives, clearly. A warped style of due process. Ethnic groups targeted. Private economic incentives behind the incarceration craze. Exploitation of the poor. Authoritarianism run amok, no checks and balances. We had it all. We had the totalitarian system, just more cleverly disguised. We had it all, but more of it.

Except there was one major difference. The people in the USSR became politically conscious, and the gulags began to be dismantled shortly after Stalin died in March of 1953. By contrast, there is no dictator in the United States whose demise will spark an end to America's mass incarceration system. Here, an entire political machine needs to be overhauled, and the political consciousness of the masses has yet to be awakened.

I had a response for Donnie.

"Donnie, man . . ." I said, "I didn't just work on guilty people's cases. I don't know quite how to explain this, but in my eyes, they were *all* innocent."

He peered at me sideways.

"They *all* got too much time. They should not have been here. Your case and mine, and all the cases I worked on, are just a few of the 1.8 million in this country who should not be locked up. They're not all wonderful people, but it was wrong to give them more time than they deserved."

The gym doors opened, and a throng rushed out, vying to be first to the dorm showers. Donnie and I brought up the rear of the column, enjoying our last stroll from the yard. I had failed him, and now there was nothing I, or anybody, could do about it. We exchanged a few parting words, and when he disappeared up the stairs of O-dorm, I knew I would probably never see him again.

I packed up that night, and left the next morning.

+ + +

January 21, 2017. Grand Canyon National Park. I turned 55 today. My risky, care-free, rock-climbing days are long gone, replaced by the less demanding challenge of hiking a long, winding path to the bottom of the canyon, then hiking back out. Cool, clean air. Pristine cerulean blue sky. Noiseless, if I keep my Timberlands still and hold my breath. Reddish-brown sandstone, scraggly brush, and a smooth strand of river far below. It took fifty million years for the river to carve this canyon, and I'll reach the bottom by noon and climb back to the rim by sundown.

I like being alone. I have almost nothing with me, no possessions, and I recall an old saying: *He who would travel happily must travel light.* On the trail headed down, I begin to forget that a world beyond this canyon exists. The world becomes just me, and rocks. I am an island of humanity far from the shores of the human continent. At my greatest distance from the buzz of the civilized world, I reach the edge of the ancient river, and drink.

Such freedom. I stay awhile, lay back, close my eyes, and sense a timeless unconsciousness, like a deep sleep. This is the perfect prescription to alleviate my case of Nature Deficit Disorder. My mind clears, then the world invades my consciousness as I realize I will have to return to it. I open my eyes. Reluctantly, I begin to head back.

I think about yesterday's newsworthy events. A new President was sworn in, and the world braced for change. He has made noise about being "tough on crime," and seems to have an authoritarian streak. Perhaps someone can convince him that "smart on crime" works better. It's more humane, and it costs less. Perhaps the President's maverick personality will lead a popular shift in the attitude toward mass incarceration, and they can get Congress to act. If Congress can incentivize high incarceration rates, like they did in 1994, then surely they can incentivize lower incarceration rates. It's possible, but as I continue my ascent I am resigned to the knowledge that the people in power will be unlikely to reverse course. Only a populist mass movement can force change.

I am here enjoying my freedom because mine was one of the few post-conviction efforts that succeeded. The facts were forceful, and undeniable, and the errors too egregious to ignore. I did more time than I should have, but the truth was finally conceded, so here I am.

The return trip up-canyon turns out to be a greater challenge than I anticipated. It's a ten-mile trail, but vertically a half-mile rise. I can't scramble like I did thirty years ago. Lost time, lost youth. A walking stick gives me leverage. I plod on, my breathing labored, and I stop to rest and gaze around the canyon. I see sparkles, getting dizzy at times, and I think I see prisoners I know, scattered across the canyon walls, trying vainly to climb the steepest cliffs. I shake these visions, clear my head, and resume my effort.

Hours pass, and the sun gets low over the far rim. I reach a strata about thirty feet below the Navajo flatland, where a narrow path winds along the base of this final tier of rock. The rock isn't reddish-brown any more – it's gray. And smooth. Unnaturally smooth. I look up: no handholds, no cracks in the wall. Odd. I traverse the footpath, looking for a break somewhere, or an avalanche of boulders I can pick through, but none appears.

Twilight dims the scene, and in my haste I begin to trot. The sky darkens, and I drop the walking stick and speed up my pace. I don't want to be stranded out here at night, and in my panic to negotiate the last thirty feet of cliff I break into a sweat.

I keep looking up, and finally I see an occlusion in the smooth-rimmed crest – a tangled overhang. It looks alarmingly like . . . concertina wire. Well, that's confusing. A uniformed man (park service?) leans out and tells me to step away from the wall.

I stop. I gather a 360 view, and a cold reality comes over me.

There's no canyon below me, no river, no trail, no setting sun. There's no sky. The air is still, and stale, and claustrophobic. There's no way up, or down, or out. I'm on my back, and I see concrete above me. Voices echo around the cellblock, and the tenor tells me it's early morning, another day dawning at Michigan City.

I roll to my side, wrap the blanket tightly around my head, close my eyes, and wish for the dream to return.

+ + +

"Why do these chains bind me and prevent me from rescuing those who are drowning?"
– Antoine de St. Exupéry, *Wind, Sand, and Stars* (1939).

AFTERWORD

"If we hope to return to the rate of incarceration of the 1970's – a time when many civil rights advocates believed rates of imprisonment were egregiously high – we would have to release approximately four out of five people currently behind bars today." – Michelle Alexander, *The New Jim Crow*, p. 230.

"Experience teaches," said Gletkin, *"that the masses must be given, for all difficult and complicated processes, a simple, easily grasped explanation."* – Arthur Koestler, *Darkness at Noon* (1941).

Ten Things to Learn from *Fifty Million Years in Prison*

1. The USA has the world's highest incarceration rate, despite a merely average crime rate.

America's incarceration rate is more than five times higher than the world average of 127 prisoners per 100,000 population. If one argues that high incarceration rates keep crime rates down, it implies that Americans are uniquely far more criminally prone than all other nationalities.

2. High incarceration rates are a political choice, unrelated to a nation's crime rate.

Political motivation is exposed by comparing demographically similar jurisdictions: comparing nations within their cultural regions, comparing states in the USA, and comparing counties within a state. High incarceration is found to not correlate with crime, but with authoritarian political ideology.

3. Within the USA, poverty (not crime) most strongly correlates to high incarceration rates.

State and county data taken in multiple states over the last 30 years consistently prove that poverty is the strongest predictor of high incarceration rates. This is not because poverty causes crime but because those in poverty are the ones most unable to defend themselves and obtain the best outcomes from the criminal justice system. If the poverty-incarceration correlation was a product of the crime emanating from poverty, then crime would correlate more strongly to incarceration than does poverty. It doesn't. Crime's correlation to incarceration rates is weak.

4. Minorities are grossly over-represented in America's prisons.

Blacks are incarcerated at a rate more than 6 times higher than whites; Hispanics at a rate almost 3 times higher. This is not because of intrinsic defects within these people, but because they are much more likely to live in poverty, have single-parent households, and reside in dense urban areas where criminal activity more easily congregates, and where authoritarian law enforcement efforts can focus.

5. Institutional racism causes minorities to live in criminogenic environments.

Active racism exercised by those in control of resources limit opportunities to minorities, through unequal access to education, employment, and housing. American public schools are primarily funded by local governments, from taxes on property values – dooming children in impoverished areas to suffer from inadequate schooling. Lesser educational achievement hampers the ability to secure well-paying jobs, as does discriminatory hiring practices. Due to globalism, many industrial jobs have fled from areas where minorities once held jobs.

6. High incarceration rates in the USA are proximately caused by excessive sentences.

The USA has a normal level of crime, but a five times higher incarceration rate because sentences are, on average, excessive by a factor of five. There is no proportionality clause in the U.S. Constitution. Sentences escalate because legislators, prosecutors and judges engage in "tough on crime" authoritarian practices, out of political and ideological motivations.

7. Authoritarian power is unchecked in the USA because the structure of American government has been fashioned to under-represent minorities and the poor.

The USA, unlike other Western democracies, does not have proportional representation of minority groups in the legislature, as occurs in other countries through parliaments. The American system is designed for a "tyranny of the ruling class." Only a two-party system can survive under the current elective format; i.e. – a third party cannot gain 20% of the seats in the legislature by securing 20% of the popular vote, so no third party can arise. The USA's two parties are centrist and rightist, fueling authoritarianism in the criminal justice system. Authoritarians cause further suppression of minority voices through gerrymandering elective districts and engaging in voter-suppression tactics.

8. The War on Drugs is responsible for half of the USA's over-incarceration.

Nationwide, 21% of America's prisoners are in for drug offenses, and 30% of all non-sex crimes are drug-related. Together, 40% of America's prisoners are in for drugs or drug-related offenses, which is half of the 80% we need to release to reverse over-incarceration. Legalization of *all* drugs would depress the prices of street drugs, take away the profit incentive, and make the drug trade not worth engaging in or fighting over. Other countries, such as Portugal, have legalized all drugs and seen crime drastically reduced. The ambition is to treat drug abuse as a health problem, not as a crime – much the same way we ended Prohibition and now tolerate alcohol abuse.

9. Reducing crime will not reduce high incarceration rates.

Any approach to relieving mass incarceration that focuses on reducing crime is doomed to fail. Reductions in the crime rate over the last 20 years have not resulted in lower incarceration rates. Once prisons are built, the authoritarian class fills them. If one wishes to reduce crime, reducing poverty would be effective, and reducing poverty requires equal access to quality education, jobs, and housing.

10. Reversing mass incarceration requires a broad, federal approach.

A state-by-state, piecemeal approach will not work because most states are politically averse to change, due to the structural factors listed above. States require incentives, which can be provided by the federal government. Congress is the only political entity with the power to incentivize states to reduce prison populations. The Mass Incarceration Reduction Act, outlined below, is proposed as a solution to end over-incarceration in 8 to 12 years.

Mass Incarceration Reduction Act

Proposed: Title 42, United States Code, Chapter 160, "Mass Incarceration Reduction Act," §18501-18509

§18501 Purpose
This act addresses the national problem of high incarceration rates, which are disproportionate to crime rates, and abnormally high as compared to incarceration rates in the world. This act provides incentives for states to reduce prison and jail populations, while also providing funds for rehabilitative services, enhancing public safety, and saving taxpayers money.

§18502 Incentive Model
(a) The federal government will provide an annual budget for states to use for prisoner rehabilitative services, equal to 10% of the state's current corrections budget; provided the state continues to reduce its prisoner population and corrections budget by 8% annually, until the state reduces its incarceration rate to below 200 prisoners per 100,000 residents.

(b) Upon achieving the targeted incarceration rate, a state will receive an annual budget for prisoner rehabilitative services equal to a fixed amount of $5,000 per prisoner per year, in perpetuity, adjustable for inflation.

§18503 Prisoner Population Reduction Mechanisms
States are free to adopt any approach that helps them achieve annual prisoner reduction goals. Suggested strategies include:
(a) Legislative action:
    (1) Reduce sentencing ranges.
    (2) Establish parole boards.
    (3) Award prisoners earned credit time for educational and rehabilitative achievements.
    (4) Decriminalize drug offenses.
    (5) Cap a sentence at two times any plea agreement offer.
    (6) Set prisoner quotas for county jurisdictions. Quotas should be commensurate with local crime rates, and a head tax should be assessed for counties exceeding the prisoner quota.

Afterword - MIRA 294

(b) Executive action – Governors:
   (1) Use commutation power in conjunction with federally-designed Prisoner Release Advisory Board.
   (2) Retroactive sentence review. Establish office to revise current prisoners' sentences downward when new sentencing ranges have been revised by the legislature.
   (3) Retroactive sentence advocacy. Establish a free advocacy office as the only agency allowed to present prisoners' claims to the Governor, to ensure equal access to the process for all prisoners.

(c) Federal assistance.
   (1) Create a Prisoner Release Advisory Board to employ analytical tools to help states determine which prisoners are the best candidates for release.
   (2) Score prisoners for: risk to re-offend, potential harm of re-offense, and length of time served on current offense.

§18504 Rehabilitative services

Every prisoner shall have an equal opportunity to participate in rehabilitative services, as his or her needs require.

(a) Education. Education shall be provided in coordination with local colleges and vocational schools; G.E.D. and literacy training shall be mandatory for prisoners who need them.

(b) Behavioral. Psychological services and training in social skills and behavior-changing programs shall be available.

(c) Pell Grant. Prisoners and former prisoners shall be eligible for all federal educational grants for colleges, universities, and vocational schools.

§18505 Prison administration

To achieve prisoner reduction goals and enhance rehabilitative services, the following should be employed:

(a) Reclassify prisoners. House prisoners in facilities where appropriate services are offered – i.e., separate facilities for prisoners enrolled in vocations, G.E.D., college, psychological therapy, sex offender treatment, drug treatment, et cetera.

(b) Close prisons. To reduce corrections budgets by 8% per year, facilities

must be closed, and assets sold.
(c) Open community re-integration facilities. Require prisoners to transition into communities, obtaining employment and residence prior to release.

§18506 Community transformation incentives
To increase economic opportunities in poverty-stricken, criminogenic environments, communities shall be transformed with these incentives:
(a) Tax incentives. A corporate tax rate of 5% for businesses that relocate to economically depressed areas, provided they employ local residents to work 50% of the business's labor hours. This 5% will be transferred in its entirety to fund the local school district.
(b) An economically depressed area is defined as a zip code area where the population's poverty rate (excluding full-time college students) exceeds 30%.
(c) Public works employment. Provide part-time minimum wage jobs on public works projects for prisoners and ex-prisoners who have not yet secured private-sector jobs.

§18507 Prisoner accounting
A state's prisoner count includes all prisoners in the state corrections department, and all prisoners in local jails and correctional facilities, excluding juvenile facilities.

§18508 Appropriations
The state is eligible to receive a grant equal to 10% of the state corrections budget immediately upon acceptance of this Act. The 8% reduction goals must be met annually on the date the initial grant was received.

§18509 Effect on Other Legislation
Prior legislative acts in contravention of this Act are superseded. See 42 U.S.C. Chapter 137, §13701-13712; et. al. (VCCLEA).

Example of how MIRA would work:

Indiana (1/1/2016 figures)

27,350 state prisoners in IDOC\
14,500 county prisoners
41,850 total prisoners
6,540,000 state population
Incarceration rate = 640 per 100,000 population
$720,000,000 annual IDOC budget

= $72 million Federal grant (et at 10% of $720 million IDOC budget)

	Year	Prisoners County	State	Total	IDOC Budget	Fed Grant	INC Rate
1	2019	14500	27350	41850	720.0	72	640
2	2020	13340	25162	38502	6625.4	72	589
3	2021	12180	22974	35154	604.8	72	538
4	2022	11020	20786	31806	547.2	72	486
5	2023	9860	18598	28458	489.6	72	435
6	2024	8700	16410	25110	432.0	72	384
7	2025	7540	14222	21762	374.4	72	333
8	2026	6380	12034	18414	316.8	72	282
9	2027	5220	9846	15066	259.2	72	230
10	2028	4528	8546	13074	225.0	72	200
11	2029	4528	8546	13074	225.0	65.37	200
12	2030	4528	8546	13074	225.0	65.37	200

Taxpayers pay into the federal grant, but save much more when the prisoner population and IDOC budget are reduced.

The annual savings to Indiana taxpayers after 12 years, as compared to 2016, is $677,000,000 per year.

12-Year Savings to Indiana Taxpayers =

IDOC: $720m/yr x 12 – $5,081.4m = $3,558,600,000

Counties: estimated at half of IDOC costs = $1,779,300,000

Federal grants, from taxes: $72m (x10) + $65.37m (x2) = -$850,740,000

TOTAL SAVINGS is $4,487,160,000.

Savings to USA Taxpayers =

This savings to taxpayers can be multiplied by 50 to get a rough estimate of the savings to all taxpayers in the United States. In the first 12 years, USA taxpayers would save around $225 billion, and $34 billion per year thereafter.

These figures do not include court costs, policing costs, the savings accrued through lower crime rates, or the increase to the economy by converting prisoners to productive citizens.

Appendix 1

Excessive Incarceration in the United States, 1980-2017
Source: U.S. Department of Justice. U.S. Census Bureau

Commentary:

Appendix 1 shows the amount of excessive incarceration in the United States since 1980, with "excessive" defined as above 125 prisoners per 100,000 population. The USA incarceration rate should be lower than the world average (127.2), due to a lower-than-average percentage of juveniles in the general population. A rate of 125 per 100,000 is a reasonable goal. The Mass Incarceration Reduction Act (MIRA) aims to reduce the USA incarceration rate to 200 per 100,000 population within 10 years. A subsequent effort to reduce the rate to 125 would most be effectively accomplished by focusing on alleviating the poverty rate, which is the strongest predictor of a high incarceration rate.

Data Sources:

1 – Bureau of Justice Statistics, usdoj.gov, "Estimated number of persons supervised by adult correctional systems, by correctional status, 1980-2014." Accessed 1-12-2016.

2 – U.S. Census Bureau, "U.S. Population by Year." Accessed 7-1-2016.

3 – Adult prisoner populations in 2015, 2016 and 2017 are author's estimates.

4 – 2012 U.S. population age 18 and over was 76.5%. See: *2014 World Almanac*, p.618; U.S. Census Bureau, "U.S. Population by Age, Sex, and Household, 2012."

Appendix 1

Excessive Incarceration in the United States, 1980-2017

Year	Prisoners	USA Population	per 100K
1980	503,600	227,220,000	222
1981	556,800	229,470,000	243
1982	612,500	231,660,000	264
1983	647,400	233,790,000	277
1984	682,800	235,820,000	290
1985	744,200	237,920,000	313
1986	815,000	240,130,000	339
1987	858,700	242,290,000	354
1988	950,400	244,500,000	389
1989	1,078,900	246,820,000	437
1990	1,148,700	249,620,000	460
1991	1,219,000	252,980,000	482
1992	1,295,200	256,510,000	505
1993	1,369,200	259,920,000	527
1994	1,476,600	263,130,000	561
1995	1,585,600	266,280,000	595
1996	1,646,300	269,390,000	611
1997	1,743,600	272,650,000	640
1998	1,815,200	275,850,000	658
1999	1,910,400	279,040,000	685
2000	1,945,400	282,160,000	689
2001	1,962,800	284,970,000	689
2002	2,033,100	287,630,000	707
2003	2,086,500	290,110,000	719
2004	2,136,600	292,810,000	730
2005	2,200,400	295,520,000	745
2006	2,256,600	298,380,000	756
2007	2,296,400	301,230,000	762
2008	2,310,300	304,090,000	760
2009	2,297,700	306,770,000	749
2010	2,279,100	308,110,000	740
2011	2,252,500	310,500,000	725
2012	2,231,300	312,860,000	713
2013	2,222,500	315,180,000	705
2014	2,224,400	317,680,000	700
2015	2,224,000*	320,220,000	695
2016	2,224,000*	322,480,000*	690
2017	2,224,000*	325,000,000*	684
total	**62,067,700**	**10,490,690,000**	

Appendix 1

Excessive Incarceration in the United States, 1980-2017

Year	Prisoners if 125/100K	Excess Prisoners
1980	284,025	219,575
1981	286,838	269,963
1982	289,575	322,925
1983	292,238	355,163
1984	294,775	388,025
1985	297,400	446,800
1986	300,163	514,838
1987	302,863	555,838
1988	305,625	644,775
1989	308,525	770,375
1990	312,025	836,675
1991	316,225	902,775
1992	320,638	974,563
1993	324,900	1,044,300
1994	328,913	1,147,688
1995	332,850	1,252,750
1996	336,738	1,309,563
1997	340,813	1,402,788
1998	344,813	1,470,388
1999	348,800	1,561,600
2000	352,700	1,592,700
2001	356,213	1,606,588
2002	359,538	1,673,563
2003	362,638	1,723,863
2004	366,013	1,770,588
2005	369,400	1,831,000
2006	372,975	1,883,625
2007	376,538	1,919,863
2008	380,113	1,930,188
2009	383,463	1,914,238
2010	385,138	1,893,963
2011	388,125	1,864,375
2012	391,075	1,840,225
2013	393,975	1,828,525
2014	397,100	1,827,300
2015	400,275	1,823,725
2016	403,100	1,820,900
2017	406,250	1,817,750
total	13,113,363	48,954,338

Appendix 2

International Comparisons, Crime and Incarceration

Commentary:
Breaking the world's countries into regions with similar demographics, cultures, and histories allows the reader to identify how political differences determine incarceration rates. The world's correlation between incarceration rates and crime rates is .054, a negligible factor. Authoritarian governments most strongly correlate to incarceration rates. That the United States' incarceration rate is higher than all of the world's most authoritarian governments makes it clear that political motivations, not crime, drive the USA's high incarceration rate.

Data Sources:

INC – Incarceration Rate, prisoners per 100,000 population.
International Centre for Prison Studies, Oct. 3, 2012.
www.prisonstudies.org/world-prison-brief. Accessed 8-24-2014.

CR – Crime Rate, on a 0 to 100 scale, low to high crime.
www.numbeo.com/crime/rankings_by_country.jsp.
"Crime Index by Country, 2014 Mid-Year." Accessed 8-24-2014.

Appendix 2
International Comparisons, Crime and Incarceration

INCARCERATION RATES BY REGION, 2012
(Prisoners per 100,000 population)

REGION	Ave	Highest	Rate
Central America	288	Cuba	510
Former USSR	243	Russia	470
East Asia	226	North Korea	600 +/-
South America	215	Uruguay	289
Islamic	137	Iran	284
Eastern Europe	136	Slovakia	188
Southeast Asia	118	Thailand	435
SubSaharan Africa	95	Rwanda	492
Western Europe	95	England	148
WORLD (w/o USA)	127	USA	707

Appendix 2

International Comparisons, Crime and Incarceration

Central America	INC	CR		Former USSR	INC	CR
Cuba	510			Russia	470	52
Belize	495	57		Belarus	335	29
El Salvador	424	64		Lithuania	322	35
Bahamas	383	68		Kazakhstan	290	46
Panama	379	43		Ukraine	271	50
Trinidad	362	77		Latvia	264	40
Puerto Rico	335	67		Estonia	228	29
Costa Rica	314	61		Turkmenistan	224	
Dom. Rep.	247	66		Georgia	219	19
Mexico	211	53		Azerbaijan	210	38
Honduras	160	70		Moldova	187	49
Nicaragua	153	43		Kyrgyzstan	182	58
Jamaica	152	69		Uzbekistan	160	64
Guatemala	105	78		Armenia	160	34
Haiti	95	60		Tajikistan	121	

East Asia	INC	CR		Others	INC	CR
North Korea	600*			USA	707	50
Mongolia	274	70		Amer. Samoa	349	
Taiwan	273	21		Israel	249	31
China	172	27		New Zealand	183	42
Philippines	113	42		Fiji	172	49
South Korea	98	20		Australia	133	42
Japan	51	15		Canada	115	37

Eastern Europe	INC	CR
Slovakia	188	34
Hungary	184	40
Albania	181	56
Montenegro	171	19
Czech Rep.	163	34
Romania	163	29
Macedonia	147	37
Serbia	142	42
Bulgaria	138	41
Poland	120	34
Greece	120	41
Croatia	108	29
Cyprus	108	34
Kosovo	93	
Bosnia	80	46
Slovenia	66	31

Southeast Asia	INC	CR
Thailand	435	37
Singapore	233	19
Bhutan	145	
Vietnam	143	50
Malaysia	133	69
Brunei	125	30
Myanmar	113	50
Sri Lanka	105	
Cambodia	100	41
Laos	71	36
Indonesia	62	48
Papua N. G.	52	81
Nepal	51	51
Bangladesh	45	62
East Timor	38	
India	30	45

Western Europe	INC	CR
England	148	41
Spain	144	34
Portugal	138	35
Luxembourg	131	34
Belgium	108	44
France	103	48
Italy	100	47
Austria	98	28
Ireland	89	52
Switzerland	87	28
Netherlands	82	36
Germany	78	29
Denmark	73	27
Norway	72	33
Sweden	60	42
Finland	58	29
Iceland	47	26

South America	INC	CR
Uruguay	289	44
Fr. Guiana	287	
Brazil	274	70
Guyana	260	77
Chile	250	45
Colombia	244	57
Peru	221	57
Suriname	194	
Venezuela	174	83
Ecuador	173	58
Argentina	149	60
Bolivia	140	68
Paraguay	136	54

Appendices

Islamic	INC	CR
Iran	284	51
Bahrain	275	44
U.A.E.	238	21
Tunisia	230	46
Morocco	221	57
Turkey	198	42
Algeria	162	54
Saudi Arabia	162	54
Iraq	139	49
Lebanon	108	45
Jordan	95	47
Kuwait	86	42
Afghanistan	83	77
Egypt	76	55
Syria	60	56
Yemen	53	70
Qatar	53	23
Pakistan	41	61
Oman	36	40
Libya	64	

SubSaharan Africa	INC	CR
Rwanda	492	19
South Africa	294	79
Gabon	210	
Botswana	204	50
Namibia	182	51
Zimbabwe	147	64
Eq. Guinea	132	
Kenya	121	79
Zambia	119	

SubSaharan Africa	INC	CR
Cameroon	115	
Ethiopia	111	41
Lesotho	107	
Angola	105	61
Uganda	102	66
Burundi	85	
Madagascar	83	
Benin	77	
Malawi	76	
Tanzania	73	66
Togo	67	
South Sudan	65	85
Senegal	64	
Djibouti	63	
Mozambique	62	
Ghana	55	47
Sierra Leone	54	
Gambia	53	
Sudan	50	40
Ivory Coast	44	
Liberia	43	
Mauritania	43	
Niger	40	
Mali	39	
Chad	35	
D.R. Congo	33	
Congo	33	
Nigeria	32	78
Burkina Faso	32	
Guinea	22	
C. Afr. Rep.	19	
Somalia		67

Appendix 3

State Comparisons, Rank in Each Category
As Compared to the Incarceration Rate

Commentary:

In the United States, the strongest correlation to a state's incarceration rate is the poverty rate, not the crime rate. One may initially theorize that a high poverty rate would cause a high crime rate, and result in a high incarceration rate, but if that reasoning held, crime rates would more strongly correlate to incarceration rates than would poverty rates. What the numbers suggest is a criminal justice system that victimizes poor defendants while allowing the wealthy to avoid incarceration. It also suggests that anti-poverty initiatives would be the most effective way to combat both crime and high incarceration rates. Education would be a key component in that fight, as the correlation between dropout rates and poverty is .696. Education has also been shown to have the most dramatic effect on recidivism.

Data Sources:

INC – Incarceration Rate, calculated from 2010 U.S. Census and the Bureau of Justice Statistics, *Prisoners in 2011.*

VC – Violent Crime Rate, from U.S. Department of Justice and FBI, *Crime in the United States, 2011.*

DO – Dropout Rate, from National Center for Educational Statistics, U.S. Department of Education, *U.S. High School Graduation Rates by State, 2009-2010.*

POV – Poverty Rates, from U.S. Census Bureau, U.S. Department of Commerce, *Poverty Rates by State*; Author combined the data from 2000, 2005, and 2010.

B – Percentage of Black population, from U.S. Census Bureau, U.S. Department of Commerce, *U.S. Race and Minority Group Percentages by State, 2010.*

MIN – Percentage of Minorities, from U.S. Census Bureau, U.S. Department of Commerce, *U.S. Race and Minority Group Percentages by State, 2010.*

C – Voting for Republican for President in 2012. From Federal Election Commission, *Presidential Election Results by State, 1960-2012.*

State	INC	POV	DO	B	C	VC	MIN
LA	1	2	5	6	8	6	8
MS	2	1	2	1	14	33	4
OK	3	7	24	25	2	10	20
AL	4	5	8	5	6	15	15
TX	5	4	26	18	15	17	2
AZ	6	8	9	34	17	18	21
GA	7	10	6	2	20	20	10
AR	8	9	10	11	7	9	5
FL	9	18	7	12	25	7	23
AK	10	37	13	37	5	29	6
WV	11	6	23	36	12	26	47
DE	12	40	14	8	44	5	17
MO	13	28	39	19	22	11	31
KY	14	12	28	24	9	41	41
SC	15	15	4	4	16	2	11
ID	16	25	41	49	4	45	38
VA	17	44	31	9	27	46	18
NV	18	27	1	23	33	4	9
IN	19	21	21	22	24	24	33
OH	20	19	32	17	26	28	32
TN	21	11	30	10	10	1	24
MI	22	20	15	15	37	12	25
SD	23	26	33	42	19	36	39
CO	24	32	27	33	28	25	19

INC – Incarceration Rate
POV – Poverty Rate
B – Percentage of Black Population
C – Voting Republican for President in 2012
VC- Violent Crime Rate
MIN – Percentage Minorities, Non-White
POP – Population

State	INC	POV	DO	B	C	VC	MIN
NC	25	14	19	7	23	23	13
PA	26	34	42	20	32	21	28
WI	27	41	49	26	34	42	37
HI	28	17	22	28	43	16	3
MD	29	45	36	3	45	8	7
WY	30	35	29	48	1	44	40
IL	31	24	35	14	46	13	16
CA	32	22	17	40	38	38	35
CT	33	47	11	21	41	32	22
MT	34	16	34	50	21	34	44
NM	35	3	3	39	35	3	1
KS	36	30	43	29	11	22	27
OR	37	38	12	41	50	31	43
IA	38	39	46	38	29	35	46
NY	39	13	16	13	47	19	12
NJ	40	48	45	16	36	27	14
WA	41	33	20	35	39	30	29
NE	42	43	40	32	13	37	36
UT	43	46	25	46	3	47	34
VT	44	42	50	47	49	49	50
RI	45	23	18	31	48	39	26
ND	46	31	48	43	18	40	45
NH	47	50	44	45	30	48	48
MN	48	49	47	30	31	43	42
MA	49	36	37	27	42	14	30
ME	50	29	38	44	40	50	49
Corr.	1.000	0.634	0.553	0.539	0.531	0.494	0.489

Corr. – Correlation to Incarceration Rate (0 is least, 1.000 is highest)

Appendix 4

Indiana County Comparisons

Commentary:

In the author's opinion, nothing more clearly reveals the cause of mass incarceration than the comparison of county incarceration rates. Differences in county imprisonment rates reflect nothing but the ideologies of those in power in the local criminal justice system.

The wide range of county incarceration rates shows that sentencing ranges set by the state legislature do not effectively control a state's incarceration rate. Local law enforcement officials – judges and prosecutors – are still able to incarcerate people far out of proportion to the need to do so. Authoritarianism at the local level is unchecked by any authority. The most determinative factor for a defendant's sentence is the political mindset of local authorities.

Two forces need to be employed to check disparate county incarceration rates. One is to establish a county quota system, limiting the number of prisoners a county may incarcerate. Second is a release mechanism, through executive or legislative authority, to force the state's incarceration down to an acceptable level. Legislative amendments to sentencing ranges alone will not work because county prosecutors and county judges will still find ways to overcharge and oversentence defendants.

To compare county incarceration rates to world incarceration rates, multiply the county rate by 1.46 to roughly account for jail prisoners.

Note that some counties are over-reporting violent crime by including all violent crimes charged, rather than reporting the number of violent incidents that may result in multiple charges.

Appendix 4

Indiana County Comparisons

Data Sources:

Only the 50 largest counties in population have been used for this appendix. Indiana has 92 counties.

Data does not include county jail prisoners.

INC – Incarceration Rate, IDOC prisoners on 1-1-2016, www.in.gov/idoc "Offender Population Report."

POV – Poverty Rate, adjusted to exclude on-campus students. U.S. Department of Agriculture, 2014. Bureau of the Census, "Small Area Income and Poverty Estimates." Accessed 2-3-2016.

VC – Violent Crime Rate, U.S. Department of Health and Human Services, "County Health Rankings and Roadmaps." Accessed 3-16-2016.

B – Black population, U.S. Census Bureau, 7-1-2013.

MIN – Minority population, U.S. Census Bureau, 7-1-2013.

C – Voting Republican for President, 2012, from *2014 World Almanac*.

Appendix 4

Indiana County Comparisons

County	INC	POV	VC	MIN	POP	B	C
Huntington	1	37	32	45	43	43	4
Dearborn	2	31	41	49	29	39	5
Madison	3	11	14	12	13	7	41
Elkhart	4	18	10	4	6	13	28
Shelby	5	28	35	34	33	32	14
Wayne	6	4	7	25	25	16	36
Grant	7	2	24	14	24	9	32
Marion	8	1	1	2	1	1	49
Henry	9	14	47	38	28	24	34
Montgomery	10	26	23	32	39	33	8
Jackson	11	17	11	27	34	35	25
Clinton	12	24	18	8	50	42	21
Cass	13	19	36	7	38	28	33
Adams	14	15	45	35	45	50	6
Vanderburgh	15	5	4	13	7	6	39
Allen	16	16	13	5	3	4	35
Howard	17	10	12	16	18	10	37
Lawrence	18	25	20	48	32	44	16
Tippecanoe	19	22	8	10	8	17	42
Bartholomew	20	29	25	22	19	25	30
St.Joseph	21	8	5	3	5	3	45
Steuben	22	23	38	40	46	37	26
Vigo	23	13	17	18	17	11	43
Gibson	24	30	30	42	47	27	20
LaPorte	25	3	21	6	16	5	47

Appendix 4

Indiana County Comparisons

County	Pop.	INC/100K	VC/100K
Huntington	36,841	979.9	89
Dearborn	48,799	905.8	63
Madison	130,380	869.1	258
Elkhart	200,591	803.6	364
Shelby	44,502	779.7	77
Wayne	67,978	754.7	283
Grant	69,044	618.4	162
Marion	928,349	599.6	1124
Henry	49,066	519.7	47
Montgomery	38,130	519.3	168
Jackson	43,436	501.9	263
Clinton	32,958	488.5	210
Cass	38,542	482.6	74
Adams	34,685	461.3	53
Vanderburgh	181,524	451.7	386
Allen	363,596	441.1	258
Howard	82,961	440.0	259
Lawrence	45,873	431.6	183
Tippecanoe	180,925	410.7	274
Bartholomew	79,549	383.4	160
St.Joseph	266,850	378.5	370
Steuben	34,924	376.2	70
Vigo	108,356	362.7	223
Gibson	33,554	345.7	109
LaPorte	111,256	338.9	182

Appendix 4

Indiana County Comparisons

County	INC	POV	VC	MIN	POP	B	C
DeKalb	26	41	26	44	36	45	18
Noble	27	34	42	15	30	40	15
Delaware	28	12	6	20	14	12	44
Harrison	29	43	34	47	37	41	31
Marshall	30	35	31	17	31	38	22
Morgan	31	33	22	50	23	47	2
Whitley	32	44	40	46	49	48	7
Floyd	33	32	19	23	21	15	38
Boone	34	47	50	41	27	31	10
Johnson	35	40	16	33	11	29	9
Kosciusko	36	27	43	21	20	34	1
Monroe	37	21	9	29	12	22	48
Lake	38	6	3	1	2	2	50
Miami	39	9	28	26	44	18	19
Dubois	40	45	29	28	35	46	24
Putnam	41	20	44	31	42	19	17
Clark	42	38	2	11	15	8	40
Jasper	43	39	39	30	48	36	29
Hancock	44	48	46	39	22	26	3
Porter	45	42	27	9	9	21	46
Knox	46	7	33	36	41	23	23
Hendricks	47	49	37	19	10	14	12
LaGrange	48	36	49	37	40	49	11
Hamilton	49	50	48	24	4	20	13
Warrick	50	46	15	43	26	30	27

Appendix 4

Indiana County Comparisons

County	Pop.	INC/100K	VC/100K
DeKalb	42,302	338.0	135
Noble	47,511	334.7	62
Delaware	118,355	332.3	339
Harrison	39,082	330.1	86
Marshall	47,037	318.9	91
Morgan	69,446	308.2	182
Whitley	33,238	294.8	64
Floyd	76,059	289.2	185
Boone	60,519	266.0	28
Johnson	145,806	261.3	230
Kosciusko	77,997	248.7	61
Monroe	142,020	248.6	272
Lake	491,403	248.1	403
Miami	36,133	226.9	114
Dubois	42,318	217.4	113
Putnam	37,532	215.8	61
Clark	112,800	214.5	589
Jasper	33,381	209.7	66
Hancock	71,096	178.6	49
Porter	166,427	164.0	127
Knox	38,064	162.9	87
Hendricks	153,644	158.8	72
LaGrange	38,067	152.4	42
Hamilton	296,828	134.1	44
Warrick	61,001	104.9	254

Appendices

Bibliography

Adorno, T.W., and E. Frenkel-Brunswick, D. Levinson, R.N. Sanford. *The Authoritarian Personality* (1950)

Alexander, Michelle. *The New Jim Crow: Mass Incarceration in the Age of Colorblindness* (2010)

Amar, Akhil Reed. *America's Constitution: A Biography* (2005)

Applebaum, Anne. *Gulag: A History* (2004)

Austin, James F. *Unlocking America: Why and How to Reduce America's Prison Population*, JFA Inst. (2007)

Beckett, Katherine, and Theodore Sasson. *The Politics of Injustice: Crime and Punishment in America* (2004)

Bennion, Elizabeth. *Banning the Bing: Why Extreme Solitary Confinement is Cruel and All Too Usual Punishment,* Indiana Law Journal, Vol. 90, No.2, Spring 2015.

Bourgois, Phillippe. *In Search of Respect: Selling Crack in El Barrio* (1995)

Clear, Todd R. *Imprisoning Communities: How Mass Incarceration Makes Disadvantaged Communities Worse* (2007)

Conover, Ted. *Newjack: Guarding Sing Sing* (2000)

Cook, Philip J. and Jens Ludwig. *The Economist's Guide to Crimebusting,* Wilson Q., Winter 2011.

Davis, Angela. *Arbitrary Justice: The Power of the American Prosecutor* (2007)

Frankl, Viktor. *Man's Search for Meaning* (2006)

Gates, Henry Louis, Jr. *Class Matters* (2005)

Gilmore, Ruth Wilson. *Golden Gulag* (2007)

Gleick, James. *Chaos: Making a New Science* (1987)

Grace, Julian. *Death Penalty Cases Squeeze Prosecutor's Budget,* Indianapolis Star, Aug. 20, 2014

Grassian, Stuart. *Psychiatric Effects of Solitary Confinement,* 22 Wash. U.J.L. & Policy (2006)

Hacker, Andrew. *Two Nations: Black and White, Separate, Hostile, Unequal* (1995)

Hall, Kenneth L., Ed. *The Oxford Guide to the United States Supreme Court* (1999)
Halliday, Paul Delaney. *Habeas Corpus: From England to Empire* (2010)
Kearney, Melissa S., et.al. *Ten Economic Facts about Crime and Incarceration,* The Hamilton Project (2013)
Kilgore, James. *Understanding Mass Incarceration* (2015)
Koestler, Arthur. *Darkness at Noon* (1941)
Levitt, Steven D. and Stephen J. Dunbar. *Freakonomics* (2009)
London, Jack. *The Call of the Wild* (1903)
London, Jack. *White Fang* (1905)
Madison, James H. *Hoosiers: A New History of Indiana* (2014)
Massey, Douglas, and Nancy A. Denton. *American Apartheid: Segregation and the Making of the Underclass* (1993)
Mauer, Marc. *Race to Incarcerate* (1999)
Mauer, Marc, and Ryan King. *A 25 Year Quagmire: The War on Drugs and Its Impact on American Society* (2007)
Payne, Ruby. *A Framework for Understanding Poverty* (2005)
Petersilia, Joan. *When Prisoners Come Home: Parole and Prisoner Reentry* (2014)
Rawls, John. *Political Liberalism* (1993)
Roemer, John. *Theories of Distributive Justice* (1996)
Rothbard, Murray. *The Ethics of Liberty* (1998)
Samizdat Publishing LLC. *Prison is For Real* (2015)
Sampson, Robert, and John Laub. *Crime in the Making: Pathways and Turning Points Through Life* (1993)
Sampson, Robert and Charles Loeffler. *Punishment's Place: The Local Concentration of Mass Incarceration,* Daedalus, Summer 2010
Sandel, Michael J. *Liberalism and the Limits of Justice* (1998)
Sandel, Michael J. *Justice: What's the Right Thing to Do?* (2010)
Scalia, Antonin. *A Matter of Interpretation: Federal Courts and the Law* (1997)
Sen, Amartya. *Democracy as Freedom* (1999)
Solzhenitsym, Aleksandr. *One Day in the Life of Ivan Denisovich* (1961)

Thaler, Richard H. *Misbehaving: The Making of Behavioral Economics* (2015)

Turley, Jonathan. *Appetite for Authoritarianism Spawns an American Gulag.* L.A. Times. May 2, 2003. B-19.

Vollen, Lola and David Eggers. *Surviving Justice: America's Wrongfully Convicted and Exonerated* (2008)

West, Cornel. *Race Matters* (1991)

Western, Bruce and Becky Pettit. *Incarceration and Social Inequality,* Daedalus, Summer 2010.

Wilson, William Julius. *When Work Disappears: The World of the New Urban Poor* (1996)

Wilson, William Julius. *More than Just Race: Being Black and Poor in the Inner City* (1996)

Xue, Lao. *The Holy Book of Modern Taoism* (2013)

Zagrans, Maura Poston. *Camerado, I Give You My Hand: How a Powerful Lawyer-Turned-Priest Is Changing the Lives of Men Behind Bars* (2012)

Zoukis, Christopher. *Pell Grants for Prisoners: New Bill Restores Hope for Reinstating College Programs,* Prison Legal News, August 2015.

Bibliography

Endnotes

Prologue
It's a fine line – uttered by David St. Hubbins, in *This is Spinal Tap* (1983).

Chapter One
Stalin's gulags – held 2.1 million at their height. Applebaum reports that just over 1 million died in the gulags over twenty years, with most succumbing during famine years, when millions died throughout the USSR.
Dillinger – *Indiana State Prison History*, C.E.C. Library, Michigan City, IN. Accessed 10-2015.
Manhattan – 2010 population was 1,527,000; island is 22.6 square miles. G-cellhouse is 19,800 square feet. USA prisoner population, including jails, could fit into 7,822 cellhouses, occupying 5.56 square miles.
Timothy Knapp – killed May 29, 2011. "Silencing the Sound of Stabbing," PrisonWriters.com, Ty Evans, 7-13-2015.
Toby Payne – *Lucio v State*, 907 N.E.2d 1008 (Ind. 2009); *Delarosa v State*, 938 N.E.2d 690 (Ind. 2010).
law library expenses – FOIA request, PCF business office, 7-31-2013.
Donald Ware – *Ware v State*, 859 N.E.2d 708 (Ind. App. 2007).

Chapter Two
curvilinear – the curve is a surge function in calculus, $f(x) = axe^{-bx}$, for the math nerds out there.
chess ratings – calculated by comparing our records against Bradford Drake, USCF Expert, who left Pendleton and won the 2012 Indiana State Championship. The author also qualifies as Expert level.
summary judgment win – *Evans v. Poskon*, 603 F.3d 362 (7th Cir. 2010).
world incarceration rates – see Appendix 2.

Endnotes 322

focus on the innocent – U. Michigan Law School reported 149 exonerations in 2015, aired by MSNBC on 2-3-2016.

judges as former prosecutors – on-line profiles of Indiana judges show former prosecutors outnumber former public defenders by 3 to 1.

David Camm – *Camm v. State,* 812 N.E.2d 1127 (Ind. App. 2004); *Boney v. State,* 880 N.E.2d 279 (Ind. App. 2008); *Camm v. State,* 908 N.E.2d 215 (Ind. 2009). In the 2009 Opinion, on page 221: "The first ground requiring reversal is the state's repeated emphasis upon speculation that the defendant molested his daughter." The dissent by C.J. Shepard credited Camm's alleged "confessions" to three jailhouse informants. Footnote 4 referenced the published news article titled, *"The Jurors Speak: Molestation evidence led to guilty verdict."*

blue pencil doctrine – *Lee v. State,* 816 N.E.2d 35 (Ind. 2004).

Melvin Tunstill – *Tunstill v. State,* 568 N.E.2d 539 (Ind. 1991); *Tunstill v. State,* 743 N.E.2d 1136 (Ind. 2001).

Chapter 3

mistaken identification – 64% of wrongful convictions of the innocent involve erroneous witness identification, per *Surviving Justice,* p. 407.

Chapter 4

innocence defined – "50 Shades of Innocence," PrisonWriters.com, Ty Evans, 4-4-2015.

Nate – conversation actually took place at Michigan City, not at Pendleton.

Louis Amalfitano – *Luigi Amalfitano v State,* 956 N.E.2d 208 (Ind. App. 2011). At 212: "For over six months, Amalfitano kept sixty-five year old A.T. locked in a utility closet."

double jeopardy – principle dates to 1688 in England, per Blackstone.

1,000-to-1 proportionality – compare to *Russell v. State,* 11 N.E.2d 938 (Ind. App. 2014) and *Russell v. State,* 34 N.E.2d 1223 (Ind. 2015). Larry D. Russell Jr. locked three adopted teenagers in a room for three months, physically tortured them (Icy Hot on genitals and rectum, urine poured on heads, waterboarded, socks duct taped into their mouths, tied to beds, food deprived, bath-

room denied, 17-year-old weighed 82 pounds when he escaped), and ended up with a 10-do-5. He could afford private counsel.
Goddie – *Oldham v State*, 779 N.E.2d 1162 (Ind. App. 2002).
sudden heat – defined at *Wilson v State*, 697 N.E.2d 460, 474 (Ind. 1998).

Chapter 5

Arturo Gallardo – *Gallardo v. State,* 908 N.E.2d 369 (Ind. App. 2009) [Unpub.].
Operation Streamline – Kilgore, *Understanding Mass Incarceration*, p. 81-83.
Shewmaker – B.A. Indiana State, 1969; J.D. Notre Dame Law, 1975. Former deputy prosecutor, Republican. 24th circuit court judge, Elkhart, 1998-2016. One million years vow is unverified by author's research.
Bill Woodford – *Woodford v. State,* 752 N.E.2d 1278 (Ind. 2001).
Robert Storey – *Storey v. State,* 830 N.E.2d 180 (Ind. App. 2005); *Storey v. State*, 875 N.E.2d 243 (Ind. App. 2007).
Roger DeLucenay – *DeLucenay v. State,* 849 N.E.2d 1011 (Ind. App. 2007).
Hispanic prisoner increase – Kilgore, *Understanding Mass Incarceration,* p.83.
David Fields – *Fields v. State,* 825 N.E.2d 841 (Ind. App. 2005); *Green v. State,* 850 N.E.2d 977 (Ind. App. 2006); *Fields v. State,* 852 N.E.2d 1030 (Ind. App. 2006). PC became final 3-6-2014.
Republican voting – in 2012 election for President, per *2014 World Almanac*, p.522.
Pendleton release dates – FOIA request, Pendleton roster sheet, 6-22-2013.
William Moore – info from IDOC website, and *Indy Star* article [title and date misplaced by author].
Michael W. Daniels – *Daniels v State*, 452 N.E.2d 160 (Ind. 1983); *State v Daniels*, 680 N.E.2d 829 (Ind. 1997); *Daniels v Knight*, 476 F.3d 426 (7th Cir. 2007); see also, "How the State of Indiana Killed Michael Daniels," PrisonWriters.com, Ty Evans, 1-21-2016.
death penalty – info from Death Penalty Information Center.

trial costs – are $449,887 for death penalty cases, $42,658 for LWOP cases. Legislative Services Agency for Indiana General Assembly, January 2010.
150,000 to die in US prisons – Kali Holloway, *There is Talk of Prison Reform, but for the 150,000 People in Prison for Life, there is No Reform on the Horizon*, Alternet, 7-15-2016; reported in Prison Legal News, October 2016, p. 54. See also: www.TheOtherDeathPenalty.org.
David Wayne Smith – *Drollinger v. State*, 408 N.E.2d 1228 (Ind. 1980); *Smith v. State*, 420 N.E.2d 1225 (Ind. 1981).
3.8 trillion to one – 1 in 15 at Pendleton get written up monthly. 14/15 to the 420 power is 3.8 trillion.

Chapter 6

Dujuan Emerson – *Emerson v. State*, 724 N.E.2d 605 (Ind. 2000).
Christopher Lewis – *Lewis v. State*, 812 N.E.2d 248 (Ind. App. 2004).
no proportional punishments in US Constitution – Justice Scalia, in *Harmelin v. Michigan*, 501 US 957, 974 (1991).
Electoral College – is another example of a disproportionate voting system. For example, Vermont gets 3 electoral votes and Kansas, with four times the population of Vermont, gets 6. States with small populations are over-represented in the tally, and states with large populations, like California and Texas, are under-represented. There is unequal representation in voting for President. If we were devising an electoral system now, it wouldn't be this.
parliaments – began in France in 13th century. The American system of House and Senate was devised to accommodate slave state interests.
substance abuse treatment – 2% of the 81% with issues get treatment, per outgoing IDOC Commissioner Ed Buss, *Indy Star* editorial page, Dec. 2010.

Chapter 7

poverty statistics – *2014 World Almanac*, p. 49-50, 618.
crime predictors – Levitt and Dubner, *Freakonomics*, p. 139.
Leo Dent, Sr. – conversation at Michigan City, September 2016.

Jeremy Gross – *Spears v. State,* 735 N.E.2d 1161 (Ind. 2000); *Gross v. State,* 769 N.E.2d 1136 (Ind. 2002). Codefendant Joshua Spears got 73 years.

Chapter 8

636,000 USA homicides – 1981 through 2014, U.S. Dept of Justice statistics.
30% of crime is drug related – "Fact Sheet: Drug-Related Crime," U.S. Dept. of Justice, Sept. 1994, NCJ-149286.
Christopher McCaster – *McCaster v. State*, transfer denied 3-2, Indiana Supreme Court, 10-25-2013.
1,000-foot rule – IDOC "Offender Population Report," January 2016.
Kenneth Elmore – *Elmore v. State*, 657 N.E.2d 1216 (Ind. 1995).
Indiana Constitution, Article 13 – *Barkshire v. State*, 7 Ind. 309 (Ind. 1856); *In re Todd,* 193 N.E.2d 865 (Ind. 1935).
KKK in Indiana – James H. Madison, *Hoosiers: A New History of Indiana* (2014).
Klan-themed Indiana state flag – author's observations.
D.C. Stephenson – *Stephenson v. State,* (Ind. 1926).
gerrymandering – redrawing voting districts to obtain seats in the legislature in greater proportion than votes cast. For example, Indiana voters in 2016 cast 54.3% of their votes for Republican candidates for the US House of Representatives, and won 7 of 9 seats. Nationally, gerrymanders favor Republicans. In 2016, of 407 contested House races, Republicans won 50.7% of the vote, but got 55.5% of the seats (226 of 407). [29 races were uncontested, 15 Republican, 14 Democrat.] Republicans got 20 more House seats than they would have been awarded under a parliamentary system. In 47 of 50 states, federal courts have had to rule on gerrymandering issues.
Republican dominance in Indiana – 2015 data on state offices held.
crack sellers and users – *U.S. v. Bannister*, 786 F. Supp. 617, 648 (E.D. NY 2011).
heroin – There were 49,714 drug-related deaths in the USA in 2014, an all-time high. The increase is attributed to opioid use, and fentanyl mixed with heroin. *2017 World Almanac*, p. 211.

Chapter 9

turning down a plea – to reduce the penalty for exercising one's right to a trial, the legislation should enact a law capping a sentence at two times the plea offer. This would also prevent the coercion of false guilty pleas with deals "too good to refuse."

Kent McDonald – beaten to death by his cellmate on April 6, 2007. McDonald had 40-do-20.

David Scott – *Scott v. State* (Ind. App. 1986).

Jerry E. Watkins – *Watkins v. State,* 528 N.E.2d 456 (Ind. 1988); *Watkins v. Miller,* 92 F.Supp. 2d 824, 92 F.Supp.2d 841 (S.D. Ind. 2000).

The Hunting Ground – aired 12-27-2015 on CNN. Percentage of sexual assault claims found to be false: 8% (1992 – Grace, Lloyd, Smith); 3% (2005 – Kelly, Lovett, Regan); 2% (2006 – Heenan, Murray); 7% (2008 – Lonswey, Archambault); 5% (2014 – Spahn, White, Tellis).

Christopher M. Stevens – *Stevens v. State,* 691 N.E.2d 412 (Ind. 1997).

Chapter 10

Ben Steinberg – *In re Steinberg*, 821 N.E.2d 835 (Ind. App. 2004); *Steinburg v. State,* 941 N.E.2d 515 (Ind. 2011).

drop in violence at Pendleton – reported on episode of *Lock-Up Raw*, aired by MSNBC, 2009.

Scottie McLean – "One Prisoner's Fight to Beat the Thorazine Shuffle," PrisonWriters.com, Ty Evans, 7-17-2015.

Chapter 11

ACA Report – FOIA request, Pendleton Accreditation Report, April 2012.

Charles Durham – *Durham v. Mitcheff,* 2015 US Dist LEXIS 129960 (S.D. Ind.); settlement reached 9-29-2015.

INSIGHT program – *Indiana Dept of Public Advocacy v. IDOC,* 2012 US Dist LEXIS 182974 (S.D. Ind.), published 12-31-2012.

PREA cameras - $250,000 for surveillance, in 2012 ACA Report on Pendleton.

Pendleton settlement decree – *French v. Owens,* 538 F.Supp. 910 (S.D. Ind. 1982); *French v. Owens,* 777 F.2d 1250 (7th Cir. 1985); *French v. Duckworth,* 178 F.3d 437 (7th Cir. 1998); *Miller v. French,* 520 US 327 (2000). Decree ended 6-19-2000. PLRA is at 18 USC 3626.

double bunks – "totality of circumstances" standard is at *Rhodes v. Chapman* (1981).

Chapter 12

Jelani, cell phone robbery – "Silencing the Sound of Stabbing," PrisonWriters.com, Ty Evans, 7-13-2015.

Roy Martin – *Martin v. State,* 779 N.E.2d 1235 (Ind. App. 2002).

Leif O'Connell – *O'Connell v. State,* 742 N.E.2d 943 (Ind. 2001).

Jason P. Davidson – IDOC website; Kosciusko County Case No. 43C01-0205-MR-70 and 43S03-0506-CR-263. Curious side note: In 2015 the prisoner referred to in this book as "Dog Bite" was solicited by Davidson via Jpay email for Dog Bite's mother's maiden name and Dog Bite's social security number.

Wyser and Brizzi – Cory Schouten, "How the Brizzi Public Corruption Case Unraveled," *The Indiana Lawyer*.com, 11-5-2013. Wyser's disciplinary proceedings at *In re Wyser,* 4 N.E.3d 619 (Ind. 2014) and 14 N.E.3d 1292 (Ind. 2014).

Timothy Durham – Sandra Chapman, "Tim Durham Sentenced to 50 Years in Fraud Case," WTHR.com, 11-30-2012. Durham's disbarment at *In re Durham,* 55 N.E.2d 302 (Ind. 2016) July 20, 2016.

Travis Roberson – *State v. Roberson,* Jennings County Case No. 40C01-0701-FA-001.

Jimmy Croom – "Help Us Help Ourselves Reduce Recidivism," PrisonWriters.com, Ty Evans, 1-21-2016.

IDOC budget – see state website, www.in.gov.

Pell grants – Christopher Zoukis, "Pell Grants for Prisoners: New Bill Restores Hope for Reinstating College Programs," Prison Legal News, August 2015, p.32-35.

education's effect on recidivism – *Ibid.*

PLUS program – Stephen T. Hall, "Indiana Implements a Faith and Character Based Housing Program," *Corrections Today*, Dec. 2008.

Chapter 13
David Camm – *Camm v. State*, 908 N.E.2d 215 (Ind. 2009). Related proceedings at *Life Insurance Co. of North America v. David Camm, et.al.*, 2007 US Dist. LEXIS 58456 (Aug. 6, 2007) and 2007 US Dist LEXIS 64454 (Aug. 30, 2007).
bar exam – author has never taken the bar exam, but scored 157 on the LSAT, good enough for acceptance into most law schools.
Ware's habeas corpus – *Ware v. Zatecky* (S.D. Ind. 2015).

Chapter 14
VCCLEA – at 18 USC 13701 to 14223. Section 13704 is for Truth-in-Sentencing Incentive Grants. (85% rule).
sewage incident – O-dorm on 3-31-2015.
Terry Riggs – traffic accident occurred on 6-19-2015.
David Smith – PC denied in Jasper County on 7-19-2015.
another day at Michigan City – author was transferred from Pendleton to Michigan City as part of a settlement agreement in a federal civil suit.
He who would travel happily must travel light. – quote from Antoine de St. Exupéry, *Wind, Sand, and Stars* (1939).

Acknowledgements

I would have never attempted to write this book if not for the encouragement, support, and advice I received from Loen Kelley and the staff at PrisonWriters.com. Thank you for selecting me as one of your contributing writers in 2014.

My professors at Ball State University deserve acknowledgement for giving me numerous writing assignments that helped me learn how to think critically: Dr. James Danglade (History), Professor Curt Hosier (Sociology), Dr. Gerald Waite (Anthropology), Dr. Benjamin Jessup (History), and Professor Elizabeth Pfeiffer (Anthropology).

I appreciate the assistance provided by: Kenneth Allen, Caylin Black, Joey Callahan, James Collins, David M. Green, Seth Hollows, Mahfuz Huq, Stuart 'Jack' Kennedy, Phillip 'Edgar' Lee, Dean Maust, Angela McGee, Matthew Thies, and Larry Warren.

An inner circle of associates concerned about mass incarceration and human rights provided insight and advice, including: Aaron M. Brown, Brandon M. Ennis, Jeremy Gross, Christopher M. Lewis, Michael P. Shannon, Will Staples, Melvin Tunstill, and Kyle D. Williams.

I appreciate the letters of support and encouragement from others dedicated to the struggle against mass incarceration, particularly: Dr. James Kilgore, John Loranger, and Jim Ridgeway.

Of course, none of this could have been written with the cooperation and candid insights from the many prisoners outlined in this book, and scores of others whose stories could add to the theme.

Last, I am most grateful to my family for their love and support during all the years I have spent in prison – particularly my mother, who did so much to help me write this book, but who did not live to see it published. My time in prison has probably been harder on them than it has been on me.

Acknowledgements 330

About the Author

Ivan Denison is the pen name of Indiana prisoner Ty Evans, #158293, who currently resides at the Indiana State Prison in Michigan City. The nom de plume was chosen as an homage to Aleksandr Solzhenitsyn's title character in *One Day in the Life of Ivan Denisovich.*

Evans is serving a 71-year sentence from Marion County for attempted murder (40 years) and resisting arrest (1 year), with a habitual offender enhancement (30 years). He began his incarceration on May 16, 2005, and his release date is November 16, 2036.

Evans is a graduate of Ball State University, Bachelor of General Studies, *summa cum laude,* with minors in History, Anthropology, and Sociology. He previously graduated from Southeastern Illinois College with a degree in Land Surveying. Prior to his incarceration, he owned and operated Centurion Surveys LLC in Indianapolis.

- May 10, 2017

Contact Information:

Direct Email:
www.JPay.com/IndianaDOC

Ty Evans #158293
Indiana State Prison
One Park Row
Michigan City, IN
46360

Comments and criticisms are welcomed and appreciated.

333

www.ingramcontent.com/pod-product-compliance
Lightning Source LLC
Chambersburg PA
CBHW052308220526
45472CB00001B/22